SPANISH POLITICS AND IMPERIAL TRADE, 1700–1789

Geoffrey J. Walker, M.A., Ph.D.

INDIANA UNIVERSITY PRESS

Bloomington and London

**Library of Congress Cataloging in Publication
Data**

Walker, Geoffrey J
   Spanish politics and imperial trade, 1700–1789.

   Bibliography: p.
   Includes index.
   1. Spain – Colonies – America – Commerce.
   2. Spain – Commercial policy – History.   I. Title.
   HF3686.W35   382'.0946'08   78-63107
   ISBN
   0-253-12150-7   1 2 3 4 5 83 82 81 80 79

For Ana

Contents

List of Illustrations and Maps

ILLUSTRATIONS

1. The explosion of the *San José*, the flagship of the Conde de Casa Alegre, off Cartagena de Indias, from *A Map of the British Empire in America. . . .*, by Henry Popple, London, 1733 (by courtesy of the University Library, Cambridge).
2. Plan of Portobello, from *The Seat of War in the West Indies*, published by G. Foster, London, 1739/40 (by courtesy of the University Library, Cambridge).
3. Plan of Cartagena de Indias, from *The Seat of War in the West Indies*, published by G. Foster, London, 1739/40 (by courtesy of the University Library, Cambridge).
4. Plan of Veracruz, from *The Seat of War in the West Indies*, published by G. Foster, London, 1739/40 (by courtesy of the University Library, Cambridge).
5. Don José Patiño, from an engraving in *Retratos de españoles ilustres*, Madrid, 1791, after a contemporary painting.
6. Don Manuel López Pintado, from a painting in the Museo de la Torre del Oro, Seville (by courtesy of the Curator).
7. View of Mexico City, from *A Map of the British Empire in America. . .*, by Henry Popple, London, 1733 (by courtesy of the University Library, Cambridge).
8. A scenographic plan of Lima before the earthquake of 1748 (from J. Juan and A. de Ulloa, *Relación histórica del viaje hecho de orden de Su Mag. a la América meridional . . .*, Madrid, 1755).

MAPS

viii

Preface

The present study began life as an investigation into the effects on the internal economy of the Spanish Empire in America of the slave trade carried on by the French and English 'Assiento' companies in the first half of the eighteenth century. Yet, as that work proceeded, I realised that a large amount of vital background information was not available and that a specialised study of the kind I intended could not be made until some basic research on the history of the trade between Spain and her American colonies in the eighteenth century had been done. For example, existing accounts of the state of the economy of the Spanish Empire in the eighteenth century proved patchy, extremely incomplete, and patently unreliable; nowhere could I find a coherent analysis or explanation of Spanish policy in those times with regard to the Imperial trade; even the skeletal pattern of that trade itself remained obscure, for there existed no full and accurate list of eighteenth-century Spanish trade fleets to America, giving details such as their years of sailing, destinations, commanders, numbers of ships, tonnages and composition of cargoes. All such information, and more besides, had to be found if the particular issue within the field was to be properly researched. With mixed feelings I now set about this task. Eventually the end was lost in the pursuit of the means. Gradually I found my work on the slave trade being superseded in favour of the fascinating and unsuspected topic which now revealed itself. It became clear that during the period under examination, 1700–1750, the principal matter of interest was the desperate struggle in which Spanish merchants and ministers had been engaged in order to retain for themselves the markets of Spain's own colonies in America. Throughout these years they faced not only the diplomatic and military hostility of their European rivals and the interloping on a grand scale of friend and foe alike, but, perhaps most intriguing of all to the historian, they encountered the stubborn reluctance of their own flesh and blood, the merchants and residents of the colonies themselves, to cooperate commercially with Spain except upon terms which were tacitly dictated to the Crown by the businessmen of Lima and Mexico City. Here then lay the basis of a study complete in itself which might not only provide background material for specialised research but could bring to light and explore a number of issues of significance in the history of the Spanish Empire in America as a whole. What was the pattern of Spain's American trade in the eighteenth century? How did the actions of foreign traders, sailors and diplomats affect it? In what way and in what terms did Spanish colonial opposition to metropolitan commerce make itself felt? In such circumstances, what, and how effective, were the policies of the Spanish Crown? Why did the ancient trading system by means of fleets of galleons finally break down and give rise to the concept of 'free trade'? These were some of the questions which presented themselves, and these plus supplementaries – are the ones to which I have tentatively suggested answers in the present study.

Detailed research in modern times into the history of Spain's transatlantic trade has been limited in the main to the sixteenth and seventeenth centuries (C. H. Haring, P. Chaunu) or has dealt with strictly defined topics in the eighteenth (R. D. Hussey, J. J. Real Díaz[1]). C. H. Haring, for example, in his *The Spanish Empire in America* spends less than two full pages on trade in the eighteenth century, while some of J. H. Parry's observations in *The Spanish Seaborne Empire* seem more to point the way towards possible future research on the period than to define Spain's problems and the attempts to solve them. Only S. Villalobos R. in his *El comercio y la crisis colonial: un mito de la independencia*, discusses in any detail the problems of Imperial trade, but his purposes are, historically speaking, quite different from my own. Several admirable works do indeed exist, however, concerning the foreign pressures brought to bear upon Spain and her Indies at this time in the fields of diplomacy and commerce (E. W. Dahlgren, G. Scelle, V. L. Brown, R. Pares, J. O. McLachlan, to mention only some of those cited in the present text). The extent of foreign contraband activities – yet scarcely at all their economic effects inside the colonies – has also been studied by some of the above, and notably by G. H. Nelson and L. Vignols. But answers to the main questions about the internal economy of the Empire and Spanish commercial policy have had to be sought from contemporary authors and principally from documentary sources.

The most abundant source of information was the papers of the Archivo General de Indias, Seville, although I also found much useful material in the Archivo General de Simancas, Valladolid, the Archivo del Ministerio de Hacienda, Lima, and the British Museum (Library), London. Six other archives in Europe and America also yielded more limited though often definitive data. Almost all the eighteenth-century Spanish treatises on historical, economic and political matters contained material of direct relevance to this study, but I feel that here comment is required on only two of them, those of R. Antúnez y Acevedo and D. Alsedo y Herrera. The works of Alsedo y Herrera are generally regarded as undependable as historical sources. Alsedo was certainly a mediocre historian and scholar, and his writings, particularly his pretentious *Aviso histórico*, which deals with Imperial history from the sixteenth century onwards, are for the most part garbled and inaccurate. However a higher standard of accuracy may be observed in the parts of his works which refer to the period 1706–40, when the author himself was actually present at many of the events he describes. Nevertheless, even here, Alsedo is not without error. In the present study I have therefore thought it wise to make use only of information which appears to be corroborated by other evidence, either documentary or circumstantial. Of greater reliability is his *Memorial informativo*. . . which he prepared in 1725. This work is primarily concerned with financial events in Peru 1706–22 of which Alsedo in his offices of *Contador Ordenador* and *Diputado de la Audiencia y del Tribunal del Consulado de Comercio de Lima* had intimate knowledge. Moreover the *Memorial* abounds in notes giving sources and authorities, and is of a much higher quality of scholarship than Alsedo's other works. A different point must be raised with regard to Antúnez y Acevedo's *Memorias históricas*. . . In his Appendix VII the author gives an accurate, if incomplete, list of Spanish trade fleets of the period, but he points out that the full records were not available to him at the time of writing. The 'Libros de registros' (AGI, Contr. 2901), on the other hand, give the individual tonnages of each of the merchantmen in the fleets and are, therefore, a complete and reliable source. In the cases of some fleets there are discrepancies between the tonnages given by Antúnez and those calculated from the 'Libros de registros'. Another incomplete set of composite tonnage figures is to be found in AGI, Contr. 5800; this corresponds with Antúnez's figures and may well be his source – or indeed his own paper. The differences between the figures of the 'Libros de registros' and Antúnez may be explicable simply in terms of arithmetical error, for often they are very slight. Such major discrepancies, as there are, appear to suggest the accidental or erroneous omission by Antúnez (and his probable source) of certain ships in the fleets concerned, or else more serious arithmetical mistakes. Throughout this study therefore the tonnage figures for the fleets discussed have been compiled (to two places of decimals) from the records of the 'Libros de registros' and Antúnez's published figure is given in parenthesis at each corresponding note.

I have converted all dates taken from English sources from old-style to new-style, with the exception of dates of publication of the English newspapers cited.

In the preparation of this study my accumulated debt to colleagues and friends, at home and abroad, remains enormous. For encouragement, assistance of all kinds and academic material my very sincere thanks go to: Dr P. J. Bakewell, Dr J. M. Batista i Roca, Dr R. Boulind, The British Council, T. W. I. Bullock Esq, Conde de Casa Alegre, Consejo Superior de Investigaciones Científicas, Dr. F. Denegri Luna, Sres Espinosa, J. Fairclough Esq, Professor P. Grases, Dr G. Lohmann Villena, Professor J. Lynch, Sr J. Mateu, Dr M. Moreyra Paz-Soldán, Dr. S. G. Redding, the staffs of the archives and libraries which I visited in Spain, Latin America and Great Britain, Dr D. Starkey, D. Stephen Esq, Dr J. Street, Professor S. Villalobos R., Professor E. M. Wilson. And last, because my greatest debt is to her, must come my inexpressible thanks to my wife, Ana, for her constant encouragement and her generous assistance in this task, from the tedious copying of documents in archives to the typing of innumerable drafts of the manuscript.

Cambridge   G.J.W.

Glossary of Spanish Terms used in the Text

Alcabala – a sales tax

almiranta – the warship commanded by the second-in-command of a fleet

almojarifazgo – a customs duty

Armada de Barlovento – the Barlovento squadron, a detachment of Crown warships stationed in the West Indies for the defense of the Caribbean

Armada del Sur – the trade fleet which sailed from Callao to Panama

audiencia – a high court of justice which, in the colonies, played a part in government and assumed supreme power on the death of a viceroy in office and in interregna

avería – a tax levied on exports and imports to defray Crown expenses in maintaining naval convoys

aviador – a merchant who specialised in supplying goods and credit to the mines and/or plantations

aviso – a dispatch ship

asiento – a contract drawn up between the Crown and a private party for tax-farming or supplying specific goods or services (Engl. 'assiento')

azogues – the small fleet which transported mercury from Spain to New Spain

Bonanza – a rich strike or period in a gold or silver mine (lit. 'good weather')

borrasca – a bad period in a gold or silver mine when a vein ran out or yielded poor ore (lit. 'a patch of bad weather')

bulas – papal bulls, specifically those which permitted their purchasers to eat meat on certain prohibited days

Capitana – the flagship of a fleet

carrera de Indias – 'the Indies run'

cédula – a decree issued by the Crown

xiii

consulado – a guild of merchants and its court (the *tribunal*)
corregidor – a district magistrate
corregimiento – the area of jurisdiction of a *corregidor*

Fiscal – a Crown attorney attached to *audiencias* and government
    councils
flota – the trade fleet which sailed from Cadiz to Veracruz

Galeones – the trade fleet which sailed from Cadiz to Cartagena de
    Indias and Portobello
guardacostas – the coast-guard vessels used in Caribbean waters in the
    eighteenth century

Junta (de comercio) – commission, committee (for trade)

Memorial – an official report on a specific subject presented to the
    Crown or high authority

Navío del oro – the ship which, in the sixteenth and part of the seven-
    teenth centuries, took merchants and treasure from northern Peru
    and Quito to Panama at the time of the fleet

Obrage – a workshop for the weaving of cloth

Palmeo – a method of calculating tax on merchandise for shipment, based
    on its volume irrespective of value or weight
papel sellado – officially stamped paper sold by the Crown for obligatory
    use in the drawing up of legal documents
patache – a small warship used as a tender and messenger in a fleet
piña – a small light-weight or porous block of silver, usually conical or
    pyramid-shaped
proyecto – a governmental or royal bill stating the conditions and
    manner in which specified actions or activities will be carried out

Quintal – a measure of weight equivalent to approximately 46 kilograms
    (1 *quintal* = 4 *arrobas* = 100 *libras*)

Real quinto – a tax levied on the product of all gold and silver mines
    amounting to one fifth of the total value of the precious metals
    obtained

registro – a merchant ship licensed by the Crown for a single voyage to a specified American port, either on its own or in the company of other vessels

residencia – a public judgment held by the Crown on an official's record of service after he had left office

Visita – a secret Crown inspection of an official's behaviour while still holding office

Abbreviations used in the Notes

AEA   = *Anuario de Estudios Americanos*, Seville
AGI   = Archivo General de Indias, Seville
   Contr.   = Sección de Contratación
   Indif. Gen. = Sección de Indiferente General
   Lima   = Audiencia de Lima
   México   = Audiencia de México
   Santa Fe = Audiencia de Santa Fe
AHR   = *American Historical Review*, New York
AMH   = Archivo del Ministerio de Hacienda, Lima
ARAH   = Archivo de la Real Academia de la Histona, Madrid
ATT   = Archivo del Palacio de Torre Tagle, Lima
BIHR   = *Bulletin of the Institute of Historical Research*, London
BM   = British (Museum) Library
BNL   = Biblioteca Nacional, Lima
COSP   = *Calendar of State Papers, Colonial Series, America and the West
           Indies, 1706—30*, London, 1916–37
EHR   = *English Historical Review*, London
HAHR   = *Hispanic American Historical Review*, Durham, N.C.
JMH   = *Journal of Modern History*, Chicago
NYPL   = New York Public Library, N.Y.
PRO   = Public Record Office, London
RHA   = *Revista de Historia de América*, Mexicð
RHES   = *Revue d'Histoire Économique et Sociale*, Paris
Simancas = Archivo General de Simancas, Valladolid
   Estado   = Sección de Estado

'. . . Mysteries which private people cannot
expect to be let into, but must wait till
Time, the Discoverer of all Secrets, takes
off the Disguises of an event, of which we
only see the outside, and which is owing
to some other Reason than is generally
imagined.'

The Flying Post
or
Post Master,
Tuesday, 28 July 1724.

Introduction: The Commercial System of the Spanish Empire[1]

The growth of Spain's Imperial power in America in the sixteenth century was accompanied by a natural increase in communications between the newly-founded colonies and the mother country. As expansion continued, supplies of stores and equipment of all kinds were sent out to the colonies more and more frequently and in larger quantities, and it was not long before the Indies in their turn were sending produce across the Atlantic, eastwards to Spain. So began the first reciprocal trade between the Old World and the New. However, despite the valuable importations of cacao, sugar, cotton, hides, dyewoods, tobacco and other American produce, current 'bullionist' economic theories caused the nation's main interest to focus upon the gold and silver, the pearls and emeralds, the so-called 'riches' of the New World. During the course of the sixteenth century the Spanish Crown became increasingly obsessed with the exploitation of the mineral wealth of the colonies as a means of financing its costly European wars. Indeed, so convinced did it become that the main economic purpose of developing the American possessions was to provide a maximum supply of precious metals to the metropolis, that before the end of the century the Crown was already beginning to regret much of the good work which had previously been done to promote colonial agriculture and industry.

For most of the sixteenth century Crown policy had been to establish agriculture and industry as widely as possible throughout the Indies, as the whole of the Spanish Empire in America came to be called. In addition to favouring the cultivation of indigenous American plants, attempts – not always successful – had repeatedly been made to introduce the vine and the olive as well as the more common European crops. The weaving industry had also been encouraged, although production was largely limited to the coarser types of cloth

1

manufactured by the Indians for their own use. Nevertheless in the viceroyalty of New Spain (modern Mexico) the silk industry too had prospered until a period of decline set in towards the 1580s. In the last quarter of the sixteenth century, however, there occurred a gradual but perceptible change in the Spanish Crown's attitude toward colonial self-sufficiency. From about that time onwards economic policy for America aimed at making the colonies as wholly dependent as possible on the mother country for supplies of consumer goods, cloth, and agricultural produce of various kinds; for every item of Spanish merchandise shipped to the Indies now came to be seen more and more in the light of the returns in gold and silver which would accrue directly to Spain as a result of its sale to the colonists. It was thus hoped to stimulate greater concentration on mining in America and a corresponding expansion of agriculture and industry in Spain. Naturally, therefore, any development of competitive agriculture and industry in America was regarded as undesirable, in that by limiting the market for Spanish exports in the colonies it reduced the returns of precious metals to the mother country to something less than the maximum. In a *memorial* of 1584 addressed to Philip II the economic thinking which lay behind this change in Crown policy was summed up in a single sentence, pointing out that

> the wine and wool industries in Peru have already lost trade representing an annual return of 200,000 ducats to the royal exchequer.[2]

In pursuance of the new policy Philip II issued orders to the viceroys and governors of the Empire instructing them to forbid the cultivation of the vines which had been introduced with so much difficulty by the early settlers. The prohibition was not heeded at first and so some years later, in 1595, the king again outlawed viticulture throughout the Indies, this time with the exception of Peru where the industry was firmly established and therefore difficult to stamp out. However in Peru the planting of new vines was strictly forbidden and a tax of two per cent was imposed on the produce of the vineyards. Peruvian wine-growing was actively discouraged over the following years, and seeing that it was still flourishing in 1614 Philip III prohibited the exportation of Peruvian wine to any part of the Empire that could normally be supplied from Spain. From 1596 the already decadent silk industry of New Spain was finally condemned as prejudicial to that of

Granada, and in the early seventeenth century large-scale production of oil from the olive, a process which had only just begun to be profitable in America, was also forbidden. An obstacle was even put in the way of American sugar production in the form of removing Indian labour from the plantations. Labour was precisely the principal problem for the colonial sugar producer and his greatest overhead cost, yet by laws of 1595 and 1601 the Crown chose to deny the American grower the only economic source of man-power available to him. On the other hand, during the seventeenth century the production of sugar increased rapidly in Andalusia, so much so that by 1650 it was considered important enough to provide a source of revenue, and a tax known as the *Millón de la azúcar* was imposed upon it.

There were no laws specifically prohibiting the manufacturing craft industries, but then there were no such industries in America large enough to offer serious competition to those of Spain. Cottage industries such as blacksmiths' and other workshops which produced bulky but low-value technical equipment, used, for example, in the mines, certainly existed in the main centres of population, with governmental consent. But such enterprises did not thrive on a large scale and concentrated on the manufacture of goods which it was not profitable to export direct from Spain in a finished state. Their continuance, and even their limited expansion, therefore presented no threat whatsoever to the export market of the craftsmen in Spain. Although the wool of the merino sheep, which had been successfully bred in the Indies, was valuable, and its shipment to Spain was encouraged by Philip II, colonial textiles were of rough quality, and the finer fabrics used by the European population of the colonies were always imported. Indeed cloth from Europe made up the greater part of the cargo of the Spanish trade fleets to the Indies. Nevertheless, the laws of 1595 and 1601 also directed Indian labour away from the *obrages*, or workshops, which were engaged in the manufacture of cloth in America. The cruel exploitation of Indian labour by the owners of these *obrages* and the sugar estates was notorious, and the Crown on several occasions expressed its genuine concern about such abuses. Yet the appearance of the laws of 1595 and 1601, ostensibly protecting the Indians from ill-treatment, does in fact coincide with other legislation which redeployed Indian labour into the most gruelling of all colonial industry, work in the gold and silver mines. At the same time, it must be noted, the Crown in Spain was making an attempt to develop and expand its home industries for the purpose of increasing its exports to the Indies.[3]

During the seventeenth and eighteenth centuries Crown policy concerning colonial agriculture and industry varied, but the overall result was one of general underdevelopment everywhere except in the mines. Industries or crops that were forbidden took time to rebuild even if prohibitions were lifted, and so a solid basis never became established for those affected. By early in the seventeenth century the American colonies were therefore forced to depend upon shipments of merchandise from the mother country for the majority of their needs, both of certain essential goods and most of their luxuries.

The method of transporting these supplies to America and bringing home the returns in precious metals evolved during the sixteenth century into a fairly regular system of fleets of galleons. The sailing of these fleets constituted the most important aspect of the *carrera de Indias*, as the whole of the shipping and trading between Spain and her American colonies was succintly called. In theory, but less often in practice, there were two fleets per year, composed of a varying number of merchantmen convoyed by a suitable number of men-of-war. Each fleet served one of the two American viceroyalties of New Spain and Peru and the respective dependencies. The fleet bound for Veracruz known as the New Spain *flota*, left Cadiz in May or June, taking with it single ships for the West Indian Islands. The other fleet, known as the Tierra Firme *galeones*, and bound for Cartagena de Indias in New Granada (modern Colombia) and Portobello on the Isthmus of Panama, left in August, taking with it ships to serve part of the Venezuelan coast.

On arrival at Veracruz the goods from the *flota* were carried overland to Mexico City where they were sold in bulk to Mexican merchants who, in turn, distributed them retail throughout the whole of New Spain. The *flota* also normally brought consignments of mercury from Spain which were so necessary in the process of smelting the silver ores from the Mexican mines. Another function of the *flota* was the shipment of military supplies for the garrisons stationed in New Spain. On the journey back to Spain the fleet took the returns, both in bullion and in American produce, from the trading in Mexico, together with the proceeds of duties and taxes collected in the viceroyalty on behalf of the Crown. However, if for any reason the *flota* was not dispatched from Spain, the mercury, always in short supply even after the discovery of rich deposits at Huancavelica in Peru, was transported to New Spain by a special naval detachment usually made up of only two vessels and known as the *azogues*. The main purpose of these ships was of course to provide the mercury, but they often also delivered military stores and occasionally served as convoy to a small number of merchantment carrying goods for general sale. On their return voyage the *azogues* took home some Mexican produce, but their main cargo was the royal treasure which had accumulated in Mexico since the last full *flota*.

The Tierra Firme *galeones* shipped merchandise for the whole of the viceroyality of Peru, including the province of New Granada. The fair at Portobello at which the cargoes of the *galeones* were exchanged for the precious metals brought up by sea to Panama from Peru became one of the most famous and richest trade fairs the world has ever known. After the Spaniards and Peruvians had completed their trading at Portobello the American produce and bullion were loaded on board the *galeones* for transportation back to Spain. After wintering in the Indies and refitting for the homeward passage the New Spain *flota* and the Tierra Firme *galeones* assembled at Havana, and, in theory if not often in practice, they set sail together into the Trade Winds that carried them back again to Europe.

Parts of the Empire which were considered too far distant from the trading ports in Central America were supplied with goods by single ships known as *registros*. These set out from Spain under special licences from the Crown with registered cargoes – hence their name – whenever it was thought they could be profitable. *Registros* sailed principally to Buenos Aires, the Venezuelan and Central American coasts and to the West Indian Islands, but since none of these areas produced large quantities of precious metals of their own, their payment for the supplies they received could only be in agricultural or animal produce. The balance of payments of these areas was therefore considered to be unfavourable, and trade with them was usually sadly neglected by the merchants of Spain. Shipments of merchandise to these places were very erratic and often consisted of non-essential or luxury goods on which speculators in Spain hoped to make high profits, rather than provide a service.

Apart from the annual fleets and their convoys, the *azogues* and the *registros*, there was another class of vessel which plied between Spain and the Indies. This was the *aviso*, or dispatch ship. It was the *avisos'* job to carry official papers and information across the Atlantic or from one colonial port to another in as short a time as possible. They were always small fast ships, and for the sake of speed they were normally forbidden to carry precious metals or merchandise of any kind. *Avisos* were sent off from Spain whenever necessary, but one of their main functions was to bear the dispatches between Spain and the Indies at the time of the fleets, announcing their departures and arrivals and carrying news of the conduct of the trade in the colonies.

Naval defences of the Caribbean were theoretically maintained by a squadron of warships based in the West Indian Islands and known as the *Armada de Barlovento*. Its main purpose was to patrol the sea routes used by Spain and keep them clear of pirates and enemy shipping. The squadron was of course of very limited value in such a vast area, but it had its uses on occasion as a supplementary or substitute convoy to the fleets, or when naval transport was required in some emergency.

The movement of transatlantic shipping was rigorously controlled by the Spanish Crown and was mainly restricted to the fleets and ships described. No ship could enter a port other than that for which it was licensed, and with few exceptions all were obliged to put in to Cadiz on their return to Spain. Except for the few approved ports, all Atlantic harbours in America were closed absolutely to all shipping. Even the approved ports were forbidden to all ships from Europe unless they carried written proof from the authorities in Spain of their permission to enter, or unless they arrived as part of the annual fleet. Inter-colonial trade was also regulated so strictly that during certain periods the limitations imposed on it amounted almost to prohibition. Movements of precious metals inside the colonies for trading purposes were subject to stringent control by the colonial authorities so as to prevent illicit commerce and to ensure a maximum of trade with the fleets from Spain.

Shipping in the Pacific consisted principally of the Manila galleon and the *Armada del Sur*, or Southern Fleet. Trade between the Philippine Islands and New Spain was carried on by means of one yearly ship which plied between Manila and the port of Acapulco on the West Coast of Mexico. Since the Philippines were the furthest outpost of the Spanish Empire, trade with New Spain was originally permitted so as to encourage colonisation of the islands which were intended to serve as the missionary base for the whole of the Far East. Moreover it was only via New Spain that the metropolis could maintain contact with the Philippines, since the direct sea route through the Magellan Straits was too dangerous and difficult to be practical. In the beginning the privilege of trading with New Spain was restricted to certain prominent Philippine citizens, Crown officials and the religious communities. But it soon became the practice for others to make private arrangements with these authorised persons, so that by the seventeenth century the trade with New Spain was in fact open to anyone who cared to partake in it. The trade was limited to one ship per year and the value of the cargo was strictly controlled, although it almost always exceeded that stipulated. Oriental goods such as silks, spices and porcelain were the most valued merchandise shipped to Mexico and they were paid for almost exclusively in precious metals, a commodity that was greatly prized in the East, then as now. However, this 'leak' of gold, and more especially silver, to the Far East was always a cause of concern to the Spanish Crown. Ways of cutting down the Philippine trade, or even preventing it altogether, were often sought by the Spanish authorities, for not only did it constitute a drain on the precious metals, but it also represented competition on the Mexican markets for some of the goods brought by the *flota* from Europe. Yet there was no real solution to the problem. To prohibit the trade would have been virtually to alienate the Philippines and cut them off from the rest of the Empire. Indeed orders imposing severe restrictions on the trade caused an uprising in Manila in the 1720s. On the other hand silver was the only acceptable payment for the merchandise brought from China. The only course open was a troublesome compromise – to permit the continuance of the trade in a highly controlled form so as to minimise its damaging effects on the Crown's economic plans for the colonies in America. To this end the exportation of Far-East merchandise from New Spain to any part of the Empire, except Spain herself, was strictly forbidden. Offenders were punishable by confiscation of their goods, ten years' service in the galleys, or exile from their homes. Indeed at times, when the spread of Chinese merchandise throughout the colonies got out of control, the Crown forbade absolutely all trade communication between Mexico and Peru in order to impede totally the infiltration of these goods on to the markets of South America.

The other major movement of shipping in the Pacific was made by the voyages of the *Armada del Sur*. As soon as the *galeones* from Spain reached American waters news of their imminent arrival was quickly dispatched from Cartagena de Indias to Lima and throughout all the provinces of Peru. The viceroy in Lima then gave orders that all the merchants who wished to take part in the fair at Portobello should bring their money, and any goods they might have for trading, to Lima to be registered and loaded aboard the ships of the *Armada del Sur* at the nearby port of Callao. The fleet then left Callao for Panama and called on its way at Trujillo and Paita in Northern Peru. On its way north it was joined by the *navío del oro* (the gold ship) bringing merchants and treasure from Quito and the neighbouring regions. By the eighteenth century, however, this practice had died out, and the

merchants who lived in Quito, New Granada and the western parts of
Venezuela were permitted to travel overland to Cartagena. There a
fair, smaller than that at Portobello, was held with the *galeones* before
the ships left for the main fair on the Isthmus of Panama. It was not
possible for the merchants of the Northern Provinces to go by land to
the fair at Portobello to join their countrymen from the Southern
Provinces, for the strip of land between Portobello and the mainland
mass of South America was impassible because of high mountains
thick forests and the tribes of wild Indians which inhabited the area.
Cartagena grew, then, from being little more than a well-fortified
anchorage for the *galeones* (Portobello was disease-ridden and
unsuitable as a long-stay harbour) into a port of certain commercial
importance, and the fair there, while never rivaling that at Portobello,
became the main supply point for the Northern Provinces of South
America. The *Armada del Sur*, of course, also brought with it treasure
belonging to the Crown, the product of the royal revenues in the
viceroyalty of Peru. Once the ships reached Panama their cargoes were
taken across the Isthmus by mule train and river boat and loaded at
Portobello into the *galeones* for shipment back to Spain. Likewise the
merchandise from Europe was taken from Portobello to Panama and
the *Armada del Sur* carried the Peruvian merchants and their goods
down the coast again as far as Paita. Winds and currents prevented the
Armada del Sur from sailing further south without making a lengthy
detour westwards into the Pacific, before returning to Callao. So the
passengers and the cargo of the fleet had to make their way back to
Lima overland from Paita.

The American trade was regulated on both sides of the Atlantic on a
strong institutional basis. In overall control of the colonies was the
Consejo de Indias, the Council of the Indies, but the day-to-day running
of commercial aspects was in the hands of the *Casa de Contratación*,
or Board of Trade. This had in fact been the very first
institution created by Spain for the administration of America, in
1503. It was established in Seville, the major city of Andalusia and the
centre of Spain's American activities, but early in the eighteenth
century the *Casa* was transferred, despite Sevillian opposition, to the
more convenient port of Cadiz. The functions of the *Casa* were to
license and register all ships, crews, equipment and merchandise
bound for the Indies, to supervise passengers and merchants, collect
and record Crown taxes and dues on out-going and in-coming ships
and cargoes, and, in short, to enforce all the laws and regulations
relating to the *carrera de Indias*. It also acted as a court of law in cases of
commercial litigation.

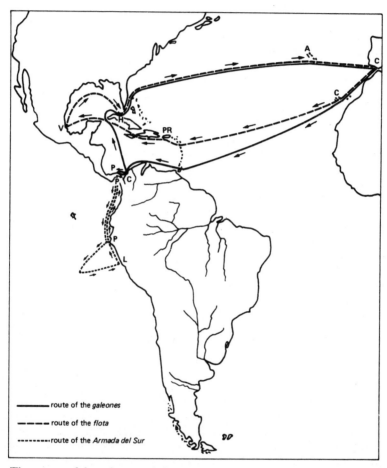

The routes of the *galeones* and *flota* and the *Armada del Sur*

Working in close association with the *Casa* was the *Universidad de los cargadores a las Indias*, more commonly called the *consulado de comercio*. In 1543 the Crown had constituted the Indies traders of Seville, at their own request, into a corporate body, and by the end of the sixteenth century this 'guild' formed an exclusive club of rich merchants which enjoyed the sole rights to conduct the trade with the colonies. The *consulado* was important to the Crown as a means of regulating the American commerce. Not only did it provide advice, ships and money (in addition to sizeable loans to the royal exchequer), but in its defense of its jealously guarded rights it also facilitated Crown control of the trade and automatically excluded interlopers from it. Later, a similar *consulado* was set up by the merchants of Cadiz, and in the eighteenth century this actually overshadowed the senior guild at Seville.

Consulados de comercio were also established in the Indies, in New Spain in 1594 and in Peru in 1613. The merchants of the American *consulados* were not necessarily colonial-born. Many of them were recent immigrants to the Indies, and a number of them were even members of the great trading families of Seville and Cadiz. Until well into the eighteenth century no distinction was made, in law or otherwise, between merchants resident in the Indies and those in Spain, and a sort of loose association appears to have existed, at least as regards certain matters, between all the *consulados* on both sides of the Atlantic.[4] The rights and privileges of the American *consulados* were parallel with those of Andalusia, although their influence upon the life of the community was more far-reaching. In Mexico and Lima the *consulados* were composed principally of the large merchants, and because of the economic power which they held they were the virtual arbiters of the commercial life of the viceroyalties. Their members were the bulk purchasers of the cargoes of the *flota* and *galeones*, and it was they who distributed the merchandise throughout the viceroyalties. They financed a good deal of the prospecting for deposits of precious metals, and advanced credit and supplies to the mines and agriculture. They also farmed royal taxes such as the *alcabala* sales tax in the areas of their jurisdiction. Another responsibility of the *consulados*, both those in Spain and America, was the collection and payment of a royal tax known as the *avería*. This was a tax levied in order partly to defray the Crown's expenses in providing escorts of warships for the *flota* and *galeones* in the Atlantic, and the *Armada del Sur* in the Pacific.

In each of the ports involved in the trade there were stationed royal officials (*oficiales reales*). In fact these were treasury agents, but they performed duties very akin to those of present-day customs officers.

Originally the royal officials were primarily concerned with the collection of customs dues (*almojarifazgo*) and the inspection of ships and merchandise on entering and leaving ports. But later, in the Indies, they assumed duties in connection with the administration of the trade fairs and shipping procedures and the running of the towns and ports in which they served. They even became involved in naval and military protocol and were appealed to for authoritative opinions on a number of matters involving commerce and the law. They were generally regarded as severe, if corruptible.

Such, in broad terms, were the economic objectives of Spain's American trade and the methods by which it was conducted.

Spain's economic and commercial policies for her American Empire followed closely the generally accepted mercantilist ideas of the time. The accumulation and retention of wealth in the form of bullion was every nation's aim, and it is likely that if any other of the European countries had discovered rich mineral deposits in its colonies, its policies would have been based on the same principles. In Spain's case, therefore, the political consequence was that the Indies and the American trade had to be preserved exclusively for subjects of the Crown of Castile. Indeed over the greater part of the colonial era Spanish legislation was as much designed to keep the foreigner out of the Indies as it was to exploit the colonies for the benefit of the metropolis. Yet in practice this monopoly was little more than an illusion. Spanish industries had never been large enough nor sufficiently developed to provide manufactures for both home and colonial markets, and during the sixteenth and seventeenth centuries, the position, rather than improving, grew steadily worse. The crippling taxes demanded by the Crown to finance its wars and its inept management of the economy were partly to blame, but the monetary inflation produced by the very importation of gold and silver which the Crown itself encouraged was responsible for Spanish prices rising above the levels in other European countries.[5] The cheaper foreign goods which came into Spain, in addition to contributing to the decline of Spanish industry, also naturally found their way on to the annual fleets to America via the operations of the *consulados* of Andalusia. So advanced did the process become that by the end of the seventeenth century the merchants of Seville had been turned into nothing more than the agents of foreign manufacturers and businessmen.

But if the apparatus of monopoly was strictly maintained in all matters relating to the *carrera de Indias*, there was one aspect of the trade that was perforce given over in its entirety to domination by foreigners. That was the African slave trade. By papal bulls of the end of the fifteenth century, ratified in the Treaty of Tordesillas of 1494, it was agreed that for the purposes of discovery and conquest the world was divided into two by means of an imaginary line drawn down the assumed centre of the Atlantic. The western hemisphere was ceded to Spain and the eastern to Portugal, and each country pledged itself not to trespass on the other's domain. Because the American Indians were accorded legal status not as slaves of the colonists but as subjects of the Crown, by early in the sixteenth century the Indies were in very great need of black slave labour. Yet the geographical arrangements agreed upon with Portugal prevented Spain from establishing her own slaving bases in Africa. The Crown was consequently obliged to enter into contracts with foreigners for the supply of Negro labour. The Portuguese were naturally the principal contractors, but over the centuries other European nations succeeded in obtaining for themselves the *Asiento de Negros*, as the slave concession was called.[6] As African slaves became indispensable to the economy of the Indies, the foreign companies which supplied them were always at an advantage when negotiating the assientos with the Spanish Crown, and they were often able to demand terms very favourable to themselves. For this reason foreign slaving vessels were usually allowed to sail directly into the ports of the Indies to sell their cargoes. Indeed black slaves were the only 'merchandise' which was not obliged to pass through the *Casa de Contratación* at Seville for registering and taxing.

The *Asiento de Negros* in fact made a mockery of the pretended Spanish commercial monopoly of the Indies. As a result of this dependence on foreigners and their being permitted to communicate directly with the Spanish colonies, the slave trade became closely linked with large-scale smuggling. Wherever there was a slaving ship in the Indies there was almost always contraband trading too, in all kinds of merchandise. For the foreign companies possession of the assiento was the most practical and profitable way of breaking Spain's exclusive hold on the American market and, for this reason, if for no other, it was greatly coveted.

Foreign contraband in the Indies, and not only under cover of the assiento, was one of the crosses which the Spanish government had to bear for practically the whole of the colonial era. The English, Dutch, and, at times, the French, in their island strongholds in the Caribbean, regarded smuggling almost as a full-time occupation. Many foreign ships also set sail from Europe direct, to transport their countries' manufactures into the Spanish Indies, without any attempt to use the legal mediation of the merchants of Andalusia. This was, after all, no more than the natural consequence of Spain's commercial policies. The heavy taxes imposed by the Crown on the Indies trades inevitably caused goods shipped to America to sell there at extremely high prices. The sorry state of Spanish industry, as already explained, meant that foreign imports made up by far the greater part of the cargoes of the annual fleets. Obviously if the colonists could buy exactly those same foreign goods directly from interlopers, often at less than a third of the prices demanded by the Andalusians, they became willing collaborators in the contraband.

But short-sighted commercial attitudes on the part of the merchants of Spain themselves also presented extraordinary opportunities to the foreign smugglers. The Sevillian businessman aimed to make as large a profit as he could on his trade to the Indies. By concentrating his business on high-value low-bulk merchandise he could reduce his overhead charges and increase his profit. Yet low-price consumer articles – wax, nails, paper, buttons, ironware and the like – were those most required in the colonies! Moreover, if the Sevillian could keep the colonial markets under-stocked with European goods, he could force prices up to his buyers in the Indies. He therefore maliciously endeavoured to delay the sailings of the fleets from Spain, for he knew that the longer the colonists had to wait between fleets, the greater would be the demand, and, consequently, the higher would be the prices he could obtain for his goods. In the interval the American mines would, of course, continue producing metals, and so, in addition, there would be more money available to purchase his cargo when it eventually arrived. To delay a fleet for a year could, therefore, mean a tripling or quadrupling of prices when the goods were finally sold in the Indies. Such self-seeking practices obviously left the Spanish Empire wide open to the activities of foreign interlopers.

By the close of the seventeenth century the *carrera de Indias*, together with all other things Spanish, had fallen into such an advanced state of decline that the colonies depended for their supplies of European goods upon the irregular and unpredictable trade of the smuggler. In the end this was merely supplemented by the equally irregular and unpredictable arrival of legal merchandise from the decrepit metropolis. Even so, only about five per cent of the cargoes of the fleets were of Spanish origin – fleets which were themselves made up of foreign (or colonial) built vessels, crewed by foreign sailors.[7] Clearly the Spanish contribution to the *total* consumption of European

goods in the Indies was negligible. A further effect of this continuing
deterioration was that, inevitably, primary and craft industries began
to develop in the Indies in a way that was contrary to the policy of the
Crown.[8]

It is evident that, in these conditions, the economy of the Indies was
gradually becoming stronger than that of Spain herself. While the
metropolis was dependent on the colonies for its livelihood – at least in
terms of precious metals – economically, by the late seventeenth
century, the colonies no longer had any real need to depend solely upon
the mother country. Although the loyalty of the Indies was not in doubt
at that time, for both American and European-born Spaniards
regarded themselves as citizens of a 'greater Spain', a certain
resentment of Peninsular attitudes was already being felt in the Indies.
This was something which the Spaniards in Spain failed to recognise.
Bernardo de Ulloa, writing in 1740, attempted to analyse why and at
what point in the past commercial relations between Spain and the
Indies had first gone wrong. He apportioned the whole blame to the
covetousness of the foreign interlopers during the early years of the
eighteenth century. While describing and condemning many of the bad
policies and malpractices adopted by the Spaniards in the seventeenth
century, he remained naïvely convinced that the Americans took no
exception to them, and deduced that it was not until the dawn of the
eighteenth century that commercial problems arose.[9] Such assertions
demonstrate how, even by mid-eighteenth century, Spain still could not
understand that for nearly a hundred years she had been endeavouring
to retain a position of commercial control over the Indies which ignored
economic realities. The increasingly powerful capitalists in Mexico and
Lima, whether Spanish-born or not, could no longer see any reason
why their weak Andalusian counterparts should be allowed to force
commercial practices upon them which patently worked against their
interests, prevented them from making a better living, and subjected
them to the outrageous price structures imposed by the fleet system.
Obviously the colonial merchant came to resent the Peninsular
merchant. Of course he welcomed the smuggler. Naturally he sought as
much freedom as possible from commercial domination by compatriots
who lived in the mother country, and who, despite their economic
impotence, thought they had the right to dictate the terms of trade.

As we shall see in the course of this study, the first half of the
eighteenth century saw this struggle for supremacy between the
merchant of the metropolis and the merchant of the colonies develop
into open economic conflict. Eventually, around 1750, a sort of impasse

was reached, but only when the Americans were within a stone's throw of victory and virtual economic self-determination.

And where economic autonomy is so nearly achieved, can thoughts of political independence lag far behind?

Part I

The Threat from France

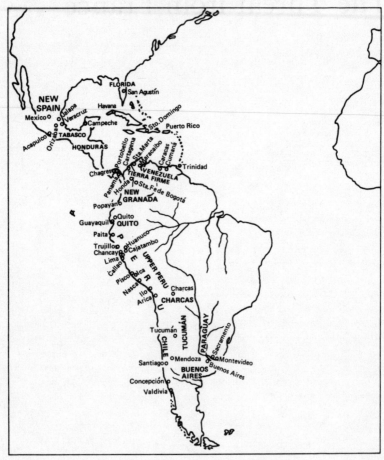

Map of places in Spanish America referred to in the text

1 Spain's American Trade, 1700–1707

The publication in November 1700 of the will of the heirless Charles II, which left the Spanish Crown to Philip, Duke of Anjou, was an event which delighted Louis XIV of France. During the later part of the seventeenth century Louis' policies of aggression towards Spanish interests in Europe and America had several times flared up into open warfare, and the uneasy Peace of Ryswick in 1697 had signified no genuine change of heart on the part of the French monarch. However, news that his grandson had inherited the Spanish throne caused Louis to change his tactics almost overnight. France straightaway took upon herself the role of the friend and protector of Spain, and Louis was confident that at long last his neighbour's vast overseas Empire had now truly fallen into his lap. The English and Dutch, on the other hand, quickly realised that the much feared family connection between the Crowns of France and Spain brought with it a serious threat to their own Spanish trade – both the legitimate trade with Old Spain and the contraband in the Indies.

The question of the continuance of these trades figures prominently amongst the causes of the outbreak of the War of the Spanish Succession.[1] As soon as it was clear that a Bourbon was to rule Spain, French influence at Madrid had been immediately used to produce difficulties for English and Dutch merchants trading in Spain. It was also learned that the French hoped to have embargoes put on the exportation of English and Dutch goods in the Cadiz fleets, so that the benefits of the Indies trade should remain entirely in the hands of France and Spain. At the same time rumour had it that French war-ships, ostensibly defending Spanish interests, would seriously impede foreign interlopers in the Indies in order to force the English and Dutch merchants and manufacturers to yield their happy position in the Spanish trades to their French rivals. It was mainly this threat to commerce which turned any sympathies the English may have had for the Bourbon prince into public support for his rival for the throne of Spain, the Hapsburg Archduke Charles. English public opinion changed over a period of months from an attitude of mild indifference to the accession of Philip of Anjou to one of resentment and antagonism. The nation therefore wholeheartedly upheld Queen Anne's decision to declare war upon France and Spain in May 1702.

For nearly half a century French goods had made up the greatest part of the foreign merchandise exported in the Cadiz fleets, and many of the articles smuggled under cover of the slave trade – especially under the Portuguese assientos – were of French origin. Although there had always been a certain amount of direct French smuggling in the Indies it had never been comparable in volume with that of the English and Dutch. The French possessions in the Caribbean were less convenient for smuggling than those of the English and the Dutch, and the French merchants, whose efforts had been mainly aimed at dominating the Cadiz trade, had neglected to organise contraband through the West Indies on any large scale. However when it was known that a French prince was to become king of Spain the subjects of Louis XIV grew anxious that their direct contraband trade in the Indies should flourish at least as much as that of their English and Dutch rivals, and they were hopeful too that their monopoly of the Cadiz trade would now become complete. Their king was urged to take full advantage of the political situation to obtain every possible commercial benefit for France. Louis was nevertheless ever cautious and discreet in pressing for French hegemony in the affairs of Spain for fear of increasing an already widespread Spanish mistrust of his motives; but he did succeed in establishing very considerable French influence in the government at Madrid and by tactful negotiations he secured for his subjects the coveted *Asiento de Negros*, lifting it deftly out of the hands of the Portuguese.[2] The assiento opened the way to increased French smuggling in the Indies, and the hostilities begun in 1702 against a united France and Spain made Spain more dependent than ever upon France for manufactured goods. One of France's aims, that of gaining complete control over the markets of Old Spain, was thus virtually achieved.

Yet Louis XIV's declared object of shoring up the crumbling walls of Spain's Empire by means of French arms and French provisions was rightly suspected by many Spaniards of being no more than a pretext to ensure France's own control of the Empire. Having entered the Indies by the large front door France would then slam it – and all the side doors too – in the faces of her rivals, England and Holland. It was feared, and with good reason, that in the guise of her protector France would become Spain's keeper.

In the Indies the French in general were resented as much as in Spain herself – if not more so. During the wars with France, before the Treaty of Ryswick, the Spanish colonies had been subjected to continual attack from France both by privateers and concerted forces. The sack of Cartagena in 1697 by French troops under the Baron de Pointis had been a hard blow, and it was still remembered when France became Spain's military ally only five years later. In the Pacific also French pirates had roved, plundering and killing. The attitude of the colonists throughout the Indies towards the French was therefore quite different from their attitude towards the English and, more particularly, the Dutch, who were welcomed as peaceful and generally honest traders.[3]

The reputation earned by the subjects of Louis XIV in Peru and Chile was soon apparent to de Terville, the commander of one of the two ships in de Beauchesne's expedition to the Pacific of 1698–1701 – the first of France's peaceful trading ventures in the South Seas after the treaty of 1697.[4] Even after his friendly overtures had been accepted by the inhabitants of Valdivia in Chile, de Terville received a surprise attack from the shore defences as he lay at anchor in the harbour, and he was indeed fortunate to escape with most of his crew and a badly damaged ship. Both de Beauchesne and de Terville were taken to be no more than pirates by the Spanish colonists who, in many places up and down the coast, even refused to sell them provisions. However, so great was the dearth of goods throughout the country, because of the extreme decadence of the legitimate trade from Cadiz by way of the Portobello fair, that some merchants, eventually believing in the peaceable objects of the expedition, decided finally to trade with the Frenchmen: even so, the colonists continued to be suspicious and were reportedly dishonest in their dealings.

The voyage of de Beauchesne was important for France. Although the returns were barely enough to cover the cost of the expedition, the beginnings of the commercial relations with the Spanish colonists, so earnestly desired by the French merchants, had now been established between the Peruvians and themselves. The two ships which returned to La Rochelle in August 1701 were, in fact, the first of numerous French ships which during the War of the Succession carried on a highly profitable trade along the coasts of Chile and Peru.[5]

But although the goods sold in the Spanish colonies by a whole host of French traders in future years were eventually welcomed by the people, it does not follow that the Frenchmen themselves were at all well received. Since 1696, no supplies whatever had been received in

Peru from Spain, and for the greater part of the War of the Succession that viceroyalty continued to be cut off commercially from Cadiz.[6] It is not surprising, therefore, that all the merchandise offered by de Beauchesne on his first voyage, even though it arrived rotted and damaged from the long journey, was gladly accepted by the ill-stocked merchants. Moreover, because of the critically low stocks of goods in the country, the Spanish viceroy even went as far as issuing a special licence to permit the local merchants to trade with the French on this occasion.[7] In the succeeding years the Spanish colonists increased their dealings with the French interlopers in the Pacific out of sheer necessity, just as, for the same reason, they accepted Bourbon rule from Madrid. There was not, as their new allies hoped, any fundamental change in their attitude.[8] This was something which the French failed to understand, and the comments of one of Louis XIV's ministers, Pontchartrain, sum up concisely both the colonists' feelings and French reactions to them. He wrote:

[I am surprised to learn of] the enormous volume of English and Dutch commerce carried on ... with the connivance of the Royal Officials; and I am amazed that two or three miserable little boats of ours are seized upon, while more than fifty of theirs are allowed to go free, and that the Spanish colonists should drive such hard bargains with our people, when it is thanks to us that they are able to continue the war.[9]

It was after all only natural that the Spanish colonists should still recall that the ships which now, during the war, came to their shores with smuggled goods had but a few years previously been cruising up and down those same coasts pillaging and robbing. In fact the French *Compagnie de la Chine* and the *Compagnie de la Mer Pacifique* were formed largely to give employment to the ships of St Malo which, until the Peace of Ryswick, had been in service as corsairs and pirates in the Spanish dominions.[10] Like the Peninsular Spaniards, the Americans found it difficult, if not impossible, to regard France as their protector and ally when for so long she had been the powerful and almost traditional enemy.

During the last quarter of the seventeenth century the unpopularity of the French in the legitimate American trade also had been demonstrated on various occasions by the seizure of goods belonging to French merchants and the imposition of high duties and special conditions on their transactions at Seville and Cadiz.[11] This was no more than normal retaliation so long as France persisted in her hostile attitude towards Spain. As Spanish industry was in such decline the transatlantic trade could ill afford to dispense with French merchandise for the provisioning of the Indies; but this did not in the least offset the strong Spanish disapproval of French policies. The efforts made by the French, therefore, in the years following Philip V's accession, to control important posts in the Indies administration, to organise the Atlantic trade according to French ideas and to become Spain's commercial partner in the Indies were resented and resisted by all Spaniards loyal to the concept of Imperial Spain and her commercial monopoly of the Empire. It seemed to Daubenton, writing to Pontchartrain on 8 August 1705,

> that the Spaniards would resolutely prefer to *lose* the American trade, before consenting to France's deriving the slightest benefit from it.[12]

On neither side of the Atlantic, so it appeared, was France's popularity as great as her own disappointment at Spain's continuing opposition.

The outbreak of the War of the Succession had, of course, the effect of retarding even further Spain's already dilatory communications with the Indies; nevertheless they were by no means severed totally. In fact New Spain received ships from Old Spain with remarkable regularity considering the circumstances. During the period 1699–1713 there were five full *flotas* to New Spain and four pairs of quicksilver ships. Commercial contact with Peru however was indeed reduced to a minimum, and between 1695 and 1713 the only fleet of *galeones* to sail to Tierra Firme was that of the Conde de Casa Alegre which left Spain in March 1706.[13] Other parts of the Empire, on the other hand, were still served by occasional vessels, and over the period 1701–13 some 26 register ships were dispatched to America making up between them some 4800 tons.[14] At least one ship reached each of the 13 available American ports except Santo Domingo. Losses of these ships by enemy action were comparatively few, amounting only to five out of the total of 26 – and, of these, two were recaptured with their cargoes intact. There were no reported wrecks on outward-bound voyages. In addition, and over the same period, 36 *aviso* ships were sent off, mainly for Veracruz and Cartagena but also usually touching at other ports. These left fairly regularly and only five of them were lost over the whole 12 years. It is therefore untrue to suggest, as do Bernardo de Ulloa and others who follow him, that the colonies were virtually isolated from the mother country during the hostilities.[15] On the contrary, contact in general between Spain and the Indies during the war was really surprisingly frequent.

But all this is not to say that communications were in any sense adequate. Both the Spaniards and the French were well aware of the serious deficiencies of the transatlantic trade which, like the lack of industry in Spain, were as much the heritage of Hapsburg rule as the result of the present war. One of the first matters to which the young Bourbon king gave his attention was an attempt to revive commerce in general both in Spain and the Indies. To this end an order was published in 1701 requiring the commercial bodies in all parts of the kingdom to submit proposals for the re-establishment of the nation's commerce.[16] Many propositions were received, and it seems that during the following years, when the question of the revival and continuance of trade and navigation was under more or less permanent discussion, recommendations on pertinent topics continued to be submitted, partly as a result of further royal requests to be informed of the opinions of the Crown's subjects on these matters.[17]

It would be wrong, however, to imagine that such measures were exclusively the result of Bourbon zeal. They were in fact merely the intensification of a process which had begun in Spain 25 or more years previously. Neither the Hapsburg government nor the merchant bodies had been blind to the increasing economic decline of the later seventeenth century, nor did they merely acquiesce in the belief that the problem, though lamentable, defied effective solution. Serious thought had indeed been given to improving the general situation of the nation. A *Junta de comercio* was set up in 1679 to consider what might best be done, and many plans and schemes were put forward touching on all aspects of Spain's economic life, and not least, of course, upon the transatlantic trade itself. The traditional Hapsburg institution of the *galeones* and *flota* even then was reportedly felt by many to be outmoded and no longer adequate as a commercial system. The great trading companies of the English and Dutch were viewed by Spaniards with envy, and proposals for the establishment of similar bodies to replace the old fleet system were naturally amongst the various schemes most favoured by the authorities. Unhappily none of these suggestions was ever really given fair trial, and the traditional method of trading persisted.[18] But the debates and the proposed reforms of the last quarter of the century do indicate that the fleet system was perhaps one Hapsburg institution whose future was already uncertain before the death of Charles II, and one which because of its evidently unsatisfactory nature seemed an obvious target for Bourbon reform from the outset.

From 1701 onwards the French, given their unprecedented opportunity to influence Spanish affairs, were naturally anxious that propositions of their own should be incorporated into any new method of conducting the American trade. Their objective was unquestionably to achieve greater and more direct participation in all aspects of the commerce with Spanish America, and to that end they directed all their suggestions and proposals.[19] Yet Spanish interests were not slow to see the danger which French influence of this kind represented to the monopolistic concept of the Indies trade. Resistance took the form of obtuseness and unwillingness to cooperate with French advisors, a dogged refusal to see reason and, above all, a relentless defense of the traditional fleet system, right or wrong. In such circumstances it was clearly impossible – and unwise – for any progressive elements there may have been in Spanish mercantile thinking to come to the fore. The one safe course for Spanish interests to follow was to dig themselves in and maintain an entrenched position with regard to the method of trading with the colonies. Any genuine Spanish desire to reorganise the *carrera de Indias* was therefore stifled by the very real fear of French domination. The old fleet system may have had recognised shortcomings, but in the present situation it had one great advantage, its exclusiveness. For this alone, it was well worthwhile retaining as an effective barrier to these attempted French incursions into the legitimate Atlantic trade. It was largely the ensuing deadlock – French determination to profit from the *carrera de Indias* faced by an equal Spanish determination not to yield an inch to French pressures in this matter – that brought about the period of increased torpor in Spain's transatlantic trade during the war. Indeed the various disasters associated with the fleet of 1706–9, to be discussed later, can largely be attributed to lack of cooperation between the two allies.

The arena in which the French pitted their guile in this matter against the opposition of sullen old-school Spanish ideas was formed by the sessions and the correspondence of the *Junta de restablecimiento del comercio* – the old *Junta de comercio* revived under French pressure to examine all matters of Spanish trade, and especially the commerce with America.[20] It was at the meetings of this body that the Spanish ministers and merchants, by tactics of procrastination and stubbornness, defended Spain's exclusive right to trade with the Indies against the power-backed diplomacy of her self-seeking ally. The course of this struggle, over the years 1705–6, constitutes one of the more interesting examples of Franco-Spanish conflict during the War of the Succession.[21]

The clash of these commercial interests had really begun at the outset of the alliance between France and Spain. Orders had been given for a joint fleet to sail to the Indies in 1701: the *flota* to New Spain under the command of Don Diego Fernández de Santillán, and the Tierra Firme *galeones* under his uncle Don José, Conde de Casa Alegre.[22] However the date of departure was put off until the following year because the long overdue New Spain fleet of 1699 under Don Manuel Velasco had still not reached Cadiz, and it was of course undesirable to dispatch another fleet before the return of the previous one. This was but the first of a series of irksome postponements of which the outbreak of war in 1702 was the major cause.[23] When Velasco's fleet eventually arrived back from New Spain in September 1702, escorted now by French men-of-war, an English squadron under Sir George Rooke inflicted terrible losses in a spectacular action at Vigo, where the Spanish ships had docked in the hope of avoiding the enemy whom they knew to be waiting off Cadiz.[24] Such a disaster showed clearly how important it was for future movements of shipping to be as stealthy as possible and above all to be fully and effectively defended. The French especially were very alive to the dangers of an attack on a large transatlantic fleet whose route was only too well known by the English and the Dutch. Nevertheless the Spanish merchants, and even the Council of the Indies, gave only a cool reception to French proposals that, for safety's sake, the Indies trade should be carried on henceforth by means of single, or at most, pairs of well-armed supply ships fitted out at intervals in Cadiz.[25] Spanish reticence was based on fears that these plans for 'free trade', as the method was called (an idea in itself contrary to the revered Spanish tradition), would quickly lead to a predominance of French warships in the *carrera de Indias* and shortly to total French domination of the trade. Troubled by this apprehension, Spanish ministers reacted with shrewdness and caution, remaining obdurate in their resistance to all changes or reforms proposed by the French, no matter how reasonable. The danger from within was judged to be greater than the danger from without. It was while discussions of the matter were being carried on that the equipping of the Fernández de Santillán fleet was delayed once again, for, not only lacking a convoy to protect it, the commanders were now unable to obtain ship's biscuit, in short supply as a result of the war. By 1703 the attempt to dispatch the fleet promptly was abandoned altogether and preparations ceased until the end of the year, although a fresh departure date was fixed for early in the following year of 1704.[26] The decision to delay the preparation of a fleet no doubt greatly annoyed the French consul at Cadiz and the many French merchants who had arrived in the port some long time before with goods for exportation to the Indies, hoping almost surely to be able to transport them directly if the 'free trade' proposals had been accepted by the Spaniards.[27]

The fact that their attempts to reorganise the Indies trade by plain suggestion had come to nothing made the French determined to resort to more subtle methods of infiltration into the Indies administration. As had been mentioned already, Philip V was persuaded to set up again the old *Junta de comercio* (under the name of *Junta de restablecimiento del comercio*) in order to settle finally the prevalent questions of the Indies trade. The various French interests were confident that by adroitly placing French and Francophile officials in the *Junta* they would be able to impose their plans for reorganising the trade with the colonies in the guise of the considered recommendations of an official organ of Spanish government. The French advisers to the *Junta* were appointed in 1704, but it was not until nearly a year later, in May 1705, that their Spanish counterparts took office.[28] In the course of the discussions and negotiations about the reformation of the American trade, the departure of the fleet from Cadiz was once again delayed, from 1704 until 1705. However, in March 1705, when the Spanish finally had made all ready for the fleet to sail, it was, surprisingly, the action of the French themselves which brought about a further postponement. The French squadron under Admiral Ducasse, which had been dispatched to Cadiz to convoy the fleet to America, hurled itself into an abortive attempt to retake Gibraltar from the British. This untimely escapade cost the French squadron dearly and, as a result, the Spanish merchant fleet at Cadiz had to wait until a new French convoy squadron could be equipped.[29] In the meantime the fruitless deliberations of the *Junta* continued around the vital issues of the abandonment or continuance of the fleet system and direct French participation in the Indies trade, or Spanish monopoly.[30] The defence of Spain's prerogatives in the sessions of the *Junta* had proved stronger than the French had anticipated.

Yet Ducasse's impetuous attack on Gibraltar was perhaps not the reckless gesture it appears to be at first sight. It is possible to perceive a remarkable cooperation at this stage between all French interests in matters involving Spain's trade to the Indies, both those at ministerial level and those at merchant and military level. From the beginning of

the alliance until 1704 the French favoured the early dispatch of a fleet
from Cadiz in the traditional form. After all, for the French merchants
trading via Cadiz, once the 'free trade' system which they urged had
been rejected by the Spaniards, the next best thing was to export their
wares to the Indies, as they had always done, aboard the regular
Spanish fleets. Consequently there was some impatience at the continual orders to delay or abandon the departure of the Fernández de
Santilláns' fleet, over the years 1701–4.[31] But the year 1705 marks a
clear change in French policy. With the setting up of the *Junta de
restablecimiento del comercio*, of which the French ministers had high
hopes, and the increased success of their illegal trading in the South
Seas, the situation had altered considerably. All French interests now
sought to *hinder* the fleet for two clear reasons. First, that while there
were no supplies from Old Spain in America, and especially in Peru,
French contrabandists in the South Seas could increase the volume of
their trade: there is evidence alleging that French merchants even withdrew goods from the Tierra Firme ships in the fleet waiting at Cadiz.[32]
Second, that for the French it was essential to delay the departure of the
fleets as long as possible so that the 'happy' outcome of the deliberations of the *Junta* – either allowing direct French participation in the
trade or relaxing the rigid commercial system – could be immediately
used to advantage with the ships then hoping to set sail from Cadiz
almost at any time. The expedition of Admiral Ducasse against
Gibraltar, at the most inopportune moment possible, may be seen,
then, not as an impetuous assault upon the enemy, but as a move
calculated to hinder further the sailing of the luckless fleet from Cadiz
until such time as a favourable decision came out of the *Junta*. The
plan is clear: whichever way the engagement with the British went,
the Spanish fleet could not depart as arranged, and the French
ministers at Madrid would thereby gain another period of months in
which to promote their designs in the *Junta*. In the meanwhile the
St Malo smugglers could also continue their profitable expeditions to
the Pacific, and further delay at Cadiz could only benefit their trade.

Just as the French attitude to the departure of the fleet appears to
have changed early in 1705, so too did the Spanish. By the spring of
that year there was already a feeling of urgency among many
Spaniards for the dispatch of the fleet. The American markets were
unstocked and the dangers of contraband were daily increasing.[33] The
ruse employed by Ducasse, himself a strong advocate of holding back
the Cadiz fleet, thus effectively delayed its leaving, yet avoided an
undesirable clash with the Spaniards on the matter. Ducasse after all,

it could be maintained, was risking his squadron in attempting to recapture Spanish territory in the hands of a common enemy. The policies of the French towards the Cadiz fleet at this time are neatly exposed in the following dispatch from the British government to Governor Handasyde at Jamaica in January 1706:

> . . . the Galeons and Flota are become almost useless, or are at least made so by the French, who choose rather to bring home the Treasure of the Indies in their own men-of-war and merchant ships, than to entrust it to the Spanish fleets. [That all goods must be registered at the *Casa de Contratación* in the names of Spanish merchants irks the French, as they] cannot divert them so conveniently to their own profitt and purposes, nor furnish the Indies so well with their own native commodities as directly from France, which is the occasion, that all possible means are used by the French, and M. du Casse in particular, to hinder the going out of the Galeons and Flotta, as it is now said the Spanish Court has been perswaded at present to putt a stop to them for this year [1705–6], which being on the one hand very injurious to the Spaniards, as well in Spain as in their American Dominions and very advantageous to the French, there is no doubt but this prohibition will cause very great discontents. . .[34]

News of considerably increased French smuggling in the Pacific during the year 1705 only served to heighten the existing anxiety of the various Spanish interests, and by the early part of 1706 their concern was converted into resolute action. Despite the advice of their French allies, the Council of the Indies gave orders for the fleet to set sail from Cadiz as soon as possible, whether or not the French had by then succeeded in equipping a new squadron of convoy ships.[35] On 10 March 1706, therefore, the combined *galeones* and *flota*, comprising 26 ships in all, under the command of the Generals Diego and José Fernández de Santillán, at last left Cadiz, but without their French escort. The *flota* for New Spain carried 2674.85 tons of goods and the *galeones* for Tierra Firme carried 3542.42 tons.[36] Fortunately the voyage to the West Indies was made without losses either through storm or enemy attack, although it is reported that the fleet narrowly escaped an encounter in the Atlantic with a British squadron under Sir John Leake, who would certainly have given a good account of himself in an uneven battle if he had come across them.[37] Nevertheless on 27 April 1706, the combined fleet put in to Cartagena de Indias after its transatlantic voyage, unharmed despite its lack of convoy.[38]

To the dismay, rather than relief, of the Spaniards the zealously French Admiral Ducasse arrived in Cartagena shortly afterwards, anxious to keep a strict control on the movements of the Spaniards.[39] Ducasse was particularly hated in Cartagena, having taken part in the sack of that city nine years earlier.[40] We are told that he had

> lived about 30 years upon Hispaniola near the Spaniards, and had used the profession of buchaneering, being well acquainted with the interests and practices of the Spaniards in the West Indies.[41]

He was no doubt now eager to give his personal attention to French affairs in the Spanish Indies. The port of Cartagena, which for so long had seen precious little activity, was thus thronged with about 40 sail, made up by the *galeones* and *flota*, the French men-of-war and the Barlovento squadron which had also recently arrived there.[42]

Within a short time of their arrival the French put out to sea once more. Ducasse himself sailed as escort to the *flota* on the second stage of its voyage, from Cartagena to Veracruz, while other ships of the French squadron sailed to Havana, where it was intended they should wait in order to convoy the Spanish fleet on its return to Europe.[43] But feelings were running high amongst the Spaniards about Ducasse's continual meddling in the affairs of the fleet. Friction between the allied officers must have been strong, for it was soon known that the Spaniards had refused absolutely to allow their ships to return to Europe under French convoy.[44] Moreover, by the time the dispute had come to a head, news of Hapsburg victories in Spain had already reached the Indies, giving the Spanish officers greater confidence to stand up squarely to the French.[45] As a result, in the summer of 1706, the French ships which had been waiting at Havana returned to France, having previously lost a large man-of-war and their senior officer, de Berville, in a wreck off the Cuban coast.[46] French naval plans to sabotage the fleet, and failing that to chaperone it closely, were little by little becoming as ineffectual as those of their ministers to force issues in the *Junta de restablecimiento del comercio*. But ironically the comings and goings of Admiral Ducasse in the Indies had involved little or no expense to France. By a *cédula* of 6 November 1706, Philip V gave an order for the payment by the Spanish Crown of 907,670 *pesos escudos de plata* to the French ambassador for the expenses incurred in equipping 'seven ships to provide an escort for the New Spain fleet, and . . . eight more for the Tierra Firme galleons'.[47]

Yet in spite of everything, by now the French had really come quite close to achieving their aims in the *Junta*, on paper at least, if still not in practice. By a series of skilful manoeuvres they had succeeded in 'making the Spaniards see reason',[48] and on 9 January 1706, the *Junta* agreed on a series of articles concerning the reorganisation of the American trade. While it was still categorically stated that the *carrera de Indias* would be reserved to Spanish vessels only and that the trading of goods in the Indies would be limited to native Spaniards, concessions were made to the French on two major points: first, it was recommended that 'friendly foreigners' should be permitted to register goods for exportation to America under their own names, always providing they were shipped in Spanish bottoms and that the foreigners did not accompany their goods on the journey; and second, the fleet system would be abandoned and the trading practices at Portobello and in New Spain discontinued.[49] These articles were of course no more than the preliminaries to the reforms the French desired, yet because of the course of events even they were never ratified. The traditional fleet in fact had sailed on its way to Portobello and Veracruz within a month of the final session of the *Junta* and, owing to the fortunes of war, it was the *Junta* itself that was suspended indefinitely, rather than the trade fairs which it had condemned.[50] By the spring of 1706 the Bourbon had been driven into a position of considerable weakness and with Lord Galway's capture of Madrid on 27 June, the triumphant Archduke Charles took over the organs of government in Spain, albeit only for a short time.[51]

It is clear from what has been said that disagreement was ever present between Spanish and French on matters to do with trade and navigation to the Indies. Indeed, if one is to value the opinions of British ministers and officers in the West Indies, the Spaniards, at least those in the colonies, were ready at any moment for the Franco-Spanish alliance to be converted by France into an attempt to take Spain and her colonies for herself by military force.[52] The view seems to be confirmed by the events in the Indies of 1706 and 1707.

It was greatly feared by the French that the news of the Bourbon defeats in Spain would lead to open support in the Indies for the Archduke Charles.[53] The prompt appearance of Ducasse at Cartagena in April 1706 had probably not a little to do with this. Later in the year matters came to a head. The British in Jamaica intercepted some French documents in which was expressed the French intention of taking over the Spanish garrisons in the Indies by force in order to hold them for the Duke of Anjou. The Governor of Jamaica immediately sent word of this to the various Spanish governors in the Caribbean. That this news was gratefully accepted, and indeed even acted upon, seems to indicate beyond doubt that Spanish fears must in any case have already been roused. It is reported that after these dispatches had been received from the British, French men-of-war, for some time at least, were strictly refused admittance to all the ports of the Spanish Indies.[54]

However, even earlier than this, the Spaniards, in their mistrust of their allies, had virtually refused to accept non-Spanish troops in their garrisons in the Indies, and the fact that the French had insisted on supplying them with French 'reinforcements' had not made them any the more welcome.[55] The Spaniards were determined to resist, by force if necessary, any French attempts at military occupation of the Indies. At Havana fighting actually broke out between the French and Spanish. In August 1706 some French men-of-war, probably the remains of de Berville's squadron, entered the harbour demanding provisions, despite the governor's refusal to allow them in. When they attempted to make a landing

> the Spanish Guard fell on them, and killed 90 odd of the French, severall Spaniards were killed, and amongst them the Captain of the Town Guard, which . . . has bred so much ill-blood that it will turn considerably to the advantage of King Charles.[56]

For the supporters of the Bourbon the situation in the Indies was serious by September 1706. Although Philip V had regained his capital in August of that year, military success in the Peninsula was not accompanied by an improvement in naval strength in America. Both the *galeones* and the *flota* were in the Indies, with a largely pro-Hapsburg population in absolute control of them and not a French warship to defend them – and the enemies of France and Spain dominating the Caribbean from their island strongholds. Moreover the Bourbon was by now extremely short of silver with which to carry on the war and there seemed to be no way of obtaining immediate further supplies.

For these reasons and contrary to expectation, an official French project to raise bullion in the Indies was accepted by the Spanish Crown in the autumn of 1706. It was proposed that six well-armed French frigates should leave Cadiz for New Spain with merchandise for sale in the colony. The benefit to the Crown in taxes, it was calculated, would be of the order of two or three hundred thousand very welcome *escudos*. So at last it seemed there was to be some degree of Franco-Spanish cooperation over transatlantic shipping, even if it did look very much as if the French were at last gaining an unprecedented share in it. But the end of the affair was as unexpected as its beginning, for the merchants of St Malo, to whom the enterprise was naturally to be entrusted, refused absolutely to participate, despite much persuasion on the part of the French Crown, and Admiral Ducasse in particular. Obviously it was much more in the St Malo interest to continue illicit trade in the South Seas than to pay considerable sums in tax to the Spanish Crown for the doubtful privilege of carrying on legal trade via Cadiz. Several precious months were lost in negotiations which finally did nothing to raise money, nor indeed to speed the return of the fleets to Spain from the Indies.[57]

It was not until 12 October of the following year 1707 that the indefatigable Ducasse put out from Brest, bound once more for the Indies, with orders for the fleets and the eventual object of convoying them back to Europe. In view of the delays and the perilous situation the services of French naval squadrons were now specifically requested and paid for by the Spanish Crown. This was essentially a Bourbon crisis plan to obtain supplies of precious metals and to hold the Indies for Philip in the face, still, of a likely pro-Hapsburg raising there. Ducasse was dispatched to New Spain with nine ships while Captain Chabert was sent with two ships via Cape Horn to Callao.[58] Nevertheless the fortunes of war once more frustrated the satisfactory completion of Ducasse's mission. Although after a prolonged wait in Veracruz he was able to afford protection to the *flota* on its return journey in August 1708, he had earlier failed to be on hand at the time of the departure of the Tierra Firme *galeones* on their short voyage back to Cartagena from the fair at Portobello. Indeed the only warships with which the unfortunate Conde de Casa Alegre and his *galeones* had any dealings on their ill-fated passage were those of Commodore Sir Charles Wager, who sighted them in the waters off Cartagena at 9 o'clock on the morning of Saturday, 8 June 1708.[59]

2 The Portobello Fair of 1708

The docking of the *galeones* commanded by the Conde de Casa Alegre in Cartagena on 19 April 1706 was not marked by the activity usual throughout the provinces of the viceroyalty of Peru and its dependencies on the arrival of the fleet from Spain. Owing to the abnormal situation in Spain and the exceptional circumstances of the sailing of the fleets, it had been impossible to send ahead of them accurate early notice of their departure for the Indies. Preparations for the dispatch of the *Armada del Sur* had, therefore, not even begun when the *galeones* put in to Cartagena, and so the ships and their crews were made ready for a long wait in port. Moreover both the illegal trade in Oriental merchandise from New Spain and the French contraband in the Pacific had increased out of necessity during the previous few years, and the well-stocked merchants of Lima were not anxious to hasten along the regular commercial routes. In the meanwhile the new viceroy of Peru, who had arrived with his family and suite in the *galeones*, proceeded on his way to Panama and eventually to Lima. He did not arrive in his capital until 22 May 1707, 13 months later, to take over the organs of government and begin arrangements for the merchants of Lima to ship their money up to Panama for the trading at Portobello.[1]

Don Manuel de Oms y Santa Pau olim de Sentmenat y de Lanuza, first Marqués de Castelldosríus and the new viceroy of Peru, was certainly a colourful character. A member of the Catalan aristocracy, an accomplished man of letters and musician, and an able diplomat, he had been both popular and effective as Charles II's ambassador to the court of Portugal. His success in Lisbon had quickly earned him promotion to the highly important embassy to Louis XIV. At Versailles he was in his element, and he soon became an intimate of the Sun King himself. It was he who in the early morning of 11 November 1700, had had the fortune of bringing to Louis XIV's bed chamber the welcome news that the king's grandson, Philip of Anjou, had inherited the throne of Spain. The famous '*Il n'existe plus de Pyrénnées*', often

34

attributed to Louis himself, were Castelldosríus' own words on greeting his new sovereign for the first time. While his countrymen in Catalonia joined the cause of the Hapsburg in the War of the Succession, Castelldosríus, on the best of possible terms with the House of Bourbon, continued to serve for three more years at the French court as the ambassador of Philip V. In 1704, as a reward for faithful service, he was appointed viceroy of Peru, where he remained from May 1707 until his death in March 1710.

The character of Castelldosríus' rule in Peru is a matter which presents something of a problem. It was he who first brought an atmosphere of culture and fashion to the somewhat remote colonial society of Lima and introduced the French ways and manners which he had so taken to at the court of Versailles. The literary and artistic activities which were a feature of the viceregal court during his short years of office must certainly be regarded as a cultural highlight of Spanish rule in Peru. But in April 1709, after close investigation of a number of serious accusations made against him by his subjects in Peru, the Crown resolved to suspend him from office. The charges ranged from gross immorality in the viceregal court and irreverence in holy places, to neglect of government affairs and corruption, including participation in the illicit trade of the French interlopers. Despite the fact that much of the evidence before the Crown seemed (and still seems) conclusive, the proceedings against him were stopped, largely as a result of the intervention of his daughter, Catalina, who was at court in Madrid, and his name was officially cleared. His *residencia* was held after his death in 1710, and the judgment, made in 1717, stated that there was insufficient evidence to prove his guilt. The historian is thus confronted by the dilemma of whether to work from the detailed evidence which the Crown had itself gathered against Castelldosríus, or to accept the more general and sometimes unexplained refutations offered by the viceroy, knowing his position to be perilous, and by his defenders at the time of and after his death.[2] Whatever the truth concerning the viceroy's alleged immorality at his court, only the charges against him affecting commercial issues are of relevance to the present study. Of these many seem to be well substantiated by definite events and facts, external to the case itself but intimately connected with commercial developments in Peru during his years of office. In the account which follows of the trading in Peru and the Portobello fair of 1708 great care has been taken to attribute to Castelldosríus only such actions as seem to be proved by events, or alternatively which result from the Crown's *own* secret investigations through five independent

witnesses of impartial and honest reputation. No account has been
taken of any of the many other witnesses and accusations which may be
open to interpretation as inspired by personal enmity towards the
viceroy himself.[3]

The Marqués de Castelldosríus was sent to Peru to take over from
the *audiencia* of Lima which had been in charge of government since the
death of the previous viceroy, the Conde de la Moncloa. But the change
of viceroy had not been caused in the first instance by the death of the
count. It has already been mentioned how the plans of the French for
dominating the affairs of Spain for their own purposes had included the
placing of officials sympathetic to the French interest in positions of
importance in the government. In 1701 already, when Louis XIV was
endeavouring to manipulate the Council of the Indies, the Conde de la
Moncloa, then serving as viceroy in Lima, had been envisaged as a
replacement for the Marqués del Carpio in the supreme office of
president of the Council. The old marquis, in any case only an interim
president, showed little inclination to allow the French the free rein
they desired, whereas it was known on the other hand that the Conde
de la Moncloa was well disposed towards Spain's allies. French
ministers had high hopes that the recall of the count from the Indies to
occupy the presidency of the Council would be most advantageous to
their interests. Unfortunately, however, the Conde de la Moncloa died
while still in office in Peru, and French ambition in this respect was
thus frustrated. Nevertheless the count's death caused an important
vacancy in the Indies administration, and such a fine opportunity as
the appointment of a new viceroy in Peru was not to go unprofited by
the French. Even before the death of the Conde de la Moncloa, Louis
XIV had succeeded in having the Marqués de Castelldosríus
nominated as the next viceroy of Peru, and his elevation to such a high
post seemed most favourable to further French commercial expansion
into Spanish colonial markets.[4] Although his rule was by no means
entirely devoted to the interests of France, the profits to Louis XIV's
subjects and to the Bourbon cause in the Indies were certainly greater
than they might otherwise have been.

Commercial activity in Peru, both that at the Portobello fair and that
of the French interlopers in the South Seas, was greatly affected by the
rule and the vested interests of the new viceroy. From the moment of
his arrival in the Indies, in April 1706, it was plain that the sympathies
of Castelldosríus were not shared by the colonial officials then under
his command. The viceroy had brought with him from Europe a large
number of French gentlemen intended to occupy positions in his

viceregal court at Lima[5] – this, in spite of the ancient law forbidding the immigration of foreigners into the Indies without the express permission of the Crown.[6] Immediately there was dissension. The governor of Cartagena refused, apparently in no uncertain terms, to allow the viceroy's party to enter the country, and even went as far as passing the word to the authorities at Portobello, the viceroy's next port of call. From Portobello a message was sent back to Cartagena warning Castelldosríus that admittance for the French gentlemen of his entourage would not be granted via Portobello either. Governor Handasyde wrote:

> The Governor [of Cartagena] told him [Castelldosríus] he himselfe was welcome there, but as for his attendants, none should be admitted that were French. He had the like message sent from Porto Bell, when notice was given there of his coming, which shews the Spaniards' inclination for King Charles' interest.

He also laconically stated:

> I am of opinion whenever the fleet [the *Armada del Sur*] arrives, there will be great alterations [in the holders of local authority].[7]

But the various officials who showed themselves ill-disposed towards the new regime had not to wait until the arrival of the *Armada del Sur* before finding their positions in jeopardy. In March 1707, even before Castelldosríus had reached Lima, Governor Handasyde again wrote:

> [There] has been lately a great alteration made in the Spanish Governments, those Governors who were supposed to be in the interest of King Charles are turned out, and their places supply'd by those in the French interest.[8]

One of the first matters with which the new viceroy concerned himself on his arrival in the Indies was making sure that he had men upon whom he could rely occupying as many positions of local authority as possible throughout the viceroyalty. He was by no means slow in seeing to this. While he was still in Cartagena he had temporarily given the *corregimiento* of Ica, Pisco and Nazca, in the south of Peru, to Don Felipe de Betancourt, a captain of infantry from Panama, with whom he had struck up a great friendship during his stay in Cartagena. The post had then become vacant because of the death of the previous *corregidor*, but even when the official new tenant of the office, appointed in Spain by the king, presented himself at the viceregal court Castelldosríus refused to allow him to take over the *corregimiento*.[9] Other office-holders were deprived of their legitimate rights by the viceroy and, after having originally paid the Crown handsomely for their posts, they now found themselves obliged to live in penury in Lima during the viceroy's pleasure. By detaining the rightful holders of office in this way and granting the *corregimientos* or governorships to men of his own choice, either as gifts or, in the majority of cases, in return for agreed sums, the viceroy quickly achieved his aim of extending his influence throughout the country. His supporters received office in the *corregimientos* of Chancay, La Vacuña, Cajatambo, Nazca, Huánuco, Ica, the ports of Pisco and Paita and many other centres of local authority. He also secured the good will of the officials at Arica, Callao, Concepción, Guayaquil and Trujillo – all principal ports of the viceroyalty on the Pacific coast.[10] Clearly, from this position of political strength the viceroy was well able to control and indeed to facilitate the illicit commerce of the French ships in the South Seas and the entry of French traders into the interior of the country. During his time in office the previous viceroy, the pro-French Conde de la Moncloa, had permitted the trade with the French to flourish to some extent, despite his obligation to suppress it.[11] But it was not until the advent of Castelldosríus that the contraband between French and Peruvians was put on to a properly organised footing.

Once Castelldosríus began to arrange his affairs in Lima his illicit trading activities were so well coordinated as almost to compel admiration. Even while the *galeones* were in port at Cartagena, the regularly thriving trade with the foreign contrabandists had not decreased. The Spaniards from the fleet themselves in fact corruptly aided the entry of illegal merchandise and acted as go-betweens for the foreign smuggling vessels anchored near the port. A small fair at Cartagena itself was held during the summer of 1706 and was attended by the merchants from Popayán, Santa Fe, Quito and the other northern provinces of the viceroyalty. Approximately one third of the merchandise of the *galeones* was intended for sale at Cartagena. After this quantity had been sold a large volume of smuggled goods was also sold on the pretext that they too formed part of the original cargo of the fleet for Cartagena.[12] Between 27 April (the day the *galeones* put in to port) and 5 October, thirty smuggling vessels arrived in Cartagena loaded with merchandise, all of which passed into the provinces of northern Peru as authentic legal supplies purchased from the fleet.[13] The new viceroy, far from taking necessary measures against the interlopers, actually aided the three French privateers which were to take him to Portobello to dispose of their illegal cargoes while they were still in port at Cartagena.[14] It was common knowledge in Cartagena that the governor of Santa Marta had secured for himself a profitable source of income in the form of a 'tax' which amounted to 10 per cent of the value of all the smuggled goods which passed through his jurisdiction,[15] and this was an example which Castelldosríus was to follow with remarkable skill and inventiveness once he had established his viceregal court at Lima.

In close association with the Marqués de Castelldosríus in Peru were two other Catalans, Don Antonio Marí Ginovés, a lifelong friend of his, and the captain of infantry, Don Ramón de Tamarit, the viceroy's nephew. Tamarit was given the command of the troops which formed the viceroy's personal guard, and Marí, as the intimate and companion of Castelldosríus, was allowed to interfere to such an extent in the affairs of state that, it was alleged, the government of the viceroyalty was left almost entirely in his hands. Castelldosríus, Tamarit and Marí, together with another friend of the viceroy, Don José de Rosas, entered into an association with one Don Bernardo Solís Bango, alleged to be the head of a 'company' which concerned itself in regulating, and to a large extent monopolising the contraband trade of the French in the Pacific. In order to do this, of course, the associates depended upon the good will of the *corregidores* and officials who had received their positions from the viceroy. It was at the small port of Pisco, some miles to the south of Lima, that the French traders knew they could be sure of the safest welcome. There Captain Betancourt was *corregidor*, and close by, Rosas, the viceroy's friend and associate, had large estates. It was here therefore that the activities of this strange 'company' were particularly centred. French traders would put in to Pisco where their merchandise was unloaded and bought by members of the viceregal group. It would then be carried away for storing in various buildings on the nearby estates of Rosas; from there the goods would be distributed and sold throughout the viceroyalty. Merchants from Lima were also allowed to take their money to trade with the French at Pisco and the business grew to such proportions that the trading there came to be known publicly as the Pisco Fair.[16]

At Pisco, however, another kind of business was also transacted for the viceroy's profit. Private merchants were only permitted to trade there providing they paid a fee to the viceroy equal to 25 per cent of their total transactions. Naturally, what with the large volume of the trade and its somewhat irregular nature, it was difficult to know which merchants had paid the 25 per cent contribution and which had not. Therefore slips of paper were issued by Don Antonio Marí Ginovés certifying that the 'tax' had been paid and that the merchant concerned should be allowed free passage with his goods. Captain Ramón de Tamarit and his force of soldiers had the job of examining the merchandise and its owners on the road out of the port, and those merchants who were found to have eluded Marí's agents had their goods confiscated and officially declared as contraband. In this case the goods were turned over to the Crown after a certain proportion of their value had been given to the informer, as the law decreed, as a reward. Either way, therefore, whether the merchant paid the stipulated 25 per cent or whether the goods were declared as contraband, the viceroy and the 'company' could be sure of a percentage on the smuggled French wares. A similar state of affairs existed at all other ports in which occasional French vessels might be found carrying on their trade with the local merchants and inhabitants.[17]

For the merchants of Lima the fact that Castelldosríus, Marí, Rosas and Tamarit had so quickly and successfully cornered for themselves a large part of the contraband trade was a cause for great concern. The speed with which their control was established would seem incredible were it not borne out by certain facts. Castelldosríus arrived in Peru in March and took over the government at the end of May 1707. The events of the next few months show clearly that before the end of 1707 the 'company' had secured a tight grip and that the merchants were already endeavouring to break the stranglehold. Whereas previously through necessity they had learned to favour the French illegal commerce along their shores for the supplies and the profits it brought them, they were now keen that the laws against interlopers should be strictly enforced. For some years the merchants of the *consulado* had lived double lives, engaging in the trade as individuals but condemning it as a body. Castelldosríus himself, in a letter to the king in August 1707, described the situation very accurately:

> The merchant body in general laments and complains quite rightly that the illegal traffic has greatly weakened it, and yet the individual members of that body are themselves the ones who cause the general decline, for they have no concern whatsoever for the common good when it conflicts with their own private interests.[18]

But by the autumn of 1707 both the 'personalities' of the merchants were equally opposed to the French traffic – at least in its present form. It was at this stage that the *galeones* of Casa Alegre and the Portobello fair became a pawn in the growing struggle between the interests of the Lima merchants and those of Castelldosríus and the 'company'.

One of the responsibilities which fell upon the viceroy of Peru was the maintenance of the *Armada del Sur*, and it was his duty to order and organise the dispatch of this fleet to Panama at the appropriate time so as to make possible the trade fair at Portobello. The purpose of the fleet, as has already been explained, was to carry the king's treasure from Lima to the waiting *galeones* from Spain and to transport the Lima merchants and their money to the Portobello fair. Before the fleet could be dispatched at all and the fair subsequently held at Portobello, three essential conditions had to be fulfilled. First, there had to be a sufficient number of ships in service to make up the necessary complement of merchantmen for the *Armada* and its convoy; second, there had to be a considerable sum in the royal treasury at Lima available for shipment to the king in Spain; and third, there had to be several Lima and provincial merchants willing to embark in the fleet and take money with them for the trade at Portobello. In 1707 not one of these conditions was fulfilled. The Marqués de Castelldosríus therefore found himself in a position of considerable difficulty.

The Crown's ships of the *Armada del Sur*, like all things naval and military in the viceroyalty at that time, were in a state of disrepair and near abandonment. The *Armada* had not been fitted out for eleven years past, and as a result the Crown's contracts with the *consulado* for the *avería* (the contribution paid by the merchants to help to cover the Crown's expenses in maintaining the *Armada* and organising and convoying the fleet) had long since been allowed to expire.[19] The viceroy had at his disposal only three warships that could be made seaworthy to lead and protect the *Armada*. These the merchants had helped to build in 1688.[20] But their crews were very much under-strength and those men there were could hardly be considered capable sailors. Otherwise there was one galleon – which was a virtual wreck.[21]

The state of the royal treasury in Lima was nothing short of chaotic. For some years receipts from the main source of income, the *real quinto* (the tax exacted by the Crown which amounted to one fifth of the produce of all gold and silver mines) had dwindled sadly. In the times of the Conde de la Moncloa by far the greater part of the French smuggled goods had been paid for in crude silver smuggled out of the mines illegally before the royal tax had been deducted. Moreover the count had paid little attention to the state of the mines and overall production had also declined. In more recent times the increased volume of French merchandise brought into Peru had prompted more and more of the products of the mines to leave the country untaxed. This, together with the all-round decreasing output of metals, had caused the treasury's receipts to be considerably reduced. Fraud of the *real quinto* became such an accepted fact, it is reported, that by 1707 the royal seals for stamping silver were passing around from hand to hand among private persons quite freely. The result was that almost all illegal silver smuggled out of the mines before it was stamped, as proof that the tax had been paid, could be easily 'legalised' and all detection of the fraud quickly rendered impossible.²² When Castelldosríus arrived in Lima the treasury was already in extreme financial straits and the new viceroy inherited a deficit of some 5,000,000 *pesos*. His fund-raising activities throughout the kingdom were, however, quite remarkable, and he laid hands on every possible source of money from parish poor-boxes to community chests. It is alleged in fact that he diverted portions of this income into the purchase of French goods for the 'company'. Whether this was true or not the fact remains that Castelldosríus raised as a matter of urgency the record total of 1,679,310 *pesos* to send off to Spain to relieve the financial distress of his Bourbon master.²³

While the country continued to be flooded with cheap smuggled goods the merchants of Lima were obviously not prepared to travel to the Portobello fair to invest their money in stock which they knew they could never sell again on their return. They therefore rejected Castelldosríus' proposals – as they had those of the *audiencia* the year before – to make ready for the sailing of the *Armada* and the trading at Portobello.²⁴ The legitimate goods from Portobello, it was calculated, would sell at two and three times more than those brought in illegally from the French ships. It was in fact more profitable to pay the viceroy his 25 per cent. The merchant body therefore, although opposed to the contraband in its present form, was even more strongly opposed to spending its money at the Portobello fair. The fair represented for them the greater of two evils.

The situation, then, which faced Castelldosríus – an ill-equipped *Armada del Sur*, a serious shortage of royal treasure for shipment to Spain, and an absolute lack of cooperation on the part of the merchants – was one which, for his own good, he had to remedy if his government of Peru was not to be unfavourably represented before the throne. Moreover before he had left Spain he had been given special instructions that he was to draw up fresh contracts for the *avería* with the *consulado* to replace those which had lapsed, and dispatch the *Armada del Sur* as soon as possible after his arrival. At the same time he had been particularly instructed to do his utmost to foster and encourage the trade of the *galeones* of Casa Alegre in order to promote the revival of the Portobello fairs, so desired by the various interests in Spain.[25] The Conde de Casa Alegre and the representatives of the Spanish *Consulados* had been long awaiting news of the departure of the *Armada* and it was now learned that Admiral Ducasse was once more in the Indies (having left Brest on 12 October 1707) with orders already for the return to Spain of both *galeones* and *flots*.[26] Yet by December 1707, there was still no definite news that the *Armada del Sur* was on its way north, and the commander of the *galeones* had become despondent about the continued stagnation of his fleet in Cartegena. There were rumours that five of his ships (probably those that had already completed their transactions at the Cartegena fair the previous year) were about to set sail for Buenos Aires in order to await there an unspecified convoy to escort them back to Europe.[27]

In these difficult circumstances the viceroy had little alternative but to come to some kind of an understanding with the merchants of Lima which would satisfactorily solve his various problems. The merchants too were anxious that for their own sakes this very tense situation should be eased. An agreement was therefore reached between the two opposing interests at some time during the late autumn of 1707. Over this the viceroy had to spend nearly three months of negotiations in and out of the port of Callao.[28] It seems that Castelldosríus on his part undertook to curtail the activities of the 'company', and moreover agreed to make every effort to prevent smuggled goods of all kinds from entering the country. In this way the Lima merchants would have a certain amount of security in the form of a guaranteed market for the goods which they would import from Portobello. Strict orders were issued that all French interlopers were to be expelled from the ports and beaches of the viceroyalty and that henceforth smugglers would not be tolerated. Naturally once these orders were known in Europe they caused the greatest consternation amongst the hitherto gleeful French adherents of Castelldosríus in Spain. Daubenton wrote to Pontchartrain:

> The orders which Castelldosríus has given concerning shipping in the South Seas have been unnecessarily severe. There is even a note of fury against France in the representations which he has made to

His Catholic Majesty and to the Council of the Indies. His disregard
of the obligations which he has to the King [Louis XIV] reveal his
ill will and his extreme ingratitude, and show that the French have
no greater enemy than him. Who could ever have imagined such
appalling behaviour?[29]

The merchants on their part agreed to help the viceroy out of his
financial troubles by making some contribution to Crown revenue and,
certainly no less important, for it was the crucial point in the whole
affair, they agreed to take their goods and money to trade at the Portobello fair.[30] In so doing, incidentally, they risked both their lives
and their riches, for the lack of fully equipped ships and the failure to
draw up the contracts for the *avería* meant that the fleet would have had
to leave Callao virtually unprotected if the merchants had not taken
some of the financial responsibility for its defence upon themselves.[31]
Besides, the viceroy's recent anti-contraband orders were likely to turn
frustrated French smugglers into potential enemies and pirates.[32] But
in spite of the physical dangers and the risk of financial loss, the
merchants cooperated, and on 19 December 1707, the *Armada del Sur* set
sail from Callao on its way to Panama and Portobello with more than
seven million *pesos* on board.[33] There were, however, other considerations, as will presently be seen, that gave the merchants an added
interest in the early celebration of the fair at Portobello, in spite of their
previous aversion to it on purely commercial grounds.

News that the *Armada del Sur* was at last really about to depart
produced more purposeful activity at Cartagena, and on 5 January
1708, the *galeones* too set sail for Portobello.[34] For Casa Alegre and his
crews a dreary wait of nearly two years at Cartagena was happily over.
In Lima the struggle between the various vested interests had eventually come to an end, and after a break of more than 10 years a fair at
Portobello was once again to be celebrated. Yet for those concerned in
the trade it might perhaps have been better if the fair had never taken
place, for the outcome was certainly more unhappy for them all than
any could ever have imagined.

The fair itself was utter confusion. For this the viceroy himself was
very largely to blame. One of the Bourbon's considerations in
rewarding Castelldosríus with the viceroyalty of Peru had been that
through that office he should be able to recuperate the personal
financial losses which he claimed to have sustained in the diplomatic
service of his country.[35] This fact alone may perhaps lend credibility to
the charges of malpractice laid against him. Castelldosríus had

borrowed the large sum of 6300 *pistoles* from the French *Compagnie de la Mer Pacifique* while in Paris, and in addition to this he had an enormous personal debt of some 200,000 *pesos* in Spain which he had left unpaid on his departure for Peru.[36] Not long after his arrival in the Indies, when he was passing through Panama on his way to Lima, he had written to his old friend, Don Antonio Marí Ginovés, who was then already established in Lima, requesting that this latter sum be advanced to him by the merchants of the city as a special personal favour. The intention was that while he was still in touch with the fleet from Spain he could arrange to have the money sent back to Spain in the first ships to return to Europe. He promised to pay back the money to his Peruvian creditors when the fair was held in Portobello. As a willing service to their new lord the Lima merchants readily agreed to help, and the money was handed over to Marí and sent on to Panama. Now that the fair was about to be celebrated Castelldosríus found himself under an uncomfortable obligation to return the borrowed money to its merchant owners and he conceived a highly irregular method of doing this.

Although no proper contract for the *avería* was in force for the *Armada del Sur* in 1708, the merchants of Lima were still obliged to pay the Crown their fixed contribution of 350,000 ducats towards the *avería* for the fleets from Spain. The money for this was collected by the *consulado* itself, through two officers elected from its own number, at a point on the way from Panama to Portobello known as El Boquerón. Here a tax of seven per cent was levied on all the precious metals going through to the fair. The proceeds of this tax were lumped together to make up the 350,000 ducats to be received by the commander of the *galeones* for shipment to Spain. The amount collected in tax was normally greater than the sum payable, and so after the dues had been handed over the remainder was divided out proportionally and returned to the merchants for their own use at the fair.[37] In 1708 the two merchants chosen to collect the money and keep the books were Don Juan Munariz and Don José de Meneses. It was with the aid of these two that Castelldosríus hoped to put his plan into action for the repayment of his debt to the merchants. The plan was this: the tax at El Boquerón would be collected in the usual way from each merchant as he passed, but when all had gone by El Boquerón and paid their dues the viceroy's personal debt of 200,000 *pesos* was to be settled with the Lima merchants in Portobello itself out of the proceeds of the duties collected from them on the journey across the Isthmus by Munariz and Meneses. All this was in fact nearly accomplished. The only snag was that, because the viceroy's merchant creditors were several in number it was inevitable that the scheme for repayment should soon become public knowledge, and news of the swindle quickly reached the ears of the commander of the *galeones*. It was not long before he discovered that the sum of tax he was to receive from the *consulado* was short. Munariz and Meneses were thrown into prison and were held until they agreed to supply full details of the fraud; for some time they refused to do this for fear of the viceroy's wrath when they returned to Lima. Yet by then each merchant had already received what was owed to him on the viceroy's account and was ready to spend money on the goods for sale at the fair. The Conde de Casa Alegre, however, suspended the opening of the fair and sent soldiers to search every house in the town with instructions that all the money found belonging to the merchants from Lima was to be brought to him where it would be held in confiscation until the Crown's rightful dues had been paid in full. Clearly once all the Lima merchants' money had been mixed together, confusion and chaos reigned. It was only when Munariz and Meneses had been released and the whole scheme divulged that the involved business of restoring to its owners that money which remained after the king's 350,000 ducats had been set aside could begin. Eventually, however, a settlement was reached, but not without a good deal of bad feeling prevailing on both sides. The Peruvians complained that the goods were poor stuff and high in price, while the Spaniards blamed the Peruvians for the unprecedented turmoil and confusion at the fair.

By the end of May 1708 the fair was over and the *galeones* left Portobello bound once more for Cartagena. But they were never to arrive, for shortly after their departure from Portobello the final tragedy struck the Conde de Casa Alegre and his *galeones*. The British in Jamaica had kept a sharp watch on all movements of French and Spanish shipping in the area. They were fully aware that after the fair was finished at Portobello the *galeones* would have to cross the Caribbean without the benefit of French protection, and for this they were prepared.[38] On Saturday, 8 June 1708, Commodore Wager, with three men-of-war and a fire-ship, met the *galeones* off Cartagena. For the Spaniards the losses were catastrophic. In the engagement the *San José*, Casa Alegre's flagship, blew up, and the commander himself lost his life. The other ships, holed, sinking or grounded, got out of range of Wager's guns, but only the *almiranta* and one merchantman succeeded in making port at Cartagena.[39] So, tragically, ended the voyage of the *galeones* of the Conde de Casa Alegre, an expedition which for nearly eight years had been the continuous victim of various sets of conflicting interests, both in Europe and America.

In early July 1708, the *flota* from Veracruz set sail from Havana for Spain with its French convoy, but without its sister fleet.[40] Once again Ducasse had failed to complete his mission, and his Bourbon master, so anxious about the treasure from the Indies, received only a portion of the amount he was expecting.

For the Peruvians the aftermath of the Portobello fair was also a disaster. On the way home from the fair the merchant fleet was twice plundered by English pirates, once by Colb on the Isthmus of Panama, and once by Rogers and Dampier in the Pacific. Moreover, contrary winds lengthened the voyage and as late as 1709 merchants were still straggling back overland from the port of Paita to Lima with portions of goods.[41] But the greatest set-back for many was that the viceroy had not only failed to prohibit the French interlopers on the coasts of Peru, as had been agreed, but had treacherously promoted the importation of smuggled goods during the merchants' absence at the fair. After the departure of the *Armada del Sur* from Callao he had enforced most strictly a total ban on communications between the northern and southern provinces of the viceroyalty. The ports were closed and travel by land was prohibited for some time between certain places in order to isolate completely the two areas of the country. This was allegedly done so as to ensure that news of the influx of French goods which the infamous 'company' was organising in the South should not reach the merchants on their way to the fair at Portobello in the North, and thus paralyse the trading. The transactions of the viceroy and his associates involved various French vessels at Pisco and Callao; but the principal scandals arose over the cargoes brought by the Captains Chabert and Fouquet who had come to Callao as part of the Bourbon plan to secure the Indies and obtain urgently needed bullion. Under the pretext of being in port on official allied business they succeeded, with the viceroy's consent, in selling large quantities of goods from their own and other private French ships.[42] The respected Don Pedro de Olaurtúa, who had recently finished a term in the office of Prior of the *consulado*, alarmed like many others by the volume of the traffic at such a time, had attempted to have a letter drawn up, signed by many of the Lima merchants, to be sent on to their representatives or colleagues in the *Armada*. In this he advised them to withdraw at all costs their money from the trading at Portobello as the viceroyalty was already flooded with illegal French goods. For this attempt to frustrate the viceroy's plans Olaurtúa was exiled to a remote part of the country and his scribe was imprisoned.[43]

The quantity of illegal merchandise which came through the Pacific ports of Peru at this time was enormous. For a month or two French goods had free rein throughout the southern provinces, and every article of merchandise sold added to the acute distress felt generally by the wretched Lima merchants once they returned from the fair at Portobello, having been plundered on their journey and betrayed while away from home. Many were ruined and many more made unparalleled losses. The market was so saturated with goods much cheaper than those the merchants from Portobello could offer that the viceroyalty was reduced to a state of commercial crisis.[44] Thus, apart from the viceregal 'company', the only ones to profit from the events of 1707-8 were the French contrabandists. Confirmation of the increased volume of French traffic along the Pacific coasts in the year of the Portobello fair is to be found in the fact that the following year, 1709, was the year in which the bullion returns to France reached their peak. In 1709 more than 30,000,000 *piastres* in gold and silver was handed over to the royal mints in France from ships which had been in the South Seas, and this figure may in fact represent something less than the total value of precious metals taken from Peru.[45]

At Cartagena the two ships which had survived the encounter with Commodore Wager in June 1708 remained in port without much prospect of an early departure. Indeed for nearly two years there was no move to supply men-of-war from Europe to bring them home. During that time relations between Spanish and French ministers in Madrid were unsatisfactory for both sides. France's continued and impertinent attempts to introduce quantities of merchandise into the Spanish colonies, even under the thin cover of convoy operations and official expeditions, were causing feelings to run high in Madrid. This, together with persistent distrust of French motives in sending warships to the Indies, resulted in a good deal of reluctance to allow France to intervene, even though Spain herself was unable to provide adequate protection to the waiting *galeones*. Indeed the Conde de Aguilar, in one outburst, is reported to have said that he would have preferred to see the treasure ships perish rather than fall into the hands of the French. In December 1709, therefore, Ducasse was officially forbidden to go out to the Indies to escort the two ships back to Europe: they were to remain in port at Cartagena until the peace, when they would make their own way back to Spain independent of French warships.[46] Of this the French were not so convinced. They had a direct interest in the cargo of the *San Joaquín* in the form of treasure belonging to the French Assiento Company and other French merchants. Governor Handasyde wrote:

> . . . the Spaniards say they will not trust [the ships] under a French convoy, therefore is [*sic*] resolved they shall stay there till Peace, but as they are the weaker Party, I expect, if a strong French squadron come, they will obleidge them either by foule means or fare.[47]

Throughout the year 1710–11 several French ships entered and left Cartagena, apparently unsuccessful in their attempts to sail as escort to the two galleons.[48] It was not until May 1711, after French interests had prevailed in Madrid, that Ducasse arrived in the Indies 'on account of the galloons' and accompanied by a number of French merchantmen.[49] Three months later, in August 1711, the French admiral slipped secretly out from Cartagena with his five men-of-war, having first taken on board the whole treasure from the *San Joaquín*, including the money belonging to merchants and the French Assiento Company.[50] Shortly afterwards the *San Joaquín* and the *patache* of the *galeones* put out from Cartagena bound for Spain but without an escort of any description. The inevitable happened. Before they were clear of the Antilles, a British squadron under Commodore Littleton sighted them, and after a brief battle forced them to surrender. The two ships were taken into port to Jamaica and it is reported that there Villa Nova, the commander of the *San Joaquín*, died of his wounds.[51] In spite of these considerable Spanish losses Ducasse himself skilfully slipped through the hands of the waiting British, and, as it turned out, successfully salvaged all that remained of the treasure brought from Portobello.

Small indeed were the returns for Spain from the official trading at Portobello in 1708, an enterprise which had cost so great an effort to effect and which had so tragically fallen victim to a multitude of vested interests on both sides of the Atlantic.

3 Spain's American Trade, 1708-1713

By the year 1708 the French had reasons to believe that they were on the point of an important break-through in their negotiations with the Spanish on the question of the transatlantic trade. It will be remembered that in 1706 the Spanish ministers of the *Junta de comercio* had finally yielded, in principle at least, to French insistence that the old system of *galeones* and *flota* should be abolished. The matter was again brought up in the spring of 1708, when a renewed French diplomatic effort attempted to implement the recommendations of the by-now defunct *Junta*. Once more French and Spanish officials sat down together to draft a revised set of regulations governing future trading practice with the colonies, based on the previous agreements of 1706. But although the French realised that tact and even compromise were still necessary if they were to gain any real advantage, they clearly hoped that at this stage the reforms would embody major concessions to their country's diplomacy. However the series of articles, when they were eventually agreed upon in July 1708, represented for the French nothing more nor less than one step forward and two steps back from their very promising position of 1706. For while it was at last accepted that henceforth *all* foreigners might participate directly in the American trade (i.e. register cargoes for the Indies in their own names and not through Spanish agents) it was still roundly declared that the trade itself would continue to be the exclusive preserve of Spanish subjects. Moreover it was insisted that any foreign nation desiring to benefit from these new privileges would be required to present a statement sworn by its sovereign to the effect that his subjects were forbidden to trade directly with the Spanish colonies and that he would outlaw and punish all contraband activities by his subjects in the Indies. Failure to comply with this would incur the withdrawal of the privilege. This of course, if ratified, meant an end to France's increasingly prosperous smuggling in the Pacific, so irksome to the authorities in Spain. But neither was the old system of annual fleets to be entirely abandoned, as the French had always insisted. Instead, and by way of compromise, a kind of Atlantic ferry service of warships would convoy small fleets of Spanish merchantmen, whenever they assembled, to the traditional ports of Veracruz, Cartagena and Portobello. The old trade fair was to be discontinued, it is true, but this was really only a minor matter. The main intention of the French had always been to secure the legal admission of their merchantmen directly to the ports of the Indies, for once their ships docked there they believed they could soon dispose of the cargoes, with or without a fair. The prices alone would ensure this. Thus French diplomatic effort over the previous four or five years had been directed towards this specific end. Yet even by 1708, despite a good deal of headway in making the Spaniards accept the need for reform, the French had still failed to achieve, even theoretically, this basic objective of their policy.

For the French ministers the provision that the trade should be open to other foreign nations as well as France was one of the least satisfactory aspects of the new regulations. They had agreed to it only in order to make a show of their own professed lack of self-interest in Spain's economic recovery; but it was certainly no substitute for the advantages they hoped to gain from their close alliance with Spain. At all events Louis XIV decided that the present stage of the war was hardly the moment to invite England and Holland to share in Spain's American commerce, nor indeed to tempt them to negotiate a peace in order to benefit from the new privilege – on equal terms with France! The matter was, therefore, brought to a halt before it got out of control, and the legislation was never put into effect, nor even published. Nevertheless rumours of the reform travelled round Holland and England and may even have played a part in the British government's initiative of entering into the secret negotiations of 1709–10 with Philip V for a peace on the basis of trade concessions in America.[1]

But if Spanish diplomatic resistance was stubborn and effective, lack of resources and strength in the field had been gradually weakening that negotiating position for some time past. We have seen how, as early as the winter of 1706, while the Fernández de Santillán's' fleets were held up in the Indies, despairing of an early return, naval inadequacy and shortage of precious metals had persuaded the Crown to accept French offers to send a fleet of six ships to trade in New Spain and bring back some badly needed treasure. France was to benefit from the supplying and crewing of the ships and from two thirds of the cargo, which could be dispatched and sold in New Spain *directly* by French merchants. Acceptance of their plan had caused not a little surprise to the French ministers. They had apparently put forward the proposals largely as diplomatic form, and were neither expecting nor prepared to have to put them into effect. When the merchants of St Malo refused to collaborate, the earnest arguments of the civil servants that such an expedition could well be the 'thin end of the wedge' made little impression. The illegal trade to the Pacific continued to produce very satisfactory profits and no advantage was seen in risking ships, merchandise and capital in a legal venture. Disappointment in French diplomatic circles was considerable, and the pressure on the St Malo merchants was continued. Eventually a compromise was reached and a form of contract between French and Spanish Crowns was agreed upon, resulting in the inclusion of several French vessels, both merchantmen and warships, in the New Spain fleet of 1708.[2] The sailing of this mixed fleet of Spanish and French ships marked in fact the maximum attainment of France in her prolonged effort to break into and dominate the legal trade to America from Spain. Never before in the history of the *galeones* and *flota* had foreign vessels sailed into the ports of the Indies, as part of the official fleet, to market goods for their own profit. France never had the opportunity again, and it was left to England in the years to come to violate, regularly and by right, the ancient monopoly of the Spaniards in their commercial relations with their American Empire.

This international fleet, then, which left Cadiz on 22 May 1708 under the command of General Andrés de Pez, consisted in all of 21 ships. There were 14 Spanish vessels, of which eight were frail little craft of less than 100 tons, and seven French, most of which were fair-sized ships averaging something over 200 tons each. Defenses were provided by the *capitana de Barlovento*, returning to her base in the Indies, a small Spanish armed ship and two large French men-of-war, both heavily laden with merchandise. All the Spanish ships together measured only 1282.98 tons, while the French merchantmen alone made up 1014.90 tons. In addition there were the sizeable cargoes of the two French warships.[3] It is clear, therefore, that French interests in the trading in Mexico in 1708 were at least as great as those of Spain, and probably greater. Perhaps it was on this account that tension between the representatives of both countries was expected to be particularly strong throughout the voyage. Official fears of strife aboard were expressed in the instructions to the fleet, which began by ordering all ranks to maintain 'the greatest possible unity and peacefulness', and ended with a lengthy exhortation to pay 'great care and attention to achieving a maximum of good relations and friendship between the two nations so that there should not arise the least discord between them'.[4]

Such orders were nevertheless of little avail, as is testified by the significant bundle of 'criminal charges' which French and Spanish filed against each other on their return to Cadiz.[5]

The movements of the fleet of 1708, like that of 1706, were seriously restricted by the waiting British squadrons in the Caribbean. Business affairs in New Spain were concluded unusually quickly in 1708, but although the fleet was ready to leave for home in February 1709, after only six months in New Spain, orders were received that it was not to sail until a French convoy arrived. Faced by increasing protests from the Spanish (and French!) merchants on board, in the following November the viceroy resolved to disobey orders and allow the fleet to attempt the voyage home under the largely inadequate protection of the two men-of-war and the one Spanish armed ship which had accompanied the fleet on its outward bound voyage.[6] As a result of the protracted ten-month wait in the Indies the condition of the ships had deteriorated considerably. This, and the absence of a French convoy of any strength, caused some concern on the part of the officers in the fleet. Yet to the great annoyance of the British – both those in the West Indies and particularly those in Her Majesty's government in London – the *flota* succeeded in slipping through the net, and towards the end of February 1710 Andrés de Pez put safely in to Cadiz on his return from New Spain. To express royal appreciation of his conduct of the mission the customary *residencia* was waived and Pez was promoted to the rank of Admiral of the Fleet.[7]

The fleet of 1708, under Pez, was the last occasion on which French participation in Spanish transatlantic shipping was a real issue. The scent of peace negotiations was in the air and the Franco-Spanish alliance was beginning to drift apart, although France was as keen as ever to foster the illegal trade of her interlopers in Spanish America at every possible opportunity.[8] Louis XIV's decision to encourage a settlement with his enemies by withdrawing troops from the Peninsula meant that Philip was obliged to continue the war with Spanish resources alone. Given the critical state of the nation's affairs and the catastrophic condition of the royal treasury, French military retirement was somewhat resented by the Bourbon's Spanish supporters.[9] Nevertheless although 1709 was a crucial year for the Franco-Spanish alliance it was now possible for Spain to set about regaining for herself full control of the *carrera de Indias* and, providing sufficient ships were available, she would be able to manage her trade without interference from the French. Yet lack of warships for service both in the Mediterranean and in the Atlantic presented precisely one of the most

serious problems which the Spanish Crown had to face at this stage. It
was publicly admitted that adequate protection could not be provided
for the American trade fleets while naval effort in the Mediterranean
was so urgent. Moreover, not only were there no suitable ships, but the
Crown was unable to afford to have any built. A royal appeal of 28
August 1708 to the people of New Spain for funds for shipbuilding had
not been immediately productive, but a general more urgent appeal
throughout Spain and the Empire in March 1710 produced 100,000
pesos as a gift from the merchants, and 200,000 *pesos* more as a loan,
raised from the returns of the 1708 fleet. The request brought in a
further 67,422 *pesos* from New Spain by 1713.[10] In the meanwhile, as a
partial but prompt solution to the pressing problem, Philip V
attempted to buy four warships from his grandfather Louis XIV; but
because the French king did not wish to prejudice the negotiations for
peace then in progress between himself and the Dutch, he refused to
sell.[11] The Spanish Crown consequently found itself obliged to make
special arrangements, based mainly on the drawing-up of contracts
with private individuals, for the continuance of the American trade.

Royal dependence upon merchants and speculators for the provision
of ships was to become the most striking feature of the *carrera de Indias*
over the next decade. Even in 1706 the Crown had had to hire a
flagship for the fleet from the merchant Don Juan de Eguilaz,[12] and
now, in 1709, for the first time, the king entered into contract with a
well known sailor speculator, Don Manuel López Pintado, for
transporting the quicksilver to New Spain.[13] The sale of mercury to be
used in the amalgam process for refining silver was a royal monopoly
and supplies had always been sent to New Spain in Crown warships
commanded by serving officers. That tradition was now broken, but
nevertheless in the summer of 1710 the two ships which plied across the
Atlantic carrying the royal quicksilver and 200 tons of merchandise for
sale in Mexico were governed once again entirely by Spanish interests.
In the autumn of that year a second little fleet carrying the new viceroy
of New Spain, the Duque de Linares, also reached Veracruz from Spain
with more quicksilver and goods for sale.[14]

But the sailing of four little ships on official business could hardly be
seen as the vindication of Spanish ministers' efforts over a decade to
maintain their country's exclusive commercial preserve in the Indies
against the schemes of the French. Clearly something more was needed
if merchants were not to face ruin through the Crown's impotence and
the continuing illegal activities of foreigners in the Indies. The
commercial bodies of Andalusia were greatly distressed in 1710 by

news that Admiral Ducasse and his squadron had again left St Malo, bound for Cartagena with cloth and other merchandise. They were positively enraged, however, by the further news that Philip had himself given the St Malo merchants permission to send four large ships to Veracruz, each with 500 tons of goods, on which he had already collected 20,000 *pesos* in duty. What was more, it was learned that the king intended to forbid anyone else from trading there for the rest of the year. As a result of all this the merchants of Seville drafted a strongly worded protest to the Crown, and in order to placate them the king announced his intention to make ready a full New Spain trade fleet for the following year of 1711. It was, of course, immediately realised just how vain such a project was, given the total lack of available warships, and anger and despondency were rife in Seville for some months. But in March 1711, as if by magic, the *capitana* of the Barlovento squadron unexpectedly put into Cadiz, bringing a million *pesos* for the royal treasury and convoying four small merchantmen from Veracruz. The preparation of a fleet now seemed feasible, and the merchant bodies left the king in no doubt about their desire to go ahead.[15]

The outcome of the negotiations which ensued was the *proyecto*, or set of arrangements, for the dispatch of a fleet to New Spain, published on 21 April 1711.[16] This was the first and most important of the series of *proyectos* and private contracts by which the Indies trade was conducted over the years, 1711 to 1720, a decade which saw a number of changes in naval and commercial affairs, culminating in the *Real proyecto para galeones y flotas* of 1720. The *proyecto* of 1711 brings in two basic innovations, the one in the organisation of the fleet, the other in the field of taxation. For the dispatching of a fleet, the usual practice had been for the Crown to announce the date of its departure to the Indies under the protection of a convoy of royal warships. Merchant ships and goods were then brought to Seville for registration and payment of duties. By contrast the *proyecto* of 1711 required six privately-owned and named ships, together with the *capitana* of the Barlovento squadron, to assemble at Cadiz to be loaded as a *flota* for New Spain. Because the Crown was unable to provide an adequate convoy it was declared that two of the merchant ships were to be equipped as warships by private contract between the Crown and their owners. In the sections on taxes and duties the document marks a significant milestone in the history of Spain's American trade, foreshadowing in its schedules the more complete piece of legislation, the *Real proyecto* of 1720. The complicated Hapsburg method of collecting duties piecemeal on both sides of the

Atlantic was simplified, and tax was to be levied in the form of a direct duty calculated solely on the volume of the goods, irrespective of their weight or value.[17] Tax was to be collected at Cadiz only, once at the start of the voyage on goods exported, and once at the end of the voyage on precious metals and goods imported. The schedules of the *proyecto* go into considerable detail, specifying both merchandise and duty to be levied item by item. The document of 1711 and the rates of duty established in it were in fact to serve as the fiscal basis for the dispatching of five of the six fleets sent to America between 1711 and 1720.

The command was given to General Andrés de Arriola, the chief of the Barlovento squadron, and the small fleet, composed now of eight vessels and not seven, left Cadiz on 3 August 1711 and carried 1596.85 tons of merchandise.[18] It reached Veracruz without incident on 5 October. The fears of the Andalusian merchants of a great influx into New Spain of contraband and licensed goods from France proved to be correct, and trading for the Spaniards in Mexico was difficult. Moreover the Manila galleon had only recently arrived, putting her much esteemed 'China' merchandise on the market in competition with the *flotistas'* goods. The business of the fleet was therefore not concluded quickly. A further complication also arose with the death of Arriola in New Spain. His subordinate, Don Pedro de Ribera, was promoted to the command, and it was he who on 19 January 1713 took the fleet out of Veracruz on the return voyage to Cadiz.[19]

Meanwhile in Spain the desire to revitalise and even reform the American trade was growing, both in government circles and among the merchants, and within seven months of the departure of Arriola's fleet from Cadiz the Crown took in hand the preparation of another *flota* for New Spain.[20] On 3 March 1712 a *proyecto* went before the Council of the Indies proposing a fleet to be composed of two large warships and two smaller warships (whose chartering and equipping were currently under negotiation with the shipowner Don Juan de Eguilaz, and with the merchant bodies) and four merchant ships belonging to specified individuals. The Crown hoped to have Arriola and the *capitana* of the Barlovento squadron back in Spain again and ready to lead the fleet by the stipulated date of departure, 31 July 1712. Unfortunately the matter did not proceed according to plan. Negotiations over the ships proved fruitless, the Seville merchant body was unable to find even one vessel (and eventually had to be permitted to load goods in other ships in the fleet), and the *capitana de Barlovento* remained at anchor in Veracruz. The Crown, therefore, thought fit to accept an offer made by Don Juan de Ubilla, an old sailor of the *carrera de Indias*, backed by the finances of the Chevalier d'Eon, head of a French merchant family based in Cadiz. A new contract, by which these two gentlemen undertook the organisation and dispatching of the proposed fleet, was signed on 15 May 1712. Ubilla himself was given the senior command with the rank of general, and Don Francisco Salmerón was made admiral in place of the Chevalier d'Eon who declined to undertake the voyage. Blank patents for the three remaining major officers were handed to Ubilla, and appointments were made by agreement with Eon. The financial arrangements for the voyage were complex, but may be resumed as follows. Ubilla and Eon agreed to supply and equip at their own cost, or by sub-contract, two warships of 50 and 54 guns to serve as *capitana* and *almiranta* and to provide the other smaller warships necessary for a fleet. They also contracted to transport in them mercury (the vast amount of 4000 *quintales* was taken) and other Crown property. The entrepreneurs insisted that the round trip had to be made within approximately 12 months from July 1712 – an almost impossible feat; but the Crown agreed to pay the expenses of any delay of the fleet in Veracruz beyond March 1713. The Crown also paid the cost of crewing and provisioning the ships for the whole voyage, and gave tax-free salaries to the general and his admiral. In order to achieve a speedy return to Spain the originally planned tonnage of merchandise in the fleet was reduced. This, it was hoped, would minimise the length of the commercial operations in New Spain. All taxes and duties on the goods carried by the fleet both ways were to be levied according to the schedules set out in the *proyecto* of 1711 for Arriola's fleet, and the outstanding charter fees for the ships were to be paid to Ubilla and Eon out of the proceeds of the taxes on their return to Cadiz.

By the end of August 1712, the fleet was loaded and almost ready to sail. But in view of the considerable personal capital tied up in the venture the veteran Ubilla was loath to set off into the waiting guns of an English squadron which was reported in the vicinity. The fleet actually left Cadiz on 31 August, but came back into port on the same day.[21] Fortunately news of the armistice ending the war, which was signed in August 1712, was soon published, and on 16 September, Ubilla judged it safe to set sail for America with his little fleet of eight ships. The tonnage of the fleet on its departure was registered as 1439.66 tons,[22] small indeed compared with some past and future fleets. Yet control of the trade was now for the second time fully in Spanish hands after the long struggle against French domination. Ironically, though, not a single ship in the fleet was owned by the Crown. One French vessel, *le Griffon*, did nevertheless have permission to go to Veracruz to coincide with Ubilla's fleet, but it was quite independent of the Spanish command. Philip V had once again granted a special licence, so resented by the Seville merchants and so prized by French diplomats, for a ship of 300 tons to trade in New Spain at the time of the fleet. It was permitted to sail from anywhere in France and return directly home without calling at any Spanish port.[23]

Ubilla put in to Veracruz on 3 December 1712. He was never to return to Spain. Immediately there began a course of events which was to lead to final tragedy. It will be remembered that following the death of Arriola in 1711 the viceroy of Mexico had appointed Pedro de Ribera to the command of his fleet, and from then on Ribera naturally flew a general's flag from his mainmast. As soon as Ubilla arrived in port he ordered Ribera to lower the flag, maintaining that his was the senior command, having been granted directly by the king, and alleging that there could be only one supreme commander in port at any given time. The dispute was put before the viceroy, the Duque de Linares, who ruled against Ubilla, but was later reproached by the Crown. The incident was significant, for the viceroy felt affronted by the upstart sailor, and the mutual dislike which followed had serious consequences.

Ubilla's fleet arrived in New Spain at the worst possible moment. The strong northerly winds which blow across Veracruz in the winter made it impossible for some weeks for the fleet even to unload its cargo on to dry land, let alone set about selling it in record time. Moreover every other circumstance worked against the Spanish merchants. Arriola's fleet had only just left port, taking with it every last *peso* possible for the treasury. The country was fully stocked with goods from that fleet and the French expeditions. The arrival at Acapulco of the Manila galleon for 1712, within days of Ubilla's fleet, only made matters worse. The situation was further aggravated by the summer droughts and excessive autumn rains of 1712 which upset the whole agricultural and mining structure of New Spain and caused a temporary scarcity of silver. Consequently it was agreed that there was absolutely no hope of completing the business of the fleet on schedule, and so Ubilla settled down to wait. Nine months later, by September 1713, things had advanced far enough to make the homeward voyage a possibility. But at this point the viceroy intervened, ordering the fleet to winter in harbour for its own safety and in the public interest. The following spring the viceroy still refused to allow the fleet to sail, alleging that he had had no order from Spain about its departure. The scent of vengeance for the incident over the flags was noticeably in the air. Despite protests from Ubilla and correspondence with the Council of the Indies, the Duque de Linares found a flow of trifling excuses to hold the fleet in port for a further 15 months. During all this time Ubilla had had his ships on and off loaded and careened three times, and the unpaid crews were beginning to desert. By the summer of 1715 the venture was clearly a resounding financial failure for both the *flotistas* and the Crown, a result, as will be seen later, which the Mexican merchants, perhaps more than the viceroy, had a veiled interest in achieving.

It was eventually 24 July 1715, 31 months after his arrival in New Spain, when Ubilla set sail on the major leg of his return voyage to Cadiz. A week later he encountered the ultimate disaster that can befall a sailor. On 30 July the whole fleet and a number of other Spanish ships sailing in its company were hit by the full force of a hurricane at Palmar de Ayx in the Bahama Channel. All the ships were smashed and there was great loss of life, thus producing a major naval catastrophe which Spain could ill afford at that moment. Ironically the only ship to escape the tragedy was the Frenchman, *le Griffon*, which was some distance ahead of the main Spanish fleet and went on to complete her voyage to France without incident.[24] A strange postscript to the whole affair is provided by a letter from the Duque de Linares to Philip V, after the tragic news was known. In it he despairingly blames himself for the delays and so, directly, for the wreck, and he claims that Divine Providence had seen fit to punish him for his behaviour by producing the calamity. By then he had received some pretty sharp words from the Council of the Indies too![25]

In 1711 the Crown had entered into a number of other naval and commercial contracts with private individuals for the *carrera de Indias*, of which the two principal ones were those with Don Manuel López Pintado and Don Antonio de Echeverz y Subiza, a merchant from Panama. The contract with López Pintado, originally to buy and transport shipbuilding materials to the Indies and set up yards there, underwent several modifications before emerging as the contract for the New Spain *flota* of 1715. That of Echeverz for *galeones* to Tierra Firme had a less complicated but more lamentable outcome, although its terms represented in fact the furthest departure which the Crown was obliged to make at this time from its traditional commercial practice with the Indies. The contract was originally drawn up shortly after the *proyecto* for the *flota* of Arriola, although it was not actually ratified until the summer of 1713. On 23 June 1711, the document was signed,

and on the following 14 October Philip V issued a decree stating that
Don Antonio de Echeverz y Subiza had leave to prepare three ships in
the port of Cadiz to sail to Cartagena and Portobello.[26] The expedition
was to be ready within four months time, and the entire cost of it, both
of the ships themselves and payment of the crews, was to be borne by
Echeverz, although the artillery for the ships was to be supplied by the
Crown providing Echeverz agreed to make good any losses.[27] The
object of the voyage was primarily to take military stores for the
garrisons of Tierra Firme, together with ten *quintales* of quicksilver, and
a supply of *bulas* (papal dispensations sold under Crown monopoly) and
papel sellado (Crown stamped paper required for all legal and official
business). The space left in the holds once these items had been put
aboard was to be filled with general merchandise for sale in the Indies.
The Crown, however, contracted to pay for all the expense of loading
and unloading the ships. It was declared that the Prince of Santo
Buono, viceroy elect of Peru, and his retinue, were also to be given
passage to the Indies in Echeverz's ships. On the return journey to
Spain Echeverz was to bring back some royal treasure from Lima,
which had not been dispatched to Europe along the regular route since
1707, after having first made arrangements for it to be brought up to
Portobello in the *Armada del Sur*. All taxes and duties for both the
outward and return voyages would be collected at the same rates and
under the same conditions as those stipulated in the *proyecto* of 1711.
Other minor points of the contract concerned the maximum duration of
the voyage, the rank Echeverz could use, and the combination of flags
he was to fly on his flagship.[28]

Since the departure of Fernández de Santillán in 1706 no attempt
had been made to dispatch the *galeones* to Tierra Firme. This was one of
the consequences of the continued French attempts to undermine the
legitimate trade to Peru for the sake of the illegal traffic of the St Malo
merchantmen. In New Spain the French contraband trade was less,
and consequently so too was their desire to hinder the *flotas*. Rather had
it been in the French interest to dominate with their own ships and
their own wares the fleets which did leave for New Spain, and this had
of course been accomplished for the first and only time in the case of the
flota under Andrés de Pez in 1708. It was not until the spring of 1712
that news was received in the Indies that a small fleet of *galeones* was
expected to set sail shortly for Cartagena.[29] Despite the condition laid
down in October 1711 that Echeverz was to be ready to sail within four
months, it was as late as 27 July 1713, when he actually left.[30] His ships
numbered four in all for he was also given permission to take a register
ship out to Havana to bring back the tobacco crop on his return. The

total volume of the small fleet was 1290 tons.[31] In the event, Echeverz did not transport the new viceroy to Peru. Delay on the part of the prince, who was not eventually to leave until November 1715, accounted to some extent at least for Echeverz's lingering in Cadiz.[32] The *galeones* put in to Cartagena on 29 August 1713, and it was at this stage that Echeverz's real misfortunes began.[33] They are remarkably similar to those of Ubilla in Veracruz, and indicate perhaps the extent to which these sailor merchantmen were resented by serving officers and Crown officials. It seems, from Echeverz's reports, that his small fleet was not at all welcome in Tierra Firme, and immediately a heated argument began between himself and the governor of Cartagena about his right to fly the Crown's naval standards on his flagship. This was followed by a dispute which lasted nearly a month about who was to pay for the unloading of the *galeones*, the royal treasury at Cartagena or Echeverz himself. In spite of his contract with the Crown, which he brandished before the royal officials, it was Echeverz who was finally forced to agree to pay; after all it was he who wanted to dispose of the cargo in order to be able to continue the voyage. Unlike Ubilla, he had 600 men to feed and pay out of his own pocket and could not afford to spend time in idle disputes.[34]

It was in this matter of the disposal of cargo and the sale of his merchandise that the reason for Echeverz's bad reception in the Indies was to be found. To understand this fully it is necessary to describe briefly commercial developments in the viceroyalty of Peru since the aftermath of the fair of 1708. The death of Castelldosríus in 1710 had by no means meant the end of the French interloping up and down the Pacific coasts of the country. The area continued to be supplied with contraband goods from France, and only a short time before Echeverz's arrival in the Indies the interim viceroy, the Bishop of Quito, Don Diego Ladrón de Guevara, a worthy successor to the Marqués de Castelldosríus, had allowed a large quantity of French merchandise to be brought into the viceroyalty more or less legally. In 1712 news had reached Peru via a royal communication that a naval squadron was being made ready in England for an attempt to invade Chile. The Crown therefore demanded immediate military precautions to be taken throughout the length of the Pacific coastline. Such measures obviously involved an expense, and the royal treasury in Lima, as always, claimed to be in difficult straits. The viceroy also complained that he was still faced by the continuous and insoluble problem of the large numbers of French smugglers in the Peruvian ports, a matter in which he as much as his predecessors showed complete hypocrisy. Prompted by the *fiscal* of the *audiencia* and supported by the merchant body, he decided to kill two birds with one stone by issuing a proclamation declaring that French vessels would be allowed to enter the port of Callao and sell their wares freely, providing that the royal duties were paid on the goods. In this way, it was considered, badly needed money for the royal treasury would be raised, and at the same time the coasts would be cleared of smugglers. The French ships in Callao would also give necessary support to the inadequate Spanish defences against the threatened English attack. Although it appears that only three ships were expected, a dozen or more Frenchmen actually dropped anchor legally in Callao in the summer of 1712, and another great wave of French merchandise was released throughout the country. This time, however, the royal treasury was reputed to have benefited to the extent of a quarter of a million *pesos* in the duties collected. Other less legal goods of course were also on sale throughout Peru. In the viceroy's *residencia* (1716–18) charges against him for having allowed contrabandists to go unpunished were substantiated, and he was fined 40,000 *pesos* on this account alone. In fact since about 1713 the Crown had been taking an increasingly poor view of Ladrón de Guevara's government, and finally, in March 1716, he was dishonourably relieved of his post.[35]

Because of the well stocked state of the Peruvian markets Echeverz had a difficult time disposing of his merchandise in Tierra Firme.[36] Like Fernández de Santillán before him he was very much the victim of French activities in the Pacific. Moreover he was hindered in every possible way by the royal officials in the Caribbean ports, who in all probability had some interest in the continuing contraband trade to that area of Spain's Empire.[37] Echeverz complained bitterly to Philip V about the treatment he had received from the royal officials in the Indies. He was held up for three months, from 29 August to 24 November 1713, in senseless argument at Cartagena; four and a half months from 3 December 1713 to 21 April 1714 at Portobello, while he waited for a shipment of treasure to be sent from Lima; and a further four months, from 15 May to 7 September 1714 at Cartagena, again attempting to settle his affairs. At last, on 7 September 1714, Echeverz left Cartagena for Havana, there to join up with Juan de Ubilla's *flota* from New Spain for the return voyage to Europe. The *galeones* reached Havana on 2 October 1714, but they were kept waiting there a further 10 months for Ubilla and did not sail finally until the fateful 24 July 1715.[38] After such a troubled voyage, bedevilled by enormously costly delays, it was indeed a cruel and ironical stroke of fate which took Echeverz and his ships through the Bahama Channel on the tragic 30 July 1715. In the hurricane which caused such extensive damage to the fleet on that day Echeverz lost all his ships and property and one of his sons, Don Manuel de Echeverz, who was in command of his *Nuestra Señora de la Concepción.*[39] Echeverz himself survived the wreck, which was more than Ubilla succeeded in doing, but from the expedition which had cost him four years of his life and a vast sum of money he 'saved nothing but the clothes [he] stood up in'.[40]

The present account of Spain's trade fleets during the War of the Succession must be complemented by a brief description of the country's trade over the years in question to areas of the Empire other than the two main ports – emphasising incidentally thereby the inaccuracy of the view that maritime relations between Spain and America were virtually severed during the war.[41] In addition to the fleets to Cartagena and Veracruz, 11 American ports were served by register ships direct from Spain at various intervals over the years 1701-13. Details of the trade may be summarised as follows.[42] For the West Indian Islands, seven ships sailed to Havana (of which two were taken by the enemy), bearing a total of some 1000 tons of merchandise; two ships touched at Puerto Rico, carrying something over 350 tons of goods; Santo Domingo fared worst – only one ship of less than 100 tons was dispatched from Spain during the whole period of the war, in 1705, and that was captured by the enemy before it arrived. On the coast of Central America, Campeche received four ships and about 700 tons of merchandise, Tabasco three ships and about 300 tons of goods, and Honduras, only one ship with less than 100 tons. On the Venezuelan coast Caracas and Maracaibo were visited each by three ships bearing a total of about 400 tons of goods, and Cumaná and Trinidad received just over 200 tons of merchandise in two ships, only one of which actually called at Trinidad. Buenos Aires received only four ships during the war, two small ones carrying mainly military supplies in 1705 and some 800 tons of goods in two ships in 1711. In addition Florida received two small shipments of arms in 1704 and 1705. Communications were otherwise maintained by a fairly regular service of dispatch ships (*avisos*), most of which carried a nominal cargo of 40 tons of Spanish produce. One or two of these ships sailed to Cartagena every year of the war except 1712, and to Veracruz every year except 1706 and 1712; they also called occasionally at Puerto Rico, Caracas or Santo Domingo. Moreover there were four fleets of quicksilver ships to Veracruz during this period: as well as the two fleets of 1710, referred to earlier, *azogues* went to New Spain under the command of Don Fernando Chacón in 1701 and under Don Francisco Garrote in 1703.

Part II
England in the Ascendant

4 The *Galeones* and *Flotas* and the English 'Annual Ship', 1713–1720

I

By the time Don Antonio de Echeverz y Subiza's little fleet of *galeones* had reached Cartagena, the War of the Succession was already at an end. As a by-product of the terms of the Peace of Utrecht of 1713 the considerable French influence on the Indies trade was destined shortly to give way to strong British pressures on the Spanish colonial markets. Just as the commercial interests of the nations had been largely the cause of the war, so too were they of importance in the pattern of the peace. Britain's illicit trade with the Spanish-American colonists at Portobello, Cartagena and all along the Tierra Firme coast, built up during the later years of the seventeenth century, had continued almost without interruption throughout the first half of the war.[1] While the *galeones* of the Conde de Casa Alegre were lying in harbour at Cartagena in 1707, the British were dispatching trading vessels to Portobello under the protection of men-of-war.[2] In May 1708, even while the trading with the *galeones* was in progress on the Isthmus, '20 odd sail of [British] trading sloops [were] at Porto Bell under Convoy of a 60 gun ship'.[3] But by 1708 the optimum moment was already past. By then British trade to the coasts had already begun to decline, for it was reported that

'. . . [our traders] can hardly sell the goods for what they cost them, but however it is supposed to be for the advantage of the trade to keep it afoot, for fear the French or any else should undermine us in it'.[4]

From 1708 business became steadily worse, as French commercial pressures and intensive smuggling in the Pacific took a stronger hold on the American markets. In spite of all, Britain found herself gradually losing those very markets which she had sought to preserve by launch-

ing herself into the war.[5] In such circumstances it seemed more profitable, therefore, that Britain should further her interests in America by
making the war-weary and impecunious Philip V an offer of peace,
provided that the terms agreed upon could be those dictated by Britain
herself. The matter was aired late in 1710 and within six months basic
agreements for a treaty had already been arranged.[6]

Of the concessions made to Britain by Spain as part of the
negotiations for that treaty, and indeed as part of the agreements
associated with the Peace Treaty of Utrecht itself in 1713, by far the
most important for Britain's trade to the Spanish Indies was the
granting of the *Asiento de Negros* to the South Sea Company. In 1702
British recognition of Philip V would have been tantamount to yielding
to France Britain's illegal commercial foothold in Spain's Indies. By
1710 the position was completely reversed, and recognition of Philip V
signified for Britain legal admittance to the Indies through the largest
and most profitable of the back-doors, the *Asiento de Negros*.

Although France had held the slave assiento from 1701–13 she had
not made full use of her opportunity to carry on illegal trading under its
cover. This is not to say that smuggling was not at that time carried on
under the shadow of the negro, but French contrabandists had had
such unprecedented facilities in the Pacific for disposing of their wares
that smuggling under the assiento was by comparison of little
importance.[7] England, however, was now preparing to take advantage
of every opportunity the French had missed and to make use of the
Asiento de Negros as no nation had ever done before her.

In obtaining the slaving contract for Her Majesty, British ministers
were not aiming solely to find a less hazardous and more efficient method
of selling British manufactures inside the Spanish Empire itself. It is
true that this was indeed a desirable objective for its own sake, but
there were other considerations too. At the time Britain was
developing, and to a certain extent had already developed, a flourishing
trade with the Far East. In this area of the world silver and precious
metals were highly prized commodities, and goods such as spices, silks
and other Oriental merchandise, bought there in exchange for silver,
fetched returns of 60 per cent or more net profit when sold in Europe
and America.[8] The English objective in the Indies was not, therefore,
only to promote trade for the sake of trade and find a market for
British manufactures, but also to lay hands on quantities of precious
metals, especially silver, with which to continue the extremely
profitable Far-East trade. The assiento would become a kind of
touchstone to convert cloth, candles, ironware and other English goods
into ready silver for trade to the East.

The Treaty of Utrecht of 1713 brought peace once more to Europe, but it also changed the balance of commercial power in the world. Britain had profited greatly both from the issues of the war and by the terms of the peace. Her European rivals had none of her advantages, for she was now dependent on no other nation but herself for the means to gain enormous riches. Because of her new-found access to a supply of Spanish silver and her enterprising naval strength she had the wherewithal to carry on world-wide trade. She also had military power and territorial empire. It seemed that in the contest for international supremacy the Treaty of Utrecht had indeed provided Britain with the title-deed to perpetually increasing wealth.

It would be natural to suppose that the ratification of the treaty in 1713 and the almost total cessation of arms in Europe should have been followed by the re-establishment of more normal communications between Spain and the Indies and the full reorganisation and revival of Spain's American trade. Some faltering steps towards restoration had indeed been taken, as we have seen, from 1711 onwards, once it seemed that peace might soon be proclaimed, but it was not really until 1720 that measures had been worked out which in any way attempted to come to grips with the basic problem of the decline of the *galeones* and *flota*. During the eight years that elapsed between the end of hostilities in 1712 and the publication of the *Real proyecto para galeones y flotas* on 5 April 1720, the Indies trade from Seville and Cadiz continued to be haphazard. In spite of enlightened measures towards the end of the decade, the general picture is in fact one of continuing decadence. In the course of the years 1712–20 no fair at all was held at Portobello – the last one had been the luckless fair of 1708 and the next was to be that held in 1722. The *flotas* sent to New Spain during the period were irregular and small in comparison with those of future years and those of the previous century;[9] and smuggling and foreign interloping increased in virtually all areas of the Empire.

The worsening of the situation and the Crown's failure to apply any satisfactory measures were in no small degree due to the unfortunate circumstances in which Spain found herself during the eight years in question. In 1713 the nation's naval resources were still extremely limited. Even at the outbreak of the hostilities in 1702 Spain had not possessed a large nor a very efficient navy and, as we know, she had been obliged to depend to some considerable extent upon French assistance at sea during the course of the war. The end of hostilities naturally found Spanish marine affairs in even worse disorder than before, and satisfactory improvement of the situation in the post-war years was seriously frustrated by two events in the Mediterranean of supreme national importance: the siege of Barcelona of 1713–14 and the outbreak of the War of the Quadruple Alliance of 1718–20.

The end of the international struggle over Philip V's throne had not coincided with the end of the civil strife that divided Spain herself. The Catalans, former supporters of the Archduke Charles of Austria, continued their war against domination by Castile and Philip V, even after Utrecht, and their resistance was centred mainly on the port of Barcelona. During the war the Catalans and their allies had depended heavily upon naval support in the form of both men and provisions which they received from Hapsburg Sicily and Naples, and from Majorca. Attempts to intercept these communications had previously been a constant drain on Franco-Castilian naval resources. Once the international war came to an end Philip V made use of every available vessel, whether merchantman or man-of-war, Crown or privately owned, to set up an effective blockade of the port of Barcelona in order to make good his army's seige by land. He was obliged to resort to all possible means of raising ships for this purpose – purchasing, attempting even to build what he could, borrowing and hiring from private persons, and requesting, as on previous occasions, both ships and men from his grandfather Louis XIV – and bestowing Spanish naval rank upon the French officers to legitimise the situation. The result of the powerful naval blockade begun in August 1713, was that Bacelona was finally taken 13 months later, on 11 September 1714. After that, in the summer of 1715, there followed the expedition to take Majorca for the Bourbon.[10] The fact that Castile had had to summon all her remaining strength and spend time and ships in the conquest of Catalonia and Majorca meant that it was not until early 1715 that Philip could turn to ruling and reorganising his realms; nor were Spain's mariners and merchants really free to look to the protection and development of the languishing transatlantic trade.

But even before two post-war fleets had been equipped and dispatched to the Indies, naval attention was once more to be distracted from the business of the regeneration of the *carrera de Indias*. Alberoni's rise to ministerial power under Philip V had the result of concentrating Spain's reviving maritime strength once again in the Mediterranean. Alberoni, a compatriot of Philip's second wife, the Italian Elizabeth Farnese, pursued policies which had as their aim, first the independence of Italy from the House of Austria, and secondly the aggrandisement of Spain and Philip V by the annexation of Sardinia and Sicily to the Crown of Castile. It was Alberoni's desire to carry on the struggle with Charles of Austria which led eventually to the outbreak of war with the Quadruple Alliance – that futile conflict which lasted from 1718 to 1720. Already in 1717, a year before the declaration of the war there had come the secret build-up of ships and men in Barcelona and the concentration of all Spain's by-now-reviving naval forces in the Mediterranean. Initially things had gone well for Alberoni, with the surprise capture of Sardinia in September 1717. Afterwards, however, a serious blow was dealt to the renascent Spanish navy in the form of the resounding defeat inflicted upon it by the English Admiral Byng off Cape Passaro in August 1718. In that action exactly half the Spanish fleet was captured or burned and the ships which did succeed in escaping were mainly the smaller, lighter craft of least importance.[11]

Spain's Mediterranean commitments, then – first the need for the suppression of the resistance in Catalonia and almost immediately afterwards the anti-Hapsburg policies of Alberoni – had meant that nearly all Spain's newly rising naval strength was deployed and eventually lost in Europe.

Apart from issues arising in the Mediterranean, the other major circumstance to have a profound effect upon Spain's American trade throughout these years was that England had at last succeeded in securing for herself the slave assiento. British merchants, after the Peace of Utrecht, found themselves in a stronger position than they had ever been in before to penetrate the forbidden markets of the Spanish Indies, and their task was made easier by the fact that Spain's true interests were being betrayed for a vital four or five years by the scheming Alberoni. The great increase in British smuggling from the Antilles under cover of the assiento and the many cunning devices used by British slavers to pass their contraband wares into the Spanish colonies have often been described in detail.[12] However one aspect of English commercial activity in connection with the assiento which deserves closer consideration is that of the place occupied by the South Sea Company's so-called 'Annual Ship' within the established Spanish commercial system of *galeones* and *flotas*.

In the light of past *Asientos de Negros*, the most striking feature of the assiento of 1713 is perhaps the second paragraph of the 42nd and last article of the treaty by which Philip V granted the South Sea Company, as holders of the assiento, permission to send a ship of 500 tons to trade in the Spanish Indies at each of the fairs attended by the *galeones* and *flotas*. The fact that this concession was given in the form of an additional paragraph at the end of a lengthy and rather complicated treaty concerning the granting of the *Asiento de Negros* would make it appear to have been almost an afterthought to which no great importance was attached. The wording of the text also suggests that the reason for its inclusion in the treaty was simply to show that Philip V had no desire to drive a particularly hard bargain:

> His Catholick Majesty, considering the Losses which former Assientists have sustained . . . and to manifest to Her Britannick Majesty how much he desires to pleasure Her, and to confirm more and more a strict and good Correspondence, has been pleas'd . . . to allow the Company of this Assiento, a Ship of Five hundred Tons Yearly during the Thirty Years of it's Continuance, to Trade therewith to the *Indies* . . .[13]

Such a concession was in fact an unprecendented relaxation of the strict principles which for centuries had kept all legitimate foreign traders out of the Spanish Empire in America.

The reasons why this exceptional concession was granted are not difficult to find. In 1707, while Britain was still fighting the Hapsburg cause, a treaty of commerce had been signed at Barcelona between Queen Anne and the pretender, Charles of Austria. Britain's powerful negotiating position had enabled her to have a secret article added to the treaty which afforded her almost carte-blanche commercial privileges in Spanish America and opened the door wide to large scale British legitimate trade in the Indies.[14] In the very favourable terms of this treaty there was no call upon Britain to meddle in the tiresome business of the *Asiento de Negros*.[15] However, even when Anne's ministers decided to desert Charles and come to terms with Philip, their position was still one of some strength. It was worth Philip's while to make peace with Britain at the expense of the assiento and a rather novel trade concession, and it was worth Britain's while to cut her losses over the war and begin to trade legally in the Indies, even if the conditions were less advantageous than those which the desperate Charles of Austria had been prepared to grant earlier. After all, Philip's control of the Indies at the end of the decade was very much more real than had been Charles' in 1707. As a result of her changed attitude, Britain had now to concern herself with the slave trade and be content with contraband trade instead of obtaining general legitimate rights. But she was still strong enough to secure for herself from Philip one legal foothold in the markets of the Spanish Indies in the form of the 'Annual Ship'. The outcome of the negotiations for ending the war and the final form of the Assiento Treaty with its Article 42 may be seen then as something of a compromise on both sides, at least insomuch as it concerns the transatlantic trade. Philip, on the one hand, was prepared to yield an unprecedented place to Britain inside the American trade in exchange for an undisputed crown; Britain, on the other, was prepared to accept less generous trading privileges from Philip, but ones that were sure to materialise, rather than continue to waste herself in war for the benefit of obtaining the wider concessions offered by Charles.

As for 'the Losses which former Assientists have sustained . . . ,' being the main reason for the clause, it is true that the slave trade had not always produced the high profits its eager assientists had hoped for, and no doubt the British in negotiating the treaty were able to make an issue out of the possible losses which the new Assiento Company might suffer. Obviously the circumstances belie the sincerity of such talk. The English had ever been intent on securing for themselves the *Asiento de Negros* and they knew very well how the profits would be made. In view of Charles' impotence to ratify the Treaty of Barcelona the English now coveted the assiento, not, of course, for its own value, but as a lever with which to prise a sizeable opening in the American commercial barricade.[16]

As Queen Anne's agent for the assiento, the South Sea Company was bound by the terms of Article 42 of the treaty to fulfil certain conditions with regard to its 'Annual Ship' of 500 tons. In the first place the ship was to be permitted to sail to the Indies only at the time of the annual trade fairs; but if for one reason or another it should happen to reach its destination in advance of the *flota* or *galeones* which were also attending the fair, a set procedure was to be followed. The factors of the South Sea Company in the American port were to be obliged to have the cargo unloaded and were to place it in storage inside a warehouse belonging to the Spanish Crown. The warehouse would be locked with two keys, of which one would be retained by the Spanish royal officials and the other would be handed over to the company's agents. The cargo of the ship was to remain in the store until such time as the *galeones* or *flota* arrived. Once the fair was ready to begin the merchandise was to be taken out of the warehouse and could then be sold freely to the American merchants in the same way as the goods from Spain. Of the profits brought home by the 'Annual Ship' one quarter was to be credited to the Spanish Crown as well as five per cent of the remaining three quarters of the net profit. In view of this arrangement the goods carried by the 'Annual Ship' were to be 'free of all Duties in the Indies'.[17]

The granting of the 'Annual Ship' to the South Sea Company is particularly interesting in that it constitutes the only example of a foreign power's effective yet legitimate penetration into the very heart of the Spanish trading system. It is true that Spain's monopoly had never been absolute. For many years past the European nations had had a large share in the American trade via Cadiz. Sometimes foreign vessels had been granted licences to make single voyages to specific American ports to sell merchandise – France had even provided naval escorts and sent merchantmen in the Spanish fleets – but never before had a foreign ship been permitted to attend the American fairs regularly, to enter into direct commercial competition with the ships of the Spanish fleets, and to enjoy the same privileges, and even greater ones than those which the merchantmen from Spain enjoyed themselves. It was precisely this sort of penetration which Spanish ministers had feared and successfully resisted throughout the alliance with France, and they were of course not slow to realise the dangers of the present situation.

The South Sea Company dispatched three of these 'Annual Ships' over the years 1713–20. The conditions laid out seem to be both simple and clear, yet considerable complications arose out of the voyages of the first two. So involved did these issues become that it was necessary to draw up a fresh treaty in 1716, which was in large measure devoted to clarifying the matter to the satisfaction of both governments.[18] Part of the trouble lay in the fact that in Article 42 of the Assiento Treaty it was taken for granted that trade fairs would actually be held annually in the Indies. As we have seen, in the years following the war Spain was hard pressed to find enough ships to make even one fair possible, let alone undertake to hold one every year. Consequently the basic problem was simply that there was no guarantee that fairs would be held with regularity for the 'Annual Ships' to attend. It was, therefore, amongst other things, to provide for this circumstance that a change in the terms of Article 42 was very necessary. And since the problems which had arisen were clearly of Spain's making, the English were quick to take every advantage when a new arrangement was finally agreed upon in May 1716. To appreciate the significance of this situation it is necessary to examine the early post-war development of the fleet system and consider the place which the first two English ships and the treaty of 1716 occupied in the changing pattern of Spain's American trade.

II

In November 1712, as part of a general desire to improve naval affairs the Crown had entered into a second agreement with Captain Manuel López Pintado, who had successfully completed his earlier contract to transport mercury to New Spain in 1709.[19] By this new agreement the Captain contracted to provide three good ships in which he was to carry to Havana all the materials, except wood, necessary for the building in Cuba of ten 800-ton ships. He was to find and buy at his own expense, in Spain or abroad, both the three ships and all the naval equipment, and find sufficient carpenters and other craftsmen to work the shipyards which he was to set up. López Pintado pledged all his personal wealth for the enterprise and agreed to raise the rest of the money amongst the other merchants. The whole cost of the operation was to be refunded by the Crown at various rates of interest when the mission was satisfactorily completed. But during the winter of 1712–13, while López Pintado was making ready at Cadiz, anxiety was steadily growing in both official and merchant circles over the urgent need to reassert Spain's commercial hold upon her precarious American markets. In theory at least, the fleets sailed annually. Arriola had gone in 1711, Ubilla in 1712, so why not López Pintado in 1713? Consequently the Captain's contract was extended in the course of 1713 to include the equipping of a full New Spain *flota*, of which the shipbuilding project was only a part. For this purpose the Captain was promoted to the rank of Admiral. A *proyecto* for a fleet was therefore drawn up on 11 July 1713, setting out the details and stipulating the complex financial arrangements by which López Pintado was eventually to benefit from the operation.[20] In general terms the document follows fairly closely the lines of the previous *proyectos* of 1711 and 1712. However, barely a week before the draft was signed, the still independent Catalan parliament voted by 78 to 45 to continue the principality's resistance against Philip of Anjou.[21] The seige of Barcelona was laid a month later. López Pintado's ships, together with every other available vessel, were requisitioned for the naval blockade, and so began the prolonged but inevitable delay of the New Spain fleet.[22]

A year and four months later the Crown was once again attending to the Andalusian merchants' fears that the American markets were now becoming dangerously neglected. On 20 November 1714 López Pintado offered to rescind the shipbuilding aspect of his contract so that undivided attention could be given by himself and everyone else concerned to the urgent dispatching of a normal trade fleet to New Spain. The Crown accepted the offer and a final agreement was reached on 17 December 1714.[23] The departure was fixed for the following February, but the ships were so slow returning from Barcelona, and repairs and other delays were so lengthy, that it was 21 August 1715 before the by-now acting General López Pintado could leave Cadiz bound for Veracruz.[24] The fleet was composed of eleven vessels, mostly small ones, and only one of which, the ubiquitous *capitana de Barlovento*, the *Nuestra Señora de Guadalupe*, was Crown-owned.[25] The total volume was 1975.91 tons, larger than that of Ubilla's fleet, but nevertheless still rather small.[26] Unfortunately the commercial situation which faced López Pintado when he put in to Veracruz early in November 1715 was certainly a good deal worse than that which he and his associates in Spain had expected to find. The arrival of another *flota* was in fact not at all welcomed by the merchants of Mexico, and the traders from the fleet actually had quite a hard time over the following months disposing of their small cargo, even at drastically reduced prices. Although the authorities managed to send the fleet back to Spain within five months, much of the merchandise remained unsold in New Spain in the charge of agents, and the financial ruin of the enterprise was thus assured.[27]

The reasons for the failure of the *flota* of 1715 must be sought in the changing economic state of the viceroyalty and the hardening attitudes of the New Spain merchant bodies in the post-war period they were now entering. The War of the Succession clearly altered the character of both the legitimate and the illicit trade in Spanish America, and the early years of the eighteenth century saw a rapid growth in the feeling of self-dependence in commercial circles throughout the colonies. This was the natural result of the irregular communications with Spain and the concomitant increase in foreign interloping. The circumstances in Peru in this respect have already been described, and in New Spain an analogous situation had developed. During the war Mexico's existing illegal trading links with the foreign islands of the Antilles had persisted, and commerce with the Far East via Acapulco had grown almost unchecked. So important in fact did the latter become during the first quarter of the eighteenth century that the merchants of Mexico came to look upon their trade with the Philippines as their principal commercial interest.[28] New Spain, open to a virtually uncontrolled trade both with the Caribbean and the Far East, was thus rarely short of supplies, and this state of affairs continued unchanged even after the war was over.[29] In these conditions there was clearly no advantage to be had for the Americans in accepting once again the rigid and less profitable system of economic colonialism, and the regular arrival of *flotas* from Spain was fast becoming a source of worry and real embarrassment to the merchants of Mexico. Of this the merchants of Andalusia were well aware. Some time before López Pintado's arrival in Veracruz, and even while the ill-fated Ubilla was just beginning to sell the cargo of his fleet in January 1713, the merchants of New Spain had already written to the Council of the Indies recommending that because stocks were so high in the country no *flota* should be dispatched from Spain until 1715 at the earliest.[30] Later in the year they came further out into the open and stated their clear opposition to any attempt to revive the system of annual fleets from Cadiz.[31] The background to this issue was complex and in fact went beyond the mere question of alternative sources of supply. Basically it concerned the Spanish trading system itself and the question of the uneasy relationship which existed between the merchants of Old and New Spain.

In the viceroyalty of New Spain no trade fair had been held comparable with that which was traditionally celebrated at Portobello for Peru. The merchandise which arrived in the *flota* was transported overland to Mexico City from the ships at Veracruz, and the *flotistas*, as those Spaniards from the fleet were called, then sold the goods as best they could in the capital itself. When stock was low in Mexico transactions between Mexican merchants and *flotistas* had normally been completed fairly quickly, although inevitably some time was lost in haggling. For most of the seventeenth century this system appears to have worked fairly satisfactorily. However, as supplies of contraband goods and merchandise from the East became more plentiful, especially in the eighteenth century, the Mexican merchant was not unduly anxious to buy goods from the *flota*, unless of course the prices were very competitive. The legitimate goods from Spain carrying high taxes were naturally as expensive as ever, and consequently the fleet from Cadiz became increasingly unwelcome in Mexico. The *flotista* (who was in reality attempting to break into an unfavourable market) therefore needed a good deal of time and considerable effort if he was to sell his wares in Mexico at anything like an acceptable price. The Mexican merchant in the meantime, living in his own home and going about his normal business, cared nothing for the expense which a prolonged stay in New Spain caused the *flotista*. His bargaining position was thus a very strong one. All was a question of time, for the Spaniard was eventually forced into reducing his prices to a fraction of the original for the sake of cutting down the expense of a lengthy stay in Mexico and, hopefully, of being able to return home with the fleet. As a result of this 'commercial blackmail' considerable sums of money were lost in Spain on the goods in the three *flotas* between 1712 and 1720.[32] On previous occasions when unfavourable market conditions had existed, unsuccessful attempts had indeed been made by the authorities to prevent this frustrating course of events from taking place. In 1683, and again in 1706, the viceroy had ordered the merchants of Mexico City to go to Veracruz to meet the fleet, agree prices with the *flotistas* and complete the purchase of the whole cargo as quickly as possible. This had been especially important during the war when money was urgently needed in Spain. But the Mexicans maintained, probably with real justification, that the Spaniards demanded exhorbitant prices, and no fair could be held.[33] When the Crown once more resolved to hold a fair at Veracruz for the *flota* of 1708 the city merchants had simply taken no notice at all of viceregal orders to travel to the port.[34]

In addition to the purely commercial disadvantages for the Mexican merchants in the reviving of annual fleets, the existing taxation system positively encouraged them in their opposition. The *consulado de comercio* of Mexico, under the terms of its *asiento de alcabalas*, was obliged to collect tax on behalf of the Crown on all goods which entered Mexico for sale.[35] From the amount collected, the *consulado* contributed annually to the royal treasury the sum of 280,000 *pesos*. It was conceded, however, that if for any reason no *flota* arrived at Veracruz from Spain, thus diminishing commercial activity, the amount the *consulado* had to contribute for that year was reduced by one third.[36] Consequently the regular arrival of goods from Europe in *flotas*, such as those of 1711, 1712 and 1715, meant that the *consulado* had no right to drop its contribution by a third and no excuse for falling short of the full annual sum stipulated by its *asiento*. Now, for the reasons just stated, the merchants of Mexico were unwilling to buy the goods the *flotistas* had brought, but for the sake of making up the 280,000 *pesos* of *alcabala* from the sales of the *flotistas* it was important that the Spanish goods should be marketed.[37] The merchant body of Mexico was thus in quite a predicament: either it over-stocked itself and lost money by buying the goods from Spain (but had less difficulty over making up the sum required for the *alcabala*) or else it ignored the *flotistas* and lost money on the *alcabala*. The second of the alternatives probably represented the smaller loss of the two, and so the *flotista* was left high and dry in Mexico with a quantity of unsaleable goods. But there was a further consideration. The prolonged stay of the *flotista* in Mexico, in some cases from one *flota* to the next, was embarrassing for the regular turnover of the contraband and the large stock of goods from the Orient. It was also clear that when the Spaniard reached home he would complain to the Crown about his losses and the unscrupulous behaviour of the Mexican merchants. The merchants of Mexico City therefore believed that the answer to their difficulties lay in the suspension of trade with Spain on the basis of a system of *regular* fleets from Cadiz. In this way there would be no whining *flotistas* to contend with, and the *alcabala* would automatically go down by the agreed third, more or less permanently. It was probably with these considerations in mind that in the autumn of 1713 the merchants of Mexico made a representation to the Crown for the suspension of regular *flotas* between Old and New Spain – this, the preliminary to a series of exchanges which was to continue well into the 1720s.[38]

In the representation and in their own appraisal of the situation to the Crown the merchants of course made no mention of either the reduction in the *alcabala* or the flourishing alternative trades. The grounds on which the request for a change in the established commercial practice was based were that the merchants of Mexico had been elbowed out of the trade of the *flota*. The inhabitants of the provinces, they pleaded, came personally to Mexico when a fleet was in New Spain and bought their supplies directly from the *flotistas*. This they did in order to avoid having to deal with the middlemen. The merchants of Mexico City maintained, therefore, that in their role of simple intermediaries between the *flotistas* and the population of New Spain in general, their business was so reduced that they personally stood to gain nothing from the merchandise of a *flota*. Any purchases they themselves made from the *flotistas* were in vain, they claimed, for the goods were unsaleable in the provinces at a retail price.[39]

There was perhaps some truth in this, but two well-established facts served to prove the basic groundlessness of the argument.[40] First: the quantity of goods an individual or a small merchant from the provinces could afford to buy at any one time from a *flotista* was minute compared with the large bulk stock purchases normally made by the powerful merchant in Mexico City. This is borne out by the admission of the *consulado* of Mexico, on another occasion, that the ambition of almost every merchant living in the provinces was to amass sufficient capital to be able to establish himself in Mexico City as a major stockist.[41] Therefore it follows that the competition from the small-time country merchants was always limited, for their very existence in the provinces was proof of their comparatively small resources. Second: when the Crown made an attempt to resolve the issue, as presented by the *consulado* of Mexico, by establishing for 1720 a trade fair at Jalapa, similar to that of Portobello, so that only large-scale buying was possible, the Mexican merchants caused it to founder, failing once again to cooperate with the authorities or the *flotistas*, just as they had earlier sabotaged the attempted fairs at Veracruz in 1683, 1706 and 1708.[42] A further indication of the insincerity of the *consulado's* case is provided by the fact that the traditional system of marketing the goods from the fleet to the merchants of Mexico City had been in use for almost a century and a half and no such difficulty appears to have arisen before. It seems incredible that in 1710, or thereabouts, the struggling merchants of the provinces should suddenly have turned *en masse* to buying in bulk directly from the *flotistas* in order to cut out the merchants of the capital. Moreover there is no reason to suppose that their economic strength had increased sufficiently to allow them to do so. No doubt the arguments which the *consulado* put forward to the Crown were not the real underlying reasons they had for desiring the suspension of regular *flotas* from Spain.

The representation of 1713, like those that followed it, was peremptorily rejected by the *consulados* in Spain and by the Council of the Indies.[43] Nevertheless knowledge that in New Spain there was opposition to the trade from Cadiz coupled with the experience of the losses sustained by the current *flotas* was alarming. On top of all the other obstacles at home to the re-establishment of regular commerce with America, the task was now seen to be further complicated by a hostile attitude to the accepted system within the Indies themselves.

In the viceroyalty of Peru enthusiasm for the re-establishment of the *carrera de Indias* was no greater than in New Spain. French vessels continued to find their way into the Pacific ports of Peru for a decade after Utrecht, and for a short time, until the infamous viceroy Bishop Ladrón de Guevara was relieved of his post in 1716, this contraband actually increased.[44] Smuggling along the northern coasts of South America naturally expanded with the creation of the South Sea Company's slaving 'factories' at Cartagena and on the Isthmus of Panama. Illegal trafficking also continued all along the remainder of the coasts from the foreign islands in the Antilles. Despite hollow protestations of good will by the *tribunal* of the *consulado* of Lima, indifference, if nothing more, to the revival of the *galeones* had developed in Peru. The *tribunal* itself, with its official voice, recorded its fervent desire for the suppression of contraband and the celebration of a fair at

Portobello. It pointed out, however, that its own membership was relatively small and declared that the majority of the merchants, especially in the northern provinces, thought differently. In the event, the *tribunal* advised the Crown that because the viceroyalty was so full of goods no attempt should be made to hold a fair until the high stocks throughout the country had been cleared.[45] In this stagnant situation in Peru it was unlikely that the attitude of apathy towards Cadiz could have changed other than for the worse.

This difficult situation was not at all helped, either for the Americans or for the Spaniards, by the fact that England at precisely this time was preparing her first legal assault on the Indies trade in the form of the first two of the 'Annual Ships'. Following the ratification of the Assiento Treaty *cédulas* were issued by Philip V to the South Sea Company on 9 May 1715 for two ships: one for the *Elizabeth*, to sail to Veracruz, and the other for the *Bedford*, to go to Cartagena.[46] By royal decree of 15 July 1715, the king advised the governors and royal officials in the Indies that these ships would be arriving, and gave orders concerning the procedure to be followed in measuring the cargo and admitting the goods. But he also warned them that the two ships were 1200 tonners and the officials must take care that only 500–600 tons of merchandise were sold. Any excess was to be confiscated.[47]

Because of their freedom from Spanish duties the goods from the English ships could sell at 25–30 per cent cheaper than those brought from Spain in the fleets.[48] But it would be a mistake to conclude from this that the cargoes of the *Elizabeth* and the *Bedford* were disposed of either easily or quickly once the ships arrived in Veracruz and Cartagena in 1715. The great days of the 'Annual Ship', when ton upon ton of merchandise poured out unhampered from her holds into the American markets had not yet begun.

No trade fair had been planned for Portobello in 1716, and so the *cédula* granted for the *Bedford* gave her permission to sell her goods at Cartagena.[49] However when she arrived in the Indies towards the end of 1715 there were no *galeones* in port at Cartagena either. Article 42 of the Assiento Treaty stipulated that the English ships were not to be allowed to sell their goods 'but only at the time of the Fair', and it was in order to fulfil this condition that a small fair was held in the port with four Spanish ships which arrived in January 1716. These were sent under the command of Don Nicolás de La Rosa, Conde de Vegaflorida. Apart from providing a fair in accordance with the terms of the Treaty of Utrecht, their purpose was to convey the belated Prince of Santo Buono to his new seat of viceregal government in Peru, and also to carry a supply of *papel sellado* and *bulas* for the colony.[50] The expedition can hardly be considered a fleet of *galeones* since it consisted of only one main warship, the count's own *Santa Rosa*, and all four ships together carried only 556.60 tons of cargo.[51] There was of course no fair at Portobello. It is interesting to note however that the essential features of the *proyecto* of 1711 were once again adhered to as the basis for the rates and method of collecting the duties on the merchandise shipped.

But before the arrival of the Spaniards from Cadiz or the sale of their goods, the *Bedford*'s troubles had already begun. The governor of Cartagena at this time and the royal officials (the same ones as those who had angered Echeverz and delayed his departure) were clearly a very smart team, well-versed in the uses of red-tape and administrative blank-wall tactics.[52] Once they had measured the *Bedford* they declared her to be almost twice the tonnage stated by the Company and the royal decree of July 1715, and they confiscated the greater part of her cargo. The South Sea Company's factors at Cartagena could make no headway and did not help themselves by insisting that in any case under the assiento there was no limit stated for the tonnage of the 'Annual Ship'.[53] At some stage the sum of 75,000 or 85,000 pieces of eight changed hands, but even this failed to do the trick.[54] The case was quickly referred back to London and from there sent on to the Crown's ministers in Spain. No doubt the *Bedford* did indeed carry a large excess over the stipulated 500 tons – hence the attempt at bribery. She probably even carried her maximum load of 1100 tons or a little over, but the pretension of the Spanish officials that she was a 2117 tonner was nothing short of ludicrous. As the South Sea Company itself pointed out in its representation to the Spanish Crown, there was as yet no ship on the seas that was capable of carrying 2117 tons of cargo. She was, the Company maintained, a 1100 tonner, and her actual cargo amounted to 537 tons.[55] Eventually the matter was resolved by the Council of the Indies on 31 October 1716, when it was decided that since there had obviously been some misunderstanding about measuring the dimensions of the ship the most gentlemanly solution was that the entire confiscated cargo should be returned to its owners.[56]

It is difficult to interpret the actions of the royal officials in this matter. Clearly they did not behave as they did in order to extract money from the English. The bribe must surely have been handed over, even if this was what the Spaniards were after, before this affair reached the diplomatic level. The measurement of 2117 tons was certainly an impossible exaggeration, made with some ulterior motive in view.

There seem to be two possibilities. Either the Spanish officials were genuinely anxious to keep the English goods out to protect their own interests on the internal markets of the country: to make a wild exaggeration in the measurement of the *Bedford* and impound most of the goods was at least a temporary solution (in which case the money handed over by the English factors was accepted in bad faith). Alternatively, the whole business amounted to an arrangement between the Spaniards and the English. The second of these possibilities seems the more likely in the circumstances. At the time of the arrival of the *Bedford*, it was known that the new viceroy of Peru was shortly to pass through Cartagena on his way to Lima. It was also known that the smuggling activities of the interim viceroy Ladrón de Guevara had been discovered and condemned by the Crown in Spain. What the attitude of the new viceroy would be towards contraband was impossible to predict. If he came determined to reform the economic state of the viceroyalty, it could well have been most unwise to have 1000 tons and more of cheap merchandise from the *Bedford* for sale at Cartagena – especially as it was realised that the merchantmen accompanying the new viceroy would have a difficult task to sell their few tons of legitimate goods from Cadiz. An honest viceroy would have received a disastrous first impression of colonial officialdom. To have an insoluble argument raging about the cargo of the *Bedford*, in which the new viceroy could hardly interfere, was a possible answer. It would be clear to all that a misunderstanding had arisen and that in time a solution would be found, and probably in favour of the English. Meanwhile the goods remained in bond until the coast was literally clear, both of viceroy and merchantmen from Cadiz. Then the English goods could be released on to the market in safety. Such an interpretation of these events is, of course, not contained in the official records of the case. Reports of the unreasonable behaviour of the royal officials exist, as do two independent accounts of the bribe, yet details of the timing and the method of sale of the contraband goods from the *Bedford* on the Peruvian markets in 1716 are naturally not forthcoming. Whatever the outcome of the affair, and whatever the motives of the governor and royal officials, the South Sea Company, as early as the New Year of 1716, was in a position to allege injustice on the part of Spanish officialdom, and to claim that the *Bedford*, instead of bringing a profit, had in fact produced a loss. As will be shown later these facts were of some importance in the negotiations for the treaty of 1716.

The result of the voyage of the *Elizabeth* was similar to that of the voyage of the *Bedford*, although the problems were of a different nature.[57] The *Elizabeth* was also capable of carrying over 1000 tons of merchandise, but no difficulties about her measurements or her cargo appear to have been encountered by the officials at Veracruz. The ship reached New Spain in time to coincide with the arrival of the *flota* of General López Pintado, in November 1715, and her goods were transported, like those of the *flota*, to Mexico City to be sold. Whether they were disposed of immediately is not clear, but what is certain is that the *consulado* of Mexico, keen to make up its 280,000 *pesos* of *alcabala*, insisted upon its right to collect the tax on the cargo of the English ship, just as it was authorised to do on the goods from the fleets from Cadiz. Obviously the *consulado* was not going to fail to take best advantage of the circumstances. The English goods were saleable in Mexico because of their low price, and at the same time the *consulado* could profit from their sale by making the English contribute a good proportion of the money required under their *asiento de alcabalas*. The South Sea Company's agents of course refused absolutely to pay this tax, referring the *consulado* to the words of the Assiento Contract which stated that the goods from the 'Annual Ships' were 'free of all Duties in the *Indies*'. The Mexicans, however, maintained that this phrase applied to port duties only, and in return referred the English to their own *asiento de alcabalas* which gave them the right to collect the *alcabala* on all commercial goods entering Mexico for sale, without distinction of any kind. A deadlock ensued. The matter was brought before the viceroy and there followed a long and fruitless court case. The English soon informed London of the matter and from there it passed to the court at Madrid. The final decision was published more than two years later in the form of a royal *cédula* of 22 January 1717 in which it was ordered that the English should after all pay the *alcabala* to the *consulado* so that it should not fall short of its 280,000 *pesos*.

But the decision of the Crown in 1717 was certainly influenced by the fact that during the course of the dispute the clarification treaty of 1716 had been signed and ratified. By it England had already eased herself into an even more advantageous position within the established Spanish commercial system. The English case, as presented to the court in Madrid during the spring of 1716, was that if the Crown took the part of the *consulado* of Mexico and obliged the South Sea Company to pay the *alcabala* on the *Elizabeth*'s cargo a condition of the Assiento Treaty would be broken. Moreover what was to stop the authorities in Peru from claiming *alcabala* on the goods from the *Bedford*? The *Elizabeth* affair had already cost the company time and money and if the *alcabala* had to be paid after /all, the profits would be negligible.

Similarly at Cartagena the *Bedford*'s goods were still lying unsold in the Crown's warehouses in the port. The Company, it was claimed, might as well have not bothered to send either of the 'Annual Ships' for all the use they had been or the profits they had brought.[58]

Armed with these facts and with several other valid complaints about Spain's behaviour in the actual business of the slave trade, George Bubb, the British envoy to Spain, set about negotiating a treaty to clarify these and other matters relating to the dispatch of the 'Annual Ship' and certain other financial questions that had arisen. Bubb was a very able minister and the negotiations were so successful for Britain that on 26 May 1716 a very advantageous treaty emerged,[59] and Bubb was commended for his skilful handling of the Spaniards.[60] He successfully convinced the Spanish court that the voyages of the *Bedford* and the *Elizabeth* had been quite worthless, and as far as the treaty under consideration was concerned these two voyages should be ignored altogether: to all intents and purposes no 'Annual Ship' had so far been sent by the South Sea Company. A further matter which Bubb was able to touch upon in his negotiations, with considerable benefit to England, was that of the regularity of Spain's own trade to the Indies by means of the *galeones* and *flotas*. England knew full well that Spain could not be relied upon to send a fleet to the Indies every year, and so another of Bubb's tasks was to release the South Sea Company from that irksome phrase in the Assiento Contract 'but only at the time of the Fair'. Both slave-trade and 'Annual-Ship' issues were mixed and counterbalanced in the treaty of 1716, but as far as the matters under present examination are concerned only the agreements reached about the 'Annual Ship' are of special interest. A résumé of the relevant paragraphs will serve to indicate the new conditions under which the 'Annual Ship' was to be dispatched from 1717 onwards.

Paragraph 1 is limited to a statement of the existing terms on which the 'Annual Ship' could be sent, as agreed in the assiento of 1713.

Paragraph 2 describes a petition made by the South Sea Company in which it points out the unlikelihood of a fair being celebrated annually in the Indies and goes on to declare that in the event of the Company's preparing a ship and no fair being held in America, the English could sustain an important loss. This would be quite contrary to the spirit of the Assiento Treaty in which the 'Annual Ship' had been granted precisely to counteract any losses brought by the slave trade (no doubt Bubb was driving home the effect of the current losses claimed to have been made by the *Elizabeth* and the *Bedford*). The Company, therefore, requested that the 'Annual Ships', after waiting a reasonable time for the Spanish fleet, should be allowed to sell their cargoes in the American ports whether a fair was held or not.

Paragraph 3 states that the Spanish Crown agreed that the English had a case, but henceforth the Crown would make sure that a fleet was dispatched from Cadiz every June and that a fair was held annually in the Indies (this indeed was a rather quixotic undertaking in view of the economic state of the Indies at the time and the lack of naval strength). Nevertheless in the event of any delay in the departure of the fleets from Spain the English ship could leave for the Indies after the end of June, but would be obliged to wait four months in the American port. If after that time no fleet from Spain had materialised, she would be at liberty to sell her goods. By this article the Spanish Crown also undertook to advise the English court of the exact date of the departure of the fleets from Cadiz.

Paragraphs 4, 5, 6 and *7* deal with the slave trade and a financial dispute over the payment of the Spanish Crown's share in the trade for 1713–14. *Paragraph 7* also states that for all practical purposes the assiento would be deemed to have begun on 1 May 1714.

Paragraph 8 again returns to the 'Annual Ship' and declares that the South Sea Company had not yet taken advantage of its permission to send such a ship (here is supreme evidence of Bubb's diplomatic ability). Since the outstanding financial questions had been amicably settled (*Paragraphs 6* and *7*), the Spanish Crown was prepared to make amends to the Company for this by taking into consideration three years' annual tonnage – that corresponding to 1714 (the new date of the commencement of the assiento), 1715, and 1716 (for which no *cédula* had yet been granted). The three years' tonnage amounted to 1500 tons and these were to be divided equally into ten portions and added to the tonnage of the next ten 'Annual Ships'. The volume of cargo of the 'Annual Ship' was thus raised by 150 tons from 500 to 650 tons. It is interesting to note incidentally how the continuing argument about the *Bedford*'s tonnage is reflected in the substance of this paragraph, for after the final mention of 'tonnage' in the document there appear in parenthesis the words,

> each Tun being to be computed at two Pipes of Malaga in Measure, and at Twenty Quintals in Weight, as is the ordinary Computation between *Spain* and *England*.

It is thus made quite clear that in future neither side would have grounds for further complaints over the way in which cargo should be measured.

It is beyond doubt, then, that by May 1716 – only three years after the official end of the war – Britain had gained for herself far greater advantages in the legal trade of Spanish America than France had succeeded in doing throughout the whole period of the war itself. Bearing in mind that at that time France had been Spain's only ally, manipulating the Council of the Indies and dominating the *Junta de restablecimiento del comercio*, the British achievement was no mean feat. It is no little wonder, therefore, that on 16 November 1716, the Council of the Indies felt itself free to recommend the Crown to order that the South Sea Company should indeed be forced to pay the 10 per cent *alcabala* on the cargo of the *Elizabeth*, so earnestly claimed by the *consulado* of Mexico. An appeal against this decision by the South Sea Company was of course refused out-of-hand.[61]

In 1716 no *galeones* or *flota* were dispatched to the Indies. A small number of armed ships left Spain for Veracruz under Commodore Francisco Cornejo, and in these the new viceroy of Mexico was given passage to America.[62] In 1716 also, General Fernando Chacón took a couple of ships to Havana to collect what treasure had been salvaged from the wrecks of Ubilla and Echeverz of the previous year.[63] But the terms of the treaty of 1716 and the undertaking to celebrate annual trade fairs in America made it important for the Crown to look to the full re-establishment of the *carrera de Indias* as a matter of real urgency. If fleets could not be made ready to sail regularly and on time from Cadiz, the English 'Annual Ship' would soon be the only official trader in the ports of the Indies and would hold those markets uncontested. Moreover, it had always to be borne in mind that the English goods, exempt from most taxes, would sell cheaper in the Indies than the Spanish. The situation was perilous. Not only had the English opened up a chink in Spain's armour of trade monopoly with the Indies, but it now seemed just possible that the monopoly itself could pass by default into the hands of the foreign nation. The Council of the Indies, immediately after the signing of Bubb's Treaty, impressed upon the king

the supreme importance of dispatching annually and alternately *flotas* and *galeones* (and especially to the Kingdom of Peru because its transatlantic trade is so run down) for if the English Company sells its merchandise at other times than when there is a fair with goods from Spain the English may obtain great profits and the Spaniards nothing but serious prejudice. . . If the Spanish fleets were to be delayed and the 30th June each year went by and the English ship set sail and four months after its arrival in the Indies sold all its goods without the Spaniards making an appearance, this would result in enormous riches for the English and the anihilation of Spanish trade.[64]

The period 1716–20 consequently was one in which a most serious effort was made in Spain to reform the *carrera de Indias*, and the important Bourbon commercial reforms for the Indies trade all date from 1716 onwards. At all events the voyages of the *Bedford* and the *Elizabeth* and the recognised dangers of the 'Annual Ship' may be seen as playing a decisive role in the future shape and development of the Indies trade. It was largely thanks to the disputes at Cartagena and Mexico in 1715–16 that Bubb was able to negotiate a successful treaty, and it was in turn mainly due to the terms of this treaty that the Spanish government was precipitated into a constructive effort to remedy the forlorn state of the transatlantic trade.

III

The signing of Bubb's Treaty, then, in May, 1716, brought with it a new phase in the life of the *carrera de Indias*. The pace had to be quickened immediately, and the Spanish authorities were galvanised into decisive action. If the English were not to gain the feared commercial advantage from the treaty, a trade fleet had to be prepared without delay. There was no time now for negotiating involved contracts with merchants and speculators. There was no time to take into account proposals and counter-proposals from merchant bodies on both sides of the Atlantic. There was not even time to get the new viceroy of Peru to prepare the decrepit *Armada del Sur* and persuade his reluctant subjects to go up to a fair at Portobello, the most languishing aspect of the trade. Within seven weeks of Bubb's signature appearing on the treaty the broad outlines of Spain's next fleet to the Indies had already been worked out. A royal decree of 15 July 1716 ordered a full fleet to be ready to leave Cadiz early in 1717.[65] Its destination, yet again, was Veracruz. But for the first time in the reign of Philip V the fleet was to sail under a full complement of royal warships. These were to be put into service with the *carrera de Indias* as a matter of prime importance, and with them were to sail six new ships at that time under construction in the reviving shipyards of the North of Spain.[66] On 30 November 1716 the command of the fleet was given to Don Antonio Serrano, with the rank of *Jefe de Escuadra de la Real Armada*.[67]

During the winter of 1716–17 a number of matters concerning the American trade came under review by the Spanish Crown.[68] Not least of these was the question of taxation. It had originally been proposed that the duties on the goods in the fleet of 1717 should again be levied in accordance with the *proyecto* of 1711, which during these years had come to be regarded as the norm.[69] Yet it was realised that the high level of Spanish taxation was one of the reasons why foreign traders were so welcomed by the colonial merchants. Indeed American opposition to the re-establishment of the Cadiz trades had not a little to do with the high prices of the goods from Spain. It was inevitable that the low-priced cargo of the English 'Annual Ship' would become the first choice of the colonial merchants at future trade fairs. So a reduction in some levels of Spanish taxation seemed desirable as a token, if nothing more, of the Crown's wish to promote both trade and good will in the colonies, and agriculture and industry at home. A new *proyecto* dated 10 March 1717, gave the results of the Crown's deliberations on this matter.[70] Although the form of the document once again followed closely that of 1711, compared with the earlier *proyecto* there was a reduction of some 11 per cent in the tax payable on certain items for export to the Indies. The new rates applied primarily to Spanish produce which was beginning to be favoured by the Crown as part of a general plan of recovery, but other essential supplies were also affected. They showed reductions of as much as 25 per cent to 33 per cent on a number of products such as olive oil or cloth made up from Flanders thread, and 14 per cent to 20 per cent on others such as paper, iron or wine. Freight charges were also reduced by a similar average percentage. The tax on other merchandise, however, such as wax, cinnamon or steel, remained unchanged, as did the general *palmeo* rates which applied to the majority of the cargo. Thus a total of some 20 per cent less was payable in overheads by Spanish merchants on certain goods for inclusion in the fleet of 1717, a factor that was bound favourably to affect their prices in New Spain. Duties and freight charges on goods carried to Spain on the return journey remained generally unchanged from the rates laid down in 1711, except that in most cases the charges were to be calculated on the net weights and volumes rather than on the gross, as previously. Thus a small reduction in costs would result. However import tax on precious metals brought home by private persons was raised, on gold from $1\frac{1}{2}$ per cent in 1711 to 2 per cent in 1717, and on silver from 4 per cent to 5 per cent. No doubt this increase was intended to offset, at least in part, the loss of income to the Crown caused by reducing the duty on goods for sale in Mexico.

The *proyecto* of 1717 thus heralds the major *Real proyecto* of 1720, and marks an intermediate stage between it and the earlier document of 1711.

At the same time as the Spanish fleet was making ready in Cadiz, a royal *cédula* was published, granting the South Sea Company permission to send the *Royal Prince*, of 650 tons, to Veracruz as its 'Annual Ship' for 1717, so as to coincide with the arrival of the *flota*.[71] The *Royal Prince* was, of course, the first ship to be sent under the new conditions determined by Bubb's Treaty, and to avoid any possibility of trouble with the American officials, such as had blown up with the *Bedford* in Cartagena, the commander of the *flota* himself was given the task of measuring and certifying the cargo of the ship in the Indies.[72] Serrano was to allow up to 700 tons of cargo to be sold, and any excess was to be confiscated. The 50 tons or less difference, between the permitted 650 and 700 tons, if found, was nevertheless to be recorded and deducted from the tonnage of the next 'Annual Ship', making her 600 tons instead of 650.[73]

The *proyecto* required the *flota* to leave Cadiz on 1 May 1717. Bubb's Treaty required the Spaniards to leave no later than 30 June in any year. Yet despite all this it was 28 July before Serrano was able to set sail.[74] He brought his fleet safely into Veracruz on 9 October 1717.[75] Although the *proyecto* stated that the *flota* would consist of three warships and seven merchantmen it was eventually made up of 14 vessels in all, with a cargo distributed between 11 merchantmen of 2840.08 tons.[76] In the company of the *flota* there also sailed two register ships with small cargoes for Cartagena.[77] This was the largest fleet that had yet sailed to New Spain in the eighteenth century, for there were high hopes in Spain that economic conditions in the viceroyalty would have improved, and the reduced level of the duties was naturally expected to facilitate the sale of the cargo.[78] Unfortunately such optimism proved unfounded. For the *flotistas*, the trading in Mexico in 1717 and 1718 turned out to be quite as disastrous as that of previous years – and things were made a good deal worse for them by the presence of the *Royal Prince* in Veracruz harbour.

The royal order of 22 January 1717, concerning the payment of the *alcabala* on the cargo of the previous 'Annual Ship', the *Elizabeth*, had been published and circulated to the relevant officials in America. This document clearly reflected the feelings of the Council of the Indies on the general question of the payment of the *alcabala* on the English goods. The Council had stated in no uncertain way that the *alcabala* should indeed be paid. It ordered, furthermore, that in similar circumstances the merchandise of *all* future 'Annual Ships' had also to pay the sales tax. Moreover, the Council declared, strictly speaking the goods from the *Elizabeth* should never even have been allowed to go up to Mexico for sale. The king had granted a *cédula* for the ship to sail to Veracruz – *not* for her cargo to be carried to Mexico City.[79] This declaration was taken in the Indies as a general order that the English goods were not to leave the ports at which they arrived, unless they had first been sold to Spanish Americans. In October 1717, the cargo of the *Royal Prince* was therefore prohibited to pass on to Mexico City for sale with the rest of the merchandise from the Spanish fleet.[80] Yet it seems that the English, as part of a plan to avoid paying the *alcabala*, never even intended to transport the *Royal Prince*'s cargo to Mexico City. The captains of the ship already carried with them printed lists of the merchandise they had on board, and copies were circulated throughout New Spain as soon as the ship reached the port of Veracruz. This shrewd advertisement of the attractively priced and carefully selected supplies brought from England caused merchants from all over the viceroyalty to hurry to Veracruz and invest their money in the *Royal Prince*'s cargo before they even looked at the goods of the *flotistas* in Mexico City.[81] Moreover the *Royal Prince* certainly sold more than her permitted 650 or 700 tons.[82] Serrano measured her himself, but there is every reason to suppose that he, like later commanders of the *galeones* and *flotas*, was handsomely rewarded by the English factors for finding the cargo of the ship to be perfectly in order, when in fact she carried many tons of excess.[83] The trading in New Spain in 1717–18 was therefore perhaps even more disappointing for the *flotistas* than it had been in earlier years. The sale of merchandise was split in two: at Mexico City and at Veracruz. The English side of it at Veracruz took the pickings of the market, while the *flotistas* were left out of the picture altogether for some time until the English ship was cleared. Their discouragement was understandably mingled with a good deal of fury, which when transmitted back to Spain served only to increase the anxiety and frustration already felt in official circles.[84]

For the next two years no shipping of any account left Spain for the Indies. In the panic following Bubb's Treaty the Council of the Indies had emphasised the importance of preparing a fleet of *galeones* for Tierra Firme for 1718 so that the English 'Annual Ship' should not be left in the Indies alone.[85] Preparations were indeed begun for such a fleet, but the international crisis of 1718 which turned into war with the Quadruple Alliance prevented the *galeones* from leaving Cadiz.[86] As a result of the outbreak of war with Great Britain the *cédula* granted to the South Sea Company for the 'Annual Ship' of 1718 was of course also stopped by royal command on its way through the offices of the government.[87] For two years, from 1718–20, while Spain was at war with most of Europe, communications with the Indies were once more held up and the official trading there, both English and Spanish, came to a halt. Not so the unofficial trading, however, for although by now the French were losing their hold on the Pacific coasts,[88] the English and Dutch in the Caribbean took advantage of the circumstances to make sure that during the years of war that followed the Spanish colonies in America did not go short of essential supplies!

5 Marine and Commercial Reform, 1713–1720

Since the last quarter of the seventeenth century Spain's ministers, mariners and merchants had regularly agreed that policies were required to revive the country's trade with the colonies and protect it from the increasing threat from foreign interlopers. Never had the need of reforms been more pressing than now. As early as 1679 the *Junta de comercio* had been set up to consider these problems, and it was further strengthened in 1683 as part of a continuing effort to achieve reforms. Many hours of discussion were devoted to a multitude of ideas, and copious reports were written about them. Some of the schemes proposed the legal participation of foreigners in aspects of the trade, while others suggested abandoning the system of trade fleets altogether and establishing in their place monopolistic trading companies on the lines of the English, Dutch and French. Some recommended a combination of both. Yet it seems that all the theories contained elements which in one way or another went against some basic Crown concept of the government of the Indies, and no progress whatsoever was made in practice. The Cadiz trades continued to decline until they reached the unprecedented depths of the last decade of the century.[1]

We have seen how, during the War of the Succession, the advent of powerful French interests within the government of Spain had the effect of paralysing any constructive movement towards reform. Spanish ministers, while fully aware that changes in the *carrera de Indias* were well overdue, had resorted to intransigence and conservatism as the best defence against the threat from France. The old fleet system, although moribund by the turn of the seventeenth century, thus survived Utrecht. But ironically Utrecht brought with it a new lease of life for the *galeones* and *flota*. If change in the method of trading had been contemplated before, it seemed less feasible now, for the international treaty itself, with the associated assiento and the 'Annual Ship', depended upon the continuation of the ancient fleet system for its fulfilment. Bubb's Treaty of 1716 had made the point abundantly clear

93

and shown just how serious the situation really was. From now on reform of the American trades, if it was to be achieved at all, had to be made within that system as it currently existed.

Essential to any improvement of the *carrera de Indias* was of course the basic reconstruction and revival of Spain's navy. In 1693 Don Francisco Antonio Garrote had presented Charles II with detailed plans for the building of ships in Spain, but the project never got beyond the drawing board. Indeed only five years later, in 1698, the office of superintendent of shipyards and forestry on the Cantabrian coast was actually abolished for the simple reason that shipbuilding had mainly died out there. Vessels were now bought abroad or were made to order for the Spaniards, particularly by the Dutch.[2] It was this policy, or rather, lack of policy, exacerbated by the War of the Succession, which took on the proportions of a national crisis, when, for example, in 1713 the viceroy of New Spain had had to lay hands on two ships in Ubilla's fleet, as a compulsory purchase, so as to be able to communicate with the Caribbean Islands;[3] or when the infamous Ducasse was created *Teniente General de Mar* for the sake of enlisting four French warships (which arrived late) for the seige of Barcelona.[4]

The earliest significant factor in the reconstruction of a Spanish navy was the arrival of the Belgian Count of Bergeyck as Philip V's prime minister in 1711.[5] Bergeyck, like several of his contemporaries, was convinced of the great importance of a marine revival for the recovery of Spain, and although it is usually understood that the matter was first considered seriously in mid-1713,[6] after Bergeyck had left office, there is clear evidence that concrete plans had already been formulated by the autumn of 1712. Bergeyck was advised by the secretary of the Council of the Indies, Don Bernardo Tinajero de la Escalera, that given the state of the shipyards in Spain, there could well be economic advantage in beginning to build in Cuba rather than in Spain.[7] Bergeyck immediately agreed, and consequently the shipbuilding contract previously referred to with López Pintado was drawn up on 11 November 1712.[8] This provided for the setting up of yards in Havana, with López Pintado as superintendent, the transportation to Cuba of craftsmen and materials for shipbuilding, and the construction there of ten fair-sized warships of 800 tons and 60 guns. These were to be brought into service essentially for the convoying of the *galeones* and *flota*, but two smaller vessels were also to be built to strengthen the Barlovento squadron.[9]

At about the same time the Crown decided 'to establish a navy and shipyard in Biscay and another in Andalusia at Cadiz',[10] and it appointed Don Antonio de Gastañeta to look after the work in Biscay. Gastañeta was a sailor and naval architect of some ability, and he was destined, together with Don José Patiño, to become one of the notable founders of Spain's new navy. Incidentally, the Cuban contract of 1712 with López Pintado must certainly be identified with the so-called 'first project' of Gastañeta, referred to and dated erroneously by Uztáriz, and others who follow him, as 1713.[11] The aims of the contract and the reported proposals of the 'first project' coincide exactly, but there is no real evidence to suggest that Gastañeta was the author of the scheme nor was at all involved beyond being asked to supply two technical drawings for the ships to be built.[12] Indeed Bergeyck said, as late as April 1713, that he had not yet met Gastañeta.[13]

Thus, by the end of 1713, with plans laid for three new shipyards and the construction of a total of 18 new ships – six in Biscay under Gastañeta and 12 in the Indies under López Pintado – great steps forward were expected. Yet the schemes were pitifully overambitious. Practically none of the necessary materials were available in Spain.[14] López Pintado agreed to go abroad to buy rope, canvas, rigging and almost all other supplies, including, if necessary, the three ships in which he was actually to sail to Cuba. England was the country preferred for this, despite the fact that at that date the peace had still not been signed.[15] The Havana project, however, came to nothing, for López Pintado's expedition, after various frustrations, became, as we know, the New Spain fleet of 1715. The other scheme for six ships to be built in Biscay did indeed go ahead, but much more slowly than expected, for in a royal decree of 15 July 1716 the Crown still referred to them as 'at present under construction'.[16] When Jean Orry returned to Spain in 1713 to take over the government from Bergeyck, who despite his great ability was falling from royal favour, he rightly decided that his predecessor's plans for naval reform were too long-term in conception. He immediately resolved, therefore, to buy 20 fully-fitted ships from France with which to build the foundations of a proper naval base at Cadiz. After due discussion of the terms of purchase and the price to be paid it seems that the operation was eventually begun.[17]

There can be no doubt, however, that the most significant event in the re-establishment of the Spanish navy was the appointment of Don José Patiño on 28 January 1717 to the new ministerial post of *Intendente General de Marina*, a post which he was to hold concurrently with the offices of President of the *Tribunal de la Contratación* in the *Casa de la Contratación de las Indias*, and *Superintendente* of the Kingdom of Seville.[18] Patiño, born in Milan of Galician parentage, had come to Spain at the age of 36, accompanying Philip V on his return from Italy in 1702. He had risen via the intendancy of Extremadura to that of Catalonia which he had administered with a firm and efficient hand following the subjection of that principality to Bourbon rule. The famous decree of 1716, known as *Nueva Planta*, finally depriving the Catalans of their traditional rights, and widely resented to this day, was largely the brain-child of Patiño.[19] But even during his time in Catalonia Patiño had become involved in naval affairs. It was he who, as intendant of the army, had been in charge of obtaining ships for the blockade of Barcelona and had gone on to provide the naval wherewithal to conquer Majorca – and even help the Venetians to winkle the Turks out of Corfu![20] In 1716, using Gastañeta's designs, he proposed the construction of two ships of the line at San Feliu de Guixols, north of Barcelona, by way of an experiment to compare the cost and result with the similar operations then in progress in the Basque country. It seems that only one of these ships, *El Catalán*, was actually built and launched in 1719.[21] It was also Patiño who, as intendant of Catalonia, began an important series of Crown contracts for the hire of private vessels. The Italian ambitions of Elizabeth Farnese and her protegé Alberoni held the sympathy of the Milan-born Patiño, and the secret build-up of naval strength at Barcelona for the campaigns in the Mediterranean of 1717 and 1718 was already in hand under him in 1715 with the hiring there of 36 small vessels belonging to owners of various nationalities. For reasons of security the contracts were of unfixed duration and for unstipulated purposes, but they culminated in 1717 and 1718, under Patiño's successor, in agreements for the hire of seven armed ships belonging to Frenchmen and Catalans and six English transport vessels.[22]

Perhaps it was because Patiño had furthered Alberoni's schemes while he was at Barcelona that Alberoni, as his influence grew, succeeded in obtaining for Patiño the post for which he is best remembered, and in which he was best able to suit the designs of the Italians, the *Intendencia General de Marina*. Before he took over his new offices Patiño had become fully conversant with the problems of the commerce of the Indies, the state of the shipyards and the current plans for reconstruction. He had already been asked to think over these matters and prepare a programme for the revival of the navy.[23] He had also attended in Madrid in 1716 the meetings of ministers gathered to review the whole question of the American trade after Bubb's Treaty, from which emerged, it will be remembered, the new *proyecto* for the *flota* of 1717 with its reduced taxation. Don Andrés de Pez, it seems, had made a special point of informing Patiño carefully and fully on various points of importance.[24] The future intendant of the navy is also reputed to have had models of Gastañeta's ships sent to him for study and to have acquainted himself with the technical complexities of them in a remarkably short period of time.[25] The shortcomings of the yards in which they were to be built were manifestly obvious to all. On his arrival in Cadiz, then, to take up his post in February 1717, Patiño knew exactly what had to be done, and he set about his work with extraordinary energy.

As Spanish industry in general had fallen into such an advanced state of decline, one of Patiño's first tasks was to re-establish in Spain the prime industries necessary for shipbuilding. This was a matter of urgency even for the maintenance of the existing fleet, for when he inspected the port at Cadiz Patiño found a number of hulks rotting on the end of their anchor chains and not a cauldron of pitch with which to make good the leaks. He soon began to travel extensively throughout Spain in order to decide upon the most suitable locations for the different industries he required. Three timber-cutting centres were started in the High Pyrenees, and huge trunks were floated down the Ebro to Tortosa for processing and distributing to ports and shipyards. Factories for tar and pitch were set set up in Aragon and Catalonia so as to draw upon the rich pine wealth of the region. The production of rope and cordage was begun in Galicia where good quality hemp was grown. Although the harvest there was insufficient for the demand it was supplemented by imports from Sweden. At Sada, also in Galicia, the manufacture of canvas was started and with the products of some of these establishments manufacture of rigging was begun in Puerto Real near Cadiz.[26] But Patiño also had within his charge the actual shipbuilding itself, the registering and hiring of craft, the supply of provisions, arms and artillery, a forestry policy for supplies of wood, and the general financial administration of the navy and its dependencies. On top of all this he was to administer the *carrera de Indias* as President of the *tribunal* of the *Casa*, and look after the general welfare of the Kingdom of Seville.[27] Thus the responsibilities of his new intendancy were neither few, nor were they light. Fortunately he was capably aided in his enormous task by Gastañeta who took over almost the whole of the practical side of the revival of the shipyards.[28] Between the two of them a formidable amount was achieved within an extremely short period of time. And so began the overnight growth of Patiño's navy, as unexpected as it was distasteful to the other seafaring nations of Europe.

Parallel with these attempts at material reconstruction are the important reforms in the reorganisation of naval affairs in general. As early as 1707 changes were envisaged by Orry in the structure and ranking of Spain's armed forces,[29] but in the navy rationalisation of rank was not started until February 1714. By a royal *cédula* of that month (the same document that gave Ducasse his Spanish honours) senior naval ranks were equated, in Spanish terminology, with those of the French navy.[30] The purpose was to standardise the multitude of ranks which had grown up in Spain over the years and restore to them their traditional titles.[31] It appears, however, that the French associations, both the theoretical and the practical, were resented in Spain, and the old ranking system seems to have continued.[32] More important changes were made in the autumn of 1714, with the removal of control of the navy from the hands of the Council of the Indies and the Council of War which had managed the service jointly. On 30 November of that year a secretariat for naval affairs was set up with the former secretary of the Council of the Indies, Tinajero de la Escalera, as its first head. He soon became Spain's first Minister of the Navy.[33] Most significant of course of the administrative reforms of these years was the creation of Patiño's post itself, the *Intendecia General de Marina*, in 1717. Although Patiño is quite rightly given the credit for the work of regeneration, it must not be forgotten that his appointment was itself only one of a number of general reforms which had been taking place over the previous five years.

A crucial aspect of the revival of the navy was also the training of officers and crews. For this purpose there had long existed in Seville the Royal College of San Telmo which took in waifs and strays, but particularly sailor's orphans, to train them in naval skills, above all those of the pilot. The college was maintained by royal grants and the proceeds of a 'charity' tax on shipping. From about 1713 the college received increased royal attention and protection, and it was extended as part of Patiño's programme of reforms.[34] In 1716 a new institution was created, the *Academia Real de Guardias Marinas*. Here young Spanish noblemen were to be taught 'to tame the forces of the elements together with [naval] tasks requiring intellect and skill'.[35] The academy consisted of seventeen training officers, chaplain, musicians etc., and had specially picked instructors to teach the exact sciences, astronomy, geography, seamanship and 'everything else important for the making of a good sailor'. It reportedly gave a boy a fine training. When Patiño took office the year after the foundation of the academy, it naturally received his special favour, and a full set of regulations for the institution was issued in April 1718.[36]

A good deal of reorganisation of manpower took place under Patiño. One of his first measures was to phase out the squadrons of galleys which Spain had operated in the Mediterranean for 200 years. They were run by means of *asientos* drawn up with private individuals, and these contracts were withdrawn so that the whole of Spain's naval strength now resided directly in the hands of the Crown. New brigades of marine artillery were formed, together with four batallions of marine fighting-men, and an engineer corps was set up whose main job was the cleaning and maintenance of the nation's ports. All the necessary administrative machinery was also created for the efficient running of a navy. Responsible officers were appointed for every aspect of the service, from stores and arsenals to the crewing of the ships and the hospitalisation of the men. Commissioners, accountants and inspectors were to oversee the lot and run the finances, and a first set of general instructions was issued, covering in 25 chapters most points of protocol and organisation and revealing an outline of the new service as it was expected to function. Rules were also drawn up concerning the licensing of privateers, so useful to a maritime nation in times of war.[37]

In the field of commerce the first reform must be seen as the *proyecto* for the *flota* of 1711, an early attempt to reorganise and legislate for the Indies trade in the first fleet to be free of French interference. However, as we know, further progress was then held up by the various circumstances which led to the Crown's contracting with private persons in naval and commercial affairs. One such agreement which has not yet been described, because it involved a new principle in the trade and was neither *galeones* nor *flota*, was that which the Crown made with the Marqués de Montesacro on 27 January 1714. A joint stock company was formed for trading to Honduras and Caracas, and merchants who wished to send goods for sale could take shares in the company and participate in the eventual total profit or loss of the venture. The Crown took about a third of these shares and found some suitable ships as part of its payment. Three vessels were made ready: one merchantman and a small ship for Honduras, and one merchantman for Caracas. They all left Cadiz on 1 December 1714. The venture turned out to be a complete financial failure. The markets of Honduras and Caracas were neither large nor lucrative ones, and such business as existed there was mainly in the hands of foreign interlopers.[38] The enterprise was of only minor significance, even within the history of the development of the later monopolistic trading companies, but it does indicate that already in 1713 and 1714 experimentation was beginning with fairly fundamental reforms in the American trade such as had previously never got beyond meetings of the old *Junta de comercio.*

Associated by chance with Montesacro's venture is one of the potentially most practical reforms of the time in the matter of the Indies trade. It was clear to Philip's ministers that firm control of commerce had to be re-established, if only for the sake of replenishing the royal treasury. Moreover the alarming attitude of the merchants of Mexico had only recently been made known to the Council of the Indies.[39] It was therefore decided to send some high authority to the colonies to survey the situation in the Indies, correct the worst abuses and report back to the Crown with a clear picture upon which future policies could be based. Accordingly a royal order of 17 August 1714 created the posts of *Oidor* and *Alcalde Visitador de la Veeduría General del Comercio entre Castilla y las Indias*, and Don Pedro Tomás Pintado and Don Antonio José Álvarez de Abreu were appointed to them.[40] Their powers were wide and the scope of their task was enormous. They were to prosecute and provisionally sentence any person involved in contraband trade, calling if necessary upon the military for assistance, to observe secretly and report to the Crown on the private lives and behaviour of all royal officers from governors downwards, and to investigate frauds and other activities in which they were involved prejudicial to the royal treasury. They were also required to report upon what goods and produce could most advantageously be exported to and imported from the colonies, and upon mineral deposits and their exploitation. In addition they were to make recommendations about the administration of royal revenue and royal justice in America. They were given authority within their fields of activity over most royal officers in the Indies and even the viceroys were ordered to assist them with their cooperation. The two new officials left Spain for the Indies in December 1714 with Montesacro's expedition. Their first and only investigation took place in Venezuela where contraband activities were blatant and where, it seems, the loyalty of the local authorities to the Bourbon was in doubt. Unfortunately the whole project ended here, for although the officials sent in a full report on the province on 25 March 1715, Álvarez de Abreu became so involved in the internal politics of Venezuela that he was still there six years later, becoming governor in 1721. The major part of his mission, concerning the remainder of the commerce of the Indies, seems to have gone by the board.

The next stage in the preparation of commercial reforms for the

American trade was the series of meetings held by Spanish ministers over the twelve months following the signing of Bubb's Treaty in May 1716.[41] Here real policies were finally forged to reorganise the *carrera de Indias*, foster Spanish industries and legislate against the besetting evils of the transatlantic trade – and it was, incidentally, from these meetings that Patiño's intendancy originated. The early years of the eighteenth century had seen a protracted dispute among the Crown's economic advisers over taxation policy. One group believed that taxes ought to be high on goods exported from Spain on the grounds that it was the foreign buyer who would really pay the tax; by the same token duty should be low on goods imported into Spain, thereby keeping prices down and reducing inflation. The other group believed quite the opposite, arguing that low taxes on exports would aid Spanish industry by increasing sales abroad, and high taxes on imported goods would keep the foreigner out and so improve Spanish industries still more.[42] The matter came to a head in the government councils in the second half of 1716, and the spectre presented by the English 'Annual Ship' had not a little to do with the final decision. The ideas of the second group seemed best suited to the present circumstances and so emerged a clear policy to encourage the growth of the nation's industry and agriculture and the exportation of Spanish produce, especially to the colonies, at lower rates of tax. The reduction of certain duties in March 1717, on the fleet of that year, from the rates originally proposed nine months earlier, marked the first stage in the implementation of the new policies. Later in the year came the abolition of internal customs duties on goods transported from one part of Spain to another.[43] The Crown itself demonstrated its firm belief in its own policies by establishing the first royal cloth factory at Guadafajara in 1718.[44] Soon after there appeared a lengthy royal *instrucción*, addressed to the intendants of the realm, requiring them energetically to promote agriculture and industry throughout the land as the means of enriching the people and developing commerce.[45] There followed a number of other measures designed to help the manufacture and sale of home-produced goods.[46] It was even proposed that the Catalans, now that they were the 'equals' of the Castilians, should be encouraged to participate directly via Cadiz in the Indies trade, from which they had been excluded for 200 years. To foster their interest in commerce the foundation of a mariners' college at Barcelona was offered, along the lines of those existing at Seville. But the Catalans' own suggestion for the inclusion of a 'Catalan ship' of 500 tons to join the fleets at Cadiz, or the establishment of a trading company for a specific area of America, apparently received no consideration.[47]

Some of the most celebrated reforms to come out of the meetings of 1716 and 1717 were concerned with the *Casa de Contratación*. The old Admiral Andrés de Pez, whose voice was important in all these affairs, had ever been anxious that Cadiz should become the administrative centre of the Indies trade and not merely the official port. During most of the Hapsburg era Seville had had a complete monopoly of the American trade and the *Casa de Contratación* had been established there. In 1680, however, it had been decided that because of the difficulties of navigating the bar at the mouth of the Guadalquivir, Cadiz and not Seville should be the only port for the Indies trade. But the *Casa de Contratación* had remained in Seville, thus causing an unnecessary complication in the dispatching of the fleets to the Indies. Under Philip V, Pez was raised to the high offices of president of the Council of the Indies, secretary of the Department (*Despacho*) of Naval and Indies Affairs, and eventually, in 1721, to Minister of the Navy, and it had long been his desire that both port and *Casa* should be brought together in one place.[48] It was he who prevailed upon Patiño, as soon as the new intendant general was appointed, to make his first objective in the reformation of the *carrera de Indias* the transference of the *Casa de Contratación* to Cadiz. The proposal caused an uproar in Seville where the illusion of the Indies monopoly was jealously guarded. Nevertheless the spirit of the reformers triumphed and by a royal decree of 12 May 1717, the *Casa* and all its dependencies were ordered to be removed to Cadiz.[49] Pez realised that there was a serious danger that this decision might be reversed in later years by vehement representations from the merchants of Seville, whose efforts indeed almost succeeded in 1722 and 1726.[50] In order to frustrate such schemes Pez persuaded Patiño that the works which had been going on for some time to join the rivers Guadalquivir and Guadalete, so as to facilitate navigation, should be stopped and the channel allowed to silt up.[51] Thus the transatlantic monopoly was irrevocably transferred to Cadiz, and port and administrative centre became one.

Various reforms in the political structure of the *Casa* and its general administration were also introduced at this time. The Crown considered that in the past there had been an excess of employees and officials concerned in the running of the *Casa*. For greater efficiency it was advisable to reduce their numbers. The offices of *visitador* and *juez oficial* were suppressed and the whole administration of the shipping for the Indies trade became the responsibility of the new president, assisted by two legal advisers, a revenue officer, two scribes and a book-keeper. Corresponding reductions were also made in the number of individuals representing the merchant bodies allowed to take part in the affairs of the institution.[52] However, even before the actual transference of the *Casa* to Cadiz was ordered, reform of the administration of the Indies trade had begun. Traditionally the supreme authority for all matters relating to the settlement and government of the colonies had resided in the Council of the Indies. But the Council, by its very nature, was so occupied with a host of other matters that it could hardly be expected to look to the details of the revival of the Cadiz trade with the urgency required in 1716–17. A royal decree of 27 January 1717, repeated on 20 September of the same year, therefore forbade the Council of the Indies to have any direct dealing in the organisation of the fleets and commerce from Cadiz to the Indies. Full responsibility was henceforth to be resumed by the Crown itself and the *Casa de Contratación*, with the new intendant of the navy in overall control.[53]

A final touch to the reorganisation came with the provision of a regular service of dispatch ships between Spain and the colonies. The Marqués de Montesacro had undertaken the running of such a service as early as 1708, under a Crown concession, but it had been abandoned after the first two ships had gone.[54] A royal decree of 29 July 1718 stated that eight *aviso* ships would be sent off to America at regular intervals each year, four to New Spain and four to Peru. Two would leave for their respective destinations in early January, two more at the end of March, another two in mid-June and the final pair at the beginning of November. This service, like the first attempt, was also administered under a Crown concession, this time by *asiento* with the merchant bodies of Andalusia.[55] Thus it would be possible to plan the cargoes of the *flotas* and *galeones* so as to obtain a maximum benefit from the trade with the colonies.[56]

By 1718, then, it seemed that Spain was ready to meet the challenge presented by Bubb's Treaty. Possibly the *Royal Prince* might be the only English 'Annual Ship' after all whose voyage, in 1717, was to profit from the chaotic state of Spain's transatlantic trade. Yet there still remained one other matter of supreme importance to be dealt with before the future of the *galeones* and *flota* could be secure – that of the growing American opposition towards the established system of trade with Cadiz. It was necessary to take measures that would effectively bring the colonies back again into Spain's economic harness. The alienation of the Indies from the Cadiz trade had been brought about by three main factors. First, in Peru, the continued and even increased contraband of the French in the Pacific after 1713, which made a successful expedition of *galeones* to Tierra Firme an impossibility. Second, the growth of New Spain's commerce with the Far East which was highly prejudicial to the trade of the *flota*. Third, the method of conducting the trade of the *flota* in New Spain, which gave the Mexican merchants considerable advantage over the *flotistas* and permitted them to manipulate the prices by practising their 'commercial blackmail'. In 1716 all this information was available at the meetings of the Crown's ministers and it was only a question of introducing adequate legislation.

The situation in Peru was the most straightforward, yet it was also the most intractable. In 1712, at the instance of the Spanish Crown, Louis XIV had forbidden his subjects to trade along the Pacific coasts of South America, and the peace treaties of 1713 had confirmed the prohibition.[57] It had had no real effect, and in 1714 and 1715 stern instructions were given to the viceroy of Peru to stamp out the illegal trading.[58] At the same time renewed demands to the French court to control its subjects resulted in a further serious prohibition in Paris in January 1716.[59] But the contraband still continued.[60] In December 1716, by agreement with the French Crown, a combined Franco-Spanish expedition was sent off to the Pacific. It consisted of two French men-of-war and two Spanish, and the sole object of the mission was to arrest any French ships found trafficking along the coasts of Peru. Six or seven offenders were eventually caught and taken captive into Callao. A relevant comment on the state of the navy before Patiño is provided incidentally by the description of this expedition.[61] The two Spanish men-of-war, commanded by Don Bartolomé de Urdinzu and Don Blas de Lezo, were so old and in such an unseaworthy condition that they were incapable of making the voyage round Cape Horn. They were so badly damaged by the heavy weather that they were forced to turn back and put in to Buenos Aires. There they were abandoned, having been judged unfit for further service. Ironically it was left to the two Frenchmen, M. Nicholas de Martinet and M. le Junquier, to carry out the mission in the Pacific. The two Spanish sea-captains went on to Lima by land![62] In view of the prohibitions published and the practical measures taken, the Crown's advisers, at their meetings in 1717, decided that nothing further could be done to improve the situation until, as the Peruvians themselves recommended, the contraband stopped and the stocks of illegal merchandise in the viceroyalty were exhausted.[63] A clear statement of policy on the matter was issued in the form of a royal *cédula* to the viceroy of Peru on 10 March 1718.[64]

Action required for dealing with the situation which had developed in New Spain had to be rather more subtle than that needed for Peru. In New Spain it was virtually a question of altering the economic *status quo* of the viceroyalty. A serious obstacle to the success of the *flotas* in New Spain had long been that country's trade with the Far East. The majority of Mexicans, even the lower classes, dressed more in the Oriental cottons and silks, brought in via Acapulco, than they did in European cloth.[65] As an important cargo carried in the *flota* from Europe was cloth, it followed that the *flotistas* could not face the competition offered by the cheaper and superior Chinese stuff. To strike a telling blow against the importation of cloth from the East into New Spain – a trade that was yearly increasing – was therefore to regain some measure of control over the Mexican markets for the *flotas* from Cadiz. This was the policy which lay behind the dispatch of certain instructions to the viceroy of New Spain on 8 and 11 January 1718.[66] The Crown commanded that a proclamation should be published stating that the cargo of the Manila galleon would henceforth be limited to china, wax, peppers, cinnamon, cloves and linen – all of them goods that were not produced in Spain. Trade in cloths, silks and other material from the Orient would be prohibited absolutely and severe penalties inflicted upon offenders. A period of six months grace was to be given for the current stocks to be used up and after that public burnings were to be held of any Oriental cloth found in the kingdom. The viceroy objected to these measures on the grounds that they were unpracticable and unnecessary. The matter was considered again in Spain, but nevertheless the instructions were confirmed by a royal order of 27 February 1719, and re-stated in further dispatches on 27 October 1720.[67] The result of the publication of these decrees was civil disturbance in the Philippines. It was reported that

the people of Manilla had made an insurrection [1722] against the Spanish governor on occasion of his publishing the King's decree, forbidding in severe penalties those people to continue their trade to Acapulco in America, which they had like there carried on to the prejudice of the European trade to the South Seas.[68]

At all events, perhaps even this was preferable to allowing the growth of economic independence to continue in New Spain at this crucial time. The success of the *flotas* was after all of great importance for the Spanish cloth industries which were precisely now awakening from their long lethargy.[69]

However, the most serious problem in New Spain continued to be the unwillingness of the Mexican merchants to cooperate with the traders from the fleet. In 1717 the group of Crown advisers under Patiño, consisting now of both officials and merchants, heard from Don Andrés de Pez that an important new measure had been approved to promote the efficient running of the trade fleets – the introduction of a fixed annual timetable to regulate the voyages of the *galeones* and *flota*. One of the results of this would be that only seven months would be permitted for the completion of all the business of the *flota* once it had arrived in New Spain. But in view of the complexity of the transactions in Mexico, the group considered that the proposed schedule allowed insufficient time to do all that had to be done. Furthermore, if the merchants of Mexico continued their 'commercial blackmail', which made the stay of the *flotistas* in New Spain even longer, the scheme would be quite impracticable.[70]

Nevertheless the occasion presented a golden opportunity for the Spanish merchants to attempt to end the Mexicans' trading advantage and at the same time curb their sense of economic independence. The commercial interests in Old Spain had attempted three times in the past to have a proper trade fair established in New Spain, similar to that at Portobello, but, as we know, the Mexicans had failed to cooperate.[71] In 1717 the circumstances were rather different. In Spain the Mexican merchants' admitted opposition to the annual fleet and the alleged grounds for it were open for discussion. The Mexicans claimed that the small country merchants were stealing their livelihood by buying directly from the *flotistas* in the capital, and this was the chance the *consulados* in Spain had been waiting for. The celebration of a formal fair in New Spain with a fixed period of duration would meet the complaints of the Mexican merchants, for a short trade fair would automatically exclude the small retailer who would have insufficient capital to buy in bulk. It would also be the only practical way of implementing the Crown's plans for a rigid timetable for an annual fleet. The merchants of Mexico City, it was argued, ought therefore to welcome the proposal, for it not only solved the commercial problems they raised, but by ensuring regular supplies in bulk from Spain it actually perpetuated the Mexicans' monopoly of the markets of New Spain. A proposal of Patiño's group that a proper trade fair should be established in New Spain was accordingly sent forward for the king's approval. Soon afterwards a royal *cédula*, of 20 March 1718, ordered that in future the business of the *flota* would be carried on by means of a trade fair to be held at the small town of Jalapa, about half way between Veracruz and Mexico City. It seemed that in this way a satisfactory solution might be found to the major problem of the New Spain trade.[72]

All was now ready for the publication of the main piece of legislation of the period, the *Proyecto para Galeones, y Flotas del Perú, y Nueva España y para Navíos de Registro y Avisos*. Although the spirit and most of the details of the reforms were elaborated in the course of 1716, 1717 and 1718, the document itself did not appear until 5 April 1720. The delay was caused by the naval operations in the Mediterranean in which Patiño and his colleagues were so deeply involved, and which resulted in that indecisive contest, the War of the Quadruple Alliance, late in 1718. However, Patiño's work for the reform of the American trades was also briefly endangered in 1719 by the Machiavellian Cardinal Alberoni. Jealous of his junior's zeal he took advantage of Patiño's absence from Cadiz and the court to use his by-now absolute authority to attempt to sabotage the plans.[73] Not only did Alberoni actively encourage clandestine trade during the war to Cuba, New Spain and Peru, in the new *aviso* ships,[74] but he also laid before the Council of the Indies three damaging decrees. One of these arbitrarily transferred the fair of the *galeones* from Portobello to Buenos Aires.[75] Hearing of this on his return to Spain from Sicily, Patiño threatened to resign. As a result, a committee of ministers began an enquiry into Alberoni's decrees and soon advised that they should be rescinded.

Fortunately for Patiño, and for Spain, Alberoni's precipitous fall from power followed soon after. Nevertheless as a result of the Cardinal's disastrous Mediterranean adventures most of Patiño's new navy was destroyed and even six half-built frigates, then on the stocks in Biscay, were lost by the action of Spain's enemies.[76] But to rebuild was not the immense task it had been originally, now that industry was reviving. Gastañeta produced a new and highly successful shipbuilding programme in 1720 and reconstruction again went ahead well.[77] It is possible even to argue that in a sense the war may have actually contributed to the revival of the *carrera de Indias*. While England was at war with Spain she could not send 'Annual Ships' to ruin the trade at the American fairs or, even worse, to monopolise the markets in the absence of the Cadiz fleets. The two years occupied in war in fact allowed a short breathing-space before the English were again in a position to insist upon their rights acquired by the treaty of 1716. Thanks also to the war the Crown was able to send the first of the 'reorganised' fleets out to the Indies in 1720 without an English

'Annual Ship' being present.[78] On the other hand, it is also true that such benefits were probably outweighed in the final analysis by the quantities of contraband goods which entered the Indies during their short period of isolation from Spain.

The *Real proyecto* of 1720, as the new document came to be called, consists of a long preamble followed by eight chapters.[79] Of these, the preamble and the first four chapters concern Crown policy over the *carrera de Indias* and the methods to be adopted for dispatching and receiving transatlantic shipping. The remaining four chapters consist of a detailed description of the taxes to be levied on goods transported to and from the Indies and the regulations for their collection. The *Real proyecto* is by no means as complete as its preamble suggests. The supplementary legislation which appeared over the years 1720–3[80] and the omissions pointed out by Gutiérrez de Rubalcava in his comments and analysis indicate some of its deficiencies, but it was nevertheless a remarkably clear statement of the Crown's policy on the matter and a valuable attempt at practical reform.[81] A brief summary of the more important provisions of the preamble and the first four chapters will serve to define the character of the measures adopted.

The king declares that upon the restoration of the peace his first concern will be to establish close and regular commercial relations between Spain and the Indies. This he regards as essential for stimulating the rising Peninsular industries, increasing royal revenue, and guaranteeing prosperity and a better life for all his subjects. The frequent and regular dispatching of the *galeones* and *flota* is considered undoubtedly the best method of achieving this aim. After first giving a general but accurate description of the ills attendant upon the *carrera de Indias* and roundly condemning past practice, the king goes on to state that henceforth he intends to take a lively interest and an active part in the dispatching of fleets on a properly organised basis. He commits himself to supplying without fail sufficient warships to convoy the merchant vessels and to facilitate, in every possible way, prompt departures from Cadiz. Weather permitting, 1 June and 1 September are stipulated as the sailing dates of the *flota* and *galeones* respectively. In future the ships will not be allowed to wait on account of merchants who are not ready for their goods to leave on the fixed dates. Bitter experience has shown that in the past delays of this kind have been very prejudicial to the trade of the fleets. Prolonged stays in the Indies too have had harmful effects upon the ships, their crews and their cargoes. It is therefore resolved that a strict timetable shall be adhered to on the voyage. A total of 50 days maximum will be allowed for the *galeones* to complete their business in Cartagena and Portobello. A stop of 15 days only will be permitted at Havana on the return voyage. Similarly, the outward bound *flota* will be restricted to six days at Puerto Rico for taking on water, and it will be obliged to leave Veracruz again for Spain by 15 April each year at the very latest. The *flota* too will be allowed a stop of 15 days at Havana on the homeward voyage. This schedule is to be rigorously observed and no excuses of any kind will be accepted from the commanders for failure to keep to it. The Crown proposes to invalidate the usual excuse for delay, that of death, sickness or desertion amongst the crews, by sending with each fleet a small ship carrying replacements for the men in the ships of the fleet to meet any contingency of this kind. No expense or effort is to be spared by the Crown to ensure the smooth and successful running of the *carrera de Indias*, but on the other hand it is made clear that an equal effort is expected from all concerned to cooperate fully with the Crown in the new venture. Instructions are laid out for the future election of the Old Spain merchants who are to accompany the fleets, and their duties are determined. The authority and the obligations which the commanders are to have are described, and rules are set out about who shall be entitled to embark in a fleet and under what conditions. Other details refer to inland customs dues in Spain, the control and registering of goods, the duties of the royal officials at Cadiz and Seville, the loading of the ships and the dispatching of *registros* and *avisos*. With all these precise regulations it is intended that the *carrera de Indias* shall become a properly controlled institution which will bring profit to the Crown's dominions on both sides of the Atlantic.

The *Real proyecto* sets out clearly the Crown's economic intentions. Apart from the requirement in chapter one that, except in special circumstances, only Spanish-built vessels will be admitted in the fleets, thus supporting the Spanish shipyards, the four chapters which set out the new taxes to be levied on the merchandise are significant. A comparison of the rates of tax and freight charges in the three *proyectos* of 1711, 1717 and 1720 (see Appendix III) reveals a continuing policy of reducing duties and charges on Spanish produce for export to the Indies. The *proyecto* of 1717, however, seems to indicate some uncertainty at that stage in the mind of the Crown over which goods should be so privileged. Then tax on cloth woven from Flanders thread, for instance, was lessened, tax on cinnamon and pepper (usually imported from Holland) remained unaltered, whereas tax on such patently Spanish produce as wine, spirits (*aguardiente*), raisins and oil, for example, was noticeably but not greatly reduced. The *Real proyecto* of

1720, on the other hand, shows a good deal more confidence and clearsightedness. Tax on cloth made from Flanders thread is brought back up to the 1711 level, that on cinnamon and pepper is considerably increased, while the duty on all Spanish produce is dropped, in some cases by as much as 85 per cent, from the 1711 levels. It is important to observe, however, that the main rate of tax (*palmeo*), levied on fine and manufactured goods in crates and packets, which comprised the bulk of the cargoes, remained at five and a half *reales* per cubic *palmo* in each of the three *proyectos*. As regards freight dues, although the intention has clearly been to lessen the burden on Spanish produce, a certain rationalisation of the charges is also introduced in the *proyecto* of 1720, under which certain bulky or heavy goods are indeed obliged to pay more for transport to America. On this question too some uncertainty of policy seems evident in the *proyecto* of 1717. A comparison of the duties to be imposed on the fleets on their return to Cadiz in the three *proyectos* is also significant. Although the rates of tax on most American produce remained the same in all three, the duty on precious metals imported into Spain was raised in 1717 to 2 per cent on gold (from 1½ per cent in 1711) and 5 per cent on silver (4 per cent in 1711). The *Real proyecto* of 1720 continued the rates established in 1717. Freight charges for the return journey remained virtually unaltered in all three documents.

Thus a fairly clear picture emerges of the development of a new economic policy for the Indies trade over the years 1716–20. After the shock of Bubb's Treaty and the prompt decision on the matter of taxation theory, cautious changes were introduced into the *proyecto* of 1717. Their aim, as we know, was to facilitate the sale of Spanish goods in America, and at the same time guarantee Crown revenue by increased taxes on imported gold and silver. The next major step took the form of further and more substantial tax concessions on outgoing merchandise in the *proyecto* of 1720, which were *not* matched by correspondingly higher taxes on the return to Cadiz. As a result of the reorganisation of the tax system established by the *Real proyecto* of 1720, costs to the exporting merchant were cut still further. Quite apart from the reduced rates of the schedules themselves it was also declared that the majority of minor taxes and port dues, collected on the various stages of the journey, were abolished, or rather were deemed to be included in the specified duties payable. All port dues at Cadiz for both outward and homeward bound voyages were so included, and only one set of such dues still remained payable in the Indies. Even so a supplementary royal order of 20 April 1720 abolished *all* duties outside the schedules (except the *alcabala* which remained payable everywhere) on the cargoes of the *galeones* in order to give special assistance to that particularly moribund trade.[82] Thus if the burden of taxation was relieved only in part by the actual schedules of the *Real proyecto* (remembering that the *palmeo* rate remained constant) it was considerably lessened by the overall effect of the reforms.

It seems therefore something of an exaggeration to suggest that the *Real proyecto* of 1720 was mainly an attempt to simplify a troublesome revenue process and was not intended to diminish the weight of taxes.[83] Uztáriz, in his comments on the measures of the period, makes the specific point that at this stage the Crown was anxious to abolish illogical taxes on the fleets and reduce levels generally as a means of benefiting industry and commerce in the Peninsula.[84] Certainly the documents examined seem to bear this out. Nevertheless such apparent enlightenment may easily be misinterpreted. No new basic economic principles had yet evolved, and Patiño especially saw the promotion of trade and industry simply as a means of obtaining more revenue in specie, of which a greater part would remain inside Spain. It seemed to him quite acceptable in the years ahead, as we shall see, to force the merchants of Andalusia to trade in very unfavourable American markets merely for the sake of securing Crown revenue. Unquestionably the *Real proyecto* and its complementary legislation were drafted in such a way as to suit current policy, the object of which was quite simply to promote an 'export drive', and not to ease taxation as an act of indulgence. Evidence of this is found in a royal letter addressed to the intendants of all the provinces of Spain on 23 May 1720:

> It is expedient that [the Indies trade], at least the greater part of it, be carried on with the goods and produce of Spain. . . Bearing in mind this policy and explaining it to the manufacturers and business-men of these realms, you should do your utmost to persuade and encourage them to send to Cadiz as great a quantity as possible of produce, cloth and other Spanish-made goods for exportation to the Indies, either by means of their own agents or else by entrusting them to those of the *carrera de Indias*.[85]

The Crown was clearly intending that the *Real proyecto* should also serve as a foundation upon which to base a wider improvement of Spain's general economic fortunes.

It is against this background of reformist legislation that an assessment of the Spanish attitude towards the English 'Annual Ship' may best be made. It has sometimes been suggested that the importance of the

English 'Annual Ship' in the gradual break-up of the Spanish
commercial system has been greatly exaggerated.[86] The arguments
contributing to this thesis are perhaps valid, but one cannot accept the
final conclusion without some misgivings. With good reason it has
been pointed out that the quantity of contraband merchandise taken
into the Indies via the 'Annual Ship' was appreciably less than that
introduced by various other methods during the period of the English
assiento; also that in any case most governments in the eighteenth
century had come to accept smuggling as part of commercial life – and
especially so the Spanish. Therefore, it is alleged, the attention paid to
the 'Annual Ship' by the Crown and its ministers (and by later
historians) was out of all proportion. The few thousand tons of goods
smuggled by the 'Annual Ship' over some 20 years was in fact a drop in
the ocean compared with the major illicit operations of the period in
the Spanish Indies. Thus, it is concluded, the 'Annual Ship' was quite
simply a very obvious aspect of English smuggling upon which the
Spanish authorities could pounce with dramatic effects.

Yet this view of the matter places the question of the 'Annual Ship'
and the American markets out of its true perspective. The fury of the
Spanish merchants and Crown was not basically directed at the
contraband *per se*, introduced by the 'Annual Ship', although truly this
was the object of their protests. What really incensed the Spaniards,
merchants and ministers alike, was that the 'Annual Ship' was capable
of destroying what little remained of their existing trade to the Indies.
The 'Annual Ship' was not undermining the trade from Cadiz by its
contraband, but by its very presence – by the fact that, whether with a
100 tons or 1000, it could command a market in America when the
galeones and *flotas* from Cadiz could not! The effect of contraband was
reasonably calculable. Its seriousness was a function of its volume. The
'Annual Ship' – with or without its contraband – struck at the very
nerve centre of the whole system. It further alienated the American
merchants from their partners, the *galeonistas* and *flotistas*, at precisely
the critical moment. The *Royal Prince* affair of 1717 is a classic, if early,
example of this. The fact that she may have carried a few hundred tons
of excess cargo only helped to make things worse; it was not the root of
the trouble. The real fear had been touched upon by the Council of the
Indies in its letter of 6 August 1716 in which it had referred in
near-panic terms to 'the annihilation of Spanish trade' by the 'Annual
Ship'.[87] The panic came not over its contraband activities, which at
that time had hardly begun, but because of the favoured place the ship
would inevitably hold in the American markets. The 'Annual Ship'

would nourish the growing feeling of economic independence in America, and this, it was realised, endangered the very system of trade with the Indies. It was, therefore, this fear of the commercial alienation of the Indies that prompted the Crown to complain so bitterly and to find excuses, if it could, for not issuing the annual *cédula* to the South Sea Company. It was the eventual fulfilment of this same fear that, years later, caused López Pintado to write to Patiño:

> I tell Your Excellency that if . . . an efficient remedy is not found [to the arbitrary practices of the colonial merchants], the King will lose authority over both places [Tierra Firme and Peru].[88]

A comparable threat to the Cadiz trade during these years was made, as has been mentioned, by the sale of goods from the Manila galleon, for this too alienated the colonial merchants from the Cadiz trade. Here the Crown was free to act, and it adopted ruthless measures to cut down the trade from Manila. Public burnings of Chinese goods were ordered, and merchants who were found trafficking in Oriental merchandise were threatened with heavy fines and the loss of property.[89] No doubt the Crown would have been happy to introduce similar measures to deal with the trade from England, but signed treaties prohibited such brutality. The volleys of complaints over the years to come about the activities of the 'Annual Ship' were, in reality, vain and furious protests about the calamity which had been foreseen by the Council of the Indies as early as August 1716.

It seems quite wrong, then, to suggest that the 'Annual Ship' was not really very important because her contraband activities may not have been really as consequential as has frequently been made out. The 'Annual Ship' was of supreme importance, for – contraband or no – she dealt a hard blow from *within* at the Indies trade from Cadiz. The outcry against the 'Annual Ship' was even more vehement and bitter because of the failure of the various trade fairs between 1720 and 1735 – failures aggravated and sometimes caused by the presence of the 'Annual Ship'; failures which frustrated and invalidated the reforms in the *carrera de Indias* elaborated by Spain's ministers, principally over the period 1716–20.

The *flota* for New Spain did indeed leave during the summer of 1720, as planned, but it was not until the following year that the *galeones* were ready for Cartagena and Portobello. The new legislation certainly looked impressive and business-like on paper, but its results in practice, as we shall see, were disappointing.[90]

6   The *Flotas* to New Spain, 1720–1726

The first fleet to leave Spain under the new regulations provided by the *Real proyecto* was the *flota* commanded by General Fernando Chacón Medina y Salazar, consisting of 19 ships which carried between them a cargo of 4377.68 tons.[1] This was by far the greatest volume of merchandise to leave Cadiz in a single fleet since the previous century. Besides being the first fleet to sail under the new regulations, Chacón's was also the first *flota* to be governed by the *cédula* of March 1718, ordering the sale of its merchandise by means of a properly established trade fair at Jalapa, thus finally doing away with the traditional practice of the *flotistas'* selling the goods from the fleet piecemeal in Mexico City. For the first time then, the whole cargo had to be transported to a formal fair, and the sale of merchandise at any other place than Jalapa was strictly forbidden.[2]

The reforms, however, did not get off to a very promising start, for Chacón put out from Cadiz on 7 August 1720, already more than two months later than the date stipulated by the *proyecto* for the departure of the New Spain fleet. He arrived safely in Veracruz on 26 October.[3] Unfortunately unforeseen circumstances caused the fleet's timetable to fall even further behind the schedule laid down by the royal orders. Because of continuous high winds and storms at Veracruz it was impossible to unload the ships until January 1721, and it was February before all was ready for the celebration of the fair at Jalapa.[4] It therefore became extremely important that the final financial arrangements for the trading should be made quickly. Moreover, the fair itself and all the other business had also to be concluded with all possible speed if the *flota* was to set off again for Spain by 15 April as the law now required. Consequently, on 3 February 1721, the viceroy of New Spain, the Marqués de Valero, arrived in Jalapa to preside over the meeting of the *flotistas* and the representatives of the merchants of Mexico – a meeting called together by royal instructions to decide the prices at which the cargoes of the *flota* would be sold. Agreement was not however forthcoming. For eight days the viceroy sat through hours of fruitless argument and haggling between the Spaniards and the Mexicans. When it was clear that agreement would not be reached even with further discussion, Valero ordered each side to draw up a list of the maximum or minimum prices which they would be prepared to pay or to accept for the various goods on sale at the fair. The *flotistas* handed their list to the viceroy on 9 February and the Mexican delegates gave theirs in on the following day. There was as much as a 40–50 per cent difference between the prices demanded by the *flotistas* and those the Mexicans were prepared to pay. Nevertheless on the basis of these two lists the viceroy, with the aid of a mathematician skilled in this kind of calculation, was able to produce a final price-list which showed a workable compromise between both sets of prices. Yet in spite of this the merchants of Mexico City refused to leave the capital and cooperate in the fair. The compromise prices agreed upon by their representatives were still higher than they intended to pay, and for some three weeks there was virtually no sale of goods at the fair. Eventually Valero, exasperated by the continued deadlock and lack of activity, and conscious that the departure date for the *flota* was drawing nearer, decided to act. Taking advantage of the insignificant phrase in the original *cédula* establishing the fair at Jalapa, which stated that the fair should be 'similar to that held at Acapulco' (where no tiresome price agreement had to be arranged), the viceroy declared that henceforth both buyers and sellers would be free to make their own private transactions, irrespective of the official price list. Furthermore it was ordered that as an encouragement to the trading the *alcabala* would be waived on all goods sold at the fair. Having issued these instructions he set off for his capital to attend to his business, part of which was to persuade the merchants of the city to participate in the bargaining at Jalapa.

In spite of the viceroy's actions, the selling of goods at the fair continued to be slow and only a very small quantity of the total cargo was disposed of by the beginning of April. Petitions to the viceroy requesting that the departure date of the *flota* should be delayed were in vain. In the event it was only because of the late arrival in New Spain of the homeward-bound viceroy of Peru, the Prince of Santo Buono, who was to be taken back to Europe in the fleet, that the stay of Chacón in Veracruz was prolonged past the fixed date of 15 April – until 29 May.

When it was realised throughout the viceroyalty that Valero was determined to get the fleet off with as little delay as possible, sales at

Jalapa suddenly increased. The merchants of New Spain, now taking advantage of the situation hurried to the fair with the intention of securing last minute bargains from the *flotistas* who were anxious to return home with the fleet. In this the Mexicans were eminently successful and more sales were effected between 4 May and 29 May than during any other period of the fair. The *flota* eventually set sail for Spain at the end of May, although the fair at Jalapa had still not properly ended. Of the 72 *flotistas* 41 were obliged to remain behind at the mercy of the New Spain merchants to try and get rid of their goods at the best prices they could obtain.

Trouble of this kind however had clearly been anticipated by the Crown, for in a *cédula* of 28 September 1720 it was declared that the *flotistas* would be permitted to sell merchandise not bought at the fair anywhere in the viceroyalty providing the usual *alcabala* was paid. Unfortunately, for reasons which he could not properly understand, Valero had not received this royal instruction until May 1721, when it was too late to order a change in the proceedings at Jalapa. However, after the *flota* had left he declared that the 41 *flotistas* who remained were free to sell their goods where they chose. Therefore, from July 1721 the *flotistas*, although released from the limitations of an indefinite residence in Jalapa, found themselves once again obliged to submit to the 'commercial blackmail' of the merchants of Mexico. As the volume of merchandise in the fleet of 1720 was nearly twice that of a normal *flota* as a result of the recent diligence of the Crown in these matters – and less than half of it had been sold at Jalapa – the situation was now virtually unchanged from that of earlier years. Some 2000 tons of goods, the equivalent of a normal fleet, remained in the hands of the *flotistas*, and there was very little likelihood of their selling them. The business contracted at the fair had of course decreased the chances of further sales to the already well-stocked merchants of the viceroyalty and three years later some of the *flotistas* had still not managed to return to Spain.[5]

The reasons for the Mexican merchants' failure to cooperate in the fair of 1721 are complex, but basically they all derived from the same cause, the fact that the supplies brought in the *flota* were simply not required in New Spain. Bearing in mind this situation it is not difficult to see how and why the various vested interests in Mexico contributed to the unsatisfactory developments at Jalapa. It is reported that at the time of the arrival of the *flota* in 1720 the viceroyalty was already plentifully supplied with merchandise. This had come from three sources: the Manila galleon, the English 'Annual Ship' of 1717 and the smuggling of the South Sea Company, and from the previous *flota* of 1717, whose cargo, even in 1720, was still largely unconsumed owing to the volume of cheaper goods launched on to the market by the first two.[6] Throughout the war of 1718–20 supplies had continued to reach New Spain from the Philippines and a short time just before the fair at Jalapa the Manila galleon for the current year had held its fair at Acapulco. At the time of the ship's dispatch from the Philippines the strict limitations on the trade imposed by the royal *cédulas* of 1718, 1719 and 1720 had not yet been put into effect, and so the volume of cloth and merchandise which it brought was as great as ever.[7] The merchants of Mexico City invested their usual large sums of money in Oriental goods with the result that when the time came to celebrate the fair at Jalapa they were well provisioned with saleable merchandise and had no desire to buy over-priced inferior goods from Spain. Moreover just at this time a shortage of silver, and particularly of specie, was beginning to affect the merchants' buying policies. Owing to lack of economic planning throughout the country scarcity of silver was to become so great over the next months that it eventually caused a fairly serious crisis in the viceroyalty.[8] The Manila galleon of course was partly responsible for the shortage, for, as always, it took with it large sums of silver in payment for the merchandise brought to Acapulco. But another contributory factor was the sizeable quantity of coin removed from the country in 1720 when Generals Guevara and Serrano had arrived with a small naval squadron on an urgent financial errand on behalf of the Crown.[9] Further shipments of silver were also sent out of New Spain via the Barlovento squadron which at that time took two years' overdue pay to the Spanish garrisons stationed round the Caribbean.[10] However probably the most important cause of the scarcity of silver was the drop in the production of the mines which, as will be shown shortly, was curiously enough the direct result of the merchants' overstocking the country with goods.

The glut of merchandise and the shortage of silver were the two important obstacles which stood in the way of the success of the fair at Jalapa, but there were other considerations too. It was greatly in the interests of the merchants of Mexico City to sabotage the trading at Jalapa. The establishment of a trade fair with a limited duration effectively broke their control of the *flotistas'* prices, as indeed the Cadiz merchants had hoped it would. However, since there were already plenty of goods for sale and money was scarce, a boycott of the fair could harm no one but the *flotistas*. It is certainly true that such behaviour gave the small country merchants of New Spain an opportunity of buying supplies directly at the fair, which was what the Mexico City merchants had continually grumbled about, but this danger was very slight. No small merchant would be reckless enough to buy at the high prices demanded at the fair when the large merchants were imposing a boycott. The chances were that the action of the capitalists would in time force the prices of the *flotistas* right down, so that the little man who had foolishly invested earlier would lose money in the long run. This accounts for the period of complete stagnation during the first two months of the fair. The eventual attempt on the part of the viceroy to improve the situation by removing the *alcabala* and granting the liberty to bargain made considerable price reductions possible. As a result buying and selling began. But the removal of the *alcabala* not only had the effect of cutting prices, it also got rid of one of the minor reasons for the boycott. The fact that the fair was being held at Jalapa meant that the *alcabala* was not payable, as normally in the past, to the *consulado* of Mexico, because that body's jurisdiction ended outside the territorial limits of the capital. Thus the *consulado* would have fallen short in its collection of the agreed sum of tax under its *asiento*.[11] The waiving of the *alcabala* automatically reduced the *consulado*'s commitment to pay tax and therefore effectively removed further cause for resentment on this score.

By the end of March silver was beginning to be more plentiful again in New Spain, and it is reported that in the attempt to provide coin for the transactions at the fair the mint in Mexico City was working at maximum capacity, producing 50,000 *pesos* per day.[12] During the last two months of the fair business became brisker. In spite of the fact that the bargain-hunting country merchants outnumbered those from Mexico City by two to one, by far the largest sales were made to the merchants of the capital. It was estimated that eventually a total of over six million *pesos* was brought to the fair by the city merchants alone, compared with only about a million by those from the interior.[13] This in itself is confirmation that the trade and the manipulation of capital in the country continued to be controlled by the merchants of Mexico City in spite of their sophisticated protests to the contrary.

Although the *consulados* of Andalusia felt frustrated by the events in Mexico in 1721, they were soon to look back to the fair of that year with some satisfaction. At Jalapa, after all, they had sold about half the fleet's cargo. This was in fact the equivalent of the tonnage of a normal eighteenth-century *flota*, and its sale represented a feat they had not accomplished for many years past and were not to accomplish again for some years to come. Nevertheless the disappointment of the moment caused the first fair at Jalapa to be seen in Spain as such a complete disaster that it was considered imperative to avoid its repetition in future years.[14] Accordingly a *cédula* was published on 16 May 1722 cancelling the future holding of fairs at Jalapa. The royal order of 6 June 1723, advising the new viceroy of Mexico, the Marqués de Casafuerte, of the imminent dispatch of a *flota* from Cadiz, declared that the sale of its goods in New Spain should be conducted by the same method as had always been practised before the *flota* of Don Fernando Chacón.[15] For the moment, then, there appeared to be no way of breaking the independent control which the merchants of Mexico City held over commercial affairs within the viceroyalty.

II

Allusions have already been made to the special relationship which existed between the merchants of Mexico City and those in the interior of the country, to the effect of quantities of English goods on the Mexican market, and to a drop in the production of the mines owing to a glut of merchandise in the viceroyalty. All these matters were very closely linked in the economy of New Spain in the 1720s and it is impossible to appreciate the commercial situation over this period without first understanding the connection which existed between all these elements. The basis of Mexican commercial life was the trade which linked the miners, the country merchants who traded with them, and the capitalists in Mexico City. Some explanation must therefore be given of the ties which bound these three groups together into commercial interdependence.[16]

In the great enterprise of exploiting the mineral wealth and developing the agriculture of Spain's Empire in America no direct effort was ever made by the Crown to supply the capital outlay necessary for providing the materials and equipment for the work. Consequently a vast investment of private capital was called for if mines were to continue to be discovered and worked, and the land cultivated. From the seventeenth century almost all the capital available in the required quantities in New Spain was in the hands of the businessmen established in Mexico City. It was upon them that the task fell of supplying the capital requirements of materials and provisions and the day-to-day needs, often in money as well as in equipment and stores, of the miners, prospectors and farmers in the outlying and far-flung areas of the viceroyalty. Indeed it is true to say that without the initiative of these city merchants and their willingness to extend terms of credit, agriculture to a certain extent, and mining in its entirety, except for the small number of Crown-owned mines, would have been in great difficulties. In the remoter parts it would probably never have succeeded in developing on any appreciable scale.

The Crown's policy was that the development of mining should be considered absolutely, as far as possible, as a matter for private interests and private investment, although the royal treasury always received a direct 20 per cent share in the results of mining in the form of the tax known as the 'royal fifth'.[17] This concession to the individual was considered to be a great privilege, but there can be no doubt that in the long run it was the most profitable way of running the mines for the Crown's own benefit. The 'royal fifth' was collected quite irrespective of the expenses of working the mines, which the miner himself had to bear. Certainly if the strike proved a rich one the miner made a tidy fortune, but if the vein was only moderate his continued expenses and contributions to the Crown meant that he was lucky to make a reasonable living. However, if the mine proved barren the prospector was ruined, for the fruitless initial outlay fell entirely upon him. The risk of such misfortune as this was not one the Crown itself was prepared to run. The treasury of course could never profit from large-scale mining operations of its own or from organised prospecting.[18] It was much safer to collect the 'royal fifth' on the product of all the mines and exact punitive taxes thereafter almost every time the metals changed hands. If the Crown had not given its subjects a direct interest in the mines in this way it is doubtful if the discovery and working of the deposits of precious metals could ever have been accomplished. But without the credit and equipment supplied by the merchant classes the prospectors would never have opened new mines in the first place, and the enterprises already begun would very quickly have come to an end.

The men engaged in the day-to-day trading at the mine-head were never the wealthy merchants themselves, but smaller traders who acted as their agents, or themselves depended, like the miners they supplied, upon advances of capital from the larger merchants. The work of supplying the mines with stores and equipment was gruelling and unpleasant. It was necessary for the merchants of the interior to live for long periods in remote and often wild parts of the country, inhabited sometimes by warlike Indians, in a community of men unsubjected to law and order, who normally represented the lowest level of colonial society and who abandoned themselves for the most part to vices of all kinds. Frequent long and arduous journeys had to be made by the trader from the remote mining centres to Mexico City to collect further supplies of goods for transportation out to the pit-head trading-posts. Sometimes it was possible that the goods were not even saleable on arrival, owing to some change in mining fortunes or local requirements. And of course these journeys themselves, because of travelling conditions and the wild country, were usually full of hazards both for the trader personally and for the goods he was carrying. It was only to be expected, then, that merchants who possessed large capital sums and flourishing business in Mexico should hardly be prepared to leave their comfortable city lives in order to engage in such dangerous and unattractive trade. Consequently the only men who were willing to do so were the small traders who, for financial reasons, could not establish themselves in Mexico City. Yet these traders could not provide capital on the scale required, and they were therefore obliged to enter into financial agreements with the principal merchants or business houses, in order to equip themselves with the goods or money necessary for carrying on the trade to the mines and the country districts. However, in view of the conditions in which this trade was carried on and the hardships that had to be endured, the one aim of these merchants, or *aviadores* as they were called, was to retire from the business of mine-supplying as quickly as ever they could, that is, as soon as they had made enough money to be able to pay off their debts to their financiers and launch themselves with a 'respectable' business of their own in Mexico City. It is true to say, therefore, that the *aviadores*, probably with few exceptions, regarded themselves as doing the job only temporarily. As a result they operated their trade with an unscrupulousness mingled with caution characteristic of a man who is anxious to make large profits as quickly as possible and yet whose great fear is ruination through imprudent investment.

In many cases it was necessary for the *aviador* to supply equipment and stores to the miners and prospectors on 'open' credit. Because of the miners' and workmen's depraved condition they squandered all their profits on luxurious living, drink and vice, and consequently hardly ever possessed sufficient means to purchase their needs outright, especially if they had debts to settle for their initial equipment and supplies out of the proceeds of their first *bonanza*.[19] Moreover, they could offer no security whatsoever except the promise of the precious metals which in time they hoped to obtain for their labours. Obviously for the *aviador* the risk was great, and so, in view of this, the profits he required and the prices he demanded were proportionately high – and often very disproportionately so. The *aviador* was therefore generally considered by the miners to be ruthless and grasping and enjoyed a reputation of fickleness and disloyalty. It was generally accepted that no matter how great the profits the *aviadores* derived from a connection with a miner, they usually abandoned him in time of *borrasca*.[20] This was natural enough, however, since the *aviador*, who traded only for his own benefit had not the slightest intention of supporting any but the surest prospect he could find. The question of loyalties was for him a matter of little or no concern. So anxious were the *aviadores* to finish their work and return to civilisation that in some cases once they had made sufficient money to do just this they simply abandoned their miners and left them without means to carry on further excavations. But in many more cases this same act of 'abandonment' must also have been the result of the *aviador*'s finally managing to collect long-outstanding debts from miners who had been particularly bad payers, as were the majority, and consequently refusing to extend them any further credit.

Although the *aviador* would not help a miner through a difficult period, on the other hand whenever a rich strike was made in any part of the country no matter how remote or wild, the *aviadores* arrived in their numbers as fast as they could to take advantage of the circumstances. In such cases the miners would have plenty of silver to trade with but there would be comparatively few goods to be bought, and so the *aviador* was able to raise his prices to extortion level and make enormous profits at the miners' expense. It was common also on such occasions for the *aviador* to accept unrefined silver (*piñas*) illegally from the miners, at rates which were well below the standard. The miner, isolated from civilisation and in need of equipment and provisions was more or less obliged to take what he could get from the merchant.

But although the *aviador* was doubtless a profiteer and an unscrupulous businessman, the miner was by no means his helpless victim, for when conditions favoured, he, in his turn, knew also how to take advantage of the *aviador*.[21] His principal aim was to secure for himself a guaranteed source of credit which would provide him with supplies of equipment, stores and money for as long as he required, whether his vein was rich or only moderately so. In short he was anxious to guard himself as far as possible against being 'abandoned' by his *aviador*. In order to do this the miner endeavoured to obtain from his creditor as large an initial advance of supplies and equipment as he possibly could, on the grounds that he had struck a rich vein. Sometimes the ore which he produced in evidence of his rich strike even came from other mines.[22] After a time he would pay back a small portion of his sizeable debt out of the proceeds from his mine, but sufficient only to be able to persuade the *aviador* that his was indeed a rich vein, and to enable him, the miner, to obtain even further credit from the *aviador*. All future ores or *piñas*, however, would be secretly smuggled away from the mine and disposed of, unknown to the *aviador*, who was in the meanwhile inveigled into extending credit still more by the miner's tales of a temporary *borrasca* which would certainly soon be over, once a particular new series of excavations had been undertaken. Miners sometimes embarked upon whole new excavation projects which they knew would be fruitless with the sole object of involving an unwary *aviador* as deeply as possible, and ultimately of getting him into debt with his financial backer in Mexico City. If this happened, then even if the unfortunate *aviador* wanted to cut his losses and 'abandon' the miner, he was powerless to do so because his own debts in Mexico could only be covered by the payments that were due to him from the miner. The miner, however, once he had tricked the *aviador* into this situation would always be careful to continue to make payments only large enough to prevent the *aviador* from going bankrupt, so that in this way the wretched man was trapped into being a mere 'runner' to serve the miner with supplies and equipment. He was permanently involved in debts which he could never quite manage to pay in full, and in the meanwhile made not a penny profit for himself. He would become in fact the lackey of the miner, while at the same time attempting to serve his master in Mexico City.

The real danger of the situation lay in the fact that if a *borrasca* did really befall a mine and the vein became truly barren, the miner could no longer continue his payments to the *aviador*, no matter how politically small they may have been before. In this case ruin faced both miner and *aviador* alike. As a result, a loss, usually a substantial one, was sustained also by the merchant in Mexico City who had provided the initial capital outlay for the bedevilled project. Here then was the reason for the great caution so bitterly complained of by the miners; so, too, the unwillingness to finance all but the most secure of projects and to 'abandon', at the slightest sign of danger.

To trap the merchant classes in the way described was the goal of the majority of the miners, but although it was the most unscrupulous, it was not the only trick used by them to deceive the merchants into giving more credit than they were really prepared to advance for the projects. It was also common practice for the miner who was threatened by a *borrasca* or who had not yet 'struck it rich' to tempt the *aviador* into allowing him further credit by signing over to him in advance all the *piñas* his mine produced until his total debts for equipment and provisions had been paid off in full.[23] On occasion, no doubt, the contract must have proved profitable to the *aviador*, but since the practice was illegal there were many cases of flagrant breaches of contract, and as many, probably, of total failure to produce anything but worthless ore.

In such circumstances, with the grasping *aviador* intent only on making money at the miner's expense, fast enough and in sufficient quantity to be able to retire to the city, and the relentless miner, concerned only for his continued excavations and pit-head life of vice and riotous living, while at the same time endeavouring to condemn the *aviador* to a life of debts and toil – in such circumstances, therefore, it is hardly surprising that relations between the two groups were never very cordial, to say the least, in spite of their close and inevitable dependence upon one another.

Financial disasters brought about as a result of this kind of sharp practice between the miner and the *aviador* had far-reaching repercussions throughout all sections of society in colonial Mexico. It was common for religious communities and charities, widows, spinsters and other private citizens to invest their savings and small capitals with either individual merchants or more often with established business houses, with the idea that their money should be reinvested in the mine-supplying trade. It needed only one or two of these disasters to occur to each of the important capitalists for the majority of these people's savings to be halved or even completely lost, for it seems certain that the merchants and business houses must have allowed the greater part of the losses to fall upon their investors' capital rather than on their own. This state of affairs was particularly serious in the years round 1720.

Yet the device of deliberately delaying payments was not used exclusively by the miners against the *aviadores*, for if they were able, the *aviadores* took advantage of their own creditors in the same way. Because of the capital outlay involved in buying goods at Acapulco or in Mexico City from the *flotistas* the great majority of the cargoes were always bought up, as has been shown, by the wealthy merchants of Mexico City. The most important re-sale of merchandise which they made outside the capital was that to the *aviadores*, both those concerned in mining and those concerned in agriculture, and these formed the bulk of the so-called 'merchants of the interior'. Although the capitalists provided the *aviadores* with the initial means to carry on their trade, goods were provided to them either for an immediate cash settlement usually out of an original loan, or on direct credit. In either case the price fixed for payment would be equivalent to the full market value of the merchandise, and the *aviador* received no special reductions. The prices the *aviador* subsequently charged the miners were of no concern to the capitalist who had made his profit on the original sale of the goods to the *aviador*. These sales to the *aviadores* and other small merchants in the towns, quite apart from interest on any capital loans or other charges, made up a very important part of the business of a Mexican merchant or business house. Now, if an *aviador* could manage to amass a sufficient quantity of capital by delaying payment of his outstanding debts to his capitalist creditor, he would use the money to buy directly from the *flotistas* if he needed European goods and they were at a convenient price – always providing of course that the *flotistas* were still in the process of being 'blackmailed' by the capitalists of Mexico City. It was this state of affairs which had been the basis of the *consulado*'s continued complaints about the traditional method of trading in Mexico. Of course the situation had really been created by the capitalists themselves who forced the *flotistas* to remain in Mexico for long periods, and this gave the more enterprising of the *aviadores* the chance to do business with them. The least threat to their commercial monopoly caused anxiety to the merchants of the city, and certainly it must have been very annoying to know that one's debtors were working against one and using owed money to finance their speculations.

In the early eighteenth century it would certainly have been difficult for this practice to occur on a scale large enough to prejudice the affairs of the capitalists seriously. Their control over the whole of the commerce of the viceroyalty was virtually absolute. Yet for all that, harsh measures against the *aviadores* were ill-advised. The merchants were after all dependent upon the *aviadores* for the distribution of their stocks to the mining and agricultural communities outside the capital, and experience had shown that to discontinue associations with the *aviadores*, because of this kind of sharp practice, brought more trouble and losses than it was worth. To attempt to carry on the trade without the *aviadores*, who knew local conditions and were more or less always on the spot, led to the accumulation of unsaleable goods. Moreover, it would have been foolish and highly imprudent deliberately to strain relations with a man who owed considerable quantities of money. The city merchant was not slow to realise that by taking matters too far, he stood to lose not only an obviously capable agent – and new ones were not easy to find – but also fairly large sums of invested capital. In this way there arose a curious and anomalous situation in which the creditor was tolerant and sometimes afraid of his debtor – even when the debtor worked directly against the creditor's own interests, and moreover did so illegally by means of the very credit he had been granted and was so flagrantly misusing. For the merchants of Mexico City the most practical method of safeguarding this exclusive control over the markets which they considered their own was to remove the Spanish *flotista* from their midst altogether, for he was a nuisance both with his trade fair at Jalapa and as a whining competitor on the streets of Mexico City. It is here that one may find the origin of the alleged grounds of all the Mexicans' representations to the Crown from 1713 onwards for the suspension of fleets and, indeed, the origin of the increasing bad feeling between merchants on both sides of the Atlantic. This too, although it was never fully realised in Spain, was the basic matter behind the sea of correspondence, the claims and counter-claims, the legislation and its countermands, which made the New Spain trade such an issue for Patiño and his advisers over these years.

However, a breakdown in the existing commercial relations of the viceroyalty through lack of cooperation between capitalists and *aviadores* would have caused hardship not only to the miners and farmers of the country, but also to other citizens of Mexico City who depended indirectly upon the business of the country merchants. The same capitalists who financed the *aviadores* often also financed small factories in Mexico City itself where goods were produced which were necessary for the mines and the estates, articles such as metal bars, stone-hammers, gads, bellows, flue-tubes for use in smelting the ores, special cloth for quicksilver, spurs, brakes, coulters, cables, shoes and many other articles of daily use which were not brought from Europe in a manufactured state, nor were made outside the capital. A stoppage at any point in the established channels of trade could of course also result in the unsaleability of further products from these factories, and could naturally bring about their eventual closure. Hence the capitalist would be involved in an unnecessary loss of outlay and his employees, associates and investors would all be affected. It must not be thought from this that the trade to the mining centres was exclusively in technical equipment. Indeed sales of the fine Oriental fabrics and of expensive goods of all kinds formed a very lucrative part of the business.[24] The mining communities, although barbarous and uncivilised were nevertheless given to luxury and vice, and it was from the supplying of these goods on credit that a high proportion of the profits – or losses – were to be made.

It was essential then for all sections of society and for the royal treasury that this commercial mechanism of interdependence should continue to function, for it was the only method of putting the silver extracted from the mines into circulation and collecting all taxes other than the 'royal fifth'. Just as the miner was dependent upon the *aviador* and the capitalist, so too were these dependent upon each other – and both in turn depended for their own livelihood upon the trade to the estates and mines. Obviously any new factor which could upset this delicate balance of interests and alter the existing distribution mechanism was a major threat to the economy of the viceroyalty.

The over-stocking of the viceroyalty in an around the year 1720 with goods from three sources – contraband, the Acapulco trade and the *flota* – did in fact upset this delicate commercial balance. An abundance of merchandise on the market led to greater competition in sales, and this naturally forced prices down all round. This state of affairs accounted in part for the low prices offered by the Mexicans during the initial negotiations at Jalapa. In order to produce a turnover the merchants of the capital were obliged to increase the credit of the *aviadores* and even to take on additional creditors. The *aviadores* were themselves also forced into keener competition with each other. The only members of the community to benefit from these events were the miners, who now found it a simple matter to secure advances of credit and to obtain supplies and luxuries at greatly reduced prices. The miners were, of course, notoriously bad payers, and now that they had the advantage over the *aviadores* and the commercial bodies in general they became even more negligent in their payments and purposely increased the credit which their luckless *aviadores* had no option but to give them. They also began to work less and intentionally undertook barren excavations with the object of obtaining further advances of supplies and merchandise. The result was that large sums of capital were invested in fruitless enterprises, the miners lived well without work and the production of precious metals steadily decreased. Moreover the low prices at which goods were sold caused the returns in silver when they did come to fall correspondingly. Consequently the amount of money that found its way into general circulation grew progressively less since the trade to the mines was the only way that silver could be brought out on to the market. This lack of activity in the mines, together with the large exportations of metals from 1719 to 1721, culminating in the seven or eight million *pesos* taken back in the *flota* of

1721, produced such a scarcity in 1721 or 1722 that the inhabitants of New Spain were reduced over a period of months to bartering for the necessities of life. In the absence of sufficient coin, jewelry and *objets d'art* were used as money to buy food and everyday needs, and as a result sales of other merchandise were brought to a complete standstill.[25]

Such a situation could hardly have been anticipated by the Crown in 1718–20 in its new legislation for the *carrera de Indias*. The *Real proyecto* of 1720 had clearly not promoted the immediate improvement in the Cadiz–New Spain trade which the Crown and the merchants had expected. It is not surprising therefore that after the disaster at Jalapa the merchant bodies of Spain should petition the king that no more *flotas* should be sent to New Spain until 1726 at least. Such a measure, it was reasoned, would give time for existing stocks in Mexico to be used up and allow the recent laws concerning the trade of the Manila galleon to have their effect.[26] Ironically, then, just two years after the publication of the *Real proyecto*, the merchant bodies in Spain were joining their cousins in Mexico in requesting a run-down in the trade of the *flota* – albeit for entirely different reasons. However, the delaying of a *flota* for such a long period could not be contemplated by the Crown in the present circumstances, for three reasons. First, because the regular dispatching of the trade fleets to America formed the basis of the policy of re-establishment of the *carrera de Indias* as laid down by the *Real proyecto*; second, because the English were already objecting in serious terms about the Spanish Crown's falling behind in the yearly *cédulas* for the 'Annual Ship' (the last had been that for 1717);[27] third, because the principal object of reviving the trade, as far as the Crown was concerned, was to procure increased royal revenue from the taxes it produced. Indeed this last consideration was already becoming such an important part of Patiño's policies that it was shortly to override the true commercial interests of the Cadiz merchants.[28] Accordingly royal orders were drawn up for both *flota* and English 'Annual Ship' to be sent to New Spain in 1723.

If this decision disappointed the *consulados* of Andalusia it was even more disturbing for the merchants of Mexico City. The arrival of another *flota* so soon after the last was for them not a serious worry in itself. Although the arrival of more goods on an already glutted market would certainly cause a prolongation of the crisis in the trade to the interior of the country, the major losses would inevitably be shouldered in the long run by the *flotistas*. The real cause of their anxiety was the English 'Annual Ship', for as a by-product of certain negotiations between England and Spain the future of the Mexican capitalists had now truly become perilous in the extreme.

It has been explained how the *cédula* of 22 January 1717 concerning the payment of the *alcabala* on merchandise from the *Elizabeth* in 1715, had implied that the royal officials had been in the wrong to allow the English goods to be taken up to Mexico for sale; it has also been shown how that *cédula* was interpreted as a royal order that the 'Annual Ship' should sell its goods only at the port of arrival, and how this had been observed in 1717 with the cargo of the *Royal Prince*.[29] The desire on the part of Spanish officialdom to restrict the free movement of merchandise was very much resented in London, and the South Sea Company was not slow to lodge complaints about this matter with the Spanish court. The basis of the protest was the clause in the Assiento Contract which stated that 'the English, during the whole Time of the Assiento, shall be regarded and treated as if they were subjects of the Crown of Spain'.[30] The result was that on 27 September 1721, Philip V issued a further *cédula* directed to the royal officials at Veracruz, Portobello and Cartagena in which he clarified the matter by stating that it was not and never had been his intention that the sale of English goods should be restricted to the ports.[31] According to Spanish law Spanish subjects normally had the right to take goods that were not disposed of at the fairs to any part of the country they chose to sell them and the English had been granted the same privilege. The royal officials were henceforth ordered not to hinder or prevent the English from passing inland to sell the goods from the 'Annual Ship' in precisely the same way as the Spanish merchants were permitted to do. The principal English factor at Veracruz immediately moved out of the port and took up residence in Mexico City, incidentally contravening other conditions of the assiento, and English agents established themselves in other parts of the country and principally in the mining districts.[32]

The publication of a *flota* and 'Annual Ship' for 1723 in these circumstances was tantamount to an order for the ruination of *flotistas* and Mexican merchants alike. It was feared, and with good reason, that the English factors, exercising their right to sell goods where they chose would take the cargo of their ship directly to the mining communities and compete with the *aviadores* for the trade. The royal instruction of 6 June 1723, previously quoted, cancelling the trade fairs at Jalapa and declaring that there should be freedom of movement for all, confirmed the likelihood of this. The miners, thus given the opportunity of alternative transactions, could be relied upon to desert the *aviadores* and use their silver to buy goods from the English, instead of paying off outstanding debts to the *aviadores*. In this way the *aviadores* would not only be forced out of business but their creditors would also lose capital. Moreover, it would be the English who would benefit from the Mexicans' investments and the English who would carry off most of the silver from the mines. This could easily provoke another silver shortage of the kind which had already produced one financial crisis in the viceroyalty.[33]

In the knowledge that this situation would certainly develop as soon as the *Royal Prince*, the 'Annual Ship' for 1723, arrived in New Spain the *consulado* of Mexico drew up a paper expressing its deep concern. This it placed before the viceroy in October 1723.[34] It requested most fervently that the royal *cédula* of 27 September 1721 should be revoked; otherwise, it maintained, the existing economic structure of the viceroyalty would break down completely and both Spanish and Mexican merchants would be faced with considerable losses for several years to come. The matter was treated with great seriousness by the Marqués de Casafuerte who sent the document off to Spain on 13 November 1723 with a covering letter supporting the petition of the *consulado*. On 11 March 1724, in reply to this representation and a similar document presented by the Spanish merchant bodies in April 1723, the Crown issued a further *cédula* on the subject of the English trading rights inside the Indies.[35] It stated that irrespective of any orders that there were to the contrary, and especially the *cédula* of 27 September 1721, the English were no longer to have permission to take their goods inland to sell them. Henceforth they were to be limited to the ports of the Indies and would not be permitted to reside anywhere except in the ports where the Company had its factories. But in spite of the uncommonly swift actions of the Spanish authorities the English still had time to cause havoc on the internal markets of New Spain in 1723 and 1724.

Despite the earnest requests and the advice of the merchants of Spain and the worrying news of overstocked markets brought back by the quicksilver ships of 1722,[36] the *flota* left Cadiz for Veracruz under the command of General Antonio Serrano on 9 July 1723. The cargo of the fleet, 4309.98 tons, turned out to be somewhat larger than expected and was distributed among fifteen merchantmen which were convoyed by the traditional three men-of-war.[37] The main *flota* put in to Veracruz on 20 September, and two of the merchantmen which had strayed in a storm in the Caribbean arrived a month later. Once again it was found impossible to keep to the timetable laid down by the *Real proyecto*, and it was 21 May 1724 – not the stipulated 15 April – when the ships left for Europe.[38] In the early months of 1724 the Spaniards had much better commercial success in New Spain than any of them had dared to hope. The silver situation had unexpectedly improved and demand for goods was consequently picking up. Added to this, rumours were about that the Manila galleon had been postponed for that year, and this had the effect of raising slightly the selling price of the merchandise from Spain.[39] By the spring of 1724, much to the *flotistas'* surprise, approximately half the cargo of the fleet had been sold in return for the handsome sum of about ten million *pesos*.[40] Yet at about that time the Spaniards' luck ran out. The Manila galleon did in fact arrive at Acapulco bearing, as usual, large quantities of Oriental goods, and the relative abundance of silver proved to be short-lived thanks to this and the easy sale of the cargo of the English 'Annual Ship'. Prices in Mexico for the goods from the fleet fell sharply and its merchandise became unsaleable.[41] The old familiar pattern of 'commercial blackmail' began to repeat itself once more. Those *flotistas* who had not completed their business by May 1724 were in for a long stay in New Spain.[42] In fact two years were to elapse before they were able to find their way back to Cadiz in the next fleet returning home from Veracruz.

On 22 April 1723 the *Royal Prince* left Deptford on her second voyage to Veracruz as the South Sea Company's 'Annual Ship'.[43] After a lengthy stay at Jamaica, during which she took on more goods illegally, she reached New Spain on November 10, some weeks after the arrival of the *flota*.[44] The trade of the *Royal Prince* in 1723–4 proved to be more profitable than that carried on by either of the two previous English 'Annual Ships'. She was responsible for the introduction of well over 1000 tons of merchandise, and eye-witnesses affirmed that she unloaded about half the volume of the whole of the Spanish *flota*.[45] Since the English had a good six months in which to sell their goods inside the country before the publication of the Spanish Crown's *cédula* of 11 March 1724 restricting them to the ports, a large proportion of the cargo was sold directly in the mining communities, thus fully justifying the worst fears of the Spanish and Mexican merchants. This accounted for the great quantity of silver which the English were able to acquire in an extraordinarily short period of time. It also accounted in part for the rapid drop in the amount of silver in circulation on the commercial market. On her return to London in December 1724 the *Royal Prince* carried silver estimated to be worth six million *pesos*, and indeed in London her precious metals were valued at over £500,000.[46]

After the initial elation caused in Spain by reports of the good trading in New Spain during the winter and spring of 1723–4 the news brought home by the returning fleet in July 1724 of shortage of silver and unsaleable goods was a severe and unexpected blow to the Crown and the merchant bodies. In the knowledge of this intolerable situation, and after due discussion, the merchants of Andalusia once again resolved to request the king most earnestly to delay indefinitely the preparation of another *flota* for Veracruz until the glutted markets of New Spain were reasonably free. The news that more ships were to set out from Cadiz with goods for the viceroyalty would be sufficient in itself to knock prices further down in Mexico where the remainder of the cargo of the previous *flota* was currently selling at less than cost in Spain. The extent of the losses was also increased on account of the duties and expenses which had been incurred in shipping it to the Indies. It was thought that nothing but disaster could result from further dispatches of merchandise to New Spain.[47]

III

The petition which the merchants made to the Crown on 11 October 1724 embodied four main points: first, that the next *flota* should be postponed; second, that the volume of merchandise carried in that next fleet, whenever it sailed, should be limited to a specific number of tons; third, that sales should once again be effected by means of a formal trade fair held at some point on the road between Mexico City and Veracruz; fourth, that every effort should be made to cut down the excesses and interloping of the English. Patiño himself, as President of the *Casa de Contratación*, forwarded the document to the Council of the Indies with a covering note supporting all the requests made except, characteristically, the first. He considered it imprudent from every point of view to cancel the fleet for 1725.[48]

The Council of the Indies discussed the paper at length, and on 10 November it produced its reply to each of the merchants' points. Under no circumstances was it prepared to allow the postponement of the fleet. The object of the *Real proyecto* of 1720 had been to establish the *regular* dispatching of fleets to the Indies as this was considered to be in the best interests of all concerned. With the exception of 1722 this had so far been accomplished – 1720, Veracruz; 1721, Portobello; 1723, Veracruz; 1724, Portobello. It was therefore unthinkable, if the *Real proyecto* was to mean anything, that the *flota* should be indefinitely suspended. But apart from the Crown's own fiscal interest in the fleet (which is nowhere mentioned to the merchants) there was also another overriding interest, deriving directly from the panic caused in Spain by the cleverly negotiated Bubb's Treaty of 1716. The Council clearly indicated this in its reply to the merchants:

> . . . the attorney (*fiscal*) insists that His Majesty's decision should be upheld and the fleet be sent . . . thus avoiding the damage that would be done by the importation of foreign merchandise in the 'Annual Ship' which His Majesty has granted, for if it happened that that ship arrived alone and in the absence of a *flota* she would be the only supplier of goods to New Spain and would sell her goods at whatever price she chose, and the following year it would be more difficult to sell merchandise from Spain, for the merchants of New Spain would again be well stocked and the *flotistas* would be obliged to sell at low prices because of the continuing abundance of goods in the country.[49]

The Council was well aware too that the English would easily exceed their stipulated 650 tons and were quite capable of selling over half the volume of a reduced Spanish fleet. As no excuse could be found for refusing the South Sea Company its ship for the year in question it was a matter of supreme importance that the fleet should leave Cadiz too, irrespective of the state of the markets in the Indies. Thus it is seen that the terms of the treaty of 1716 had as important an effect upon the pattern of the *carrera de Indias* as did the *Real proyecto* of 1720. The Council agreed to the other three requests of the *consulado* – to limit the tonnage of the next fleet, to re-establish a trade fair, and to repress the English. The matter of the site of the fair was the subject of some trivial debate. Eventually Orizaba and not Jalapa was chosen, as conditions there were deemed to be more satisfactory.[50]

On 23 November 1724 the *consulado* of Cadiz again wrote to the Crown suggesting 3500 tons as the total maximum volume of the fleet and, rather surprisingly, asking that in view of the Crown's unwillingness to postpone the fleet the order establishing a trade fair should be revoked.[51] This paradoxical request was actually sound commercial sense. If the *flotistas* were to be obliged by the Crown to try to sell on the very unfavourable Mexican market of 1725, nothing but disadvantage could come from their being fenced in for six months at a trade fair. This would certainly result in large quantities of unsold merchandise and an unnecessary waste of good time which could profitably be used in trading elsewhere. It was therefore preferable to have the freedom to roam the viceroyalty, perhaps by-passing the Mexican capitalists altogether, and even competing with them by offering the goods from the fleet to the country merchants and *aviadores* directly. After all, this was what the English had so successfully done only six months before in the spring and summer of 1724. After further lengthy consideration of the matter the Council of the Indies agreed to this plan and a royal order of 14 April 1725 gave the Cadiz merchants the concession they desired.[52] Thus the struggle between the Mexican capitalist and *flotista* entered a new phase in which there was apparently some hope that the former's stranglehold on the commerce of New Spain could be broken. Indeed, if the merchants of Mexico City did not moderate their attitude it even seemed possible that they could largely be cut out of the trade altogether!

But long before the Crown had reversed its original decision to hold a fair at Orizaba a royal order had been sent to the viceroy of New Spain requiring preparations to be made for the reception of the fleet and the celebration of the fair. This was published in Mexico on 13 April 1725.[53] News of the arrival of yet another *flota* was not greeted with enthusiasm by the merchants of the capital and they decided to hold a meeting to discuss what should be done. The result was a petition to the Crown dated 15 May 1725, in which the *consulado* of Mexico protested its members' innocence in the matter of the 'commercial blackmail' of the *flotista*, alleging that if, as in times gone-by, the Spaniards would again leave their unsold goods in the hands of agents in Mexico and return home in the *flota* in which they had come, the hostility between the two merchant bodies would disappear. It was, they maintained, only the Spaniards' new-found greed that caused them to tarry in New Spain in the hope of cutting in unfairly on the rightful markets of the Mexicans. The *consulado* therefore made three recommendations to the Crown in respect of the *flota* for 1725: first, to forbid the *flotistas* absolutely from selling their wares at any place or to any person whatsoever outside the official fair at Orizaba; second, to oblige the *flotistas* to go straight back home to Spain at the end of the fair in the same fleet as that in which they had come; and third, to force them to leave any unsold merchandise in the charge of appointed agents in New Spain. The *consulado* of Mexico agreed with the *consulado* of Cadiz that it was a very good idea to limit the size of future fleets, and, as far as they were concerned, the smaller they were the better.[54] In view of the development of this conflict over the previous decade it seems clear from the self-confident tone of this document that the Mexican merchants imagined that they were now within a stone's throw of breaking down the institution of the *flota* and achieving the independence they sought in order to become the sole arbiters of the commercial life of New Spain. Their requests, as it happened, were of no avail, for the paper did not reach the Council of the Indies until October 1725, almost a month after the fleet in question had docked in Veracruz.

The *flota* of 1725, once again commanded by General Antonio Serrano, left Cadiz on 15 July. It consisted of two warships and twelve merchantmen carrying between them a cargo of 3744.50 tons, some 200 tons more than the volume recommended by the *consulado* of Cadiz, but a good deal less than that of the previous two fleets.[55] A disastrous fire on board the flagship, the *San Bartolomé*, during the crossing destroyed all the official papers of the fleet, including the royal order of 14 April 1725, cancelling the fair at Orizaba and allowing the *flotistas* to sell their cargoes where and as they chose. As the viceroy of New Spain had no previous knowledge that the fair was to be cancelled, a dispute of a fairly serious nature broke out between, on the one hand, the viceroy and the Mexican merchants and, on the other, the officers of the fleet and the *flotistas*. After a full inquiry the viceroy ruled in favour of the *flotistas* – much to the dismay of the Mexican merchants who expected to be able to keep the Spaniards cooped up at the fair and away from the real market.[56] Relations between the two groups of merchants therefore reached a very low point indeed in the winter of 1725–6 as the *flotistas* prepared to disperse themselves throughout the viceroyalty in search of buyers for their wares. However, the country was still well stocked with goods. The unfortunate *flotistas*, despite high hopes of their direct competition with the Mexicans on the open markets of the provinces, had a difficult time and their merchandise proved every bit as difficult to sell as the *consulado* had predicted in 1724.[57]

For all that, the situation they faced could have been a good deal worse. The South Sea Company's 'Annual Ship', *Prince Frederick*, reached Veracruz on 25 October 1725.[58] The *Prince Frederick* was accompanied by two 'supply ships', the *Spotswood* and the *Prince of Asturias*, both of which succeeded in off-loading their cargoes on to the 'Annual Ship' to be included in the permitted merchandise for sale in New Spain. It seems clear that, not for the first time, bribery had a place in such operations.[59] However in response to the paper from the merchants of Cadiz who had been in despair about English commercial penetration inside the viceroyalty in 1723, the Crown had issued the royal order of 11 March 1724, forbidding the English to sell their cargo on the same basis as the *flotistas* and confining them to the port of Veracruz.[60] Thus the *flotistas* obtained a distinct advantage over the English traders from the *Prince Frederick*, for while the Spaniards, in an agressive mood, aimed to elbow the Mexicans out of their own market, the English, restricted to the port, had to wait for business to come to them. The position was eventually even further improved for the *flotistas* by the various tensions that were building up between England and Spain on the diplomatic level. As a result of these international disturbances open hostilities soon broke out on the high seas between the ships of the two nations. Within a few months the *Prince Frederick* and most of her cargo were impounded by the Spanish authorities at Veracruz as a reprisal, and the sale of her merchandise ceased altogether. The restitution of the *Prince Frederick* loomed fairly large as an issue at the Congress of Soissons of 1728 and was the subject of an article of the Treaty of Seville of 1729; for even after the peace had been re-established in Europe Spain wished to retain the 'Annual Ship' and her cargo as token payment for the damage the British had done to her precarious American commerce over the previous years. The fact that the *Prince Frederick* was claimed as symbolic retribution by Spain's diplomats provides further evidence of that special kind of resentment reserved for the 'Annual Ship' by the Spanish authorities, for in the eyes of many it was she, perhaps more than the smugglers, that was undermining the American trade and, directly or indirectly, was responsible for many of its current evils.

The story of the New Spain *flota* from 1720–6 is thus seen to be essentially one of frustration and hopes dashed. Despite legislation, reforms and experiment, it is no more than the story of the inability of the Spanish merchant to hold his former position on the markets of New Spain. The continued influx of goods from the East, the success of British commercial activities in the viceroyalty, the increase of contraband from various sources all contributed to the failure of Spanish policy. Yet basically the problems were created by the merchants of Mexico who, in their growing independence, refused to allow manipulation from Spain of markets they considered their own. The Spanish Crown now found itself obliged to think again, and to think hard. This it did in 1727, when under Patiño's presidency a series of meetings was called which involved commercial experts and advisers from both sides of the Atlantic. Their purpose was to discuss solutions to the many problems of the whole of the Indies trade in general, for if in New Spain things had gone from bad to worse over these years, the situation certainly gave as much cause for concern when it came to a review of the present state of the trade with Peru.

7 The *Galeones* to Tierra Firme, 1720–1726

I

At the time of the publication of the *Real proyecto* in 1720 twelve years had gone by since the celebration of the last fair at Portobello – and twelve more years had separated that last fair of 1708 from the previous one held in 1696. Thus in nearly 25 years – a whole generation – the merchants of Lima had only traded once with *galeones* at Portobello. Throughout the entire period, naturally, the commercial affairs of the viceroyalty of Peru had been conducted internally with little direct reference to Cadiz or even to Madrid. Meanwhile the country was kept well supplied with goods from three sources: first, the contraband activities of foreign interlopers, principally the French in the Pacific, but later too the English via the agents of the South Sea Company at Buenos Aires and on the Tierra Firme coasts; second, the illegal trade between New Spain and Peru consisting mainly of merchandise from the Manila galleon; and third, the occasional register ships from Spain which reached Tierra Firme or Buenos Aires.[1] Economic necessity had sometimes forced the colonial authorities into semi-acceptance of illegal merchandise on Peruvian markets. Often enough they had confiscated contraband goods, either directly from the foreign smuggler or from the purchasing merchant, and sold them publicly for the profit of the royal treasury. Sometimes too French interlopers had even been permitted to land their cargoes and sell them openly providing the appropriate duties were paid to the Crown. Viceroy Ladrón de Guevara, for instance, proudly informed the Council of the Indies that between May 1711 and September 1713 he had collected 138,318 *pesos* in *alcabalas* and 15,209 *pesos* and 7 *reales* in *almojarifazgos* on French goods.[2] The semi-official entry of French merchandise continued and even increased after 1713 – in addition to huge quantities of contraband. We know, for example, that as late as 1720, in direct contravention of viceregal decrees, the authorities at the port of Ilo were permitting the sale of a large and profitable French cargo.[3] In view of the unorthodox economic situation of Peru it is not surprising therefore that the merchant classes of Lima should have felt that by 1720 they had very largely achieved the commercial independence from Spain to which their counterparts in Mexico City were still aspiring.

The basic commercial structure of Peru differed little from that of New Spain. As in Mexico, the *consulado de comercio* formed the official link between the Crown and the merchants of the country who likewise consisted of large capitalists in Lima and smaller traders spread throughout the country. The *consulado* of Lima played a similar double game with the Crown as that of Mexico. On the one hand it cherished royal interests when these coincided with its own, lending and giving money to the Crown and contracting to farm taxes on its behalf, while on the other hand, as we have seen earlier, protecting the commerce of its individual members to the point of explaining away participation in smuggling and other illegal practices under a cloak of protested loyalty and obedience to the Crown. But whereas in New Spain the traders in the fleets from Spain usually took themselves and their goods off to the viceregal capital, and, if necessary, out into the countryside, in Peru this had never been possible. The holding of a fair at Portobello had always meant that the whole commercial operation of the *galeonistas* had been carried out at a point which was nearly 2000 miles away from the centre of the viceroyalty. For reasons of time, distance and economy, it was obviously highly impractical for them to employ the alternative method of travelling down to Lima except for the sale of the left-overs from a fair. The holding of a fair at Portobello had also always meant that the small Peruvian merchants could not really afford to participate, although often they clubbed together or borrowed money in order to be able to attend.[4] The natural outcome of this was that the large Lima merchants could never feel that their monopoly of the internal home markets was in any sense threatened by direct competition from Spaniards, as did the merchants of Mexico City. Nevertheless the arrival of *galeones* from Spain could still be a nuisance to them, as it had been in 1708. In a country well stocked by interlopers there was no market for expensive legal goods. In New Spain, in these conditions, the large merchants had refused to be cornered in a fair at Jalapa: in Peru, as we have seen from the events of 1708, the merchants had been most unwilling to go to Portobello.

In Peru the struggle between large and small merchants centred around the question of who was to corner the *illegal* merchandise which came into the country. During the great period of French interloping in the Pacific the capitalists had nearly always won the day. The French captain, anxious to sell his cargo and be away, preferred the large merchants who would buy in bulk to the smaller buyers who haggled for a few items at a time and thereby protracted his stay in port. In such operations the scale and speed of the sale always worked against the small trader. But from about 1717 onwards the gradual decline of French trade and the concomitant increase in English contraband through Buenos Aires tended to upset the *status quo*. With the excuse of the assiento English agents were now constantly bringing small consignments of merchandise into Upper and Lower Peru and selling their wares directly to the locals. In this way troublesome inroads were made into the monopoly of the Lima capitalists. The Lima merchants greatly resented this encroachment of traders from Buenos Aires on part of their territory, and over the years to come they lodged earnest petitions to the Crown, sometimes backed by viceregal support, demanding the total closure of Buenos Aires to all shipping. However, the Crown refused to accede, and the trade through Buenos Aires continued to be a cause of bitterness and complaint amongst the Lima merchant classes for three decades.[5]

The question of the tax contracts, and especially that of the *asiento de avería* for the *Armada del Sur* was an important aspect of the commercial history of Peru at this stage.[6] It will be remembered that one of the concessions which the Marqués de Castelldosríus had been forced to allow the merchants, back in 1707, was a very indulgent *asiento de avería*. This had been necessary to enable him to win the *consulado's* cooperation and persuade the merchants to travel to the fair at Portobello in unfavourable commercial circumstances. Because of its unsuitability the Crown had cancelled that *asiento* in 1713, and in 1720 no subsequent contract had had Crown approval. In 1717, when the *consulado* of Lima was informed of the Crown's intention of preparing a fleet of galleons for the following year, the merchant body recorded its jubilation at the prospect (it could not do otherwise!), but hastened to point out to the Crown the enormous obstacles which it considered stood in the way of the commercial success of such a venture. There were, it said, considerable stocks of contraband goods in the country, and the illegal purchase of these had produced a shortage of specie. Moreover, the few ships available to make up an *Armada del Sur* were in a state of disrepair; and, last but not least, there were no contracts currently in force for the *avería* and time would be needed to draw up new ones. The *consulado* therefore advised that the *galeones* should be delayed until 1720. Negotiations for new _asientos_ were begun in 1717–18, but fortunately for the merchants the outbreak of war in 1718 forced the Crown to cancel its plans altogether and so for a short time the Peruvians were able to relax again. But in 1720, following the publication of the _Real proyecto_, the Crown advised the viceroy of Peru of its determination to re-establish the regular dispatching of _galeones_ to Cartagena and Portobello and announced the departure of a fleet for the following year of 1721. This information reached the _consulado_ of Lima via the viceroy on 19 July 1721. The news was given a lukewarm reception and the problems indicated in 1717 were again referred to by the merchants. However, by that date the _galeones_ were already on their way to Cartagena and so both viceroy and _consulado_ had no alternative but to compromise with each other and work towards the drawing up of the necessary _asientos_ and the preparation of the _Armada del Sur_.

The bargaining which took place over this matter involved the consideration of a host of complex factors, fiscal, economic and political, but the essence of the new agreement may be outlined as follows. The Lima merchants would go to Portobello and participate in a fair providing _a_) that the viceroy would not insist upon immediate payment of the _consulado_'s accumulated _alcabala_ debt of 719, 084 _pesos_, _b_) that the authorities at Panama would not have the right to open the Peruvians' boxes of money on their way through to Portobello or their merchandise on the return (this was to avoid the proper assessment of tax or the collection of debts), _c_) that severe measures would be enforced to exclude absolutely all interlopers from the viceroyalty so that the goods from the galleons would be saleable on arrival in Peru, and _d_) that the rates of taxes should be fixed at an acceptably low level. The _consulado_ for its part undertook to refit the _Armada del Sur_, accepting a viceregal grant of 100,000 _pesos_ in part payment of costs, and to do its best to encourage a good attendance at the fair and a maximum sum of precious metals for trading with the _galeones_.

These first _galeones_ to be dispatched from Cadiz after the publication of the _Real proyecto_ were originally required to set sail in October 1720.[7] The true ineffectiveness of the _proyecto_ had immediately been displayed, for owing to certain difficulties it was found impossible for the fleet to be ready until June of the following year, 1721. One of the recent commercial reforms in Andalusia had involved the setting up of new customs posts in the Jerez district. Most of the goods for exportation to the Indies were obliged to pass along the roads on which these posts were situated, and although it had not been intended that duties should be collected on such merchandise, the new officials insisted that merchants with goods for the *galeones* were obliged to pay on their wares just like any other merchants and travellers. This had not occurred in the case of goods for the *flota* under Chacón, as the new posts had seemingly not begun to function until the later part of 1720. When it was explained to the merchants that they were required to pay duties at Jaretas, Jerez or Lebrija, irrespective of the dues at Cadiz, the majority of them turned round and took their goods back home again. The loading of the *galeones* was thus brought to a halt. It was not until December 1720, that the matter was cleared up by means of a royal order to the effect that the Jerez customs were not to interfere with merchandise being transported for inclusion in the fleets, which was to pass freely to Cadiz.[8] Once this difficulty had been overcome the slow business of loading the *galeones* could begin again. In June 1721, eight months behind schedule, the fleet of 13 ships was at last ready to sail, with a cargo of 2047.03 tons, under its commander General Baltasar de Guevara.[9]

In order to make sure that the *Armada del Sur* would be prepared quickly so that the *galeones* would not lose time waiting in the Indies for the arrival of the merchants from Peru, Guevara sent a dispatch ship ahead of him from the Canaries to warn the viceroy that the *galeones* were on their way.[10] However the general's diligence was of little avail. The *galeones* themselves reached Cartagena on 5 August 1721, but it was November before meaningful discussions were begun in Lima to draw up the necessary *asientos*.[11] In addition to the bargaining over the terms of the *asiento* which went on between viceroy and *consulado*, there was also the technical problem of the contracts themselves. It had been so long since the *Armada del Sur* was dispatched under suitable contracts that no one could be found who was competent to advise on the form they ought to take. For some time officials scurried around looking up seventeenth-century *asientos* in order to provide some sort of acceptable model on which to base the current ones.[12] Finally, on 24 January 1722, the new *asientos* were approved by the contracting parties and the preparations for the dispatching of the *Armada* could begin.[13] The *galeones* had now spent some five months tied up at Cartagena. But when it came to an examination of the ships that were to make up the *Armada* it was discovered that they were in a far worse state than had been anticipated. Extensive and expensive repairs were needed to make them seaworthy. As a result of further negotiations between the *consulado* and the viceroy the merchants agreed to careen, repair and equip the two Crown ships of the *Armada*. This was in March 1722.[14]

Yet despite the agreements reached and the enforcement of strict prohibitions against foreign interlopers, the Peruvian merchants were extremely apprehensive of leaving Lima and going off to trade with the *galeonistas* at the Portobello fair. The lessons learned in 1708 from the treacherous behaviour of the Marqués de Castelldosríus and the involvement in contraband of his successor Ladrón de Guevara were clearly in the minds of the merchants.[15] Moreover, the danger of continuing contraband in the viceroyalty while the Peruvians were at Portobello was brought into sharp focus at precisely that time, while the *Armada del Sur* itself was being made ready. A group of six French ships, under the command of a Monsieur St Jean, were cruising up and down the coasts of Peru endeavouring to sell a large cargo of illicit merchandise. It was St Jean's contention that after the peace of 1720 France and Spain were once again allies, and there was no reason why French ships should not trade in the Pacific as they had done before Utrecht.[16] However, the strict prohibitions of the viceroy against interlopers were proving effective and St Jean was becoming more and more angry as the weeks went by.[17] He eventually sent word that he would attack the *Armada del Sur* when it left Callao if he were not allowed to sell his cargoes in Peru. It was only with great difficulty, therefore, and after repeated guarantees of good faith, that Viceroy Morcillo succeeded in persuading the *consulado* to participate in the dispatching of the fleet.[18] Fortunately for the merchants St Jean's threats proved to be as vain as their own fears about the viceroy were groundless. Archbishop Morcillo was not the Marqués de Castelldosríus. A contemporary account testifies to the honourable behaviour of the viceroy in this matter:

> The Sieur du Chaine is arrived at Brest from the South Sea with another ship belonging to the Squadron of M. St Jonan. . . These six ships have brought back to the value of seven or eight millions of *livres* in goods, which could not be disposed of by reason of the strict order of the Viceroy of Peru, given to prevent their trading in those parts. However they have found means to put off goods to the value of two millions and a hundred thousand pieces of eight, but the getting them on shoar has cost them no less than four hundred thousand by way of gratuity. . .[19]

Despite all the difficulties of its preparation and dispatch, the *Armada del Sur*, commanded by that great Spanish sailor of the eighteenth century, Don Blas de Lezo, reached Panama safely towards the end of April 1722.[20] In the event it was not as rich as had been hoped, and it

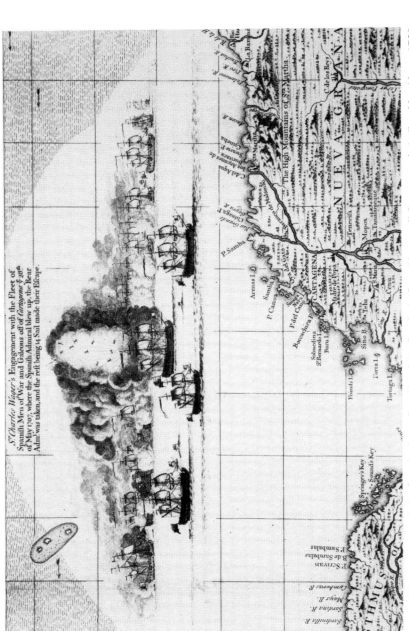

Sr Charles Wager's Engagement with the Fleet of Spanish Men of War and Galeons off of Cartagena ye 28th of May 1708, where the Spanish Admiral blew up, the Rear Adml was taken, and the rest being 14 Sail made their Escape.

NUEVA GRANADA

The High Mountains of Sta Martha

CARTAGENA

ISTHMUS

Plate 1.   The explosion of the San José, the flagship of the Conde de Casa Alegre, off Cartagena de Indias, May/June, 1708.

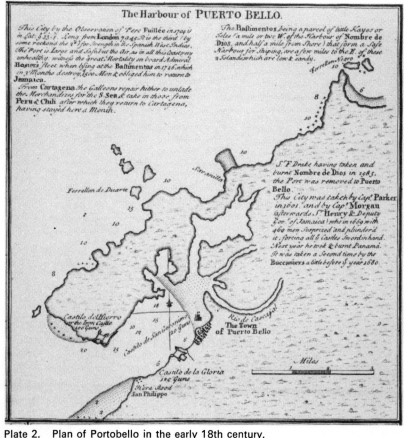

Plate 2.   Plan of Portobello in the early 18th century.

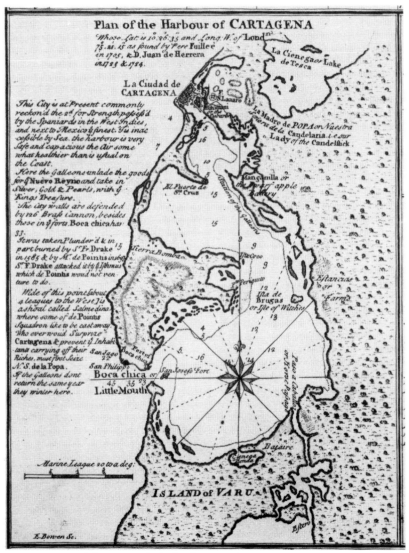

Plate 3. Plan of Cartagena de Indias in the early 18th century.

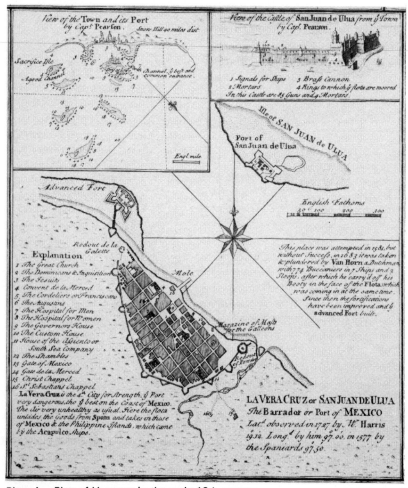

Plate 4. Plan of Veracruz in the early 18th century.

Plate 5.   Don José Patiño.

Plate 6.   Don Manuel López Pintado.

Plate 7. A view of Mexico City in the early 18th century.

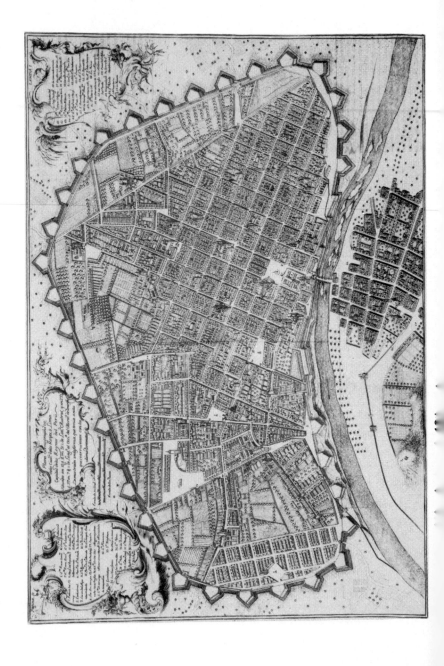

carried fewer merchants than had been expected.[21] Moreover, the year or so preceding the departure of the *Armada* had been a bad one in the mines of Peru. A serious water shortage had greatly affected the mining processes. Consequently whatever the state of the markets and the attitude of the merchants had been, it seems unlikely that the *Armada* of 1722 would have been a very rich one.[22] But further problems were immediately encountered on arrival at Panama. Relations between Peruvian merchants and the Crown authorities on the Isthmus had traditionally been hostile, for the royal officials there had always been keen to collect the rightful taxes on the passage of money and merchandise, a levy which the Peruvians considered unjust.[23] In 1722 unfamiliarity with the procedure to be followed for receiving the *Armada del Sur* at Panama and the celebration of a fair at Portobello meant that serious confusion and misunderstandings once again dominated the relations between the two groups.[24] The seventeenth-century regulations which still governed certain aspects of this procedure were incompatible with some of the recent orders of Viceroy Morcillo and with parts of the new *asiento de avería*. There were also several misinterpretations and deliberate illegal practices on the part of both the merchants and the officials. All this held up considerably the passage of men and money across the Isthmus. Another hazard proved to be the navigation of the River Chagre. The upper reaches of this river were used for carrying merchants and their property on part of the journey from Panama and Portobello as an obligatory alternative to the smuggler-infested coast road. During the many years that had elapsed since the previous fair the River Chagre had become obstructed and the obsolete contracts which provided for its clearance had not been honoured. Consequently several of the small boats overturned, there was some loss of life and considerable loss of goods and money, and, of course, further delays.[25]

Yet those contingencies were nothing compared with the disorder and confusion which was to reign throughout the fair. News of the arrival of the Peruvians on the Isthmus was welcomed not only by the *galeonistas* but also by the large numbers of foreign interlopers who had anchored in readiness in the many bays and inlets near Portobello. The activities of these foreign smuggling vessels, including the English 'Annual Ship', the *Royal George*, were almost entirely to blame for the eventual failure of the fair, and the lamentable fact was that by far the greater part of the Peruvians' money, intended for the trade with the *galeones*, was used in buying contraband goods from the foreigners. The somewhat experimental terms of the *asiento de avería*, which had worked out greatly to the advantage of the Lima merchants, permitted their goods and money to go unregistered as far as Panama.[26] There the merchants were required to state how much money they had brought with them, but since the royal officials at Panama were forbidden by viceregal orders to interfere with the packages and cases, it was impossible to prove the truth of the merchants' declarations.[27] This gave them ample opportunity to divert their money from its route to Portobello so that it could be taken to the Atlantic coast of the Isthmus to be employed in illicit trade with the foreigners. In spite of official attempts to stop this fraud, including the execution of one offender on the spot,[28] about half the money intended for Portobello never reached its destination.[29] Because of these illegal diversions of precious metals from an already relatively poor *Armada del Sur*, the quantity of specie transported to the fair was insufficient to buy all the merchandise brought in the *galeones*, and it was impossible to begin real trading in Portobello until 30 June when three other ships reached Panama from Callao with money which had not been ready at the time the main fleet had left.[30]

The trading at Portobello, which had been due to begin on 1 June 1722 was accompanied by one long and continuous argument between Lima merchants and *galeonistas*. The illegal trading all round Portobello and the consequent lack of money at the fair itself caused the Peruvians to offer extremely low prices for the cargoes of the *galeones*. The presence of the Spaniards was openly resented and the Lima merchants were not prepared to allow the official trading to interfere with the illicit. A most illuminating impression of the Peruvians' sense of economic independence is gained from General Baltasar de Guevara's account of the remarks made by the Lima *consulado* at a fiery meeting of Peruvian merchants and *galeonistas*. Facing the accusation that the Lima merchants were openly trading with the foreigners and ruining the fair,

Don Martín de Bazarrate [one of the Lima delegates] had the effrontery to say, in the presence of the Governor and Captain-General of the Province of Panama, Commodore (*Jefe de Escuadra*) Don Francisco Cornejo, the Commissioner for War, Don Antonio López Márquez and the Royal Officials of Panama . . . that the Peruvians had come up to meet these *galeones* more in order to obey His Majesty's Royal Orders than for any possible commercial advantage. . . He went on to say, out loud and in the presence of all (as they have personally confirmed to me) that the merchants of Lima had paid 300,000 *pesos* in taxes and this gave them the right to

commit *whatever outrages they chose* for the whole of one year, and if they
were not to be permitted to exercise this right, why then their money
should be returned to them and then they would be prepared to be
guided by the authority of the Royal Officials. No one was
disinclined to believe him because the despotic and authoritarian
manner in which Don Juan López Molero [head of the Peruvian
delegation] behaved when they came up [to Panama]...had
pre-empted any action by the Governor and Royal Officials and
excluded them from taking any part in these matters.[31]

Tempers rose still further, but there was no way of making the
Peruvians understand that the contribution of duties did not entitle
them to trade with the foreigners.[32] During the interval of 14 years in
which no *galeones* had come to Portobello a remarkable change had
clearly taken place in the Peruvians' conception of the purpose of the
asiento de avería and the fair at Portobello. The Spaniards remained
incredulous and felt somehow hurt by the Americans' attitude.
Guevara wrote:

> ...I am preparing my return voyage to Spain...and I can assure
> Your Excellency that I am moved to desire it not so much out of love
> for my country and the prospect of the nearness of relatives and
> friends as by my wish to be gone from these lands where the
> behaviour of the people generally is so iniquitous.[33]

One trade at the fair of 1722 which was certainly brisker than most
was that of the English 'Annual Ship'. The *Royal George* brought almost
1000 tons of merchandise to the fair and all of it was disposed of
quickly.[34] The English had had no difficulty in unloading their excess
cargo and putting it on sale. Presents of a diamond ring, mirrors, gold
watches and other gifts given in Cartagena had produced a statement
from General Guevara that the cargo was all in order at that port
and a repeat performance of the comedy occurred at Portobello.[35]
Nevertheless the shortage of money seems also to have affected the sales
from the *Royal George*, for a good deal of the merchandise was given on
partial credit. The English offered terms which amounted to a 25 per
cent down payment on all goods and the remainder on credit to be paid
to the representatives of the South Sea Company in the Indies.[36] This,
together with their very much cheaper prices of course, gave the
English an enormous advantage over the *galeonistas* who could offer
neither the credit which the Peruvians demanded nor competitive

prices.[37] But the trade of the *Royal George* was small compared with that of the smugglers outside Portobello: while the fair was actually in progress there were no fewer than 21 foreign merchantmen doing business in the nearby bays of Puerto Leonés and Bastimentos.[38] However, the 'Annual Ship' was certainly responsible for the removal of a considerable amount of silver that might otherwise have been used in trade with the *galeonistas*. In April 1723 the English press jubilantly informed its readers that 'last week a great quantity of silver brought from the South Sea Company's ship the *Royal George* was sent to the tower to be converted into specie'[39].

Although the fair at Portobello was due to end on 31 July 1722, the confusion, the endless arguing, and the unsaleability of the Spanish goods meant that General Guevara was obliged to extend the closing date until the end of August. Even so little further advantage was gained. Only a small part of the Spaniards' merchandise had been disposed of at the fair, although even at its close the Peruvians had still not spent all the money they had brought to Portobello.[40] Those *galeonistas* who had succeeded in selling their wares had done so at very low prices. Those who had not now found themselves forced to try and sell elsewhere, as the law allowed for the usually small portions of merchandise left over after the fairs. Some went back to Lima with the *Armada del Sur*, while others were given permission to remain longer in Portobello to attempt to sell after the official trading was over. Eventually however these latter had no alternative but to join the rest of the fleet at Cartagena with their goods still unsold. The blatant contraband trading continued. For some time after the fair had closed activity on the Isthmus was intense, and the roads and tracks were busy with the movement of loads of illegal merchandise and chests of illegal gold and silver.[41] Financial arrangements were also made between the South Sea Company's factors and those at the fair by which money which would have gone back to Spain in the *galeones* was put aboard the *Royal George*. The English issued letters of credit, and for a fee of eight per cent, guaranteed payment of the money in Spain. The advantage of this arrangement to the Spaniards was considerable. Precious metals which had been smuggled from the mines untaxed, and were therefore unstamped with the royal seals, could be used in the transactions since they would not be seen by the officials at Cadiz. Although the fee of eight per cent collected by the English was higher than the duties at Cadiz on imported gold and silver it also included the cost of a special all-risks insurance premium. Under this, money sent via the 'Annual Ship' involved no risk whatsoever for its owners, whereas that sent in the *galeones* or *flota* was lost completely in any disaster at sea, for even if the 'Annual Ship' went down, the money would still be paid in Spain by the South Sea Company's agents.[42]

In earlier times it would have been difficult for the Peruvians to transport large quantities of smuggled merchandise back to Lima in the *Armada del Sur*. The royal officials at Chagre and Panama would have been empowered to inspect the goods as they passed through their jurisdiction. However the Lima merchants insisted upon their right to move their goods back and forth across the Isthmus without having to submit to an inspection by the royal officials. They had originally gained this right by a royal *cédula* of 25 November 1717,[43] although the terms of this were intended to apply only to the movement of goods from register ships at Portobello in the years when no *galeones* could be sent. However, as we know, the Peruvians had obtained an extension of this privilege to include the *galeones* of 1722, as part of their guarantees from Viceroy Morcillo, and it was this which had caused so much of the bad feeling of the authorities at Panama. Although official attempts were in fact made to open packages and denounce smugglers, it was difficult to prove anything and the thousands of tons of illegal merchandise therefore reached the ships at Panama without a great deal of trouble.[44] But the royal officials were determined to do their best to rectify the abuses committed at the fair. The royal *cédula* of 27 September 1721,[45] which gave the English permission to sell goods from the 'Annual Ships' inland, had been flatly rejected by the viceroy of Peru. Before the fair began he had therefore commanded that in spite of the royal *cédula* the English were *not* to be allowed inland to sell their goods. Such non-compliance with Crown instructions was unavoidable if he was to honour his agreement with the merchants to keep the markets of the viceroyalty free for the sale of goods from the *galeones*.[46] The royal officials at Panama seized upon this opportunity to hold up the departure of the *Armada del Sur* by alleging that the viceroy's order forbade the entry of all goods from the 'Annual Ship' whether already bought by the Peruvians or still unsold. As most of the smuggled merchandise was certainly English this was no doubt an attempt to prevent its passing on to Lima. The argument which followed lasted for four months, but in the end the royal officials were forced to yield and allow the fleet to return to Peru.[47]

Those four months of discussion at Panama may not have stopped the contraband entering the viceroyalty, but they did immense harm to the subsequent trade of the Lima merchants once they reached their homes. In the meantime, despite Viceroy Morcillo's precautions, the country had been well supplied with goods from two other sources. A fair had as usual been held at Cartagena during the winter before the *galeones* passed to Portobello and the merchants of New Granada and the Northern Provinces of Peru had attended, as was their right and custom.[48] Smuggling had been carried on very widely at that fair also, and not least by the *Royal George*.[49] After the *galeones* had gone to Portobello the merchants of the Northern Provinces lost no time in taking their sizeable stocks of goods to the South of the country and cutting in on the future markets of the Lima merchants.[50] Moreover the lengthy delays at every stage in the trading at Portobello had favoured their enterprise. But there was a further set-back for the Lima merchants on their arrival home. At the same time as the fair was being held at Portobello a very successful fair was also being held at Buenos Aires with two ostensibly very well provisioned register ships from Spain.[51] In fact the arrival of these two ships proved most timely for the agents of the South Sea Company, for with the connivance of the local population they were able to release on to the market a considerable volume of illegal merchandise under the pretext that it was part of the cargo of the two register ships.[52] The merchants of La Plata, therefore, like those of New Granada, took advantage of the absence of the Lima capitalists and the seller's market being created by the viceroy of Peru. It became an exceedingly profitable venture for them to transport as much of this merchandise as possible over the Andes into Peru where prices were good and sales were now easy. Thus the Argentines found the opportunity of capturing an important part of the trade of the Southern Provinces of the viceroyalty just as the New Granadans were cornering that of the North. The commercial prospects of the Lima merchants returning from Portobello were therefore only marginally better than they had been in 1708, and this slight difference was only by virtue of the fact that most of what they brought back with them was also contraband! Indeed the country was by now as well stocked with European goods as it had been for some time, and although these had not come from French smugglers in the Pacific – which was what the Peruvians had feared – the effect was the same as if M. St Jean had been given free access to the interior markets of the country.[53] But naturally those who faced the greatest problems arising from the present commercial state of Peru were the *galeonistas* who had joined the *Armada del Sur* with whole cargoes of unsold merchandise, hoping to dispose of them directly from Lima.

In the past such large quantities of Spanish goods had never been left over from the Portobello fair[54] and once the news was known in Spain the *consulados* of Andalusia declared themselves to be incensed by the events on the Isthmus and the attitude of the Peruvians towards the trade of the galleons.[55] General Guevara handed in a report in which he deplored the abuses committed at the fair,[56] although he himself had been by no means blameless. Not only had he accepted presents to facilitate the entry of many tons of excess cargo from the *Royal George* both at Cartagena and Portobello, but neither had he made any attempt whatsoever to pursue the smuggling vessels along the coasts, claiming that his warships were undergoing an extensive refit throughout the time of the fair.[57] In the knowledge of most of the relevant facts the *consulados* of Andalusia lodged a strong complaint with the Crown in which they roundly condemned all concerned in the business – foreign smugglers, the South Sea Company, the Peruvians and the royal officials – and they even launched an attack against the viceroy of the new viceroyalty of New Granada whom they alleged had ignored royal orders and actually encouraged the contraband.[58]

From the Spanish point of view, then, it was clear that by 1723 the trade of the *galeones* to Tierra Firme was more out of control and in worse disarray than that of the *flota* to New Spain.

II

The news of the disasters at Portobello and in Peru reached Spain in the autumn of 1722 at precisely the time when the *consulados* of Seville and Cadiz were petitioning the Crown to suspend the *flota* temporarily in view of the appalling commercial conditions reported from New Spain. It is not surprising therefore that the merchants should make a similar request for the postponement of the next set of *galeones* too, scheduled to leave Cadiz in 1723. As they expected, the Council of the Indies replied to their suggestion in very much the same terms as it had used over their proposals for the suspension of the *flota* – that it was important to maintain the regular transatlantic trade as ordered by the *Real proyecto*, that the English 'Annual Ship' should not be allowed alone in the ports of the Indies, etc., etc. However, as in the case of the *flota*, the Council recommended that the merchants should themselves decide the tonnage of the next set of *galeones*. This reply had been anticipated in Cadiz, and indeed the *consulado* had already recommended a maximum of 2000 tons for the *galeones* of 1723.[59] But a certain note of criticism had crept into the merchants' representations about the *galeones*, which had been absent from their letters on the subject of the *flota*. While loyally acknowledging that the Crown was doing its utmost to restore the Indies trade to its erstwhile prosperity they sarcastically pointed out that Crown policy on this matter

> . . . has become the ruination rather than the relief of the merchants of Spain and the Indies, because obviously the regular dispatching of *galeones* is the most efficient [aid] there can be to the entry of contraband goods into America, for [smuggling] is conducted with greater liberty when the *galeones* are in the Indies than when they are not. . .[60]

In a sense criticism of the Crown itself was more justified in connection with the Peruvian trade than it was with the trade to New Spain. Was it not, after all, because the king's warships had failed to rid the coasts of smugglers that the fair at Portobello had produced such losses? Was it not because the *asientos* of the Lima merchants were so concessionary that they had been permitted to behave as they chose at Panama? Was it not because international treaties were being broken and Crown officials were corrupt that French vessels were continuing to use the Pacific ports of Peru? All these were Crown matters. In New Spain Spanish *flotista* and Mexican capitalist were locked in a struggle for the same market, but at Portobello an established trade fair already existed which was simply being laid waste by disloyal subjects and foreign opportunists.

Patiño was not slow to react to such criticism. As soon as possible he ordered the equipping of a squadron of warships to patrol the coasts of the Caribbean, seize foreign interlopers and prevent a repetition of the scandals of 1722 at Portobello. The Andalusian merchants readily agreed to contribute a sum equal to six per cent of the total value of their imports from the Indies to offset the expense involved.[61] Thus were founded the famous *guardacostas* which in future years were to cause so much trouble to the indignant English and lead eventually to the declaration of the War of Jenkins' Ear. So much for direct naval action against Caribbean smugglers. But there was also a need for harsh measures in Peru to deal with the waywardness of the merchants and the Crown authorities there and the impertinent insistence of the foreigners in the Pacific. The first step was to instruct the newly appointed viceroy of Peru, the Marqués de Castelfuerte, that his primary concern must be to impose a firm rule on the viceroyalty and bring both the merchants and the authorities to heel.[62] The second step was to cut the Lima merchants down to size by closely examining the *asiento de avería* drawn up between them and Viceroy Morcillo, and eventually rejecting it as too soft.[63] Of course none of these measures could take immediate effect, for it would be at least a year before the coast-guard ships could be got into service in the Caribbean and the new viceroy was himself due to travel to America in the next set of *galeones* which had not yet even begun to made ready.

Although the merchants of Spain were naturally consoled by these developments they were still not anxious to collaborate commercially in the dispatching of the proposed *galeones* for 1723. The Crown however insisted on the last day of August 1723, as the departure date for the fleet (the *Real proyecto* stipulated 1 September) and fixed the closing date for registering goods for shipment as one month earlier. The preparation of the galleons proceeded much more slowly than the Crown wished, thanks to the procrastination of the Andalusian merchants, who considered that delay could only favour their interests in that it afforded greater opportunity for the glutted markets of Peru to become free. In June 1723 they requested that the command of the fleet should once again be given to General Guevara, since they felt that with his experience and his fiery temperament he would best be able to deal firmly with the Peruvians.[64] In the event the command went to an Italian sailor, favourite and compatriot of the queen, General Carlos Grillo.[65] This appointment did not increase confidence, and at the end of July, when the register should have been closed, it was found necessary to give 'ten days grace . . . to allow any interested foreigners to inscribe themselves in the fleet'.[66] Such a measure was obviously contrary to the spirit of the *Real proyecto*, which strove to stimulate Spanish exports precisely and also declared that the fleets would on no account be held up for late-comers. From this it may reasonably be deduced that the merchants of Spain were unwilling to risk their *own* capital on such an unsound investment and it was probably found difficult to make up sufficient tonnage. By the end of August the *galeones* were still not ready to sail and it was moved that their departure should be put off until December or even later if possible.[67] Within a few days, however, General Carlos Grillo arrived in Cadiz bringing personally a royal command for their sailing without fail on 30 September.[68] But even this was of no avail, for the departure of the fleet was after all successfully delayed until the end of the year. Evidently the delay had the desired effect of increasing commercial confidence in the venture, for the *galeones*, when they eventually sailed on 31 December 1723, carried not the 2000 tons of goods recommended by the *consulados*, but 3127.79 tons distributed among the impressive number of 18 sail.[69]

Some time after General Grillo's arrival in the Indies on 17 February 1724, the English 'Annual Ship', again the *Royal George*, put in to Cartagena with another huge cargo of goods for sale at the fairs. The original draft order for her sailing had been made out on 14 August, but the Spaniards refused to issue final permission until December 1723. The postponement, they alleged, was intended as a protest against English smuggling activities in the Indies. Since permission for an 'Annual Ship' had been (illegally) withheld in 1722 because Spain was unable to send a fleet to America in that year, the Crown was under the obligation of issuing papers for two South Sea Company ships in 1723. The *Royal Prince* had gone to New Spain earlier in the year to coincide with the *flota* of General Serrano, and it was intended that the *Royal George* should leave at the same time as the *galeones* which were due to sail in August. But because of the difficulty of preparing the Tierra Firme fleet for August, it was essential for Spain that the *Royal George* should be kept out of the Indies until Grillo was ready to sail. Clearly this was the real reason why the Crown delayed her sailing orders until December. The pretention that she was stopped as a protest was certainly no more than an excuse to prevent the 'Annual Ship' trading in America when no *galeones* or *flota* were present, for the fear that at some stage this might happen was constantly in the minds of those interested in the re-establishment of the *carrera de Indias*.[70]

Both the 'Annual Ship' and the *galeones* were ready to start trading in the Indies by the spring of 1724. However at that time the procedure for the dispatching of the *Armada del Sur* had not even begun. The new viceroy of Peru who had come with the fleet did not reach Lima to take over the offices of government until 14 May 1724.[71] The *galeones* had already been in port for three months by that date. As soon as Castelfuerte reached his capital he set about the tasks the Crown had commended to him with determination. His immediate concern was to stamp out the contraband trade which was recognised as the prime source of the economic evils of the viceroyalty. Straight away, therefore, he re-published the severe royal *cédula* of 31 December 1720, prohibiting smuggling on pain of death, and issued a still more strongly worded royal *cédula* of 7 September 1723. Even royal officials and Crown authorities were subject to the maximum sentence for disobedience. To these orders he added his own statement that he intended to impose the law strictly and meant to achieve the objectives which the Crown had entrusted to him. A lengthy document containing all these threats was printed in Lima on 19 June 1724, and was read out by mulatto and negro town criers throughout the viceroyalty.[72] The firmness of his resolve and the strictness of his measures became international news. *Mist's Weekly Journal* reported:

> The Viceroy of Peru . . . has been vigilant at land in suppressing this clandestine traffick, for he has published new prohibition against it on pain of death and confiscation of estates and effects along the whole coast of Peru, both on the North and South Seas, on the latter he has caused all the habitations to be demolished, and sent the inhabitants with all their cattle and effects 40 leagues up into the country.[73]

Castelfuerte meant business, and everyone knew it! Within a few months the illegal trading in the Pacific which had plagued the viceroyalty for more than 20 years was virtually at an end.[74]

The viceroy's next task, a good deal more intractable than the first, was to tackle the merchants and the *consulado* of Lima. At the heart of this problem lay the question of the *asientos*, for once Castelfuerte could force the merchants into financial commitments with the Crown, it would no longer be in their interest to boycott the *galeones* at Portobello. But, for all his harsh determination, the viceroy was unable to achieve this objective. The *consulado* of Lima had already written to the authorities in Spain informing them of the inadvisability of sending *galeones* to Portobello in 1723–4. The markets of Peru, they declared, were completely glutted with unsaleable Spanish goods from the previous fleet, and the situation was steadily worsening because of the large quantities of foreign merchandise still entering the country and preventing the sale of that left over from the *galeones*.[75] The *consulado* naturally was not at all disposed to negotiate fresh and more exigent *asientos* with the new viceroy. Moreover it had every hope that Alsedo y Herrera would succeed in having Morcillo's *asientos* approved in Madrid. Castelfuerte's bargaining position was therefore weak, and, as the Crown later pointed out to him, he could not *force* the merchants into tax-farming contracts, nor could he oblige private citizens to enter into trading which they did not wish.[76] From this position of strength, then, the merchants made known to the viceroy their disinclination to participate in the imminent fair at Portobello.[77] There followed over 18 months of discussions, threats and cajoling, during which time Castelfuerte wrote several times to Spain impassionedly informing the Crown of the disgraceful attitude of the merchants.[78] The deadlock over the *asientos* was eventually broken by the receipt and publication in June 1725 of a royal order cancelling Morcillo's *asientos* and placing the current ones instead in the hands of the royal officials at Callao.[79] Thus the *consulado*'s position was at least marginally undermined.

From the first Castelfuerte had exerted pressure on the *consulado* to hasten the departure of the *Armada del Sur*. He began by requiring its members to provide a loan of 200,000 *pesos* to cover the costs of the *galeones* waiting in port, forbade the movement of all precious metals by sea, prohibited trade between New Spain and Peru, and all but totally closed the ports of the viceroyalty. He then began a constant bombardment of the merchants with orders for the departure of the fleet for Panama. These were accompanied by a number of threats against the merchants' property and for the immediate collection of Crown debts, all of which he himself knew he was powerless to keep.[80] But the *consulado* was always one jump ahead of him. First it pointed to the existing large stocks of goods in Peru as a reason to delay the fair; then it alleged that the refitting of the Crown's warships (which Morcillo had contracted with the *consulado*) was taking longer and costing more than expected. Next there was the question of the still unconfirmed *asientos*; then the merchants complained of a general shortage of money; then they refused to leave during the rainy season – and so on and so forth, until such time as the stocks in the country were beginning to reduce and the viceroy had been forced into a more conciliatory attitude.[81] By the end of 1725 dilatory preparations were being made for the *Armada del Sur* to sail, but not before Castelfuerte had been persuaded to draw up tax *asientos* with the royal officials which greatly benefited the merchants. He was also compelled to give in to them on a number of minor matters.[82] It was not without personal experience that he wrote in his *Memoria*:

> This matter [of commerce] is the most extraordinary of all those that can come before this Government. In dealing with it it is necessary for a command to go dressed in the clothes of a request.[83]

Finally, on 14 January 1726, the *Armada del Sur* sailed for Panama. In the event it turned out to be twice as rich as either of the previous two fleets of 1707 and 1722.[84] Castelfuerte showed himself to be quite encouraged by the results he had obtained. He had extirpated foreign interloping in the Pacific and at least come to honourable terms with the merchants. Moreover, his exertions in Peru had been complemented by the Crown's alacrity in putting two coast-guard ships into service off Tierra Firme under the Conde de Clavijo and news of their effectiveness was well known in Lima.[85] In a report to the king the viceroy was therefore able to record his conviction that given the continuance of firm measures the trade of the *galeones* at Portobello could once again be made to work to the Crown's satisfaction.[86]

After the usual squabbling between the Peruvian merchants and the authorities at Panama the fair at Portobello was ready to open in June 1726, almost two-and-a-half years after General Grillo's *galeones* had first reached Cartagena.[87] Unfortunately, however, the trading on the Isthmus was to be as great a disaster in 1726 as it had been in 1722, for it was completely disrupted by the appearance of the English Admiral Hosier and his squadron off the coasts of Tierra Firme. The differences between England and Spain which eventually led to the outbreak of war in 1727 were already apparent, and the British government sent Hosier to the Indies primarily, it seems, to protect the *Royal George* from being impounded, but also with the aim of causing trouble. Having first called at Cartagena to confer with the South Sea Company's factors in the port, Hosier stationed himself in the Bay of Bastimentos just outside Portobello. From there he proceeded to interfere with any Spanish shipping that came near, hinder the celebration of the fair by blocking the Portobello-Panama road, and cause anxiety by insisting that the Spaniards should embark their money on the *Royal George* and take advantage of the insurance scheme offered by the South Sea Company.[88]

The arrival of Admiral Hosier and the British squadron was in fact welcomed by the Lima merchants, for although they withdrew to Panama and took their money with them, they refused now to pay the prices previously agreed upon at Portobello for the cargo of the *galeones*.[89] In their perfidy they were counting on the British men-of-war to protect the smuggling vessels which had been successfully kept away from the coasts over the previous months by the vigilance of the *galeones* themselves, the Spanish coast-guard ships and the penalties for smuggling imposed by Castelfuerte. Their expectations were not in vain. The presence of Admiral Hosier had the effect of completely neutralising all the Spanish measures against contraband. For the second time in four years smuggling vessels thronged the bays and inlets around Portobello at the time of the fair, and the merchants of Lima, only too delighted by the course of events, once again spent their millions in the illegal rather than the legal trade.[90] Thanks to two years of zealous government the viceroy had succeeded in making the Portobello fair a fairly rich one, and yet by a single stroke of bad fortune most of that good work was undone. Once more the Lima merchants came off best.

The galleons were trapped in the Indies for a further two years by the threat of the English navy, during which time, incidentally, their commander, General Grillo, died in port at Cartagena.[91] As soon as the prospect of international peace seemed to be a certainty a naval expedition was dispatched from Cadiz under General López Pintado to take command of the *galeones* and bring them back to Europe. López Pintado left on 8 May 1728, but by the time he reached the Indies, Hosier had been called off and the general had a relatively trouble-free mission before him. He had the king's treasure brought from Panama, where it was being held for safe-keeping, loaded it on to the ships at Portobello, and from there he passed on to Havana to collect other stranded vessels, including the homeward-bound quicksilver fleet of Don Rodrigo de Torres. The combined fleets reached Cadiz on 22 February 1729 where, to López Pintado's great joy, he found Philip V in person, together with the royal family, Patiño and all the court, waiting on the quay to receive him.[92] Although between them the fleets brought home 24,000,000 *pesos*, the returns on the investment in the *galeones* were not a cause for jubilation on the part of the merchants of Andalusia. The ships had been in the Indies for five years and the expenses were enormous, to say nothing of the diminished returns resulting from the Peruvians' second act of treachery in the trading on the Isthmus.[93]

The fair of 1726 was a significant one at this stage in the history of the *galeones*. It seemed at that time that it was indeed within Castelfuerte's power to make the Portobello fairs successful once again and thereby regain for Spain some of her declining control over the Peruvian merchants and their markets. The arrival of Hosier on the scene at the most inopportune moment was unwisely regarded in Madrid merely as an unfortunate set-back. Perhaps the immediate obstacles to the trading placed there by Hosier prevented Spain's merchants and ministers from gaining a true understanding of the nature of the real problems which faced them. Whatever the case, the current debate about the American trades produced little that was new and led in fact to action that was destined in the end to cause further commercial disasters of the kind which were becoming all too common in the eighteenth century.

III

The End of the System

8 Discussions and Decisions, 1726–1733

The ejection from office in 1726 of Spain's Chief Minister, the Duque de Ripperdá, a Dutch adventurer who had succeeded Alberoni at the court of Philip V, marked the beginning of Patiño's rise to real power within the kingdom. In May 1726 Patiño was promoted to the post of Secretary of the newly formed Indies Office (*Despacho Universal de Indias*) to which was added overall responsibility for the navy. Soon afterwards Amaza, Philip's Treasury Minister, brought about his own dismissal by giving vent to a petulant outburst against Patiño and his brother, the Marqués de Castelar, who had recently been appointed Minister of War. Patiño was himself given the post of his defamer and consequently in the summer of 1726 he took over the control of Crown finances in addition to his other royal offices. A few years later, in 1731, while his brother was ambassador to France, Patiño also accepted temporarily the Ministry of War. From about that time too he was already taking over the Secretaryship of State from the failing Marqués de la Paz, and with Paz's death in 1732 Patiño finally became Chief Minister of the Crown, adding foreign affairs to his already enormous burden of home ministries. He discharged his widespread and exacting responsibilities with remarkable energy until his death in 1736.[1]

Throughout the decade in which Patiño reached the height of his career commerce with America continued to be a vital issue in Spain's affairs. In the person of Patiño the Indies trade became even more closely linked, if that seems possible, with the question of royal finances in general. The dynastic ambitions, the military excesses and the public luxury of Philip and his Italian wife produced considerable demands upon the treasury – and upon the ingenuity of Patiño – all of which he did his utmost to meet. Immediately upon assuming the Ministry of the Treasury Patiño was requested by the Crown to prepare a report on how royal revenue could best be increased for the following year of 1727. After a brief but thorough examination of the matter Patiño presented a paper to the Crown outlining his ideas.[2] Important among his proposals were a new method of collecting customs duties and

159

measures to eradicate the fraud and illegal practices which he found to be scandalously widespread throughout the existing tax system. But perhaps most significant was the section of the paper dealing with royal expenses and income resulting from the American trade. Patiño proposed that for one year only the Crown should arbitrarily seize for its own use 25 per cent or 30 per cent of the total value of the returns of the *galeones* and *flota* whose arrival from the Indies was currently awaited. This was to be a temporary measure only, intended as a stop-gap until such time as a new tax system (which Patiño himself had originally put forward in 1723) could be brought into effect. In his paper Patiño then went on to reveal that in his opinion the Crown contributed disproportionately to the cost of the Indies trade by escorting the American fleets, sending dispatch ships, policing and defending the trade with *guardacosta* ships and the Barlovento squadron and assisting the merchant classes to carry on commerce which was essentially for their own profit and not the Crown's. Moreover, since the Crown had raised the real value of money by $12\frac{1}{2}$ per cent in 1718 by reminting and revaluing much of the coinage, the merchants, Patiño maintained, had benefited greatly.[3] In view of all this they could not reasonably object to the increased contributions he proposed to exact on the returns of the current fleets. Finally, Patiño promised that after 1728, when his 1723 proposals came into force – proposals which had lain ignored by previous ministers – royal revenue from the Indies trade would increase by as much as 500 per cent or 600 per cent, from one million to some six million *pesos* annually. Clearly, Patiño the specialist on naval and commercial affairs, and semi-mentor of the *consulados*, had became Patiño the politician and royal minister in charge of Crown finances.

By and large Patiño's proposals were put into effect.[4] In 1728 the value of the coinage was once again increased, enabling the Crown to lay its hands on a greater proportion of the precious metals from the Indies at the same rates of tax. In 1729 the administration charges at Cadiz (*Consulado*) were raised by 4 per cent. Although it seems Patiño was unable to seize the 25 per cent or 30 per cent of the value of the current American fleets on their return to Spain, as he had intended, he did succeed in obtaining a sizeable loan for the Crown on very favourable terms from the Andalusian merchants. At the same time the merchants were forced to agree to an overall 3 per cent increase in the duties paid on goods imported into Spain from the Indies. In short, as a contemporary British diplomat observed:

by all the little tricks that a thorough knowledge of the whole detail could suggest to him [Patiño] got His Catholic Majesty as great a share of these effects [from the American trade] as he possibly could.[5]

Although Patiño had always believed that the economic purpose of the colonies was to promote the economic well-being of the mother country and provide Crown revenue, in his early years at the *Casa de Contratación* he had been concerned to reform and foster the Andalusian trades with the Indies as the best method of achieving these aims. The fiscal and administrative character of the *Real proyecto* of 1720 is clear indication of this policy. However, by 1726 the realisation was growing that this policy was failing – and chance had it that this realisation happened to coincide with Patiño's own elevation to the Ministry of the Treasury. A change in Patiño's attitude to the Andalusian merchants and the operation of the trade with America consequently becomes apparent at this time. From now on the privileged position of the Andalusian merchant bodies, allowing them to dominate all aspects of the American trade, began, however minimally, to decline. In view of the fleets' failure to monopolise and increase the Indies trade since 1720, the hegemony of the commercial interests of the *consulados* of Cadiz and Seville over all other colonial trading interests now became less sacrosanct. This was not out of any wish to favour the colonial merchants specifically, but merely as a matter of pragmatism in a sphere in which the *galeones* and *flota* were proving themselves eminently unsuccessful. Patiño's hardening attitude towards the Andalusian merchants, indicated, as we have seen, by his own words and actions from 1726 onwards, must in any case also be seen within the context of an atmosphere of reappraisal and re-examination of the whole mechanism of the Indies trade over the years 1726–8.

It will be recalled that one of the chief obstacles to the trade of the *flotistas* in New Spain had been the influx of high quality and reasonably priced goods from the Orient via the Manila-Acapulco galleon. Like that of the *flota* and *galeones* the principal cargo of the Manila galleon was good quality cloth and fabrics. The legislation of 1718, 1719, 1720 and 1722, severely restricting the importation of Chinese fine cloth and ordering the public burning of excesses, had been aimed at clearing the New Spain markets in readiness for the introduction of European cloth on a larger scale by means of the reformed *flota* after 1720. Not surprisingly the inhabitants of the

Philippines, supported by the royal authorities there, protested vigorously to the Crown in Spain. The potential success of the Manila–Acapulco trade contrasted strongly with the increasing failure of the *flota* in New Spain. Moreover, in the face of the reported civil disturbances the Crown had no wish to sacrifice the Philippines to the cupidity of the Cadiz traders. The ban against Chinese cloth was therefore partially raised in 1724 and this was followed on 15 September 1726, within a short time of Patiño's promotion to the treasury, by a new set of provisions regulating the trade between the Philippines and New Spain.[6] By these each galleon from Manila was in future to be permitted to take Oriental goods to the value of 300,000 *pesos* and was allowed to return to the Philippines with goods and silver to the value of 600,000 *pesos*. Despite the enraged protests of the Cadiz merchants this regulation remained in force, and in 1734 the quotas were even raised so that Oriental goods to the value of 500,000 *pesos* could be imported into New Spain and the value of the returning goods and silver was fixed at a maximum of 1,000,000 *pesos*.[7]

But if greater freedom for Chinese cloth on the markets of New Spain may be regarded as an inroad into the hegemony of Andalusian commercial interests in America, a revision of the regulations for the trading of the *flota* of 1728 also led eventually to the *flotistas'* losing their decades-old struggle with the capitalists of Mexico City for control of the internal markets of the viceroyalty. One of the first matters to which Patiño turned his attention in 1726, as the new Secretary for the Indies, was the unresolved question of the trade fair in New Spain. It will be remembered that the last *flota*, that of 1725, had carried with it last-minute permission for its goods to be sold throughout the country in the usual manner, and not at a trade fair at Orizaba as had been previously stipulated. Nevertheless the original requirement that a fair be held in New Spain was still in force, and obviously a firm decision on the question was needed before the departure of the next fleet. The Crown therefore ordered Patiño to set in motion a full enquiry into this and related matters, in the course of which opinions were sought of the Council of the Indies, of Don Francisco de Varas y Valdés (Patiño's successor at the *Casa de Contratación* and as *Intendente de Marina*), of General Manuel López Pintado and the merchant bodies of Andalusia.[8] This was indeed the first part of a fairly large-scale overall review of the state of the American trades in general which took place by royal command over the years 1726 to 1728 and involved extensive consultations, reports and meetings. In the event the most important item to come out of those deliberations was the royal *cédula* of

2 April 1728, by which a trade fair was unequivocally established in New Spain, to be held, as originally proposed, at Jalapa.[9]

The principal purposes of the royal *cédula* of 1728 were first to rationalise the procedures to be followed for the holding of a trade fair in New Spain, and second to compromise between the interests of the merchant bodies of Andalusia and Mexico City in such a way that neither of the two trading parties could nurse more valid grievances than the other, and both would be obliged to cooperate in the celebration of a fair. Within the spirit of this compromise of 1728 the concept of the natural hegemony of the Andalusian merchants is once again eroded.

The *cédula* decreed that the fairs were to be conducted henceforth in the following manner. As soon as the *flota* put in to Veracruz one of its representatives was immediately to travel to Mexico City to confer with the viceroy and thereby initiate the movement of Mexican merchants and precious metals towards Jalapa. At the same time a second representative of the fleet was to travel to Jalapa itself in order to supervise proceedings there, while a third representative at Veracruz would begin dispatching the cargo of the fleet along the road to the fair. In this way the entry of illegal or unregistered merchandise would be prevented. When both goods and silver had all arrived at Jalapa the representatives of both merchant bodies were to sit down together and work out an official price list for the goods on sale. If after 30 days in conclave there was no agreement, new teams of negotiators could be nominated by their respective sides. The next matter which the royal *cédula* touched upon was in fact the thorny crux of the whole problem – whether or not the *flotistas* would be permitted to take their goods personally on to the internal markets of New Spain. The Crown's decision was that once the fair was over the representatives of the *consulado* of Cadiz would be obliged to make out a full and proper list of all the cargo which had not been sold. The merchants of Mexico City were then required to produce jointly sufficient money to buy up all the merchandise that remained, at the official fair prices, and then proceed to its purchase. Nevertheless any *flotista* who chose instead to place his leftovers in the hands of a Mexican agent for subsequent sale was to be free to do so. If, however, no money was forthcoming for the joint purchase of residues, despite exhaustive efforts to implement the procedure, and if no agents could be found to handle the goods, then and only then were the *flotistas* to be allowed to take their merchandise away from Jalapa and sell it as best they could on the open market of the viceroyalty. Finally the royal *cédula* dealt with the tax arrangements on sales at the fair. It has been previously explained that one of the main objections which the Mexicans had put forward against the holding of a fair outside the capital was that the product of the tax on transactions (*alcabala*) did not accrue to the *consulado* of Mexico as part of its own *asiento*, but went instead to the local tax farmer. For the purposes of the Mexicans' *asiento*, therefore, the royal *cédula* stipulated that Jalapa was deemed to be within the fiscal jurisdiction of the *consulado* of Mexico; but it also went on to declare, in deference to the petitions of the Andalusians, that the transactions at the fair would be free of tax to the *flotistas*. Despite the vigorous protests of the Mexicans who were the eventual losers under the prevailing tax-farming contracts, the Crown upheld this last decision. So although sales were to be made easier at the fair by virtue of the abolition of the traditional taxes, the merchants of Andalusia found that the internal markets of New Spain were in the end virtually closed to them, and the monopoly of the Mexican capitalists was effectively assured.

Of equal importance, if of less significant result, were the deliberations over which Patiño presided in an attempt to facilitate or even reorganise the Cadiz trade with the viceroyalty of Peru. A number of meetings took place over the years 1727 and 1728. They were attended by two members of the Council of Castile, Don José de Castro Araujo and Don Rodrigo de Cepeda, two members of the Council of the Indies, Don Juan José de Mutiloa and Don José de Laysequilla, and by the special envoy of the merchants of Peru, Don Dionisio de Alsedo y Herrera. It is principally via the writings of the latter that knowledge of the business of the committee may be obtained, as all its records and papers were destroyed in a fire which raged through the Alcázar of Madrid in 1734.[10]

The committee began its deliberations with a lengthy discussion of the state of the trade to Peru and the reasons for its current failure. It was agreed that the main problem was that of the contraband activities of British ships in the Caribbean and at Buenos Aires under the cover of the South Sea Company's assiento, and also those of a small number of French and Dutch interlopers who still continued to trade in the Pacific. Much thought was given to the possibility of re-routing the *galeones* either directly to Callao via the Straits of Magellan and the Pacific or, alternatively, to Buenos Aires where a trade fair like that at Portobello and Jalapa could be established. The members of the Councils of Castile and the Indies particularly favoured these proposals, especially that of using Buenos Aires as a trading point. Patiño and Alsedo, however, were less convinced because, with regard to the first suggestion, experience had shown that it was impossible to police and defend the southern tip of South America, and Spain's scant naval resources were insufficient to patrol the whole of the Pacific coasts. Patiño then commented that such a project was the equivalent of 'putting a toll-gate in the middle of open country'. Alsedo disliked the idea of using Buenos Aires as a trading centre on account of the long-standing resentment of the Lima merchants against those of the Plate who 'poached' the markets of Upper Peru whenever they could with contraband goods or the cargoes of *registro* ships which reached Buenos Aires. Moreover, it was argued, Buenos Aires was not easily accessible from Lima, and in any case it had always been considered a closed port by the Spanish authorities, off the accepted Imperial sea routes and too remote to act as a central point for general trading.

Another matter which must certainly have come before the committee at some stage, although Alsedo fails to record it, was a series of proposals drawn up by the viceroy of Peru, the Marqués de Castelfuerte, on 28 December 1725, 30 March 1726, and 30 December 1726, and which were finally rejected by the Council of the Indies on 4 December 1728.[11] Castelfuerte had been greatly annoyed by the reluctance of the Lima merchants to participate in the *Armada del Sur* in 1724 and was still smarting from the success of their delaying tactics. He complained bitterly that he had been obliged to make concession after concession to the *consulado* in order to persuade the merchants to embark their money and agree to travel to the fair at Portobello. He wrote:

the merchants of Lima have indeed gone to Portobello, but they have done so when *they* were ready and under conditions that suited *them*, and not as they ought to have done; and so the damage which the Spanish merchants and the royal treasury have suffered by the lengthy detention of the *galeones* in port is entirely attributable to *them*; and the same thing will happen again and again unless some measures are taken to counteract the policies of these merchants whose sole aim is to be able to trade in total independence.[12]

The measures which Castelfuerte recommended as a remedy to such behaviour were highly authoritarian. First he proposed that once the viceroy had decided the date for the departure of the *Armada del Sur* the *consulado* of Lima should be obliged by law to begin its preparations for the voyage to Portobello. By agreement between *consulado* and viceroy the fixed date would be open to rearrangement, but a maximum of only two postponements would be granted. The third date published for the departure of the fleet would be final. If, after that, the fleet were delayed by any action, or lack of action, for which the Lima merchants were responsible, the *consulado* of Lima should be threatened with having to pay all the expenses of both *galeones* and *Armada del Sur* from the appointed date until the date of actual departure. If for any reason this threat failed to have the desired effect, then the *Armada del Sur* should still be sent off to Panama on the published date, but empty. It would return in due course bringing with it the whole cargo of the galleons and the Spanish merchants. On arrival at Callao the *galeonistas* would be completely free to sell their goods throughout the viceroyalty wherever they chose and to cut in on the markets of the Lima merchants to the best advantage they could find. This, the viceroy claimed, would soon make the Peruvians sit up and realise that they could not defraud His Majesty of tax nor frustrate the legitimate commerce of Spain with her Empire.

The thinking of the Crown's ministers when faced with Castelfuerte's plan is once again indicative of their unwillingness at this time to protect the position of the Cadiz traders at all costs against the interests of the American merchants. First they pointed out the obvious drawbacks to the scheme in terms of shipping problems and expense. The *Armada del Sur* would have to make two voyages unladen, one up to Panama to collect the cargo of the galleons and a final one from Panama to Callao after it had returned the *galeonistas* to the Isthmus on their way back to Spain. Moreover the time scale of the commercial operations would be seriously protracted. The great advantage of the Portobello fair was the relative speed with which the business could be done. If the *galeonistas* were to go down to Peru and engage themselves in individual selling, the stay of the *galeones* in Cartagena would have to be greatly extended, probably to a minimum of three years. All this would bring further expense. And if the *galeones* were to go back to Spain empty, the expense and complications in the transport arrangements would be quite unthinkable. But perhaps most noteworthy in the Crown's reactions to Castelfuerte's proposals is its tone of moderation, which contrasts sharply with the viceroy's harshness. This is especially evident in the near indulgence which it showed in its references to the malpractices of the Lima merchants. The Crown declared itself unwilling to give the viceroy the authority he requested to impose threats upon the Peruvian traders, because

> it does not consider it necessary; nor can further powers than those which he already has be given to him to force his orders to be

obeyed, for with his present authority he is able to decide the dates of the departure of the *Armada del Sur* and enforce them, as have all his predecessors, in the same way as is practised with the merchants of Spain in respect of the departure of the *galeones* and *flota*; for one does not threaten a merchant into running risks that he does not wish to take, nor should the power of the Viceroy be interpreted as extending as far as being able to force the merchants to go and spend their money at Panama or Portobello if this is not in their own interest . . ., for commerce is attracted to where it can find profit, and it must not be imagined that if the merchants thought there was any advantage in going to the fair they would have failed to go on that occasion [1725–6]; for this is the *modus operandi* of a merchant, from which it must be deduced that it was not advantageous for them to go, and that they foresaw losses instead of profit in going up to Portobello, and all the more so since experience has shown them that even when previous viceroys have given their word in the name of His Majesty that French ships would not be allowed into the Pacific ports, they have in fact been permitted to land their cargoes and sell them illegally.[13]

Such tolerant understanding of the profession of a merchant seems extraordinary, especially if one recalls Patiño's unsympathetic attitude towards the Andalusian *consulados* in his paper of the year before, 1727, and his unwillingness to postpone the *flotas* of 1723 and 1725 and the *galeones* of 1724, as the Spanish *consulados* had requested, until the glutted American markets again became reasonably clear.

The reasons for Patiño's attitude and the rejection of the measures Castelfuerte proposed must be sought in his overall view of the situation. He was convinced that there could be no real remedy to Spain's commercial ills until 1744, the year in which the Assiento Contract with the South Sea Company came to an end. He stated publicly that while the assiento and its supplementary treaties gave the English legitimate business in Spain's Indies they would continue to commit excesses and alienate the American merchants from the Cadiz fleets. After 1744, Patiño believed, Spain would be free to review and reform her commercial practice with America to the advantage of both trading partners.[14] In the meantime, given the weakness of Spain's position, it would be improvident to experiment with new trade routes and imprudent in the extreme to alienate still further the merchants of Lima by imposing upon them a system of oppression which in fact did nothing to strike at the root of the problem. The advice of Alsedo y Herrera, present during all this time as special envoy of the Peruvian merchants, must also have persuaded Patiño that a moderate line and a show of sympathy was the best means of retaining the loyalty of the *consulado* of Lima. Even the original terms of the cancellation of the *consulado*'s recent *asiento de averías*, the reason for Alsedo's mission, were softened and the *consulado* was told that in 1744 its *asiento*, so advantageous to its members and so unfavourable to the Crown, would be reintroduced.[15]

But if Patiño felt that sweet words towards the merchants of Peru was the best short term measure, he was not as resigned to the intractability of the situation as might appear, for a threefold policy plan seems to have emerged from his deliberations and discussions. The harshness of Castelfuerte's penalties for smugglers and the vigilance of his men along the coasts of Peru was beginning to have results. So too were the *guardacosta* ships in the Caribbean, which were becoming a real nuisance to the British interlopers. In addition the current hostilities between Spain and England (1727–8) were further hampering the activities of the South Sea Company in both New Spain and South America. All this seemed to indicate to Patiño that prospects in the near future for the trade of a *flota* to Jalapa and *galeones* to Portobello would not be too bad, for by 1729 it was virtually certain that the markets of both viceroyalties would be encouragingly understocked with European goods. Consequently Patiño's first policy decision was to continue unswervingly with the traditional system of trade, dispatching for the present one fleet annually, *galeones* one year and *flota* the next. The first pair to go would be the *flota* in 1729 and the *galeones* in 1730.[16]

If care was needed in dealing with the Americans, there was much to be gained by the Crown from urging the merchants of Cadiz to participate in the proposed fleets, and moreover there was nothing to be lost by taking full advantage of them in fiscal terms. Consequently the only concession which Patiño felt it expedient to grant to the merchants of Andalusia at this time to placate them and to offset their obviously weakening position was royal approval of a new set of statutes for the *consulado* of Cadiz.[17] In these that body's privileges and rights in the Indies trade vis-à-vis those of foreigners and other Spanish enterprises were clearly defined. It was declared that all shippers (*cargadores*) of merchandise to America had in future to be voting members of that *consulado* – and early in the seventeenth century only native-born Spaniards of at least two generations could qualify for membership! Also for the first time in the history of Spain's American commerce a distinction was drawn between Peninsular-born and American-born Spaniards. Article 13 of the new statutes forbade American Spaniards to act as agents or consignees of Andalusian merchants in their trade with the Indies. Thus by the new statutes, control of the Spanish end of the trade was made the exclusive preserve of the *consulado* of Cadiz, and foreigners and Americans were legally prevented from having any further part in it whatsoever. Such was the sop given to the anxious merchants of Andalusia and such was the limit of protection which they were able to obtain for themselves in the face of the increasing commercial pressure from the Indies. The second aspect of Patiño's policy therefore consisted in promoting whatever Spanish trade he could with the Indies and using such trade as a means of obtaining the highest possible revenue for the Crown. The fiscal measures discussed earlier in this chapter and implemented from 1728 onwards are an indication of Patiño's endeavours in this respect.

The third part of Patiño's policy involved the introduction of a practically untried principle into the conduct of the American commerce, that of the trading company with specific terms of reference. As we have seen, Patiño rejected the idea of experimentation within the established fleet system for economic, political and diplomatic reasons, but this decision did not preclude experimentation with the American trade *outside* the traditional methods. Despite the enthusiasm of certain sectors of opinion the principle of monopolistic trading companies had never enjoyed much favour in Spain. Attempts had indeed been made in the past to form such companies on a small scale, but the Crown had never taken a real interest in them, and without exception they had collapsed almost before they had begun. Patiño, however, was now ready to experiment with this principle in a serious way, for a successful company could not only provide a good income for the Crown in the present strained circumstances, but it could also serve as a basis of experience for a probable reform of the whole system of trade with the Indies when the time for that came, as Patiño believed, in 1744.

Patiño's interest in the viability of such companies was undoubtedly encouraged by the success of the Ostend Company which the Austrian Emperor Charles VI had set up in 1722.[18] As early as 1723, the activities of this company had already become an issue in the complicated diplomatic bargainings which were increasingly dominating European politics, for the Maritime Powers felt that by means of his company ventures the Hapsburg was threatening their own commercial interests. In October 1723 the British Parliament passed an act against the Ostend Company, and by April of the following year, 1724, Spain was also urging Britain to press for the suppression of the company at the Congress of Cambrai, where the Dutch had already tabled the matter for discussion. In 1725, however, secret negotiations between Spain and Austria temporarily reconciled these two nations, and two years later when moves were afoot by the Emperor, who was constantly under pressure, to transfer the company from Ostend to Trieste, Patiño was not slow to offer it asylum in Spain. To this end he drew up an ambitious and far-sighted plan which was placed before the Crown. His aim was to establish in Cadiz the headquarters of the company and thereby convert the port into the principal commercial centre of continental Europe. A powerful international company operating from Spain would not only encourage commerce between Spain and Austria, but would more importantly attract to Cadiz a large volume of trade from the North of Europe, the Mediterranean and the East and West Indies, in addition to the already existing monopoly of Spain's own trade with America. The advantages of procuring the transfer to Spain of a vigorous commercial concern would soon be felt in the national economy. Moreover, the establishment of the Ostend Company in Cadiz would give the Spaniards valuable experience in the operation of such an enterprise, and it would provide a working example on the spot upon which to base the future conduct of Spain's own American trade when detailed thinking about more general trade reforms was called for, as Patiño believed, within the next 10 years or so. Such possibilities were of course in the air at precisely the time when Patiño was holding his meetings with his various colleagues on the question of the American trades. Whether they were discussed on these occasions we shall probably never know, but in view of Alsedo y Herrera's presence it seems likely that Patiño would have kept his own counsel.[19]

Patiño's project for the future of the Ostend Company in Spain was thwarted by the course of events in Europe and changing diplomatic alliances, for having forced the Emperor to suspend the company's activities in 1727 for five years, the Maritime Powers continued to press for its total abolition, which was finally achieved in 1731.[20] But failure of his plans did not prevent Patiño from putting into effect his experiment with a trading company. It was generally agreed that Spain's trade with Venezuela had fallen into such serious decline that experimentation with commercial practice in that area could hardly make things worse than they already were. For this reason, in late 1727 or early 1728, Patiño agreed to enter into negotiations with Don Felipe de Aguirre, the representative of certain Basque interests, for the purpose of founding a company to trade with Venezuela and the colonies in the immediate vicinity. It was hoped thereby to remedy the serious shortage of cacao from which the Spanish market was suffering. Throughout Europe the consumption of chocolate was rapidly increasing and Spain's dilatory supplies reached her mainly from Mexico. However the principal purveyors of cacao on the European markets were not the Spaniards, but the Dutch, who obtained it illegally from Venezuela, the major producer, via their colonies on Curaçao and Bonaire. The go-ahead Basque province of Guipúzcoa had been steadily working for some years past for parity of duties at Cantabrian ports with those at Cadiz and also for the end to specific restrictions on the importation of cacao from the colonies. The frustration of Patiño's plans for the re-establishment of the Ostend Company and the dearth of cacao proved to be a happy coincidence for the Basques, and on 25 September 1728 the privileges of the *Real Compañía Guipuzcoana de Caracas* were given the royal approval. The constitution, terms of reference, conditions of trading etc. of the new company were set out in great detail and have been succinctly summarised for the modern reader by R. D. Hussey in his admirable study of the history of the Caracas Company.[21] The shortage of cacao was brought to an end very quickly, and the Caracas Company entered into a period of real prosperity. Legarra, one of the company's founders, writing some years later (1735) almost in vindication of Patiño's experimental thinking in 1727, commented:

> and if this has happened, and we have evidence that it has with regard to the province of Caracas where lost trade has been fully restored to the hands of Spaniards, with great benefit to the Crown and the Nation (and the founding of a small company has been enought to achieve it), if this be so, what more practical proof do we need to show that another such company, with greater capital, will be able likewise to bring about the restoration of the lucrative trade with Peru and New Spain?[22]

Patiño's gratification at the early success of the Caracas Company prompted him to support a proposal made in 1731 by the merchants of Seville for the formation of a Philippine Company, which would engage in direct commerce between Seville or Cadiz and Manila. The traditional route for Spanish trade with the Philippines had, of course, been via New Spain, but trading along that route had always been hampered by official restrictions and commercial uncertainties. The plan was accepted by the Crown, but probably for financial reasons it was never put into effect by its sponsors. Two years later, in 1733, Patiño on his own initiative again brought the proposal forward, together with his own detailed plans for the operation of the new company. Nevertheless lack of support from the Andalusian merchants, who by that time were in even greater financial difficulties than previously, caused the project to founder again, much to Patiño's disgust. Moreover, there were reports that the merchants of Manila were opposed to the whole idea as they believed that privileges beneficial to the proposed company would inevitably be prejudicial to their own commercial freedom. In addition there were some spirited protests voiced via the diplomatic channel from English and Dutch commercial interests, which although impertinent were not inconsequential. In the event, more than half a century was yet to elapse before the Philippine Company was at last established in 1785.[23]

Another trading company founded during Patiño's ministry was that of Galicia in 1734. Its purpose was to take over the importation of dye-wood, which was used in Spain's reviving textile industry from the Campache region of Central America.[24] However, because of the strength of British establishments on the Honduras coast the company was unable to prosper and it soon went out of business.[25]

By 1728, then, Patiño seemed to be fairly clear in his own mind of the general lines along which he wished to develop his American trade policy, prior to the major reforms he contemplated at the expiration of the English assiento. Evidently there was also in Patiño's mind at this time the notion that he might already be able to take some immediate steps towards curbing Britain's encroachment into Spain's American markets and bringing to an end the impunity with which her diplomats supported her merchants. With such aims in view at the Congress of Soissons in June 1728 the Spaniards succeeded in buying the confidences of at least two South Sea Company officials.[26] The information these men sold about the illicit activities and contraband trade of the company was to provide useful material with which to counteract the vigorous diplomatic pressure exerted by the British in pursuance of their trading rights in Spanish America under the existing treaties. The Congress of Soissons, called by the French to sort out Spain's differences with the European powers (amongst them the affairs of the South Sea Company and her embargoed 'Annual Ship', the *Prince Frederick*) never in fact got beyond the banqueting table, and it was left to Patiño himself and Lord Stanhope, who went to Spain in person in October 1729, to hammer out in private at a country house near Seville an agreement between the two nations, which was formalised in the following month as the Treaty of Seville.[27] For the success of his negotiations Patiño was congratulated by the Crown and given the title of Councellor of State.[28] But his diplomatic efforts against the British did not end here. He continued to threaten the British ambassador, Benjamin Keene, that British shipping in Spanish-American waters would only be safe from Spanish guns while smuggling was not practised. He even held in abeyance full compliance with the treaty so long as the British misbehaved.[29] In 1732 when British frustration led to the capture by a man-of-war of a Spanish register ship as a reprisal, Patiño actually persuaded Keene that in order to avoid more serious troubles it would be a good idea for the South Sea Company to surrender altogether its right to send the 'Annual Ship' to the Indies at the time of the Spanish trade fairs. In exchange the Spanish Crown would hand over a two per cent yearly dividend on the total returns of the *galeones* and *flota* until such time as the Assiento Contract expired. A joint proposal from Patiño and Keene to this effect was duly dispatched to London, but it was angrily rejected by the Company, *as being financially inequable* – a not intangible measure, incidentally, of the value of trade, licit and illicit, carried on by means of the 'Annual Ship'.[30]

In the summer of 1729 the first *flota* after all these deliberations weighed anchor from Cadiz on its voyage to Veracruz. Because the Treaty of Seville settling the differences between England and Spain had not yet been negotiated no licence was given to the South Sea Company to send its 'Annual Ship' to the Spanish Indies.

9 Spain's American Trade, 1729-1733

I

On 9 August 1729 the first *flota* to New Spain for four years set sail from Cadiz under the command of the Marqués de Marí. It was composed of four warships and 16 merchantmen carrying between them the largest volume of goods to be sent to the Indies since the beginning of the century, 4882.23 tons.[1] Despite this high tonnage there can be no doubt that this was the most successful of the American fleets of the period. A number of circumstances combined to bring about for the first and only time the near fulfilment of Patiño's carefully laid plans and the royal orders intended to implement them. The *guardacosta* ships which had first gone out to the Caribbean in 1725 as a properly constituted force under the Conde de Clavijo had been doing a fairly good job of discouraging foreign interlopers, and the sporadic hostilities between Spain and the European nations had in any case tended to diminish this illegal trafficking.[2] Moreover, the South Sea Company with its 'Annual Ship', the *Prince Frederick*, impounded by the authorities in the port of Veracruz since 1725, had been anxious not to provoke the Spaniards by further controversial activities. The viceroy of New Spain, the Marqués de Casafuerte, had also been campaigning with determination over these years to prohibit the entry of illicit goods into the country, and all these factors eventually had the effect of producing a considerable dearth of European goods in New Spain by the time the next fleet was due to arrive from Cadiz, in the autumn of 1729.[3]

But an important element which contributed decisively to the successful outcome of the *flota* of 1729 was the wisdom and intelligence of the viceroy himself. Some time before the arrival of Marí's fleet the Marqués de Casafuerte received a royal order advising him that the *flota* was soon to leave Cadiz for New Spain and reminding him that under the provisions of the royal *cédula* of 2 April 1728 he was to arrange for its cargo to be sold in his viceroyalty by means of a fair at Jalapa. Casafuerte was already acquainted with the terms of the *cédula* and had immediately foreseen the problems which were likely to arise with the Mexican merchants, who were certain to consider the conditions to be observed as excessively favourable to the *flotistas* from Andalusia. He therefore set about modifying the Crown's regulations, seeking from his intimate knowledge of the situation to moderate the legislation and produce a compromise which would suit both the parties in the trade. The result of his deliberations was a detailed and extensive set of rules which when known in Spain was enthusiastically approved and in fact became the basis of all future trade fairs in New Spain.[4]

Essentially Casafuerte's amendments to the *cédula* were the result of the logical application of his practical experience. He decided that it was nonsense to wait for the whole of the cargo of a fleet to reach Jalapa before allowing trading to begin, when a simple system of enumeration, tallies and countersignatures for each of the packets transported would automatically exclude smuggled goods from the fair. Moreover, Casafuerte decreed, there were certain goods such as dried fruit, olives, wines and spirits, medicines and books which did not need to be sold under rigorous fair conditions, or might even perish as a result of excessive transportation or delay. These, he ordered, could be sold directly from the fleet either in Veracruz or anywhere else. The viceroy also considered it inadvisable to call together the merchants from both sides and force them to agree upon all prices before allowing business to begin at the fair. He therefore resolved that conventional trading could commence at Jalapa as soon as the first goods arrived there from the fleet and were cleared by the tally system. Thus he dispensed with the official price list and the ceremonial opening of the fair. The question of goods which remained unsold after the end of the fair, the thorniest problem of all, was resolved with characteristic practicality. The royal *cédula* of April 1728 wished to oblige the Mexican merchants to raise between them the money to buy all the left-overs from the fair. Alternatively the *flotistas* could entrust their remaining goods to individual Mexicans who would act as their agents. If either of these methods failed, then the Spaniards, as a last resort, were to be free to sell their goods as best they could throughout the viceroyalty.[5] Though intended by the Crown as a concession to the merchants of Mexico, obviously none of these procedures was very palatable to them. Casafuerte's solution was as follows. Instead of an official opening date for the fair there would be an official closing date, and this would necessarily coincide with the actual date of the departure of the *flota* on its return voyage to Spain. Until then all the goods in the fair, whether already purchased by the Mexicans or not, would remain, so to speak, 'in bond' at Jalapa. Consequently the merchants of Mexico would not be free to remove their goods and sell them to their own customers in the country until after the closure of the fair. Because of this restriction the merchants of Mexico would naturally be anxious to make their purchases at Jalapa as quickly as possible and at reasonable prices. In order to clear the stock and so bring the fair to an end they would also wish to buy in maximum quantities. In these circumstances the Spaniards too would be eager to sell quickly and at reasonable prices, because if they were stubbornly profit-conscious they would only succeed in holding up the departure of the fleet; indeed they would certainly sustain eventual losses, for in his orders Casafuerte absolutely forbade the *flotistas* to sell merchandise outside the confines of Jalapa *at any time*, even after the fleet had finally gone home. This last regulation of course specifically contradicted the provision of the royal *cédula* on this tricky matter; but it was precisely on account of that provision that the viceroy had anticipated trouble from the merchants of Mexico City. In the event both the Mexicans and the Spaniards welcomed the justice and equability of Casafuerte's ruling and accepted it as a good solution to a long-standing and bitter dispute.

So, with the activities of the English in Mexico temporarily suspended, Patiño's diplomatic success in not conceding the 'Annual Ship' for 1729,[6] other smuggling seriously curtailed, a shortage of European goods in the viceroyalty and a set of trading regulations acceptable by all the merchants concerned, everything was set for the celebration of the best American trade fair to be recorded in the first half of the eighteenth century.

Soon after the arrival of Marí's fleet in the port of Veracruz Casafuerte summoned the representatives of the Spanish *flotistas* to meet with him and the officers of the *consulado de comercio* of Mexico City. At that meeting he explained to both parties his reasons for modifying the provisions of the royal *cédula* and acquainted them fully with his revised set of rules under which the fair at Jalapa would be held. There was no point of dissent. At the fair itself the viceroy's regulations were observed to the letter and the local Crown officials who were given charge of the necessary administration turned out to be diligent and highly successful in their duties. Casafuerte had promised the merchants that he would attend the fair in person if needed in order to act as arbiter in any disputes that might occur. In fact the few minor problems that did arise were solved so easily that the viceroy's presence was never actually required, and he remained in his capital throughout the period of the fair. The mayor of Jalapa was permanently on hand to give assistance, and a detachment of dragoons from the Veracruz garrison also attended for the sake of general law and order and to prevent theft or fighting among the lower elements. The whole cargo of the fleet was sold without difficulty, and at the close of the fair Casafuerte was able to report to the Crown:

> the *flotistas* ought to be returning home content because the general feeling is that they have obtained advantages from the sale of their merchandise the like of which they have not known for many years past.[7]

The Jalapa fair of 1729 ran so smoothly and with so little controversy that from the historian's point of view it appears almost as a non-event. As such it was unique in the pattern of Spain's American trade in the eighteenth century, for never again were the merchant bodies of the New World to meet their counterparts from the Old in such mutually favourable circumstances.

II

On 26 January 1729 the viceroy of Peru, the Marqués de Castelfuerte, wrote to the Crown to say that in his opinion economic conditions in the viceroyalty would soon be right for the celebration of a rich and successful fair at Portobello. The severe measures he had been taking against smuggling in the Pacific had had the desired effect and there was every reason to suppose that the merchants of Lima would shortly have a large sum of money at their disposal for trading with *galeonistas* from Spain. Accordingly he recommended that the king should make plans for a fleet of *galeones* to set sail from Cadiz bound for Cartagena and Portobello six months after the date of the receipt of his letter. This news was greeted with satisfaction and optimism by both Crown and merchant classes in Spain.[8] Orders were promptly given for the assembly of a fleet in Cadiz and King Philip called upon that veteran of the *carrera de Indias*, General Manuel López Pintado, to look after the arrangements and take command of the *galeones* on their transatlantic voyage. The departure was originally fixed for the end of the year 1729, but preparations were continually delayed, not least by long runs of bad weather which prevented the loading operations from going ahead.[9] Eventually it was midsummer before all was ready, and, at long last, on 26 June 1730, the *galeones* finally left Cadiz. They consisted of 6 warships and 15 merchantmen carrying between them a total of 3962.06 tons of goods.[10] After a safe crossing lasting 40 days, the fleet dropped anchor in the bay of Cartagena de Indias on 8 August 1730.[11]

Following Patiño's further deliberations, López Pintado had been entrusted with a set of special instructions, and he was apparently given secret high authority by the Crown to carry them out. The precise terms of these instructions have not come to light, but from the commander's subsequent actions and his comments about his privilege it is not difficult to ascertain the general tenor of them.[12] One of the principal purposes of his mission was concerned with the maintenance, security and possible modification of the defenses of Cartegena and Portobello. To this was added the effective prosecution of abuses committed by the royal officials in the Caribbean ports in connection with smuggling activities. He was also instructed to cooperate as far as possible with the English Admiral Stewart to suppress piracy in the area.[13] Another important commission was to bring back into use the water route via the River Chagre for the transportation of goods and precious metals across the Isthmus of Panama, and to inquire into the possibility of constructing on a fresh site a new port on the Atlantic coast to replace that of Portobello. The defenses of Portobello were in considerable disrepair and the town was weakly placed strategically in times of war, as the British Admiral Hosier had amply demonstrated by his presence at the previous fair of 1726. For this last purpose López Pintado was given authority to levy an extra tax on the merchants at the fair so as to begin a building fund for work on the new port. In view of the recent discussions which Patiño had been holding about the conduct of the American trades, López Pintado was also ordered to consult closely with the representatives of the Lima merchants in order to discover their views at first hand on the best ways of reviving and regularising the trade of the *galeones*. He was to ask them how often the *galeones* should be sent and what tonnage of Spanish merchandise they would consider saleable at future Portobello fairs.[14] Finally the commander was given earnest instructions to make sure that a large quantity of cloth which he was carrying and which had been produced at the newly established royal factory at Guadalajara was sold to the best possible advantage. The Crown had particular interest in obtaining a good price for this, for not only was it participating itself with its own merchandise in the actual trade of the fair, but it was especially concerned to foster the growth of its own recent manufacturing enterprise.

As soon as López Pintado arrived in Cartagena he was greatly perturbed to discover that the royal officials there had arranged a time and place for a public auction of merchandise which had been captured by some roving *guardacostas* and brought into the port.[15] The law specifically forbade such a procedure and declared that prizes of this kind had to be kept under lock and key until they could be put on general sale together with the cargo of a fleet of *galeones*. Immediately a dispute broke out, and López Pintado was obliged to use his secret authority to overrule the insubordinate governor and officials. Cartagena had been well known to the Crown for many years as a particular point of corruption and illegality, and behaviour of this kind had been going on there to its knowledge since 1708.[16] The commander discovered a whole network of corruption in high places, and revealed to the Crown the existence of a secret company in Cartagena functioning in much the same way as that of the Marqués de Castelldosríus had done in the ports of the Pacific during the first decade of the century. López Pintado compared the set-up in Cartagena with that which had apparently existed until recently in Veracruz. It was also clear that the local *guardacostas*, under a certain Captain Justiniani, were actually neglecting the smuggling haunts along the coast so as to benefit the 'company' and were instead seeking out prizes on the high seas with which to supplement its supplies. Enraged by the affair López Pintado wrote to Patiño:

> I am sending you this news by special messenger so that if it reaches you you will know just what the royal officials in the Indies are like. I have often told you personally . . . that in these parts they neither recognize the King nor do they execute his orders, and even those who should most observe them take no account of them.[17]

Patiño replied by imposing the enormous fines of 44,000 *pesos* on the governor, 22,000 *pesos* on each of the royal officials and 2000 *pesos* on the official scribe for not making out the correct documents. López Pintado used his special authority to oblige the *guardacostas* to do their proper job and even sent his own warships to join them so as to keep an honest watch on the local coast-line.[18]

Despite Castelfuerte's optimism about the success of the forthcoming trade Patiño remained unconvinced of the willingness of the Lima merchants to go up to Portobello to trade at a fair. On their return to Lima after the events of 1726 the Peruvian merchant body had lodged strong protests with the Crown about the way its members had been treated by the president and royal officials of Panama, with whom of course they had traditionally had extremely poor relations. They alleged that on that occasion they had been forced to give bribes, pay trumped-up taxes on their way across the Isthmus and suffer the confiscation of property before they had been allowed to continue their journey home to Peru.[19] Following his conciliatory policy of the time towards American merchants, Patiño had accepted their complaints, removed the offending president, Don Manuel de Alderete, and replaced him with the Marqués de Villahermosa. The marquis and his subordinates were instructed henceforth not to interfere in any way with the passage of the Lima merchants through their jurisdiction, not to search their belongings nor open their packets of merchandise, and to collect only the specified taxes.[20] This of course gave the Peruvians a much freer rein than they had ever enjoyed previously, and, incidentally, facilitated contraband to them on the Isthmus. But on the other hand Patiño needed to foster their good will and cooperation in his anxiety to hold a successful trade fair in 1730. However, quite correctly anticipating the Peruvians' reluctance to trade with the *galeonistas*, even after such concessions, Patiño thought it prudent on this occasion to order Castelfuerte to send the *Armada del Sur* up to Panama immediately so as to have the treasure on the Isthmus already by the time the fleet arrived from Europe. He thus hoped to avoid the usual prolonged delays in dispatching the *Armada del Sur* and the consequent interminable and costly detention of the *galeones* in port at Cartagena.[21] Once the Lima merchants heard of the plan, in May 1730, they raised all kinds of objections. They pointed out that if for any reason the *galeones* were delayed it would be dangerous for them to wait around in Panama with large sums of money, for this would be to invite attack by pirates. Moreover, they protested, what if the *galeones* were captured or wrecked and never reached the Indies at all?[22] Although Castelfuerte remained firm in his resolve, and menaced the merchant body with having to pay itself the expense of delaying the departure of the *Armada del Sur*, he was eminently unsuccessful in his enterprise. There then began the familiar sequence of threats on the part of the viceroy and procrastination on the part of the merchants. Gradually Castelfuerte was obliged to resign himself to the intractability of the situation, and the merchants succeeded in delaying their departure for Panama for more than eight months.[23]

Apart from their growing desire to trade with whom and where they pleased, which Castelfuerte condemned on more than one occasion,[24] the merchants of Lima still had more lucrative business channels than that of the Portobello fair with its swingeing taxes and high prices, to say nothing of the perils and expense of the long journey to Panama. Castelfuerte had indeed exterminated the contraband trade along the coasts of his viceroyalty but he had not been able to stop the traffic in smuggled goods which came across the Andes from the River Plate, nor from the Caribbean down the River Magdalena in New Granada.[25] The South Sea Company was active wherever it could find a route, and especially now, under the cloak of the Spanish register ships to Buenos Aires, two of which had arrived in 1728-9 and provided cover for a fresh influx of English goods into Peru over the following two years.[26] There was also the semi-legal trade carried on sporadically between Peruvians and Mexicans by means of the Pacific sea route.[27] In these circumstances even a few months procrastination before leaving for Portobello was advantageous to the Lima merchants. Not only would it serve to drop the prices demanded by the *galeonistas*, anxious to return to Spain, but it would also play upon the nerves of the viceroy, who would be content to see rather less than a maximum sum of merchants' money embarked in the *Armada del Sur* in his eagerness to have the ships finally weigh anchor from Callao. On both accounts money would be saved for use in more favourable business dealings.

On 7 January 1731 the *Armada del Sur* set sail for Panama. It carried a good deal less treasure than had been anticipated, and although an extra ship was dispatched later, bearing a further million *pesos*, of the 14 million which eventually reached the Isthmus only nine million was available for trade with the *galeones*. The other five million consisted of money for the Crown and the Church, the salaries for garrisons and Crown officials, and private sums sent to Spain in payment of debts or as advances on specific goods.[28]

Having received news of the sailing of the fleet from Peru, on 26 January López Pintado escorted the *galeones* out of Cartagena, and two days later they reached Portobello. After employing his men for the next 10 days on necessary building works on the wharf of the port the commander then set about having the ships unloaded in readiness for the fair. Within a few days, on 10 February, there arrived in Portobello the South Sea Company's 'Annual Ship', the *Prince William*.[29] Despite Patiño's diplomatic manoeuvres with the English he had been unable to wriggle out of issuing a *cédula* for the ship in 1730, although at the time it was rumoured that he had succeeded in outsmarting the English over the Portobello ship just as he had done over the Veracruz ship the year before.[30] As soon as the *Prince William* docked in Portobello López Pintado went to work on the English officers, checking their papers closely and warning them that they would not get away with any smuggling nor even the slightest evasion of the terms of their assiento. He even reported that he had actually obtained their agreement not to sell their merchandise at the fair at cheaper prices than those stipulated by the Spanish *galeonistas*![31] Such naïveté seems incredible. The *Prince William* had already taken on tons of extra cargo beyond what was permitted before she reached Portobello, and the English were certainly not prepared to yield their commercial advantage over the prices of the Spanish goods.[32]

Six days later, on 16 February, the *Armada del Sur* reached Panama. López Pintado was greatly dismayed by news of the small amount of treasure which it brought for use at the fair, and he was even further disturbed by rumours emanating from the Peruvians themselves that the *galeonistas* were sure to have a great deal of unsold cargo left on their hands after the fair had closed.[33] He immediately got in touch with the representatives of the Lima *consulado* and told them of the royal order directing them to ship their treasure and goods by the water route, via the River Chagre and then by sea to Portobello, under convoy of his warships. The advantage of this route was that it represented a saving of several weeks in the time taken for the complete transport operation. The Peruvians, anxious as always to waste the *galeonistas'* time for their own commercial advantage, refused outright, alleging that they had already contracted muleteers for the journey overland. So began the first of a prolonged series of tempestuous quarrels destined to ruin the fair of 1731. In the end, by having recourse to his secret authority, López Pintado was able to have his way. After imposing upon him very rigorous terms for their military and naval escort the Peruvians eventually reached Portobello by the water route. The commander was later proud to report that the operation had been completed in record time, thus saving both *galeonistas* and the Crown considerable expense.[34]

In the meantime López Pintado had already begun negotiations with the senior members of the Lima consulado, who were by now in Portobello, about the contribution of half a per cent of the value of the treasure they had brought with them to a building fund for the proposed new fort and harbour of San Cristóbal, which were to replace those of old Portobello. After protests, excuses and attempts to share the burden with the Church and other parties, the Lima *consulado* was reluctantly forced to hand over 55,000 *pesos*, and in due course the commander was pleased to be able to send a sum of 87,000 *pesos* into the safe-keeping of the president of Panama as an initial payment towards the building costs.[35] His efforts in fact were in vain, for over the coming years no positive steps were ever taken to begin work on the projected new port.

The next matter upon which López Pintado had to consult the Lima *consulado* was that of future policy with regard to the trade of the *galeones* – how often they should sail and with what tonnage of merchandise. Far from being able to ascertain the views of the merchants on this matter, as the Crown had requested, he was once again faced with a total lack of cooperation. The Peruvians refused to commit themselves on the grounds that all the merchants of the viceroyalty would need to be consulted since all had a direct interest in 'this grave and important matter'. Those present at the fair could on no account make recommendations on behalf of their absent colleagues, and they argued that over the coming two years the *consulado* would have time to conduct a meaningful enquiry throughout its membership. Meanwhile,

> they were satisfied that the mercy of His Majesty would never force them into impossible [commercial transactions] . . . and although the obedience to which all were resigned obliged them to defer to even the slightest insinuation of their sovereign with the utmost fidelity, to comply at the present time would only produce opinions which had no value or effect . . . and which could be the cause of infinite disputes in the future.[36]

Once the treasure and the main body of Peruvian merchants had arrived in Portobello the representatives of the *galeonistas* and those of the Lima *consulado* settled down aboard the commander's flagship to the usual series of meetings to discuss the business of the fair in general and the vexed question of prices in particular. They were of course presided over by López Pintado. However, despite several days of hard discussions, it was clear that no agreement would be reached. The value of the tonnage of merchandise brought by the *galeones* simply exceeded that of the treasure available for its purchase. The lists of prices offered by the Peruvians differed so greatly from those of the *galeonistas* that compromise was impossible. The main stumbling-block was the extremely high prices which the commander, as the king's agent, demanded for the large cargo of cloth shipped from the Crown's factory at Guadalajara. Carrying out his instructions to the letter he insisted that the royal cloth should be sold before any other merchandise at the fair and that its prices would not be subject to discussion nor even to existing market forces. The Peruvians of course could not agree to such conditions, maintaining that not only were the prices exhorbitant and the volume excessive, but that the cloth itself was of mediocre quality and the colours in bad taste. López Pintado on the other hand was convinced that the low prices offered in general by the Lima merchants resulted from their bad faith and that their refusal to buy the king's cloth was nothing short of disloyalty. Once again tempers flared in Portobello. Eventually after much private deliberation the Peruvians decided to offer the Crown a present of 30,000 *pesos* in exchange for not having to take the royal cloth which they considered could bring them nothing but trouble and losses when they tried to sell it in Peru. López Pintado and the president of Panama, who had by now been drawn into the affair, were much incensed by this proposition, and replied by placing the head of the Peruvian deputation, Don José Nieto de Lara, and the other senior representatives under house arrest and threatening them and all their colleagues with sizeable fines. Immediately the Peruvians were forced to yield, but not without serious consequences for the trade of the *galeonistas* and for future relations between the Lima merchants and the Crown.[37]

While these disputes were in progress, and in order to prevent avoidable delay, López Pintado had been obliged to allow normal trading at the fair to proceed on the basis of bargaining and haggling, and a small amount of business had been done between *galeonistas* and Lima merchants. But naturally the Peruvians had given their attention primarily to the English 'Annual Ship' which had succeeded in selling the whole of its cargo, comprising large quantities of both legal and illegal merchandise. Either because he was so involved in his zealous pursuit of the Peruvians or, more likely, perhaps because he had received a large sum of money as a bribe from the English, López Pintado failed to measure the cargo of the *Prince William*, and once again the South Sea Company was able to dispose of many more tons of merchandise than those permitted under the terms of its assiento.[38] Not only did the English fail to maintain their prices up to the level of the Spanish prices at the fair, as they had promised López Pintado, but they actually reduced them by 10 per cent in comparison with those of previous 'Annual Ships', in recognition of the shortfall in the treasure from Peru. They quickly sold nearly 1000 tons of goods and contracted to transport large sums of money to Europe for private persons (under their famous all-risks insurance scheme). Thus they succeeded in carrying off up to half of the nine million *pesos* which had been brought for trade at the fair.[39] As soon as it was known that official coercion would oblige the Peruvians to buy the royal cloth in its entirety, and at unreasonable prices, all trading with the ordinary *galeonistas* came to an absolute halt. Thanks to transactions already completed there was now not enough treasure on hand to purchase all the king's cloth and raise any further cargo from the *galeones*, no matter how low the prices of the latter fell. The situation for the *galeonistas* at the fair thus became desperate. One of them, Don Gerónimo de Balsagón, it is reported, had been so affected by the English presence that he had 'died a sudden death'![40] But by now López Pintado was most anxious to return to Spain with what remained of the treasure so as to avoid further costly delays and in order to be able to explain fully the state of affairs personally to the Crown.[41] Therefore he commanded the Lima merchants to accept the king's cloth and hand over their money without more ado. To comply with his orders the Peruvians found themselves obliged to make complicated financial arrangements with each other, lending and borrowing money to make up the total sum demanded. They decided that their only course was to remove the cloth in bulk in the name of the *consulado* and attempt to sort out their finances and their proportional shares of the cloth on their return to Lima.[42] There was now not the remotest chance of any further business being done with the *galeonistas* who were thus stranded with the majority of their wares unsold when López Pintado set sail for Spain with all the treasure he could gather on 14 June 1731.[43]

If the actions of the commander, backed by the authority of the president of Panama, appear to have been precipitate and overbearing, they were on no account the result of mere petulance and sheer officiousness. From the outset it had been clear to López Pintado that the nine million *pesos* of treasure brought by the *Armada del Sur* would be quite insufficient to raise the cargo of the *galeones*. Moreover, from the uncooperative attitude of the Lima merchants and the eager way in which they had rushed to buy the English cargo, it was obvious that, come what may, the Spanish merchants, including on this occasion the Crown itself, would be certain to sustain an enormous financial loss. A simple arithmetical calculation made this conclusion inevitable. In these circumstances López Pintado's actions were entirely logical – force the sale of the Crown cloth at the required price, thus assuring profit for the nascent cloth industry in Spain, and thereby also laying hands on an optimum amount of the treasure before it could be spirited away into further illegal transactions with the English. His objective was simply to avoid continuing losses in this impossible situation by acting swiftly and with determination.

As early as 14 May López Pintado had realised the futility of attempting any longer to agree prices with the Peruvians, and on that day, before a notary, he set out formal arrangements for the relief of the *galeonistas* whose eventual plight he could already foresee plainly.[44] By this document, in which he exceeded his own authority, he gave the *galeonistas* permission to leave Portobello after his departure for Spain and to establish themselves with their unsold cargoes in Panama City. At the same time the viceroy of Peru was requested to send more merchants with more treasure to buy up the merchandise, and provisions were made for the celebration of a continuous fair at Panama. As soon as these arrangements were formalised the commander sent off one of his frigates back to Spain informing the Crown of the impossible and unprecedented circumstances, and passing on the *galeonistas'* own request to be allowed to travel where and as they wished throughout the Empire, selling off their goods to whatever buyers they could find.[45] Having made these emergency plans López Pintado considered it his duty to coerce the Peruvians into buying the royal cloth and hurry back to Spain himself to consult with the Crown. In fact his return was much longer delayed than he ever expected, for like many a sailor before him he was hit by a fierce hurricane in the Bahama Channel and his ship was so badly damaged that extensive repairs had to be carried out in Puerto Rico. He did not finally reach Cadiz until over a year later, on 21 June 1732.[46]

When Castelfuerte heard of López Pintado's dispositions for the establishment of the *galeonistas* in Panama and the continuance of piecemeal trading between Lima and Panama, he became very worried.[47] He was well aware that the repeated movement of ships with money and goods up and down the Pacific coast-line would soon revive all the contraband activities and the illegal exportation of precious metals which he had done so much to eradicate over the previous decade. What would now be simpler for the Lima merchants than to allege that both outgoing silver and incoming goods formed part of the trading with the *galeonistas*, when in fact, under this cover, trade could be carried on with anyone almost anywhere, especially in view of the concessions the Peruvians had won from the Crown virtually prohibiting the president of Panama to interfere in their affairs at all? Moreover, precisely at that time, Castelfuerte was himself again involved with the Crown in heated correspondence over the need to clamp down hard upon the increasing independence and impertinence of the Lima merchant body.[48] The viceroy decided to consult on the matter with members of the *consulado* who had remained in Lima. They naturally opposed López Pintado's arrangements, being embarrassed by the continuing presence of the *galeonistas* in Panama and the consequent obligation upon themselves. Hypocritically agreeing with the viceroy about the dangers of renewed contraband, and protesting that in any case there was no more money in the country with which to trade at Panama, they proposed that López Pintado's plan should be allowed to run for a period of four months only, after which time all merchandise from the *galeones* found in transit should be confiscated by the authorities. As it was impossible for any further trading to be done within such a short time, this proposal was clearly aimed solely at removing their own obligations to buy from the *galeonistas* while at the same time clearing the tiresome residue of Spanish goods from the market once and for all, and at no expense to themselves. Castelfuerte saw that this was not a just solution and therefore resolved that for a period of one year, starting from 14 June 1731, the date of López Pintado's departure, any Peruvian merchant would be free to go to trade at Panama and any *galeonista* would be free to travel to Lima, or any other part of the viceroyalty, to sell his goods as best he could. Because of the dangers of smuggling, after 14 June 1732 any merchandise still in transit would be confiscated.

No sooner was this resolution put into practice than it was superseded by a royal *cédula* from Philip V dated 9 November 1731.[49] Although López Pintado himself had been unable to reach Spain as planned, his frigate, commanded by Don Luis Lozano, bearing the *galeonistas'* request to be allowed complete freedom of action, had indeed arrived there safely. So too had the commander's own dispatches sent in various ships during the summer of 1731.[50] Immediately realising the dangers of the situation Patiño, the author of the royal *cédula*, decided to follow the recommendations of López Pintado and granted the permission sought by the desperate Spaniards in Panama. Thus, by the *cédula*, the *galeonistas* were given the right to travel freely throughout the whole of South America to sell their goods; and all Crown officials were strictly instructed not to interfere in the least with their movements or their business activities. All the traditional restrictive laws were temporarily suspended and the merchandise was declared free of duty and sales tax (*alcabala*) once it had left Portobello. In this remarkable document the Crown openly admitted that if these unprecedented measures were not taken the ruination of the Andalusian trades would be inevitable and many years would have to elapse before there could again be any question of sending the next fleet of *galeones* to Tierra Firme.

Soon after the *galeonistas* received this royal licence they set about their daunting enterprise. Some moved off into the interior of New Granada, to Popayán, Santa Fe de Bogotá and Quito, where the royal *cédula* specifically encouraged them to go. Others eventually decided to travel down to Lima where they hoped to compete advantageously with their Peruvian rivals, who still had a proportion of their capital tied up in the expensive Crown cloth. Once they reached Lima serious disputes naturally began to break out between the two bodies of merchants, and in 1734 the Spaniards resolved to set up their own *consulado de comercio* to protect their interests in the face of the hostility of the Peruvians. Finally Castelfuerte, realising the likelihood of further trouble between the two groups, found it necessary to step in and forbid the *galeonistas* to form a rival body.[51] Thus the victory of the Lima merchants was assured and the Spaniards were forced to continue their impossible task without the official help or protection of the viceregal government. Indeed, over the months, the situation had steadily been worsening for them, for the South Sea Company, taking advantage of the unprecedented opening of the ports for the benefit of the *galeonistas*, had used every possible ruse and device to put further quantities of illegal merchandise through their 'factories' and out on to the colonial markets.[52] Failing in their unachievable objectives, many of the *galeonistas* were totally ruined, the majority sustained enormous losses, and a number even ended their lives transporting their unwanted wares along the jungle trails of the interior of New Granada. Over the coming years they made their dejected way in a gradual trickle back to the Atlantic ports, and it was not until five years later that the last of them were able to return to Spain, ruined and broken men, in a *guardacosta* ship which left Cartagena in 1737.[53]

III

Encouraged by the success of the Jalapa fair of 1729 even more than he was yet disturbed by the events in Portobello in 1731, Patiño considered it would be advantageous to trading to send the next *flota* to New Spain as soon as it could be made ready. Command of the fleet was given to Don Rodrigo de Torres, and, consisting of 4 warships and 16 merchantmen, one belonging to the Crown itself, the *flota* left Cadiz on 2 August 1732.[54] Between them the ships carried 4659.06 tons of merchandise[55] for sale at a fair to be held in Jalapa under the same skilful regulations as those drafted by the Marqués de Casafuerte for the previous fair of 1729. But success was not to crown the viceroy's

efforts in the same way for a second time. When he received advice of
the volume of goods which the fleet was bringing, Casafuerte's
apprehensions began to grow.[56] The country was still well provisioned
with the record cargo of the previous fleet, together with that of the
Manila galleon, and the viceroy could not see how the market would
stand further stocking. His fears were even more aroused by the news
that the South Sea Company had been granted a *cédula* to send its
'Annual Ship' to Veracruz in 1732, the absence of which in 1729 had of
course greatly contributed to the happy outcome of the fair in that year.
Indeed events in Mexico in 1732-3 were to show conclusively just to
what extent the 'Annual Ship' was responsible for the ineffectiveness
and frustration of the best of Spanish legislation to recover and regulate
the American trades. While the fair of 1729, at which no 'Annual Ship'
was present, had proved most satisfactory, that of 1732 resurrected all
the problems and conflicts between Mexicans and Spaniards which
Patiño had been attempting to resolve for a decade or more. The
reappearance of the English 'Annual Ship' in 1732 was unquestionably
a prime cause of this deterioration.

On 24 November 1732 Casafuerte published his orders for the
holding of the trade fair.[57] Soon afterwards the trains of pack animals
began the business of transporting the cargo of the fleet, at anchor in
Veracruz, overland to Jalapa, and the *flotistas* and Mexican merchants
began the process of offers and counter-offers which Casafuerte had
decreed would replace the official price-fixing as practised at
Portobello. But agreements proved hard to reach and even by January
1733 no significant headway had yet been made.[58] The reasons were
simple. In conditions of well stocked markets the Mexicans naturally
wished to strike harsh bargains; but there was another factor also.
Whereas by Casafuerte's rules all the *flota*'s merchandise was
imprisoned in Jalapa until the termination of the fair, the cargo of the
English *Royal Caroline* was quite free to be removed from the port of
Veracruz. Not only were the English goods so much cheaper than those
at Jalapa, but Casafuerte's restriction on the movement of the Spanish
goods actually gave the English further commercial advantage.
Merchants, both large and small, thronged the harbour at Veracruz to
buy from the *Royal Caroline*, and the situation *de facto* became that which
was provided for by Bubb's Treaty of 1716, namely that if the Spanish
fleet was not in port within the specified time the South Sea Company
would have unrestricted freedom to sell its merchandise to the colonial
merchants.[59] Paradoxically, then, Casafuerte's dextrous regulations
had led to the pass most feared by Patiño and which indeed had

prompted the legislation of the *Real proyecto* of 1720 – the English right of legal access to the markets of the colonies without competition from a Spanish fleet!

Although Casafuerte, for obvious reasons, wished to keep his regulations intact, the protracted discussions and the lack of agreement at Jalapa, originating mainly from the situation described, eventually forced him to give way on the most basic of his rules – the restriction of movement of merchandise from the fair, whether sold or not. By an order of 22 January 1733, he lifted this prohibition and thereby returned the trading to the state of affairs which had caused all the earlier conflicts between the interests of the *flotistas*, the large Mexican merchants and the smaller country merchants.[60] The raising of this restriction favoured the small merchant who could not afford to leave capital tied up in goods 'frozen' at Jalapa. Consequently trading began between *flotistas* and a number of small merchants who were prepared to pay high prices to the Spaniards for a few packets of merchandise which they could then put on sale directly to their own customers. In fact they probably had to pay less to the Spaniards than they would eventually have done to the large city middlemen who would otherwise have been their normal source of supply. By mid-March some two million *pesos*' worth of the cargo had been sold in this way, which although a small volume in relation to the whole was enough to annoy the larger merchants. They too then began to buy, until eventually goods to the value of about 15 million *pesos* changed hands at the fair. But after this, trading came to a halt. When Casafuerte closed the fair and the fleet set sail again, on 25 May 1733, there remained in Jalapa a number of disappointed *flotistas* with unsold cargo worth about seven million *pesos*.[61]

At this point there arose again, and inevitably, the question of what would happen to this sizeable residue of merchandise. Casafuerte's rules obliged it to remain in Jalapa even after the end of the fair, and to make matters worse, once the fair was over the *flotistas*' further sales became liable to tax (*alcabala*). The merchants of Mexico were thus given commercial advantages which they had never dreamt possible before: they had a constant source of supply for Spanish goods, legally trapped in Jalapa; they had no need to invest capital in their purchase, for they could be bought and paid for as required; they were in an unbeatable position as regards bargaining for prices; and they could even rely upon a contribution from the *flotistas* towards the payment of the *alcabala* which they farmed on the Crown's behalf. As was only natural, the Spaniards protested vigorously about their situation to both the viceroy himself and to the Crown in Spain. The *consulado* of Cadiz also joined in the chorus.[62] However since Casafuerte had been the author of the new regulations, Patiño deemed it only right that he should be the author also of the solution of the problem, and left the matter entirely in his hands.[63]

Casafuerte decided he must take the bull by the horns. He warned the *flotistas* that if they wished to continue holding trade fairs in New Spain they would have to resign themselves to the present conditions; if, on the other hand, they preferred in future to go back to the old system of taking their goods for general sale in Mexico City and submitting themselves again to the notorious 'commercial blackmail', he would give them freedom to leave Jalapa. It was correctly pointed out that once the Mexicans realised that goods remaining after a fair could be sold off around the country by the *flotistas* themselves there would be no hope ever again of getting them to attend a trade fair. The only possible way of continuing a fair at Jalapa for the future was by guaranteeing to the merchants of Mexico the *absolute monopoly* of sales of goods from the fleet throughout the whole of the viceroyalty. With utmost reluctance both *flotistas* and commercial interests in Spain had to agree that characteristically Casafuerte had touched upon the heart of the matter. After all, since it was the Spaniards who wanted the trade fair there was no sense in ruining its prospects for the coming years by endeavouring in the short term to save a few million *pesos*.[64] In March 1734 Casafuerte died. The stranded *flotistas* immediately tried to wheedle minor concessions out of his successor, Archbishop Vizarrón, but rather to their surprise he too appreciated the gravity of the consequences of yielding, and refused to give an inch.[65] The victory of the New Spain merchants was thus complete.[66]

The Jalapa fair of 1732-3, then, turned out to be a qualified disaster, although it was nothing compared with the full-scale calamity which had occurred in Portobello the year before. On both occasions the English 'Annual Ships' had played significant roles. While *galeonistas* were roving round South America with unwanted goods, and *flotistas* were trapped in Jalapa as victims of their Mexican consumers,

the *Prince William* in 1730 [did quite well], and according to the accounts [of the South Sea Company, the profits of] the *Royal Caroline* in 1732, beat all records.[67]

Nor was the fate of the *flotistas* who sailed homeward with the fleet in

1733 to be envied, for like López Pintado before him, Rodrigo de Torres was also hit by a hurricane in the Bahama Channel, and there was much loss of life and property.[68] Luckily for the royal treasury and the Andalusian merchants a Crown-financed diving expedition in 1734 succeeded in bringing home most of the treasure.[69]

Fortune was certainly not smiling upon Spain's transatlantic ventures. It was now time again for Patiño to deliberate what measures he could possibly introduce to prevent ruination from overtaking the whole of the American trades.

10   The Continuing Crisis, 1734–1740

I

It is evident that although Patiño was the Crown's chief minister and primarily responsible for the conduct of the American trades he was by no means the only person to be deeply concerned by the serious condition into which they had fallen. Apart from the Spanish merchants themselves and their trading partners in Lima and Mexico, all of whom were writing to the Crown protesting, condemning, or pleading, the viceroys of Peru and New Spain were also informing Patiño of the hopeless morass in which the colonial trades had become immobilized. Casafuerte in Mexico, and Castelfuerte in Peru were of course in the best positions to appreciate, and indeed sympathise, with *both* the conflicting sides in the continuing commercial struggle. Their many words on these matters reveal their true understanding of the impossibility of making a system work in conditions that simply would not support it. Perhaps Castelfuerte expressed the dilemma most succinctly when he wrote, '. . . for he who purchases cannot be given the blame for the seller's cloth being too dear'.[1]

Both viceroys saw the only solution, if the system was to survive, in terms of imposing controls and obligations upon the merchant bodies in ways that they would be unable to resist. Realising its own weakness and, if López Pintado's opinions were given an ear, possibly fearing political repercussions too, the Crown itself preferred to keep silent on this matter.[2] Casafuerte had been required to use his own authority at Jalapa, and in allowing no concessions to the *flotistas* it was he who had brought them hardship, humiliation and losses and not the Crown directly. Castelfuerte, the more authoritarian of the two, had twice been unable to force the measures he proposed on the Peruvians because the Council of the Indies, in its fear of further alienating the Lima body, had told him yet again, 'commerce is a free practice and there are already enough restrictions'.[3]

193

Preoccupation with the Indies trade had by now also started to extend well beyond the sphere of those immediately concerned in it, and economic theorists of the time were increasingly putting their ideas into print. The great treatise of Gerónimo de Uztáriz, *Theórica y práctica de comercio y marina* . . . , had initiated the process, appearing as it did in 1724 in the wake of the commercial legislation of the twenties, and this work was highly regarded by a generation of economic thinkers.[4] However, soon after, in 1731, the Marqués de Villadarias, differing from Uztáriz's principles, published a 'Proyecto para una Compañía General de las Indias Españolas', the essence of which was that

> there ought to be established a Company board based on Mexico, with a higher authority in Spain, composed of businessmen and also of experts in sea and land warfare and in politics and the law, and also two smaller councils, subsidiaries of Mexico, in Peru and Chile.[5]

The Marqués de Santa Cruz de Marcenado included this in his *Rapsodia económica-política-monárquica* of 1732 together with his own 'Comercio suelto y en compañía general y particular en México, Perú, Filipinas y Moscou'. Also following this line, and realising the ineffectiveness of the *galeones* and *flota* as a viable trading system, Miguel de Zavala y Auñón produced in the same year, 1732, a *Representación al Rey N. S. Felipe V, dirigida al más seguro aumento del real erario*. . . Prompted by the worsening situation of the 1730s there appeared in 1740 Bernardo de Ulloa's lengthy analysis, *Restablecimiento de las fábricas y comercio español. Errores que se padecen en las causas de su decadencia, cuáles son los legítimos obstáculos que le destruyen y los medios eficaces de que florezca*. Three years later, in 1743, José Campillo y Cossío, a successor of Patiño as Philip's minister, was preparing his famous *Nuevo sistema de gobierno económico para la América, con los males y daños que le causa el que hoy tiene*. . . . Although this work was not to reach the press until 1789 under its own author and title, it is important to note that the second part of Bernardo Ward's celebrated *Proyecto económico* . . . of 1779, the part which deals with American matters, is essentially the work of Campillo y Cossío and was drafted before 1744, the year of Campillo's death.[6] A fair number of other less significant pieces of economic literature were also produced over this decade and a half, most of which circulated in manuscript form.[7]

As we have seen, Patiño was quite prepared to encourage experimentation with the idea of the trading company, but, following Uztáriz, he remained unconvinced that it could yet replace the traditional system as an acceptable alternative on a major scale. Whether the large company was what was eventually required or not, the diplomatic and financial policies of the Crown made such a change hazardous for the present. The magic date of 1744 and the end of the English assiento still seemed to be the earliest possible moment for major reform. Nevertheless the current critical state of the Indies trade made some sort of review urgent.

As soon as Patiño was fully informed of developments at Portobello in 1731 he decided that he should meet with the Peruvians himself in order to clarify the issues properly. On 30 October 1731, he wrote to Castelfuerte in the name of the Crown requiring the *consulado* of Lima to elect two delegates to come immediately to Spain to confer with him. However the disaffection of the Peruvians even extended to disobeying this order, and they maintained that in the aftermath of the fair of 1731 there was nothing they could profitably discuss with Patiño. But Castelfuerte used his viceregal authority to insist that they should proceed to elect delegates as ordered. After a month's delay, two of their number eventually agreed to go to see Patiño on the *consulado*'s behalf, and after much procrastination they set off. One of the two, Don José de Conderena, died in Panama, and the other, Don Juan de Berria, did not reach Spain until the end of 1733, more than two years after the Crown had required them to journey to Spain *immediately*.[8]

By the time Berria arrived in Spain Patiño knew not only of the disaster in Portobello in 1731, but also of the troubles in Jalapa in 1733. Consequently in April 1734 he summoned together a much enlarged commission of experts to discuss yet again the whole basis for the future conduct of all the American trades.[9] This was composed of General Manuel López Pintado, as a special adviser, his brother, Don José López Pintado, *Cónsul de la Universidad de cargadores a Indias* and elected representative of the Spanish merchants, Don Juan de Berria, representing the merchants of Peru, and 'ministers of integrity, devotion and experience' amongst whom must be numbered some of the new generation of theorists. For several months this group followed Patiño and the court debating the grave issues.[10] As a result of their deliberations, on 21 January 1735, there appeared the *Real Cédula sobre el despacho de galeones y flotas, y método de comerciar los residentes en Indias con España*.[11] It begins:

The King: inasmuch as experience has shown that the just and multiple measures applied at all times for the benefit of trade, both that with Peru, Tierra Firme and the other provinces of those

possessions and that with the kingdom of New Spain and the Windward Isles, have not been sufficient to remedy the abuses of the
dishonest, nor the illicit trafficking which has been practised in those
places, nor to establish the trading and intercourse in which fleets of
galeones and *flotas* may go and return with the regularity which my
Royal interests require, redounding to the benefit of the merchant
bodies here and in the Indies; wishing to find the remedy, which is so
important, and to avoid the great delays which until now have been
experienced, . . . and informed of all that which has been placed in
my Royal cognizance on this important matter, I have resolved the
following. . .

The *cédula* continues with nine sections setting out the new regulations.

The first three sections deal with the trade to Peru. It will be remembered that López Pintado had been ordered to find out from the Lima
merchants how often they considered the *galeones* should be sent to
Portobello and that they had refused to commit themselves on the
matter. Castelfuerte in the meanwhile had been making these enquires,
and his findings were on hand to Patiño's group. On 9 October 1731,
the merchants in Lima had held a meeting at which they declared that

it has never been possible to make a fixed rule which could balance
the amount of money taken [to the fair] from Lima against the merchandise brought from Spain, and the latter has always been the
greater. This imbalance has been due primarily to the mistaken idea
which the Spanish merchants have about the inexhaustible supply of
gold and silver from this Kingdom.[12]

It was certainly true that for a variety of reasons the production of
precious metals in Peru was on the decline,[13] and it was felt that the
best way of establishing the frequency with which the *galeones* should be
sent was by relating it directly to the output of the mines. Castelfuerte
summed up the conclusions:

In present times . . . the shortest interval to which the *galeones* can be
reduced is triennial, because as is well known the product of the
Kingdom only reaches four millions [annually], three of them in
silver and one in gold, of which there remain only three for business
dealings after Crown expenses and payments to Spain have been
deducted. Thus an interval of three years is necessary before another
fair can be held in Portobello (leaving aside three millions more

which New Granada produces), to which consideration there must be added the logical saving in the cost of the *galeones*, for if in a period of twelve years there were to come six sets of *galeones* there should only come four, and conversely if they came every two years [as under existing regulations] the treasure would be small and the expenses high. Given that this is so, it is declared that in order to regularize the trade fleets the route which leads from the Upper Provinces to Buenos Aires must be closed, as must that which leads from Portobello to England: in this way order will follow naturally, without the need of coercion. That these large fleets were formerly sent every two years was because the regular profit from shipments at this interval came from the opulence of the Kingdom and its high expenditure. This today is impossible because production in Peru has fallen while the amount of treasure that is removed has increased.[14]

Despite Castelfuerte's recommendations, which were those proposed by Berria also, Patiño's commission was not prepared to accept as a norm that the *galeones* should sail only once in every three years and exporting then no more than 12 million *pesos'* worth of goods – three millions for Cartagena and nine millions for Portobello. This would be in effect to limit Spain's trade with her glittering viceroyalty to a paltry four million *pesos* per year. In the first section of the *cédula* of January 1735 the Crown therefore legislates on the question of the frequency of sailings in such a way that is apparently conciliatory to the Peruvians but yet does not commit the Crown to any fixed or limiting schedule. Enforced cooperation and rational planning are the two means by which Patiño hopes in future to secure the optimum of trade with Peru. For the present, the *cédula* states, *galeones* to Tierra Firme are suspended altogether, until such time as trustworthy news arrives confirming that the residue of the fair of 1731 has been consumed completely. However, it is declared, if in the meantime it seems worth-while sending register ships to Cartagena they may sail; also if news comes in from the viceroy of Peru, the *consulado* of Lima and the representatives of the *galeonistas* in Lima that the markets there could take more goods, register ships or *galeones* may be sent to Portobello too. In this latter case it will be incumbent upon the Peruvian merchants to consult with the Crown, via their representatives in Spain, in order to decide upon the tonnage of merchandise to be shipped and the date of departure of the fleet. At the discretion of the Crown the merchants of Andalusia may also be brought into the discussions. In the second section of the *cédula* the

Crown again insists (as it had done in 1730) that the *Armada del Sur* should arrive in Panama at the same time as future fleets of *galeones* reach Cartagena. To meet the Peruvians' former objection that the *galeones* might be delayed or wrecked, an elaborate system of *aviso* ships is to be established, first to collect and bring back commercial information to Spain about the markets of Peru, then to take news, seven months ahead, of the sailing of the fleet, and finally to confirm its departure from Cadiz. This procedure, it is hoped, will 'encourage' the merchants of Lima and considerably speed up the round trip of the *galeones*. In the third section, recognising the serious consequences for trade of the falling output of precious metals from the mines of Peru, the Crown declares that in that viceroyalty the tax of one fifth on the product of the silver mines (the *real quinto*) will be dropped to one tenth, and that on gold mines to one twentieth.

In the fourth section of the *cédula* the Crown touches upon a matter which had increasingly been troubling the merchants of Spain. There had never existed any law prohibiting colonial merchants from sending money back to Spain in one fleet for the purchase of specific merchandise to be transported in the next. Indeed most of the money which the English took in the 'Annual Ships' under their 'all-risks' insurance policy was remitted for this purpose. Naturally the procedure was resented by the *flotistas* and *galeonistas*, the volume of whose trade at a fair was affected in consequence. Moreover, the setting aside of money at a fair for shipment to Spain obviously reduced the sum available for current trading, and the prices of the Spanish merchandise on sale were thereby lowered. By the 1730s as much as a quarter or one third of the tonnage of the fleets was taken up by goods purchased directly in Spain by this method. The fleet merchants, as middlemen, were thus excluded from this business in much the same way as the large Mexican merchants complained they were cut out by the country merchants when these traded directly with the *flotistas*! The representative of the *consulado* of Cadiz was most diligent in bringing this matter up for discussion at the meetings of Patiño's commission, and it was thanks to him that the fourth section of the *cédula* was approved.[15] In it the Crown declares that henceforth colonial merchants will not be permitted to send money to Spain for purely commercial purposes, nor will fleet merchants be allowed to transport goods away from the trade fairs in order to serve them to merchants resident in other places. Punishments and fines are threatened to all those who attempt to evade this prohibition.

In fact once this order was known of in the Indies a storm of protest arose, and further disputes between American and Spanish merchants broke out. Eventually the Crown was forced to retreat and a second royal *cédula* of 20 November 1738 rescinded this fourth section of the *cédula* of January 1735, although it strictly limited the colonial merchants to making their advanced purchases only via registered business houses in Cadiz involved in the Indies trade. Still not content with this the Americans demanded total freedom to send their money to Spain to buy whatever they wished from whomever they chose, and to have their goods shipped to them in a fleet or register ship without interference by the Crown or the merchant bodies in Spain. For more than a decade this matter was a cause of contention between the merchants of the New World and the Old. Finally the Crown was obliged to yield yet again and a royal order of 20 June 1749 gave the merchants of the Indies the total liberty they sought. The only minor restriction still to remain, in spite of Mexican opposition, was that when pre-purchased goods were transported in a *flota* they were not permitted to be removed from Jalapa until after the fair had closed.[16]

The fifth, sixth and seventh sections of the *cédula* are concerned with the regulation of the *flota* to New Spain. In view of the unhappy commercial outcome of the last Jalapa fair and the likelihood of unfavourable market conditions continuing for some time, the Crown was at last forced to concede ground to the dictates of reality. Section V therefore restricts the tonnage of future *flotas* to 3000 tons, and this reduced volume of goods is to be carried in seven or at most eight merchantmen, thereby keeping freight and transport charges to a minimum. How different is this provision by contrast with earlier Crown policy, and particularly the *Real proyecto* of 1720 when Andalusian merchants were encouraged, even coerced, into exporting a maximum volume of goods to America, and ships were chartered wherever possible to accommodate them.[17] Indeed section V not only limits the tonnage and number of ships in a *flota* but actually goes as far as prescribing severe monetary penalties on any person who even *requests*, verbally or in writing, the *consulado* to exceed the specified 3000 tons. Sections VI and VII set out the rules for distributing the cargo among the vessels and stipulate that 2000 tons may consist of general merchandise, but that 1000 tons *must* be made up of Spanish agricultural produce. This proportion of one third was of course that introduced by the *Real proyecto* and its supplementary legislation.[18]

The final sections of the *cédula*, VIII and IX, state that the rules for the distribution of cargo and freighting will apply to any future fleets of *galeones* and affirm that the foregoing paragraphs are officially declared to be law.

Fifteen years, then, had sufficed to reduce Patiño's plans of 1720 for the development and reform of the American trades to a state in which the sailing of the *galeones* had to be suspended for the foreseeable future and the complement and volume of the *flota* was strictly limited to eight vessels and 3000 tons of merchandise.

II

Despite his full realisation of the circumstances, and ignoring opposition on the part of the Andalusian merchants, Patiño decided that the state of the royal treasury was such that a *flota* should be sent to New Spain without delay.[19] Accordingly General López Pintado and Don Francisco de Varas y Valdés were given the charge of preparing it. By the autumn of 1735, after considerable difficulties, all was ready. López Pintado, at a late stage and very much against his will, was once again ordered to take the naval command of it, and in spite of the risk involved on account of bad weather he set sail for Veracruz on 22 November 1735.[20] The *flota* carried 3339.27 tons of goods and was composed of four Crown warships and eleven merchantmen.[21] Although over 1000 tons less than either of the previous two fleets, the *flota*, in the event, still slightly exceeded the latest royal regulations both in volume and number of vessels.

López Pintado reached Veracruz safely on 18 February 1736. One of his small warships, the *Santa Rosa*, was lost due to her captain's bad seamanship on entry to the port, but by 2 March the last of the fleet was moored and the unloading and transportation of the cargo to Jalapa was achieved in record time.[22] Viceroy Vizarrón was under orders to run the fair exactly according to the rules laid down by his predecessor, and so *flotistas* and Mexican merchants were free to begin their trading whenever they wished, although the goods on sale were, of course, confined to Jalapa until the termination of the fair.[23] Unfortunately for the *flotistas* no such transactions were entered into, for once again the merchants of Mexico were unwilling and slow to meet the Spaniards at Jalapa.[24] The reasons for their reluctance to trade are not difficult to find. Not only was the viceroyalty well stocked with merchandise from the previous fleet, but the tail-enders of that *flota* were actually still in Jalapa with the left-overs of 1733, and clamouring for purchasers. But the Mexicans were loath to begin trading with the Spaniards for another reason too. The English 'Annual Ship' had not yet appeared in Veracruz, although it was known that a *cédula* dated 31 March 1735, had been dispatched to London authorising the South Sea Company to send the *Princess of Orange* (formerly *Royal Caroline*) to coincide with the current *flota*.[25] Until such time as the English goods were on view the Mexicans could hardly be expected to begin serious dealings with the *flotistas*, especially given the already glutted market conditions.

The course of events in England in fact meant that the merchants of New Spain would never see the expected 'Annual Ship' – nor, indeed, would any Spanish-American merchant ever see one again. For some five years past the shareholders of the South Sea Company had been discontent with the unsatisfactory profits which the company was handing them and were increasingly in favour of treating with Spain for a monetary equivalent of the remaining years of the assiento.[26] The directors of the company on the other hand opposed this movement. Under Patiño's instructions Spain's representative in London, Don Tomás Geraldino, was continuing to press the question of an equivalent, and by 1735 he had almost succeeded in drawing up an agreement for the termination of the assiento in exchange for monetary compensation. The terms of the proposed settlement were similar to those which Patiño and Keene had submitted in 1732 – 2 per cent of the profits of each Spanish trade fleet to the Indies to be ceded to the South Sea Company in lieu of its privileges in the Spanish colonies. Despite the resistance of the directors to the scheme, the shareholders supported it and voted that it should go before the British Crown for acceptance. However, the directors found allies among government ministers and the move was unsuccessful. Nevertheless both shareholders and directors were agreed in their reluctance to send an 'Annual Ship' to the Indies in 1735, a time when war between Spain and Portugal seemed likely, with possible British involvement. Moreover Geraldino had skilfully delayed plans for the dispatch of the ship, alleging that the terms of the contract forbade the 'Annual Ship' to carry foreign goods. In the event the *cédula* of March 1735 was not used by the company and the *Princess of Orange* never left Deptford.

By early summer 1736 it was clear to the Mexicans that the 'Annual Ship' would not reach Veracruz that year. But its absence still did not incline them to do business with the *flotistas* under the rigid regulations of the fair. While the viceroyalty was well stocked there was simply no point in tying up capital in immovable merchandise at Jalapa. In the meanwhile López Pintado had been diligently surveying the harbour installations at Veracruz, on the Crown's behalf, with a view to improving them. He had also collected together, as a matter of urgency, Crown dues and Mexican produce worth more than three-and-a-half million *pesos*, and these he sent back to Spain in two of his ships on 10 June.[27] But still the main business of the fair at Jalapa had no real prospect of beginning. López Pintado must have imagined he was in for another nightmare situation such as that which he had witnessed at Portobello in 1731 (it was almost certainly on precisely this account that he had been unwilling to accept command of the *flota* in the first place). After three months of inactivity, without doubt some radical action was needed very soon if the complete failure of the fair was to be avoided. López Pintado was in constant contact with Vizarrón, and as a result the viceroy decided that it was in the best interests of the languishing trade of the Spaniards to countermand Crown instructions and reverse Casafuerte's celebrated rules restricting goods to Jalapa. By a viceregal order of 16 June 1736, Vizarrón therefore lifted the ban on the movement of merchandise from the fair while it was still in progress, with effect from 1 July.[28] This immediately had the desired consequence, and Jalapa was thronged with country merchants making small purchases and removing their goods for immediate resale. The larger Mexican merchants disturbed to see their own clients once again buying their goods at source hurried to join the trading. For a while the business of the *flotistas* boomed until the moment when, keen to recoup the cost of their wasted months at Jalapa and no longer fearing competition from the English, the Spaniards raised their prices by 18–25 per cent. Once more trading came to an abrupt halt.[29] Although business began to pick up again slightly over the ensuing months, it was obvious to López Pintado that trade would never recover enough to allow the whole cargo of the fleet to be cleared within the immediate future.[30] It seems that at this stage he and the *flotistas* entered into a conspiracy the object of which was to protect the interests of Andalusian business against the obduracy of the Mexican merchants and the impotence of Crown policy to deal with them. The plan appears never to have been revealed either to the viceroy or to the *consulado* of Mexico. It worked as follows.[31] The *flotistas*, still prevented by the law from moving out of Jalapa themselves (even after the termination of a fair), managed to persuade a number of small New Spain merchants to act secretly as their agents in the viceroyalty. A procedure of sham sales was then gone through, after which the Spanish goods were released from bond in Jalapa to the merchants in question. These in turn were now free to take the goods for retail sale throughout the country. The returns from their transactions (presumably less commission) were eventually brought back to the *flotistas* waiting in Jalapa. In this way the Spaniards succeeded in obtaining virtually direct contact with the internal markets of the viceroyalty and reverting to the trade practice whose abolition the middlemen capitalists had insisted upon as the price of their collaboration in a fair. The process took some four months to complete, but López Pintado was well satisfied that the scheme had worked, for he was able to set sail for Cadiz again in June 1737 with 16 million *pesos* of treasure instead of the scarcely four millions which had been taken up till January.[32] In his correspondence the archbishop-viceroy Vizarrón commented rather naïvely upon the unexpected and inexplicable success of the fair.[33] López Pintado in his paper of some years later to the Crown tells of his diligence and ability in arranging the trade to the *flotistas'* benefit and remarks on the praise he received for it at court on his return; but he omits critical detail.[34] Only in his private correspondence with Torrenueva (the successor of Patiño who had died during López's absence) does the commander reveal how the device had worked.[35]

The possibility of carrying on even a modest trade with New Spain under the present conditions was thus plainly seen to be receding. The Andalusian merchants had in the end found themselves obliged to resort to illegality, trickery and, no doubt, corruption to achieve the derisory sale of 2000 tons of merchandise every two years, in what was after all their rightful preserve – a legitimate and major colonial market.

The commerical prospects of the Spanish on their other principal American market were certainly no brighter. Since the disastrous fair of 1731 no trading whatsoever had been attempted with Peru. Even when the Marqués de Villagarcía went out in 1735 to replace Castelfuerte as viceroy in Lima it was thought pointless to use the occasion to send cargo for sale in Tierra Firme and Peru, given that *galeonistas* from the previous fair were still in commercial difficulty. During these years portions of treasure had been brought back to Spain from Peru by *guardacosta* ships, and by 1735 it was important that the four vessels which had performed this service, and had remained in Spain, should be returned to station.[36] Two of these ships, *El Conquistador* and *El Incendio*, were therefore used to transport Villagarcía to his post in America. But perhaps more noteworthy is the fact that there also sailed in them two young Spanish officers, Don Jorge Juan and Don Antonio de Ulloa, travelling to South America at the start of their famous scientific and geographical expedition.[37]

The distinguished Basque sailor, General Blas de Lezo, was especially insistent that the *guardacosta* defenses of the Caribbean should not be allowed to run down, for he was a great believer in the principle that naval strength was the only sure base on which to sustain Spain's commercial activity with America. He believed also that Spain's principal trade links should be forged along routes which were adequately defensible by naval power. Thus he supported Patiño's objection of 1727 to the opening-up of the southern route via Cape Horn to Lima and voiced criticism of the way in which the fleet system had been allowed to decay, in his view, through lack of sufficient naval potential to deal with interloping foreigners.[38] In 1736 Blas de Lezo was given command of the two remaining *guardacosta* ships in order to return them to their action stations in the Caribbean.[39] However, probably with his full approval, eight merchantmen were added to his detail to proceed not as *galeones*, but as register ships to trade in the Indies.[40] Two of these ships were for Puerto Rico and Cumaná, but six of them were to sail with Lezo to Cartagena and on to Portobello for the celebration of a normal trade fair with merchants from the *Armada del Sur*.[41]

The origins of this trade fleet are remarkable – illustrative perhaps of the small-mindedness and cupidity of the merchant bodies and, indeed, of the Crown itself. It seems that in 1735 one of the merchants of Cadiz, foolishly encouraged by the arrivals of *guardacostas* with returns of treasure from López Pintado's last *galeones*, applied for a licence for a register ship to try his luck again on the markets of the viceroyalty. Other merchants, while ridiculing this initiative, were anxious that one of their number should not by any chance steal a march on them all, and in order to prevent this the merchant body as a whole hurried to apply for permission to send corporately a number of merchantmen under the escort of Lezo's *guardacostas*. The Crown, welcoming as always any opportunity to collect tax and agreeably surprised by the merchants' readiness to engage in the American trade, approved the project, though limiting the size of the cargo to 2000 tons.[42]

Clearly there were considerable misgivings about the viability of this venture, contravening as it did the explicit provisions of the *cédula* of 1735. On the one hand it was certainly true that more than six years had passed since any attempt had been made to trade with the Peruvians, time enough, surely, for the markets to have cleared. On the other hand no *aviso* ships had been sent, as required by the recent *cédula*, to ascertain the commercial state of the viceroyalty, and Don Juan de Berria, the Peruvian representative at the Spanish court, was not encouraging. He pointed out to the Crown that if the Spaniards were again intending to impose goods at fixed high prices, as had happened under López Pintado in 1731, the trading was doomed to failure. Freedom of commercial choice and unrestricted bargaining between both bodies of merchants would be essential prerequisites.[43]

Despite disagreements in England about whether the South Sea Company should attempt to wind up its affairs with regard to the Spanish-American trade, and if so, upon what terms, the British ambassador in Spain, Benjamin Keene, felt it was his duty to insist upon his country's right to send the 'Annual Ship' to Portobello to trade with this current fleet of '*galeones*'. Patiño succeeded in convincing him that it was not a fleet of *galeones* in the accepted sense which was in course of preparation, but a set of register ships under *guardacosta* escort.[44] The matter was not pressed by the British, although it was clear that other disagreements over financial settlements involving the South Sea Company, rates of currency exchange, compensation for reprisals, disputes over prizes at sea and a host of other matters, were leading to dangerous tensions between the two nations. The conciliatory attitude of the Marqués de Torrenueva, Patiño's successor, and the pacifist policy of Walpole, culminating in the unfulfilled Convention of the Pardo of 5 January 1739, were, in the event, unable to clear the atmosphere of inevitable war which for a variety of reasons had been gradually building up over the previous years.[45]

Against this background of diplomatic uneasiness the wisdom of sending a cargo of merchandise to Portobello was even more questionable than for commercial reasons alone. The rather undue haste which Torrenueva imposed upon the departure of Lezo's fleet was no doubt the result of his correct appreciation of the likelihood of international conflict.[46] The ships left Cadiz in the midst of a spell of bad weather as and when they could. Four left with Lezo on 4 February 1737, but one of them, the *Nuestra Señora de Belén, San Antonio de Padua y San Francisco de Asís*, the register ship for Puerto Rico, launched on the day of its departure, ran into trouble a short way out from Cadiz, turned back and foundered in the bay with disastrous losses. On 6 February three more vessels ventured out, and on the day after the *almiranta* accompanied by the two remaining merchantmen finally left port.[47] The total volume of the cargo, excluding the 224.17 tons lost in the wreck, was 1891.37 tons.[48] On the outward passage the *capitana* began to take in water and Lezo was obliged to leave the rest of the fleet and hurry on to make port at Cartagena alone, arriving there a week before the merchantmen and the *almiranta*.[49] By 20 March 1737, however, all the ships in the fleet were safely at anchor in the bay of Cartagena.[50]

News of the preparation of this small fleet in Cadiz had reached Lima in November 1735, by means of a messenger from the Marqués de Villagarcía who was newly arrived at Cartagena.[51] The retiring viceroy, Castelfuerte, once more began the unenviable task of persuading the merchants of Lima to gather together money and make the journey up to Panama in the *Armada del Sur*. Their immediate response was totally negative. The fact that the ports and roads of virtually all South America had been open for the previous four years to allow the *galeonistas* of 1731 to dispose of their wares had given rise to an unprecendented influx of contraband goods of all kinds from the European nations. Via the shores of the Caribbean, along the length of the Pacific coast, through Buenos Aires and up the tracks and rivers of the interior, English, Dutch and Portuguese were supplying eager colonial merchants with all their requirements, and such Spanish authorities as did not secretly condone this traffic were in a state of serious demoralisation.[52] The merchants' reluctance to comply with viceregal requests and orders to prepare for a trade fair was of course mainly due to their desire to conserve their money for the purchase of contraband. As a result of this attitude fierce arithmetical disputes were engaged in by the new viceroy and the *consulado* concerning the production of the mines and individual merchants' wealth. But the *consulado*'s unwillingness to travel up to Panama arose also on account of the high risk involved at that time in view of the impending hostilities between England and Spain, news of which was reaching Lima in almost every dispatch. For more than three years Villagarcía reasoned and threatened, coaxed and cajoled the merchant body.[53] Early in 1739, when the merchants presented a grand total of two and three quarter million *pesos* for shipment in the *Armada del Sur*, instead of the 12 millions which Villagarcía calculated there should be, he formerlly charged the whole *consulado* with 'wickedness and disloyalty to the Crown', illegal conduct and false declarations. These accusations he threatened to send directly back to Philip V. The resentful *consulado* was thus finally forced to capitulate, and by June 1739 an acceptable *Armada del Sur* was ready to leave. At the last moment the merchants earnestly requested Villagarcía to allow the fair to take place at Panama and not Portobello because of its greater security in time of war. This the viceroy refused to do on the grounds that it was only the merchants' refusal to cooperate that had prevented the fair from being held earlier in Portobello in relative security. What he did not say was that in any case he knew that Blas de Lezo was carrying secret instructions for both goods and treasure to be locked up in the Castle of Chagre in the centre of the Isthmus if the trading was endangered by war.[54] At long last, on 28 June 1739, the *Armada del Sur* set sail from Callao, bearing 11,734,192 *pesos*[55] – a small figure relatively, but very close to the 12 millions which Villagarcía had all along maintained should be available for shipment. The fleet reached Panama safely just over a month later.[56]

In October 1739 war was formally declared between Great Britain and Spain. In an international conflict in which the defence and security of transatlantic trade interests was a basic issue it was only natural that naval forces should be those principally deployed. As early as May 1738 a British fleet under Admiral Haddock had been stationed in Gibraltar and the Mediterranean, and a year later he was menacingly cruising off Cape St Vincent with the open object of interfering with Spain's American shipping. In the summer of 1739 Haddock was joined by Admiral Ogle with another detachment which took up a position off the coast of Portugal. By now the Spanish government was responding to these preemptive acts of hostility, first by suspending, in May 1739, the South Sea Company's assiento, and then by refusing to pay the £95,000 settlement which had been agreed in the terms of the Convention of the Pardo earlier in the year. But despite this, the British government, under pressure from its parliamentary opposition and public opinion, was nevertheless obliged to continue this bellicose naval policy. One of the strongest advocates of increased harassment of Spain was Admiral Edward Vernon. For some months past he had made it his business to express his views forcefully in government circles, and in July 1739 he at last obtained orders to sail with a squadron to the Caribbean to 'commit all sorts of hostilities against the Spaniards in such manner as you shall judge the most proper'. Having reconnoitered the area and gathered tactical information, Vernon reached Port Royal, Jamaica, on 12 October 1739, where he met with Governor Trelawny to consider how best he could accomplish his mission. After due deliberation it was decided that Portobello should be the object of a major assault, for not only was the place a focal point of Spanish trade but it was also the port from which the hated *guardacosta* ships fitted out.[57]

At that time the 12 million *pesos* brought by the *Armada del Sur* were still in Panama awaiting transportation to Portobello. However the

Spaniards were apprehensive of moving the treasure across the Isthmus because of certain ominous developments. Although they had no firm news about open hostilities between the two countries, the absence of South Sea Company ships at Portobello and the recent evacuation of the company's factory in the port made them suspect that serious trouble would not be long in coming. Moreover the virtual disappearance of smuggling vessels from the coasts, and the failure of Blas de Lezo's patrols to sight foreign ships in the area, caused their fears to grow. The treasure was therefore delayed in Panama and the merchantmen remained in Cartagena, although it was hoped that a fair could be held in Portobello in January 1740.[58]

Around midday on 2 December 1739, Vernon reached the bay of Portobello with his six warships.[59] The Spanish garrisons, despite earlier requests for supplies and reinforcements from Panama, were totally unprepared. Depleted and underprovisioned, they could offer little resistance from their crumbling fortifications, and the cannon of the three main English ships soon forced the disorderly defenders into ignominious surrender. Vernon stayed some two months in Portobello during which time he maintained courteous but threatening correspondence with both Blas de Lezo and the president of Panama, although he committed no further acts of aggression beyond the capture of Spanish ships and armaments. Later in the spring of 1740 he returned to complete his mission – the systematic destruction of all the fortifications of both the port itself and the entrance to the River Chagre, the first leg of the traditional water-route over the Isthmus to Panama. Thus he rendered Portobello useless as a site for a fair and, as fate would have it, thereby brought to an end a trading pattern that had lasted for almost two centuries.

News of the fall of Portobello was greeted with panic in Panama, and by no one more than the Lima merchants who realised the immediate danger to their treasure. After a flurry of consultations with all the parties concerned, it was decided to send the *Armada del Sur* back down the Pacific Coast to Guayaquil. From there the treasure was to be taken to Quito and then on to the town of Honda in New Granada. The goods from the ships at Cartagena were to be transported down the River Magdalena as far as Honda, which was the furthest point to which the river was navigable. At that point, it was hoped, a makeshift fair could be held with *galeonistas* and Peruvian merchants.[60] The *Armada del Sur* left Panama on 14 May 1740 bound for Guayaquil, but it did not sail away with as much treasure as it had brought. Over three million *pesos* had been removed. Most of this money went northwards to Sonsonate,

Acapulco and Realejo under a licence which the president of Panama gave to a Lima merchant for the purchase of cacao in New Spain, and the remainder had been spirited away for use in other illegal dealings.[61]

The proposed fair at Honda, however, never really took place. The *galeonistas* on the one hand, distressed by the high cost of their three-year-long wait in Cartagena and in any case mindful of the bitter experiences of their predecessors at the fair of 1731, were eager to cut their losses and sell their goods wherever they could at the best obtainable prices. Few were prepared to travel to a distant fair and risk becoming once more the victims of avaricious Lima merchants. They therefore decided to spread out throughout New Granada and Peru and sell their wares as best they could. The Lima merchants on the other hand had no great wish to buy the goods from Spain, and the majority of the treasure eventually found its way not to Honda, but back to Lima. The movement of money and the taxes collected on it, the trading of the Spaniards and the taxes due, the losses sustained by the Crown, the Peruvians and the *galeonistas*, all were the subjects of protracted and resentful disputes over the years to come between the viceregal government, the *consulado* of Lima and the *galeonistas*.[62]

Thus what turned out to be Spain's final attempt to trade with Peru along the traditional trade route was once again an unqualified disaster. The events of 1735–40 came as a fitting and natural climax to the story of Spain's failure in this field. The two factors which over the years had contributed most to the downfall of the *galeones* – Peruvian commercial resistance and English intervention – then coincided on an unprecedented scale. The merchants of Lima had taken nearly five years to answer their summons to the fair, and the English finally arrived in Portobello not in their 'Annual Ship', or even as a naval escort for it, but in six men-of-war with guns blazing away.

In Spain, the *flota* for Veracruz consisting of two warships and 13 merchantmen, under the command of the Conde de Clavijo, which was being prepared in 1738–9, was unloaded on the outbreak of war and never left Cadiz.[63]

11   The Final Years

The war between England and Spain, which lasted from 1739–48, is nowadays memorable for three particular events: Vernon's capture of Portobello in 1739; his failure to take Cartagena in 1741, thanks to the heroic stand of its defenders under Blas de Lezo, in which action Lezo himself lost his life; and the circumnavigation of the globe by Admiral George Anson, a voyage which began in 1740 as a mission to harass the Spaniards in the Pacific.[1] Future hostilities extended to involve most of Europe as the Anglo-Spanish conflict merged in the multinational War of the Austrian Succession. Eventually, after a decade of strife, normal relations between Great Britain and Spain were restored following the general peace of Aix-la-Chapelle in 1748, and a new commercial treaty was signed between the two countries on 5 October 1750.[2] Some four years of hard work had gone into the agreement of terms for this treaty, for it touched upon almost all aspects of Anglo-Spanish trade. Not least important of its provisions was the termination of the South Sea Company's 'Slave Assiento' which had of course been a cause of bad relations between the two countries for nearly 40 years. The first two articles of the treaty dealt with this matter. By them the British right to enjoy four more years of the assiento privilege was relinquished in exchange for a cash settlement of £100,000 payable within three months. In article 3 all claims of the South Sea Company to supplementary compensation were declared at an end and were forbidden to be raised at any later date. The remaining articles established the conditions of trade between Spain and England and laid the basis for what turned out to be seven years of successful and friendly relations between the commercial interests of both countries.[3]

But the decade of international hostilities altered the commercial relationship between Spain and the Indies in a basic and unexpected way. Whereas over the previous 30 years both Mexicans and Peruvians had increasingly failed to cooperate with *flotistas* and *galeonistas* – to such an extent that the merchants of Andalusia became ever more reluctant to risk investing in the fleets – now, at the end of the war, the Americans were anxious to re-establish the traditional fleet system and were actually petitioning the Crown for its restoration.[4]

The change came about as a consequence of the manner in which the American trades had been forced to operate during the war. Given the strength of British naval power it was unthinkable that fleets of merchandise and treasure should attempt to cross the Atlantic in time of peril, even if market conditions in the Indies had favoured the dispatching of regular fleets – which they clearly did not. The use of register ships was therefore extended to all areas of the Empire, including New Spain and Peru, as the sole method of commerce between Spain and the Indies. Not only were single merchantmen more likely to thwart enemy vigilance than a full trade fleet, but at that time every available warship was urgently needed by the Spanish navy to contribute to the national defenses. The Crown, ever anxious to promote transatlantic commerce so as to reap the profits in cash which accrued from it, was not ungenerous with the licences for register ships which it issued to businessmen willing to invest in cargo for sale in the Indies. Some 120 such ships sailed from Cadiz during the first five years of the war, although it is reported that 69 of them were lost on the round trip.[5] Because of the strain on Spain's resources, caused by the war, a fair number of these ships were foreign-owned, foreign-commanded and foreign crewed, and for greater security sailed under neutral flags. Much of the merchandise transported in them was foreign too, particularly French, and so in many cases the merchants of Cadiz became for a second time little more than mere factors of foreign (even English!) entrepreneurs.[6]

In the American viceroyalties the arrival of register ships on such an unprecedented scale produced a total distortion of the existing commercial pattern. In New Spain the irregularity of the register ships, with their few hundred tons of cargo at a time, naturally made trade fairs at Jalapa both unpractical and unnecessary, and formal trading arrangements of this kind were discontinued. The Spanish merchants or their agents were consequently again permitted to take their wares inland to Mexico City, or wherever they chose, in order to sell them on the open market. The situation thus reverted to that which had caused such trouble between Mexicans and Andalusians a quarter of a century before, when the Spaniards' direct access to the internal markets of the country was so resented by the Mexicans. In these circumstances the capitalists of Mexico City once more found their function of profiteering middlemen greatly diminished. Nor were they able in the present conditions to make use of their infamous 'commercial blackmail' tactics. The Spaniards were not now seeking to sell their cargoes in bulk in their haste to return in a *flota* but were quite prepared to set up business in New Spain and allow their predecessors who had completed their trading to return in the waiting single ship. A number of Spaniards even remained semi-permanently in Mexico to make a career out of acting as agents for the goods from Cadiz. In 1755 there were some 60 such agents in Mexico, a number of whom had been there since the last *flota* of 1735, looking after Cadiz interests. Six of them had shops open for the sale of goods from Spain. Certainly, as before, the Mexican capitalists had the option of buying up complete cargoes from the register ships and competing with the Spaniards, but this had two drawbacks. First they had become used to large and easy profits and it was not within their concept of business to struggle for what would obviously be smaller pickings. For this reason during the years of war many of them turned exclusively to investment in agriculture and mining. Second, as they complained to the Crown, the sporadic arrival in Veracruz of register ships with previously unknown cargoes meant that any bulk investment involved them in intolerable risks. It was perfectly possible that after the purchase of a whole cargo of goods in short supply had been made from a register ship, with good commercial prospects, a second register ship could arrive with a similar cargo, thus knocking the bottom out of the original investment. Moreover, it followed naturally that no one would be prepared to buy the cargo of the second ship *in toto*. For the most part, then, the Mexican capitalists left the Spaniards themselves to bear the commercial consequences, good or bad, of their haphazard speculations on the markets of the viceroyalty. Given the state of war, of unpredictable duration, there was nothing to be gained by protesting to the Crown. All that could be done was to formulate petitions requesting that once the peace was re-established the system of *flotas* should also be restored – a situation that was evidently not without its profound irony![7]

In South America a similar situation obtained.[8] The rich merchants of Lima were of course those whose livelihood was most jeopardised by the new commercial order. The sack of Portobello, followed by the destruction of its defences and the continued strength of the British navy in West Indian waters, made the northern route to South America especially hazardous for Spanish shipping. The register ships from Spain were therefore obliged to take the southerly route to Peru, via Buenos Aires or round Cape Horn. This radical change in the traditional commercial pattern had the effect of developing Lima's long-standing resentment of River Plate trading into a particularly bitter inter-colonial dispute. The merchants of Buenos Aires had for years poached the commercial preserves of the Peruvians in Charcas and Upper Peru with merchandise from both smugglers and occasional register ships, but despite constant demands from Lima, the Crown had never agreed to close the river port completely to all shipping. Now, on the contrary, to the distress of Lima, Buenos Aires suddenly became the major trading port of the subcontinent. In addition to the increased number of register ships specifically licensed to go there, and the smugglers they attracted in their wake, a number of register ships bound for the Pacific alleged or genuinely found that their passage round the Horn was impeded by heavy weather, and used Buenos Aires as their port of unloading. A steady stream of goods was therefore making its way on to the markets of Peru from which the capitalists of Lima derived no profit whatsoever. This in its turn greatly deterred the latter from investing in the merchandise which did actually reach Callao in register ships, for, like their counterparts in Mexico, they were never sure what the state of the internal market would be in a given commodity after they had committed themselves in a bulk purchase. In these circumstances the men from the register ships had no alternative but to establish themselves on shore, take the risk themselves, and distribute their goods throughout the viceroyalty as best they could. This practice, like the action of the merchants from the Plate, effectively cut out the capitalist middlemen of Lima and brought to an end their role within the commercial cycle. Over the ensuing years the *consulado* of Lima raised complaints and protests, but ironically the only hope for their survival seemed to be in their demands for the return of the *galeones*, the very system against which they had constantly worked for the past quarter of a century.

It is perhaps important to point out the clear distinction which must be made between the interests of the Peruvian and Mexican merchants in earlier times, when the fleet system was in operation, and in the present years, during which the fleets were suspended and replaced by an alternative method of trading. We have seen how over the previous 25 years the commercial freedom of the Peninsular Spaniards, who traded by means of the fleets, had been increasingly eroded, even to the point of restricting the actual movement of Spanish merchants or their agents to specific physical locations when they were in America. Such limitations were of course very much the result of the pressures exerted on the Crown by the merchant bodies of America, who were thus gradually obtaining their own eventual objective – the total monopoly of all business activity within the bounds of their respective commercial territories. In the twenties and thirties, the delay or cancellation of a trade fleet from Spain had been for the most part a welcome event for them. During the years in which fleets were absent from the Indies the American merchants had been free to manipulate the prices of existing stocks, regulate the quantities of given commodities on the market, replenish them as and when the opportunity arose from low-cost smuggled cargoes, and trade, often illegally, from one district to another with native-produced goods or crops. Moreover, while the fleets stayed away specie was plentiful and so prices remained high. Specific supplies from Spain were certainly required from time to time, but not with the frequency, in the volume, or under the conditions which the Crown sought to impose. In short, what best suited the colonial capitalist was the continuance in *theory* but the failure in *practice* of the traditional fleet system, for such a situation represented the nearest thing to complete commercial independence to which he aspired. The suspension of the fleets in 1739 and their replacement by register ships meant, for the American merchant, the end of the relative independence he had achieved and the curtailment of the exclusivity which by shrewdness, diplomacy and courage he had forced the Crown to concede to him over the previous two decades. Now, with Peninsular Spaniards all around him legally marketing legal goods in the capital and interior of his country, he saw his livelihood being taken from him, and his only recourse was to find alternative areas of investment or risk increased dealings with the smugglers. Of course the very status of the smugglers as illegal foreigners precluded them from ever becoming anything more than fly-by-night delivery men. The haste with which they liked to complete their business in order to disappear had always been a factor which had favoured the monopoly of the moneyed merchant and reinforced his control over his markets. Yet the continuous presence of Peninsular merchants in the colonies during the current war not only inhibited contraband activities of all kinds, but because of the direct selling the Spaniards engaged in, cutting out the middlemen wholesalers, it considerably reduced the price of legal European goods to the consumer, thus also making contraband less profitable.

Contraband nevertheless increased during the war. The British navy did its best to protect and support English smugglers all along the coasts of the Caribbean,[9] and the Portuguese, French and Dutch did their utmost to take advantage of the new and relatively freely open door of Buenos Aires, making use of the infamous Isla del Sacramento in the River Plate.[10] The crews and masters of the foreign-owned register ships also benefited themselves from the circumstances, passing goods of their own into the colonies under cover of the Spanish-registered goods they carried in their ships. Unfortunately for the capitalists of Lima and Mexico only a small proportion of this contraband needed their mediation to effect its sale. Once the emergencies of war had forced them to forgo their virtual monopoly of the trading in their areas, not even the smuggler was obliged to deal with them, as the prevailing commercial disorder within the colonies made it easy for him to legitimise his goods within the general confusion.[11] Cruel indeed was the stroke of fortune which brought the War of Jenkins' Ear just at a time when the American merchant bodies seemed to be within arm's length of achieving the capitulation of the Crown in its attempts to regulate commerce in the Indies by policies imposed from Spain.

But if the American merchants soon saw their own future prosperity in terms of the re-establishment of the old trade fleets, the Spaniards too became no less anxious for a return to the traditional system.[12] Certainly the suspension of the fleets during the war produced for them conditions in which they were able to achieve their aim of dominating the American markets and virtually excluding the colonial middlemen from the trade. However, within a few years, it was clear that the present practice was not all what suited them best. Under the fleet system it had been possible to carry as great a volume of goods in a single convoy as now took several years to transport in register ships. Moreover, constant arrivals of merchandise in unplanned quantities could be most damaging to trade, as the American merchants already knew: with fleets it had been possible, at least in theory, to regulate supplies from Spain in order to force prices up in the Indies. With register ships, as well as the commercial risks, there was the added drudgery of having to spend long periods in America setting up temporary shops, selling here and there and disposing of cargo piecemeal. Thus the Spaniards came to the conclusion that in the long run their interests were better served by using the capitalist middlemen of the Indies than by carrying on a multitude of lengthy and small-scale operations within the commercial disorder which the register ships seemed necessarily to involve. The *consulado* of Cadiz therefore joined those of Lima and Mexico in recommending to the Crown that on the restoration of the peace both *galeones* and *flota* should be re-established.[13] Finally both sets of merchants realised that the covetous objectives which all had been pursuing over the past 30 years or more were in fact no more than will-o'-the-wisps. The American had resisted trade with the fleets, and the Spaniard had struggled to edge the middleman out of that trade. Now it was clear to both parties that each needed the other.

Once the Treaty of Aix-la-Chapelle had been concluded, Spain was again free to turn her attention to domestic and colonial commercial affairs. In 1750 the Marqués de la Ensenada, in the name of Ferdinand VI, called together a group of merchants and economists, men who had experience in the Indies trade, to debate about how best to bring to an end the commercial disorder of which all were complaining. After taking into account a variety of opinions solicited from different sources the group made its recommendations.[14] It was resolved that the *flota* to New Spain should be restored as soon as possible – 1753 was the earliest proposed date – although there was disagreement as to the frequency of future sailings and the maximum tonnage of goods the *flotas* should carry. It was also decided that the *galeones* to Tierra Firme should likewise be re-started, but in this matter more serious problems were apparent. First, the volume of merchandise which had recently gone out to South America in register ships was considerable; in addition, seven ships were currently preparing to sail directly to Peru and five more to Buenos Aires with permission to trade inland. From this information it was deduced that the viceroyalty would be well stocked with European goods for some years to come.[15] The second problem concerned the reconstruction of defences. At that time the Crown was especially hard pressed financially by building works, for not only had Vernon virtually destroyed Portobello, but an earthquake in 1746 had caused a great deal of damage to Lima, and in particular to the fortifications of Callao.[16] Clearly it was unthinkable that *galeones* should begin to run regularly again until the defences of Portobello could be adequately re-constructed, for the existence of quantities of treasure and merchandise in an unprotected and isolated port constituted an open invitation to attack by pirates or foreigners. Although Alsedo y Herrera had been sent out in 1743 to take over the presidency of Panama, with the specific commission of rebuilding Portobello, he had been unable to do more than raise a few earthworks and construct wooden stockades. These were nevertheless sufficient to resist two semi-piratical attacks from Jamaica in 1744, but obviously were unsatisfactory as permanent defences.[17] However it was not until 1753 that the Crown gave orders for proper works to begin. Even so money was short and progress was slow.[18] Serious thought was also given to the idea of using Buenos Aires as the American port for the *galeones*, and Mendoza, at the foot of the Andes, was proposed as a new venue for the traditional trade fair. The road from Buenos Aires to

Mendoza was easy, if long, and the town enjoyed a benign climate and absolute security from foreign attack. The scheme was soon rejected however, for three reasons. First, because Buenos Aires was alleged to be physically unsuitable as a port for handling a large number of merchantmen at one time; second, because lack of timber and other naval supplies in the area would have made the repairing and servicing of ships impossible on a large scale; and third, because although Mendoza was suitable as a town for the fair, it was too far distant from Buenos Aires to be practical.[19] One cannot avoid speculating that the long-standing rivalry between Lima and Buenos Aires must also have inclined commercial circles in Spain to anticipate problems with the Peruvian merchants if it were feared in Lima that Buenos Aires could gain advantage from such innovations. Consequently, for the present, and indeed for the foreseeable future, trade would have to continue to Peru by means of register ships.

When the Conde de Superunda took over the viceroyalty of Peru from the Marqués de Villagarcía in 1745, he was soon convinced, as were the members of the local *consulado*, that the only way to restore due commercial hegemony to Lima was to re-establish the *galeones* and the fair at Portobello. From this there naturally followed a desire for the complete closure of Buenos Aires as a port, for the encroachment of merchants from Buenos Aires into Charcas and Upper Peru was impoverishing the viceregal capital. Not only were the merchants of Lima being forced out of business, but a sizeable proportion of the mineral wealth of the region was now flowing eastwards towards Tucumán and Buenos Aires. In a letter of 10 May 1749 the viceroy placed before the Crown his strong opinions on these matters. On 12 January 1750 the Marqués de la Ensenada acknowledged his letter, assuring him that his counsels would be taken into account in the forthcoming discussions on the American trades, and informing him that in any case henceforth any register ships that were licensed to go to Buenos Aires (and they would be few) would under no circumstances be allowed to trade their goods beyond the River Plate Provinces, Tucumán and Paraguay.[20] The attitude of the Crown thus seemed to hold some promise for the languishing commerce of Lima. Yet despite hopes and intentions on both sides of the Atlantic, the *galeones* were of course never to return to Portobello. Indeed a series of administrative reforms started off by the recreation of the viceroyalty of New Granada in 1739 meant that the once flourishing *audiencia* of Panama was abolished two years after Alsedo's recall, in 1751. Such judicial and administrative business as remained was transferred to the new capital of Santa Fe de Bogotá.[21]

However by 1761, the year in which Superunda wrote his *Memoria*, to the delight of the viceroy and to the relief of many of the merchants, the situation had improved beyond all possible expectation, and without the re-establishment of the *galeones*. In fact by then Superunda was recommending not only the closure of the port of Buenos Aires, as usual, but also that of Panama.[22] The royal order of 20 June 1749, had provided the solution. It was this order, it will be remembered, which after 14 years of disputes had finally given American merchants the freedom to remit money to Spain for the direct purchase of specific merchandise.[23] The businessmen of Andalusia had naturally fought against this practice for many long years and thought they had won the day with the *cédula* of 1735, but finally the Crown had been forced to concede victory to the Americans in 1749. Despite initial disgruntlement in Spain, under this provision close and cordial contacts were now gradually built up between merchants in Lima and those in Cadiz, resulting in increased and mutually beneficial trade. In the absence of *galeones*, the Cadiz merchant, in his turn, also found that he was able to forge sound business links with colleagues in Peru and receive firm orders from them. Thus over the decade 1750–60 a new relationship between Cadiz and Lima flourished, and relative prosperity returned to the viceroyalty and to the merchants of Andalusia.[24]

In Peru two principal advantages were obtained. First, the cost of goods from Spain was considerably reduced.[25] Never again was it necessary for the Lima merchants to incur the expenses involved in travelling up and down to Portobello, plus payment of taxes and freight charges in the *Armada del Sur*, and a lengthy stay away from home. Nor were they forced to empty their coffers at the viceroy's demand and haggle, not always to advantage, at the fair. Moreover, the removal of the overhead costs of a fleet of *galeones*, including commissions to agents and factors, meant that the Andalusian merchants were now able to offer the Peruvians much reduced prices at source. Second, the facility of ordering specific goods from Spain gave the Peruvian merchant much greater control over his own business. He was not now subjected to the speculation and capriciousness of the Cadiz merchant, sending out cargoes of unknown contents, volume and price, and unpredictable saleability. He could in future limit his supplies to merchandise he knew he could sell, and was even able to expand his operations to take in goods which he had not previously dealt in, but for which there was a market. As a result there was a great increase in the importation into Peru of household goods and furniture from Spain, including even an appreciable number of Spanish-built coaches, all of which would have been difficult to ship via Portobello, to say nothing of the high freight charges that would have been involved. Trade in other luxury goods such as silks and fine fabrics also improved, for all was transported, in the words of Superunda, 'at less cost than that for shipping iron'.[26] Thus lower costs all round, predictability of prices and approximation of supply and demand, made trade in this manner a viable enterprise.

The Cadiz merchant was also pleased. No longer did he need to speculate with his own choice of goods on an erratic market. No longer did he have to travel to Peru in a register ship, or employ agents, trekking around the viceroyalty to sell goods with difficulties. Even less was he required by the king's orders to prepare his merchandise to be ready to sail on a given day in the *galeones*, nor did he have to pay convoy charges and suffer interminable delays in the Indies. For him too, prices could be lower, business could be better, profits could be higher.

It is difficult to ascertain just what influence Campillo y Cossío's doctrines may have had upon the newly developing pattern of Spain's trade with Peru at this stage, but the conclusion must be drawn that it had none or very little. Although Campillo's work, *Nuevo sistema de gobierno económico para la América* of 1743, was circulating in manuscript form and was later to become the inspiration of much economic reform under Charles III (via Ward's *Proyecto económico* of 1762, published in 1779) it would be misleading to regard the improvement and simplification of the Cadiz-Lima trade in the 1750s and 1760s as anything but the fortuitous result of the circumstances of the moment. In any case Campillo's view that Spain's trade with her colonies should be as unrestricted as possible and increased to a maximum so as to exploit the under-developed commercial potential of the Indies for the benefit of Spain, had for some time past also been that of Spanish ministers. On several occasions the Council of the Indies had stated, before Campillo did, that 'freedom of trade' was essential for commercial prosperity, and Patiño himself had envisaged significant changes after 1744.[27] In this respect at least, Campillo was therefore expounding an ideal which was already currently accepted in various quarters a decade or more before he himself put pen to paper.[28] Campillo's consequent proposals for the conduct of trade were in many ways simply the logical extension of his view of commerce, which was still broadly based on principles of Colbertian mercantilism, but they nevertheless captured the attention of the later reformers. At all events the notion must be resisted that the improvement in commercial relations between Spain and Peru after

1750 was the result of the partial application of Campillo y Cossío's theories. The commission which the Marqués de la Ensenada had brought together in 1750 to ponder the future of the American trades had in fact recommended a course of action which directly opposed another important principle of Campillo's with regard to the American trades. Campillo had written:

> It may be necessary to use the fleet system in times of war, but in times of peace it only serves to turn that trade into the monopoly of vested interests.[29]

It was precisely the reintroduction of that system which was proposed for both Peru and New Spain following the re-establishment of the general peace of 1748.

Only in the case of New Spain was it found possible to implement this plan. To resume *flotas* to Veracruz after the war was actually a reasonably simple matter. All that was needed was for the viceroyalty to clear itself of stocks built up by the register ships, and given the expressed desire of the *consulado* of Mexico for the return of the *flota*, it seemed likely that the merchants' future cooperation would guarantee the success of the trade. In the case of Peru, the disastrous results of the last two fleets of *galeones*, the destruction of Portobello and the distance of Lima from the Atlantic coasts meant that a whole new system with new regulations and arrangements would have to have been devised. In New Spain no such problems arose. There even existed Casafuerte's set of successful new rules for the fair at Jalapa, unused for more than a decade, and just waiting for readoption. Consequently, on 11 October 1754, Ferdinand VI issued a royal order to Viceroy Revillagigedo, declaring that henceforth New Spain would be supplied from Cadiz on the basis of one *flota* every two years, that between one fleet and the next no register ships would be licensed for New Spain, nor would the quicksilver fleets that might sail between *flotas* be allowed to carry cloth for sale in the viceroyalty. The first fleet, it was announced, would leave for Veracruz in 1756.[30]

In fact the fleet did not leave until 11 February 1757 because the *consulado* of Mexico had requested the Crown to delay its departure, for the reason that the markets of the country were still over-stocked – a discouraging beginning indeed to the return of a system which was to prove as unsatisfactory in its second lease of life as it had done in its first. More than 20 years had elapsed since the departure of the last *flota*; the present delay was therefore utilised for the clarification of a number of issues concerning the celebration of a fair, a process by now largely unfamiliar to the merchants of Cadiz. Several basic points needed to be established: first, that the fair was to be held in Jalapa and nowhere else, and under Casafuerte's rules; second, that the *flotistas* would be exempted from payment of the *alcabala* not only during the fair itself but also for eight weeks after its closure; third, that in no circumstances would goods unsold at the end of the fair be allowed to leave Jalapa; and fourth, that Spanish merchants resident in New Spain as a result of the former commerce of the register ships would either have to bring their stocks to Jalapa for sale at the fair or else register themselves as Mexican merchants with the *consulado* of Mexico. They were not to be permitted the best of both worlds, enjoying the freedom of the internal markets and avoiding the restrictions of the fair.

The *flota* of 1757, under the command of Don Joaquín Manuel de Villena, carried 7069.70 tons of merchandise in ten merchantmen, escorted by two warships. All went according to plan and the fair at Jalapa proceeded without incident and subject to the rules laid down by Casafuerte. The only problem, amazingly unforeseen as it was, was that the volume of cargo for sale was obviously too large, and the complaints and charges of Spaniards against Mexicans and vice versa became as much a part of life for the new generation of *flotistas* as it had been for their elders. However the device of sham sales to colluding Mexicans, as practised by López Pintado in 1736, was again employed by the desperate *flotistas* as a means of getting their cargoes out of Jalapa and on to the open markets of the viceroyalty. To allow this process to work, the date of return of the fleet had to be postponed until 2 May 1758. Even so, at the end of the trading 25 *flotistas* remained trapped in Jalapa, with goods worth two and three quarter million *pesos*. The situation was all too familiar! The only significant difference from the past was that the greater part of the transactions at the fair of 1757–8 were done with the small merchants of New Spain. The numbers of large capitalists involved in the trade with Spain had undergone serious decline during nearly two decades of register ships, and now these were no longer the dominant merchant class at the fair. In this respect, if in no other, the years without *flotas* had changed the commercial structure of the viceroyalty.

The next fleet, that of Don Carlos Regio, left Cadiz on 29 June 1760, carrying 8492.75 tons of cargo in 13 merchantmen, with an escort of two warships. There were also in its company six register ships for Havana, Caracas, Santo Domingo and Honduras. Trading at Jalapa was again extremely slow because of existing high stocks and remaining unsold cargo from 1758. Also, it was feared in New Spain that fresh diplomatic trouble with England could easily lead to another war and the reintroduction of register ships, and this had a deadening effect upon business. Once more the return of the *flota* to Spain was delayed, but nevertheless a huge volume of merchandise was still left unsold at Jalapa after the fleet eventually went home in April 1762. The capture of Havana by the English in August of that year caused Viceroy Cruillas to believe that an attack on Veracruz was imminent, and so he ordered the *flotistas* to pay 6 per cent *alcabala* on the value of their goods and take them up to Mexico for safekeeping and sale. This sudden freedom conceded to the *flotistas* to leave Jalapa and dispose of their cargo themselves threw the Mexicans into confusion, for it was what they most feared. The Spaniards again had access to the internal markets of the viceroyalty and it is reported that they engaged in direct commerce with the mines themselves. Fifty years of confrontations and manoeuvring on both sides had not sufficed to resolve the basic problem of the New Spain trade.

The Crown, increasingly disposed as it was at this time to initiate reforms, decided that here was a situation which bore serious investigation. Thus it was that Don José de Gálvez, the celebrated Visitor-General of New Spain, who sailed in the next fleet, that of 1765, was ordered to look into the matter of the Jalapa fairs. Significantly, given the fiscal motivations of Charles III, he was required specifically to discover what frauds were being practised in connection with the fairs and not by what means the commercial deadlock could be broken. The fleet of 1765, commanded by Don Agustín de Idiáquez carried the sizeable cargo of 8013.62 tons and so provided Gálvez with an excellent example both of the workings of the fair and the impossibility of the system. The Visitor-General did indeed find all the abuses the Crown suspected concerning the evasion of duties, the illegal movement of merchandise and the like. But the changes Gálvez imposed were few: the establishment of a strict customs control with official marking of goods as they were unloaded at Veracruz, and the provision that the *alcabala*, when chargeable, should be levied at 4 per cent instead of 6 per cent – and on goods entering Jalapa instead of on those leaving the fair. Gálvez did not attempt to modify the actual method of trading. Like many in Spain he was becoming convinced that nothing could be usefully achieved in this matter. As the new doctrines of physiocracy and economic liberalism advanced, hand in hand with changing political criteria, Gálvez joined the ranks of those who came to favour a more rational solution of the problems of the American trades. As

Minister for the Indies he was to give his full support to the Free Trade Act of 1778.

Three more *flotas* were yet to reach Veracruz before the fleet system was to disappear for ever. That of 1768, commanded by the Marqués de Casa Tilly, carried 5588 tons of cargo; that of 1772, under Don Luis de Córdoba, 7674.75 tons; and finally that of Don Antonio de Ulloa, in 1776, with 8176 tons. In each case the same problems persisted and augmented, and as merchandise from one fleet piled up at Jalapa the proportion of the cargoes of successive fleets which became unsaleable increased to an intolerable degree. It was not until the spring of 1782 that the unfortunate *flotistas* of 1776, having thrown themselves on the king's mercy, were finally allowed to remove their goods from Jalapa and try to sell them on the Mexican markets. To the bitter end the New Spain *flota* had continued to defeat its own object.

Great damage was also done to the trade of these last three fleets by the operation of a royal instruction of 16 October 1765, which gave 'free trade' to the Leeward Islands, Cuba, Santo Domingo, Puerto Rico, Trinidad and Margarita from nine authorised ports in Spain. Under this legislation ships bound for any of these destinations had only to register their sailing plans in Spain, collect documents for exhibition on arrival, and pay a simple *ad valorem* duty on their cargoes when they reached port in the Indies. The response to this measure was great, and between June 1766 and April 1768, for example, 20 ships left Spanish ports for Havana alone, loaded with cargo which, for the most part, found its way illegally on to the markets of New Spain. The extension of this 'free trade' to cover Louisiana in 1768 and Yucatán and Campeche in 1770 had of course increasingly detrimental effects upon the trade of the remaining *flotas*.

But although the practice of 'free trade' went quickly spreading throughout Spain's Empire, culminating in the famous Act of 1778, ironically New Spain, for a decade to come, was specifically excluded from the provisions of that legislation. The reasons for this are simply explained. The unsatisfactory nature of the Jalapa fair in its second phase had of course not escaped the attention of the Spanish government, and while no remedial action had yet been taken, the matter was under intermittent discussion in the Council of the Indies. In 1771 the Council's papers on the New Spain trade were passed to the Accountant-General, Don Tomás Ortiz de Landazuri, for study and report. On November 22 of that year he produced his findings. The main material of his paper was firmly within his terms of reference, and consisted of various suggestions to improve the working of the fair as it was currently constituted. But almost as an afterthought, Ortiz also pointed out what he considered to be the root cause of the trouble in New Spain – the persistence of the fleet system itself. He recommended that the traditional trade fleet should be discontinued and replaced by the same system of commerce as that which was proving so satisfactory for Peru and Tierra Firme. If the Crown so required, he went on to say, he was willing to make his suggestions as to how this change should be effected. Much pleased by Ortiz de Landazuri's report, the Crown called on him to inform more widely about his ideas for the American trades in general, and after further lengthy study he produced a second voluminous and highly apposite report on 6 December 1776.

In this report we find a realistic and fairly complete catalogue of the causes of the failure of Spain's trade with her Indies, following in many respects the diagnosis of Campillo y Cossío. According to Ortiz they were as follows: the monopoly of the Cadiz merchants; the system of *galeones* and *flota*; the fiscal criteria and the methods of taxation; the decline in the cultivation and manufacture of native produce in Spain and the Antilles; the inobservance of Crown laws forbidding the cultivation of the vine and the olive in America and the manufacture of cloth, all of which provided the staple exports of Spain to America; the existence of intercolonial trade which caused Spain's own trade with her colonies to diminish; confusion in the tax system in which private interests were not distinguished from public; and contraband, which Ortiz considered to be a serious cause of trouble, but also, rightly, a natural consequence of the way in which trade had been conducted for so long. He might have added as well the continued failure of Spain's ministers to understand the true nature of commerce or to balance the commercial interests of one set of merchants with those of their trading partners on the other side of the Atlantic. But, even in the 1770s, this was perhaps not yet fully apparent.

Ortiz's remedies – the opening up of many more ports in Spain and America to mutual commerce, the termination of the monopoly of Cadiz, simplified regulations for shipping, tax reforms, increased population and development of the Empire and greater exploitation of mineral resources, and the eradication of smuggling – formed the basis of the Free Trade Act of 1778. Yet in his second report, and in the Act itself, 'free trade' for New Spain is not included. The Act also withheld this privilege from Venezuela. The reasons for these exceptions, resulting from a deeper consideration of policy, are clear. One of the principal purposes of the new Act was to promote the economic development of the poorer regions of the Empire. If New Spain had been included in the reform this objective would have been largely frustrated, since that viceroyalty, being the most prosperous and developed of the colonies, would have attracted a large number of register ships to the detriment of other areas. Moreover, as the only port of importance in Mexico was Veracruz, constant vigilance there would more easily succeed in curtailing the activities of the smugglers. New Spain was nevertheless to benefit from the fiscal reforms introduced by the Act, and section VI of the document promised new regulations to govern the trade with the colony. In the meanwhile the *flota* would continue as in the past. In the case of Venezuela 'free trade' was withheld because that province was considered to be the exclusive preserve of the Caracas Company.

Another war between England and the allied Spain and France in 1779 ensured that the next *flota* did not sail from Cadiz to Veracruz, and between 1779 and 1783 register ships once again carried the trade to New Spain. But even after the Treaty of Versailles of 1783 the viceroyalty was still not to enjoy proper 'free trade'. Certainly the project of yet another revised set of rules for the *flota* and the fair was now abandoned, but the Crown, in accordance with its current policy, instead limited the total maximum tonnage which could be shipped to New Spain in register ships, allocating specific volumes to individual Spanish ports. The cargoes were fixed at 10,000 tons for 1784, 12,000 tons for 1785, 12,000 tons for 1786 and 6000 tons for 1787. Thus while trade to the less developed areas of the Empire was increasing and prospering in these years, that to New Spain was restricted and comparatively neglected. Protests and complaints soon came to the Crown from all sectors of commerce, and in 1787 the Council of State decided to look into the matter again. Opinions were sought from merchants in a number of Spanish ports, from the *consulado* of Mexico and from the intendant of Veracruz. All were agreed that 'free trade' had to be conceded to New Spain and to Venezuela as it was to the rest of the Empire. On 28 February 1789 Charles IV therefore declared that the Free Trade Act of 1778 was now extended to include the viceroyalty of New Spain. The fleet system had finally and irrevocably come to an end.

Appendix I

INDIES-BOUND SHIPPING OUT OF CADIZ, 1700–40
[from 'Libros de registros', AGI, Contr., 2901]

Table 1   Volume, frequency and constitution of Indies-bound shipping ex Cadiz, 1700–40.

Table 2   a) Trade and quicksilver fleets, 1700–40.
             b) New Spain fleets, 1757–76.

Table 3   *Registro* ships, 1701–40.

Table 4   *Aviso* ships, 1701–40.

TABLE 1   Volume, frequency and constitution of Indies-bound shipping
ex Cadiz, 1700–40

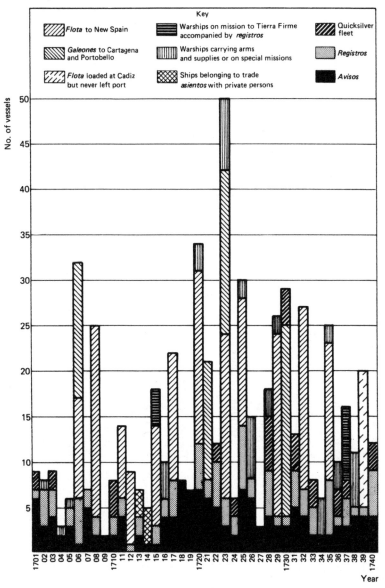

TABLE 2   a. Trade and quicksilver fleets, 1700—40

Year	Fleet	Commander	War-ships	Merchant Ships	Tons of Merchandise	Fair	English 'Annual Ship'
[1699	flota	Manuel Velasco y Tejada]					—
1701	azogues	Fernando Chacón	2	—	F	—	—
1703	azogues	Francisco Garrote	2	—	F	—	—
1706	flota	Diego Fernández de Santillán	4	7	2674.85	(V)	—
1706	galeones	José Fernández de Santillán, Conde de Casa Alegre	5	10	3542.42	P	—
1708	flota	Andrés de Pez	4	17	2297.88 +	(V)	—
1710	azogues	Manuel López Pintado	2	—	F + 200	—	—
1710	azogues	Duque de Linares	2	—	F + ?	—	—
1711	flota	Andrés de Arriola	4	4	1596.85	—	—
1712	flota	Juan de Ubilla	5	3	1439.66	—	—
1713	*galeones	Antonio de Echeverz y Subiza	—	3	1290	—	—
1715	flota	Manuel López Pintado	3	8	1975.91	—	*Elizabeth*
1715	*galeones	Conde de Vegaflorida	1	3	556.60	C	*Bedford*
1717	flota	Antonio Serrano	3	11	2840.08	J	*Royal Prince*
1720	flota	Fernando Chacón	3	16	4377.68	—	*Royal Prince*
1721	galeones	Baltasar de Guevara	4	9	2047.03	P	*Royal George*
1722	azogues	Fernando Chacón	2	—	—	—	—
1723	flota	Antonio Serrano	3	15	4309.98	—	*Royal Prince*
1723	galeones	Carlos Grillo	4	14	3127.79	P	*Royal George*
1724	azogues	Baltasar de Guevara	2	—	—	—	—
1725	flota	Antonio Serrano	2	12	3744.50	—	*Prince Frederick*

1728	azogues	Rodrigo de Torres	2	4	F + ?	—	—
1729	flota	Marqués de Marí	4	16	4882.23	J	—
1730	azogues	Rodrigo de Torres	3	1	F	—	—
1730	galeones	Manuel López Pintado	6	15	3962.06	P	*Prince William*
1731	azogues	Pérez de Alderete	4	—	—	—	—
1732	flota	Rodrigo de Torres	4	16	4659.06	J	*Royal Caroline*
1733	azogues	Conde de Bena	2	1	F + ?	—	—
1735	flota	Manuel López Pintado	4	11	3339.27	J	—
1736	azogues	Andrés Regio	2	1	330.50	—	—
1737	azogues	Daniel Huvoni	2	—	—	—	—
1737	*galeones	Blas de Lezo	2	6	1891.37	(P)	—
1739	flota	Conde de Clavijo	2	13	departure prevented by war	—	—
1740	azogues	?	3	—	—	—	—

b. New Spain fleets, 1757–76

1757	flota	Joaquín Manuel de Villena	2	10	7069.70	J	
1760	flota	Carlos Regio	2	13	8492.75	J	
1765	flota	Agustín de Idiáquez	?	?	8013.62	J	
1768	flota	Marqués de Casa Tilly	2	8	5588	J	
1772	flota	Luis de Córdoba	→14←		7674.75	J	
1776	flota	Antonio de Ulloa	2	15	8176	J	

*	= Officially described as *registros*
( )	= Unsuccessful attempt to hold a fair
C	= Cartagena
F	= Unspecified volume of Spanish produce (dried fruit, oil etc.)
J	= Jalapa
P	= Portobello
V	= Veracruz

TABLE 3 Registro ships, 1701–40 (figures represent tonnage per ship)

	Buenos Aires	Campeche	Caracas	Cartagena	Cuba	Cumaná	Florida	Honduras	Maracaibo	Puerto Rico	Sto Domingo	Sta Marta	Tabasco	Trinidad	Veracruz
1701	—	—	—	—	—	—	—	—	149.4	—	—	—	—	—	—
1702	{288.8 / 1M}	276.4	—	—	303.3	136.1	—	—	—	276.4	—	—	—	136.1	—
1703	—	—	—	—	102.4E	—	1M	—	118.75	—	—	—	101.0	—	—
1704	—	—	—	—	—	—	1M	—	—	—	—	—	—	—	—
1705	—	—	—	—	{112.7 / 139.7E}	91.2	—	—	—	—	99.8	—	—	—	—
1706	—	262.4	305.1	—	—	—	—	—	—	—	—	—	122.6	—	122.6
1707	—	148.4	—	—	{148.4 / 112.7}	—	—	—	—	—	—	—	—	—	—
1708	—	—	—	—	—	—	—	{276.4 / 84.6}	—	{276.4 / 84.6}	—	—	—	—	—
1709	{462.8 / 356.2}	—	—	—	—	—	—	—	—	—	—	—	—	—	—
1710	—	178.6	—	—	—	—	—	—	—	—	—	—	135.6	—	135.6
1711	—	—	—	—	—	—	—	—	165.02	—	—	—	—	—	—
1712	—	—	165.02	—	180.75	—	—	—	—	—	—	—	—	—	—
1713	—	—	99.4	—	—	—	—	—	—	—	—	—	—	—	—
1714	—	—	—	—	—	—	167.75	—	—	—	—	—	—	—	—
1715	—	—	167.75	167.75	88.4	—	—	—	—	—	—	—	—	—	—
1716	—	215.75	—	—	212.2	—	—	—	—	—	—	—	—	—	—
1717	{462.8 / 356.2}	—	—	{368.25 / 1U}	—	—	—	—	—	—	—	—	—	—	368.25
1718	—	—	—	—	—	—	—	—	—	—	—	—	—	—	—
1719	—	—	—	—	—	—	—	—	—	—	—	—	—	—	—
1720	—	—	221.5	—	—	—	—	—	—	—	—	—	—	—	4FU

Year														
1721	{474.5 / 312.2}	—	—	—	—	—	—	—	—	—	—	—	—	116.4
1722	—	*176.4*	251.75	*127.6*	154.33	—	—	—	154.33	154.33	—	116.4	116.4	—
1723	—	233.75	—	—	—	—	309.33	97.1B	—	154.33	—	—	—	—
1724	—	—	—	—	140.8	—	—	—	68.1	—	—	—	—	—
1725	—	213.5	—	{266.1 / 95.5F / 170.6M}	30.5	98.2	—	198.75	—	—	—	—	98.2	—
1726	—	—	—	—	4M	—	—	—	—	—	—	—	—	—
1727	{279.1 / 264.66}	—	—	—	—	—	{201.12 / 124.2}	—	—	—	—	—	—	—
1728	—	—	{220.09 / *315.9*}	233.75	*315.9*	—	—	—	—	—	—	—	—	—
1729	—	—	—	—	113.25	—	—	—	—	—	—	—	—	—
1730	—	—	—	—	233.75	—	—	—	—	—	—	—	—	—
1731	—	186.6	189.0	—	—	—	—	{141.0 / 98.9B}	—	—	212.2	86.1	—	—
1732	{279.1 / 121.16}	—	—	—	*272.97S*	—	—	—	—	—	—	—	—	—
1733	—	212.2	—	—	233.75	—	—	—	—	—	212.2	212.2	—	—
1734	—	—	—	—	—	—	—	—	—	—	—	—	—	—
1735	—	212.2	—	—	227.0	—	{235.1 / 113.25}	{95.75 / 98.9}	—	—	—	—	—	—
1736	—	—	—	—	{174.37 / 3M / 148.33}	60.33	—	—	—	—	—	—	—	—
1737	—	—	—	—	—	—	—	—	—	52.75S	—	—	60.33	—
1738	—	—	—	—	—	—	—	95.75	—	—	—	—	—	—
1739	—	—	—	1U	—	—	—	—	—	—	—	—	—	—
1740	—	—	—	1U	—	—	—	—	—	—	—	—	4U	—

Figures in italics or bold print indicate that the same ship called at each port. B = Building materials for new colony. E = Ship captured by enemy before arrival. F = Spanish produce. S = Wrecked before arrival. 1M = One ship with military supplies only. 1U = One ship of unknown tonnage. 1FU = One ship with Spanish produce of unknown tonnage.

TABLE 4 *Aviso* ships, 1701—40 (figures represent number of ships in each year; figures in brackets represent tons of Spanish produce allowed in each ship)

	Buenos Aires	Campeche	Caracas	Cartagena	Florida	Havana	Peru (via Cape Horn)	Portobello	Puerto Rico	Sto Domingo	Sta Marta	Veracruz
1701	—	—	—	2(40)	—	—	—	—	—	—	—	4(40)
1702	—	—	—	2(40)	—	—	—	—	—	—	—	1(40)
1703	—	—	—	2(40)	—	—	—	—	—	—	—	2(40)
1704	—	—	—	1(40)E	—	—	1	—	—	—	—	1(40)E
1705	—	—	—	1(40)	—	—	—	—	—	—	—	1(40)E
1706	—	—	—	1(40)	—	—	—	—	—	—	—	—
1707	—	1(20)	—	{1(40) / 1(U)}	—	—	—	—	1(U)	—	—	{1(U) / 1(40)E / 1(U)}
1708	—	—	—	*1(40)*	—	—	—	—	—	—	—	*1(40)*
1709	—	—	—	1(40)	—	1(40)	—	—	—	—	—	1(40)
1710	—	—	—	1(40)	—	—	—	—	—	—	—	1(40)E
1711	—	—	**2**	{1(40) / 1(40) / *1(40)*}	—	—	—	—	**2**	{1(40) / 2}	—	{1(127.4) / 1(125.25)+50G}
1712	—	—	—	1(40)	—	—	—	—	—	—	—	—
1713	—	—	—	—	—	—	—	—	—	—	—	1(40)S
1714	—	—	—	—	—	—	—	—	—	—	—	1(214.75)
1715	—	—	—	—	—	—	—	—	—	—	—	1(U)
1716	1	—	—	—	—	1(157.8)	—	—	—	—	—	{1(127.4) / 1(135.25) / 1(157.8)P}
1717	—	—	—	1	—	2R	—	—	—	—	—	1
1718	—	—	—	{1 / 1E}	—	2R	1	—	1	—	—	2
1719	2R	—	*1*	1	—	2[U]G	—	—	—	1	—	1R

Year											
1720	2	—	1(U)	—	—	—	—	—	—	{3 / 1(U)}	—	—
1721	1R	—	1R	—	—	—	—	—	—	3R	—	1R
1722	2R	—	—	—	—	—	—	—	1R	3R	—	1R
1723	—	—	—	—	—	—	—	—	—	1R	—	—
1724	1R	—	—	—	—	—	—	—	—	1R	—	—
1725	2R	—	—	—	—	—	—	2R	—	{2R / 1RM}	—	—
1726	2R	—	—	—	—	—	—	1R	—	2R	—	1R
1727	1R	—	1R	—	—	—	—	{2R / 1R}	—	2R	—	—
1728	1R	—	—	—	—	—	—	1R	—	{2R / 1R}	—	—
1729	1R	—	—	—	—	1R	—	1R	—	{1R / 1R}	—	—
1730	—	—	—	—	—	—	—	2RM	—	1R	—	—
1731	—	—	1R	—	—	—	1RM	1R	1RM	{1R / 1R}	—	—
1732	{1R / 2RD}	—	1R	—	—	—	—	1RM	—	1RM	—	—
1733	—	—	—	—	—	—	—	—	—	{1W / 1(U)}	—	—
1734	1R(U)	—	1R(U)	—	—	—	—	{1R(U) / 1R(U) / 1RD}	—	1R(U)	—	—
1735	1(U)	—	—	—	—	—	—	—	—	1(U)	—	—
1736	—	—	—	—	—	—	—	1R(U)	—	{2R(U) / 1R(U)}	—	—
1737	—	—	—	—	—	—	1R	1R	—	1RC	—	1R
1738	{1R(U) / 1R / 1R}	—	1R(U)	—	—	—	—	{1R(U) / 1R}	—	{1W / 1R}	—	—
1739	1	1	—	—	—	—	—	{2 / 1}	—	1	—	—
1740	1	1	—	—	—	—	—	1	—	1	—	1

Figures in italics or bold print indicate that the same ship called at each port. C=Secret papers. D=Dockyard supplies. E=Taken by enemy. G=General merchandise. M=Military supplies. P=Taken by pirates. R=Royal dispatches. S=Wrecked before arrival. U=Unknown tonnage of produce. W=Wine.

Appendix II

[from E. Cooke, *A voyage to the South Sea and round the World*, London, 1712, vol. II, pp. x–xvii]

A compleat List of all Commodities transported from any Parts of Europe, *to the* Spanish West-Indies.

From FLANDERS.

Picotes, a Sort of Woollen Stuff.
Ditto half Silk.
Palometas, half Worsted.
Ditto half Thread, half Worsted.
Damasks all Worsted.
The same half Thread.
Lanillas white.
Ditto black.
Mix'd *Quinietas*.
Hollands.
Baracanes.
Womens woollen Hose of *Tournay*.
The same for Boys and Children.
Hair Chamlots of *Brussels*.
Lamparillas half Silk, half Worsted
White Thread Lace.
Black Silk Lace.
Precillas, brown course Linnen.
Ditto white.
Bramantes brown.
Ditto white.
Ditto fine.
Hounscots of three, four, and five Seals.
Strip'd Linnen of *Gant*.
Gant Linnen fine.
The same of *Courtray*.
Damasks of Silk and Thread.
White Thread ordinary.
Ditto fine of few Numbers.
Ditto courser of many Numbers.
Thread of all Colours.
Thread Laces or Twists.
Cotton Ribbon.
White Filliting.
Red Tape.
Whip-cord large.
Ditto small.
Hair-buttons.
And several other sorts of Haberdashery.

From HOLLAND.

Pepper.
Cloves.
Cinnamon.
Nutmegs.
Serges in Grain.
Black *Leyden* Says.
Ditto of *Delfe.*
Fustians.
Broad *Hollands.*
Ditto narrow.
Strip'd Linnen.
Thread of all sorts.

Sail Cloth.
Cables and Rigging.
Ropes and Pack-thread.
Pitch and Tar.
Benjamen.
Motillas of Silk.
Ditto Wooll.
Borlones.
Ditto branch'd or flower'd for Quilts.
Velvets, and
Plushes.

From ENGLAND.

Mix'd Serges.
Long Ell-broad *Perpetuanas.*
Long Yards *ditto.*
Cheneys printed and water'd.
Silk Hose.
Colchester Bays, dy'd and white.
Worsted Hose fine.
Ditto second sort.
Woollen Hose for Men, Women, and Children.
Wrought Pewter.
Tin in Blocks.
Black Hounscot Says.

Ditto white.
Fustians.
Scotch Linnen.
Benjamen the second sort.
Lead.
Cloths broad.
Ditto narrow.
Scarlet Serges.
Calicoes dy'd.
Pepper.
Musk.
Amber, and
Civet.

From FRANCE.

Velvets.
Brocades.
Sattins.
Roan Linnen.
Ditto Blancartes.
Ditto Florettes.

Ditto Cofres.
Cambricks.
Kenting broad.
Ditto narrow.
Morlaix Dowlas broad.
Ditto narrow.

Creas broad.
Ditto narrow.
Ditto of *Gascony*.
Coletas broad.
Ditto narrow.
Cotences fine.
Ditto ordinary.

Sail-Cloth.
Combs.
Haberdashery.
Gold and Silver Lace.
Silk Lace.
Fine Thread Lace, or Bone Lace.

From HAMBURGH.

Pipe-staves large.
Ditto small.
Ordinary Boards of *Norway*.
Ditto of *Sweden*.
Great Planks.
Platillas, or, blue Paper Slesies.
Bocadillos.
Estopillas.
Capadereys.
Cresuelas white.
Ditto brown.
Checker'd Linnen in Rolls.
Vestualias.
Bed-Tickin fine.
Ditto ordinary.
Napkins and Table Linnen.

Esterlines.
Fustians double.
Ditto single.
Latten Wire.
Starch.
Powder-blew.
Gilt Leather.
Leaf-gold.
Pins.
Brass Wire.
Brass Weights and Scales.
Brass Kettles and Pans.
Yellow Wax of *Dantzick*.
Barbary Wax whiten'd.
Cases of Bottles.

From ITALY.

Ribbons of all sorts.
Hair Chamlots.
Silks flower'd with Gold and Silver.
Naples Silk.
Shags.
Velvets, one and half, and two Piles.

Grograms of *Messina*.
Men, Women, and Childrens Stockings of *Naples*.
Genoa Paper.
Hose of course Silk, call'd *Capullo*.
Mohair Stuffs from *Smyrna*.
Genoa Thread.
Ditto of *Salo*.

Iron Wares of *Genoa*.
Rice of *Milan*.
Hard Soap of *Genoa*.
Hoops.

Wheat of *Sardinia*.
Alom.
Brimstone.
Anniseed and other Seeds.

From PORTUGAL.

Musk in Cods.
Amber-grease.

Civet.
Fine Thread.

From SPAIN.

Taffaties of *Granada* double.
Ditto single.
Ditto of *Jaen*.
Ditto of *Antequera*.
Black Silk of *Granada*.
Ditto colour'd.
Sattins flower'd.
Ditto plain.
Toledo silk Hose.
Mix'd Serges of *Ampudia*.
Saffron of *Villa Alva*.
Hard Soap of *Alicant*.
Almonds of *Alicant*.
Ditto of *Valencia*.

Wooll.
Wheat.
Barley.
Xeres Wines.
Tent Wine of *St. Lucar*.
Oil of *Sevil*.
Figs.
Raisins of *Arcos* in Barrels.
Ditto in Frail.
Salt.
White Wax.
Iron Ware from *Biscay*.
Steel.

A List of Commodities brought from the Spanish West–Indies *into* Europe.

Pearls.
Emerauds.
Amethists.
Virgin Silver.
Ditto in Pigs.
Ditto in Pieces of Eight.
Virgin Gold.
Ditto in Doblones.
Cochinilla of several sorts.

Grana Silvestre, or, Wild Scarlet.
Ditto of *Campeche*.
Indigo.
Anatto.
Logwood.
Brasilette.
Nicaragua Wood.
Fustick.
Lignum Vitae.

Sugars.
Ginger.
Cacao.
Bainillas.
Cotton.
Rod Wooll.
Tobacco in Roll.
Ditto in Snuff.
Hides raw.
Ditto tann'd.
Ambergrease gray.

Ditto black.
Bezoar.
Balsam of *Peru*.
Ditto of *Tolu*.
Cortex Peruvianus, or, *Jesuit*'s Bark.
Jallap.
Mechoacan.
Sarsaparilla.
Sassafras.
Tamarinds.
Cassia.

Appendix III

The following four tables show the rates of taxes and freight charges made on goods and precious metals in all trade fleets on departure from and return to Cadiz over the period 1711–20. The first columns apply to the *flotas* of 1711, 1712 and 1715, and to the *galeones* of Echeverz in 1713 and the Conde de Vegaflorida in 1715. They originate from the *proyecto* of 1711. The second columns come from the *proyecto* for the *flota* of 1717, and the third columns set out the taxes stipulated in the *Real proyecto* of 1720. The list of goods specified in the *Real proyecto* of 1720 is very much more detailed and varied than the lists of the other two *proyectos* and consequently the tables are complete only insomuch as comparability allows. Also for the sake of comparability weights and currency denominations have been standardised.

(1 *quintal* = 4 *arrobas* = 100 *libras*; 1 *peso* = 8 *reales*)

239

TABLE 1   *Duties payable outward bound from Cadiz*

	1711		1717		1720	
Palmeo levied on all goods uninspected in crates, packets etc.: on each cubic *palmo*	$5\frac{1}{2}$	*reales*	$5\frac{1}{2}$	*reales*	$5\frac{1}{2}$	*reales*
Iron bars, per *quintal*	6	,,	5	,,	4	,,
Nails, per *quintal*	10	,,	10	,,	10	,,
Steel, per *quintal*	$18\frac{2}{3}$	,,	$18\frac{2}{3}$	,,	16	,,
Blocks of wax, per *arroba*	13	,,	13	,,	10	,,
Paper in bales, per ream	$2\frac{1}{3}$	,,	2	,,	2	,,
Untreated linen, per length	6	,,	5	,,	1	,,
Cloth woven from Flanders thread, per *libra*	$\frac{3}{4}$	,,	$\frac{1}{2}$	,,	$\frac{3}{4}$	,,
Cloth woven from hemp thread, per *quintal*	50	,,	25	,,	10	,,
Cinnamon, per *quintal*	15	*pesos*	15	*pesos*	20	*pesos*
Pepper, per *arroba*	8	*reales*	8	*reales*	12	*reales*
Raisins, per *quintal*	40	,,	32	,,	6	,,
Almonds, per *quintal*	40	,,	32	,,	32	,,
Wine, per $1\frac{1}{4}$-*arroba* jar	5	,,	4	,,	1	,,
,, per $4\frac{1}{2}$-*arroba* barrel	20	,,	16	,,	5	,,
,, per $27\frac{1}{2}$-*arroba* barrel	72	,,	72	,,	28	,,
Spirits (*aguardiente*), per $4\frac{1}{2}$-*arroba* barrel	28	,,	24	,,	7	,,
Spirits (*aguardiente*), per $27\frac{1}{2}$-*arroba* barrel	14	*pesos*	14	*pesos*	$4\frac{3}{4}$	*pesos*
Olive oil, per *arroba*	4	*reales*	3	*reales*	$1\frac{1}{2}$	*reales*

TABLE 2 *Freight charges payable outward bound from Cadiz*

	1711		1717		1720	
On packets etc. taxed by *palmeo*: for each 37½-cubic *palmos*	$\frac{7}{12}$ *pesos*		$\frac{7}{12}$ *peso*		$\frac{9}{12}$ *peso* (in Crown ships) $\frac{8}{12}$ *peso* (in private ships)	
Iron bars, per *quintal*	11	*reales*	10	*reales*	10	*reales*
Nails, per *quintal*	4¼	,,	4	,,	4	,,
Boxes of steel, per *quintal*	14	,,	12	,,	14	,,
Blocks of wax, per *arroba*	20	,,	20	,,	20	,,
Paper in bales, per 24 reams	24	*pesos*	20	*pesos*	22	*pesos*
Untreated linen, per length	10	*reales*	8	*reales*	8	*reales*
Rough cloths, per *libra*	1	,,	1	,,	1	,,
Cinnamon, per *quintal*	20	*pesos*	20	*pesos*	20	*pesos*
Pepper, per *arroba*	14	*reales*	12	*reales*	12	*reales*
Raisins, almonds, dried fruit, per *quintal*	22	*pesos*	(unspecified)		20	*pesos*
Wine, per 1¼-*arroba* jar	18	*reales*	(unspecified)		20	*reales*
,, per 4½-*arroba* barrel	9½	*pesos*	8	*pesos*	10	*pesos*
,, per 27½-*arroba* barrel	40	,,	40	,,	50	,,
(Spirits at same rates as wine)						
Olive oil, per ½ *arroba*	10	*reales*	8	*reales*	10	*reales*

TABLE 3 *Duties payable on return to Cadiz*

	1711			1717			1720		
Gold	1½% of value			2% of value			2% of value		
Silver	4% ,, ,,			5% ,, ,,			5% ,, ,,		
Indigo, per *arroba*	11	*reales*		12	*reales*		12	*reales*	
Refined cochineal, per *arroba*	40	,,	(gross wt.)	41½	,,	(net wt.)	44	,,	(net wt.)
Vanilla, per *arroba*	30	,,	(,, ,,)	31	,,	(,, ,,)	64	,,	(,, ,,)
Roucou, per *arroba*	12	,,	(,, ,,)	12	,,	(,, ,,)	10	,,	(,, ,,)
Sugar, per *arroba*	3	,,	(,, ,,)	4	,,	(,, ,,)	2	,,	(,, ,,)
Tobacco leaf, per *quintal*	6	,,	(,, ,,)	6	,,	(,, ,,)	6	,,	(,, ,,)
Snuff, per *quintal*	10	,,	(,, ,,)	10	,,	(,, ,,)	10	,,	(,, ,,)
Raw cocoa, per *quintal*	2	*pesos*	(,, ,,)	2	*pesos*	(,, ,,)	2	*pesos*	(,, ,,)
Brazil-wood, per *quintal*	5	*reales*		5	*reales*		5	*reales*	
Tanned hides	2½	,,	(each)	2½	,,	(each)	2	,,	(each)
Raw hides	2	,,	(,,)	2	,,	(,,)	1½	,,	(,,)
Unspecified goods	5% of value			5% of value			5% of value		

TABLE 4   Freight charges payable on return to Cadiz (all weights gross)

	1711	1717	1720
Gold	$\frac{1}{2}$% of value	$\frac{1}{2}$% of value	$\frac{1}{2}$% of value
Silver	$1\frac{1}{2}$% ,, ,,	$1\frac{1}{2}$% ,,	$1\frac{1}{2}$% ,,
Indigo, per *arroba*	7 *reales*	7 *reales*	7 *reales*
Cochineal, per arroba	9 ,,	9 ,,	9 ,,
Vanilla, roucou, sugar, refined chocolate, per arroba	8 ,,	8 ,,	8 ,,
Unrefined cocoa, Jalapa purge, per *arroba*	10 ,,	10 ,,	10 ,,
Tobacco leaf, per arroba	8 ,,	8 ,,	8 ,,
Snuff, per *arroba*	8 ,,	8 ,,	8 ,,
Hides, raw and tanned	8 ,, (each)	8 ,, (each)	8 ,, (each)
Brazil-wood	50% of value	50% of value	8 ,, (per *quintal*)
Campeachy-wood	50% ,, ,,	50% ,, ,,	4 ,, (per *quintal*)

Note: *Palmeo* rates had no application for the return journeys (i.e. tables 3 and 4) since fine goods or manufactured goods in packets were normally not brought back from America. The fleet usually carried mainly precious metals and native produce, although small quantities of Oriental merchandise were often included. See Appendix II.

Appendix IV

[Simancas, Estado 7017]

R.! George Cargo 2 Feb 1723 [/4]

96	Bales	Medley Cloth Amounting to	£9252	2	1
93	Do.	Sagathies	3562	5	—
80	Do.	Duroys	2933	6	8
5	Cases	Flanders Thred	405	3	9
127	Bales	White Cloths Dyed	11084	—	2
12	Casks	Gloves	793	13	6
252	Bales	Blewpaper Siletias	9200	4	—
360	Casks	Spanish Nails	961	9	8
1246	Bales	Colchester Bays	33443	3	4
86	Cases	Hair Shagg	3106	19	8
60	Bales	Cinnamon	1590	4	1
208	Do.	Woollen Druggets	9592	—	4
265	Do.	Serges Yd. $\frac{1}{8}$	7685	—	—
207	Do.	Do. Tenhundreds	6183	10	—
1302	Do.	Long Ells	28595	3	—
8	Do.	Embost Do.	227	—	3
1	Do.	Silk & Cotton Druggetts	94	2	3
794	Cakes	Bees Wax	9313	17	8
36	Cases	Hair Cambletts	2951	12	6
55	Do.	Black Crapes	1213	1	8
12	Bales	Caro de Oro Finos	873	9	10
331	Do.	Callimancos	12397	8	4
70	Do.	Palomettas de Holanda	2724	3	4
100	Do.	Callives	3247	3	4
100	Do.	Mixt Serges	3518	8	6
10	Cases	Sealing Wax	233	6	8
30	Bales	Palomettas Bretanicas	974	10	—
265	Do.	Sags	7719	17	6
80	Cases	White Spanish Thread	3367	—	8
65	Do.	Silk Stockings	16781	1	8
151	Bales	Worsted Hose	7748	9	7
37	Cases	Looking Glasses	600	6	10
17	Do.	Gold & Silver Ones	14626	19	2
2	Do.	Gold & Silver Brocaded Silk & Damask black	146	18	11

			£		
5	Do.	Worsted Shagg	201	5	11
18	Do.	Flanders White Thread Lace	12682	9	4
18	Do.	Gold & Silver & Silk Ribbons	8635	7	—
16	Bales	Hambro Linnen	801	16	2
2	Do.	Culsee Flannells	101	3	7
70	Do.	Worsted Cambletts	2809	19	4
50	Cases	Hatts	3494	14	7
4738	Bars	Spanish Iron	2281	10	—
55	Cases	Small or Power Blew	508	17	6
9	Bales	Calcetas	1120	—	—
18	Do.	Cambricks St. Gal	898	7	8
12	Do.	Genoa Paper	132	—	—
2	Casks	Packthread & Packing Needles	28	—	—
26	Do.	Pewter	225	1	—
2	Cases	Jews Harps*	42	10	—
5	Bales	Cambricks at Hambro	311	5	—
2	Cases	Silk Plush	110	11	6
1	Bale	Dimitys	61	15	1
246	Pieces	Osnabrigs	751	12	8
2	Cases	Patterns of Sundry Goods	1	7	—

			252346	17	3
		Freight	12617	6	10

Como ofizial de la Cia del Mar del Sur certifico que es esta es [*sic*] copia
fielmente sacada del Extracto del Inventario y cargazon del navio R!
George sacada de los libros de la Compañia.
Paris 1° de Marzo de 1729   M. Plowes

*With regard to this curious item of the ship's cargo attention is drawn to
the entry on Jews Harps on p. 487 of P. A. Scholes, *The Oxford Companion
to Music*, London, 1947: 'In the seventeenth century the Jew's harp was
used by the English settlers as a regular object of barter with the American
Indians . . .; curiously [however] the native races of America and Africa
seem nowadays to be amongst the very few peoples who do not know the
instrument.'

Appendix V

The conditions of establishment of the Caracas Company as summarised by R. D. Hussey in *The Caracas Company*, pp. 60–64

The basic provisions were as follows. The Company was to dispatch two ships annually to Caracas, each of forty or fifty guns and well equipped for war. The ships might carry what they pleased from Spain, unload what they desired at La Guayra as the port of Caracas, and carry the rest to the safer harbor of Puerto Cabello. The Company possessed full freedom to trade through both ports with the entire jurisdiction of Caracas. In order to avoid unnecessary formalities, the royal officials of Caracas were to appoint an agent to accompany the ships to Puerto Cabello and exercise the required functions there. Ships were to load for Venezuela in the Guipuscoan ports. Having received the legal papers from the *Juez de Arribadas* at San Sebastian, they might sail direct to Venezuela without making the usual required call at Cadiz. They must put into Cadiz on returning from the Indies, but the royal officials there were to exact the duties without unloading ship. Any part of the cargo desired might then be carried to Cantabria exempt from further levies. The taxes and other fees were to be those set forth in the *Proyecto*, a great body of law promulgated in 1720 for regulating the common trade of America. The special exemptions for the Guipuscoan-Castilian trade did not apply here.

The king specifically refused any promise of a monopoly. "Notwithstanding this contract," he said in article 5, "I will concede, if I find it well, to others whomsoever of my vassals similar licenses for Caracas, with equal or distinct circumstances according as it may be my royal will." The governor of Caracas as *Juez Conservador*, or Judge Conservator, of the company, possessed complete jurisdiction over everything concerned with prizes, with seizure of contrabandists, and with the operations and agents of the Company in America, "with inhibition of the viceroys, audiencias, ministers, tribunals, presidents, captains general, governors, corregidors, alcaldes *mayores* and *ordinarios*, royal officials, and other whatsoever judges and justices of the Indies, notwithstanding any laws or orders to the contrary." Appeal was allowed to the Council of the Indies.

The Company's coast guard functions were carefully prescribed. One or more of its cargo ships, and lesser craft, must be maintained in the Indies to patrol the coast against interlopers. These guard ships had full power to seize ships, from the Orinoco to the Rio de la Hacha. The Company might send out rigging, tackle, and sail-stuffs, iron of all sizes up to 400 quintals, arms, munitions, and food, without paying duty, so long as they were used to furnish small craft to follow the quarry into shallow water. Vessels or goods seized by the Company were to be sold without paying a sales tax, and the proceeds to be divided two thirds to the Company and one third among the officers and crew. Captured foreigners were to be sent to Spain to the Intendant of Marine. The Company enjoyed a preference in buying seized goods at fair prices and might sell them in Caracas as though brought legally from Spain. Need of cocoa being so great, captured ships might be used at the Company's discretion for shipments to Spain exactly as any other licensed craft. Captures made on the homeward voyage would be handled like the others except that the Juez de Arribadas in Spain would then have jurisdiction.

By way of aid at the start, foreign-built ships might be used for the first voyages without paying the duties of "foreignness". Also, with proper papers from the Caracas officials, goods left over after supplying Venezuela might be sent to Cumana, Trinidad, and Margarita, in exchange for silver, gold, cocoa, sugar, or other produce of that region legal for ordinary trade to Spain. Those ports "are so poor", explained the cedula, "that hardly can they consume a moderate cargo which goes from Spain". For the same reason, the grant was invalid if any such port was sheltering a ship when the Company's craft wished to enter. With either source of supply, commented the Crown, the inhabitants "will have no excuse or pretext for not abstaining from illicit commerce and communication with foreigners."

Several clauses guarded the Company's operations against stupid or malicious interference by other Crown agents in the Indies. The Company was declared under royal protection, and all persons were explicitly commanded to give it and its members all the privileges set forth as belonging to them. An individual paragraph ordered the commanding officers of the Windward or other royal squadrons of warships to consider the Company's vessels friendly, engaged in royal service, and entitled to all possible help. Another provided that if any ship or prize of the Company were forced into a port of Maracaïbo or Santa Marta by storm, lack of food, or other troubles, the officials must aid it, furnish it supplies at regular prices, and refrain from molesting it or trying to collect taxes. The Company, in turn, was to abstain from trade while there. Yet a third paragraph promised to send orders to all the officials or others concerned to prevent delays and evils "experienced in the last years." Finally, the cedula established the Privateering Instructions of 1674 and the Proyecto and other provisions of 1720 as basic law for matters not otherwise regulated, or unless opposed to the terms of the contract.

The organization of the Company, in distinction from this statement of its privileges and duties, was left to private enterprise. Transmission of the above terms to Guipuscoa was delayed by Patiño's desire for a last-minute inspection, but on October 11 Aguirre sent the Count of Peñaflorida, his principal, a printed version. This was probably a proof copy. Aguirre remarked that he had none left for himself, but was having five hundred more struck off, one hundred for the Naval Secretariat and four hundred for the Company. He also planned to furnish copies of the royal cedulas of 1674 and 1720 to which the fundamental law referred. On November 1, he forwarded the promised imprints. Meantime the Consulado of San Sebastian had been gathering information in and out of Spain upon the organization of companies, and especially on that of the Company of Ostend "as the best regulated, and arranged upon the bases of the others." This and doubtless other data was considered by a Junta of royally appointed Guipuscoans. They produced, on November 17, 1728, rules for the internal administration of the project.

The rules arranged for a stock company with shares selling at 500 pesos *escudos* each. As in any corporation, all ordinary business was handled by directors. There were five of these men, of whom the first were appointed by the Crown for convenience in beginning work. They received a salary of 5,000 pesos a year, must own at least ten shares, and no two might be related even in the second degree of consanguinity. At least every five years they were required to call a *Junta General* or stockholders' meeting, in which every person owning eight shares or more had the right to vote. The Junta must hear a full report of the directors' administration. It might elect or depose any official, pass rules for the general conduct of affairs, declare dividends, and carry on regular business of whatever variety. Stringent regulations guarded against members of the Company using its ships for individual trade. A special provision called for a preliminary Junta General when sufficient funds were at hand for the first ships.

On this simple foundation the Company was organized. It at once opened its books for subscriptions.

Notes

Preface

1. The present study was completed before the publication of the doctoral thesis of A. García-Baquero, *Cádiz y el Atlántico, 1717–1778*, 2 vols, Seville, 1976, a most useful contribution to our knowledge of economico–statistical aspects of the Cadiz trades in the eighteenth century.

Introduction

1. On this topic the major early authorities are J. de Veitia Linage, *Norte de la contratación de las Indias occidentales*, Seville, 1672, J. Gutiérrez de Rubalcava, *Tratado histórico, político y legal del comercio de las Indias occidentales . . . 1ª parte: Compendio histórico del comercio de las Indias*, Cadiz, 1750, and R. Antúnez y Acevedo, *Memorias históricas sobre la legislación y gobierno del comercio de los españoles en sus colonias en las Indias occidentales*, Madrid, 1797. The most comprehensive modern studies are those of C. H. Haring in *Trade and Navigation between Spain and the Indies in the Time of the Hapsburgs*, Cambridge, Mass., 1918, J. H. Parry in *The Spanish Seaborne Empire*, London, 1966, and the monumental work of P. and H. Chaunu, *Séville et l'Atlantique, 1504–1650*, 8 vols, Paris, 1955–7. Other information in this introduction is drawn from the *Recopilación de leyes de los reynos de las Indias*, 4 vols, Madrid, 1681, and from eighteenth-century documents cited in succeeding chapters of the present study.
2. Quoted by C. H. Haring, *op. cit.*, p. 129.
3. A comparison of certain laws in the *Recopilación* shows how Indian labour was redirected at this time to meet the Crown's economic requirements. A juxtaposition of the relevant titles into two groupings illustrates the policy:

> Group A (discouraging the use of Indian labour in all but basic agriculture): *Que los Indios no sirvan en obrages, ni ingenios de azúcar* (1595 & 1601, lib. VI, tít. XIII, ley viij); *Que para la Coca, viñas, y olivares no se repartan Indios* (1601 & 1609, lib. VI, tít. XIII, ley vj); *Que se continuen las mitas, y repartimientos importantes al bien común* (1609, lib. VI, tít. XIII, ley j); *Que se puedan repartir Indios de mita para labor de los campos, cría de ganados, y trabajo de las minas* (1609, lib. VI, tít. XII, ley xviiij); *Que los Indios de la Nueva España sean relevados del trabajo de los obrages, aunque cese la fábrica de paños* (1612, lib. IIII, tít. XXVI, ley iiij).

Group B (ordering and encouraging Indian labour in the mines): *Que se puedan repartir Indios a minas con las calidades de esta ley* (1589, lib. VI, tít. XV, lev j); *Que los Indios de Potosí sirvan en las mina, sin ocuparse en otra cosa* (1596, lib. VI, tít. XV, ley xv); *Que cerca de donde hubiere minas se procuren fundar Pueblos de Indios* (1601, lib. VI, tít. III, ley x); *Que cerca de las minas de azogue se avecinden los Indios, y sean favorecidos* (1601, lib. VI, tít. XV, ley xxj): *Que en la Comarca de Potosí se hagan poblaciones de Indios para servicio de las minas* (1609, lib. VI, tít. XV, ley xxj); *Que se tenga cuidado con las minas, y su beneficio* (1610, lib. IIII, tít. XVIIII, ley viiij).

4. R. Antúnez y Acevedo, *op. cit.*, pp. 297–8.
5. These matters have been studied in depth by E. J. Hamilton in a number of books and articles. Particular attention is drawn to *American Treasure and the Price Revolution in Spain, 1501–1650*, Cambridge, Mass., 1934, 'Spanish Mercantilism before 1700,' in *Facts and Factors in Economic History*, Cambridge, Mass., 1932, pp. 214–39, and 'The Decline of Spain,' in *Essays in Economic History* (ed. E. M. Carus-Wilson), vol. I, London, 1954, pp. 215–26.
6. The major work on the slave trade in the Spanish colonies is that of G. Scelle, *La Traite negrière aux Indes de Castille*, 2 vols, Paris, 1906.
7. Antúnez y Acevedo, p. 102, quoting Miguel Álvarez Osorio (1686); A. P. Usher, 'Spanish Ships and Shipping in the Sixteenth and Seventeenth Centuries,' *Facts and Factors in Economic History*, Harvard, 1932, pp. 203–5.
8. J. Campillo y Cossío, *Nuevo sistema de gobierno económico para la América*, Madrid, 1789, lib. I, cap. I, paras 39–40; 42.
9. B. de Ulloa, *Restablecimiento de las fábricas y comercio español*, Madrid, 1740, lib. II, pp. 105–10.

Chapter 1

1. The commercial, diplomatic and political issues mentioned in the opening paragraphs of this chapter are reviewed clearly by J. O. McLachlan, *Trade and Peace with Old Spain, 1667—1750*, Cambridge, 1940, pp. 37–45 (who considers these matters largely as they affected England), and by G. Scelle, *La Traite negrière aux Indes de Castille*, Paris, 1906, II, pp. xvi–xix, 108–12, 124–9, 143–4, 150–6 (who summarises Louis XIV's Spanish policies at this time).
2. The major work on French influence is M. A. Baudrillart, *Philippe V et la cour de France*, 5 vols, Paris, 1890–1900, but see also the excellent ch. 3 of H. Kamen, *The War of Succession in Spain, 1700—1715*, London, 1969. G. Scelle, *op. cit.*, II, pp. 122–9, 145–58, discusses the diplomacy of the French assiento.
3. Scelle, II, pp. xix, 128; E. W. Dahlgren, *Les Relations commerciales et maritimes entre la France et les côtes de l'Océan Pacifique (commencement du XVIIIe siècle)*. Vol. 1 (only one publ.): *Le Commerce de la Mer du Sud jusqu'à la paix d'Utrecht*, Paris, 1909, pp. 89–103.

4. E. W. Dahlgren, *op. cit.*, pp. 123–46, gives a full account of de Beauchesne's expedition.
5. Dahlgren, *passim*; L. Vignols, 'Le "Commerce interlope" français à la Mer du Sud, au début du XVIIIe siècle,' *RHES*, 13, 1925; R. Vargas Ugarte, *Historia del Perú* [III], *Virreinato (siglo XVIII), 1700–1790*, Lima, 1956, chs I–IV; S. Villalobos R., 'Contrabando francés en el Pacífico, 1700–1724,' *RHA*, 51, Mexico (1961).
6. D. Alsedo y Herrera, *Memorial informativo . . . del Consulado de la ciudad de los Reyes . . . sobre diferentes puntos tocantes al estado de la real hacienda, comercio, etc.*, without place or date [Madrid, 1726(?)], p. 8; R. Antúnez y Acevedo, *Memorias históricas sobre la legislación y gobierno del comercio de los españoles en sus colonias en las Indias occidentales*, Madrid, 1797, Appendix VIII, p. xxxiii.
7. Dahlgren, p. 142; 'Real cédula,' 11 January 1701, in R. Vargas, *op. cit.*, p. 14.
8. The majority of American Spaniards in fact favoured a Hapsburg succession, feeling nothing but hostility towards France and a Franco-Spanish union. '[The] appearance of ye French in ye West Indies makes the Spaniards very uneasy, especially those inclined to ye interest of King Charles III, wch. are ye major part of ye people, who dare not shew it, without there be a superior power to protect them against the insolencys of ye French . . . ,' Admiral Whetstone to Mr. Secretary Hedges, 18 June 1706, no. 376 in *COSP*, 1706–8 June. See also A. Borges, *La Casa de Austria en Venezuela durante la guerra de Sucesión Española (1702—15)*, Salzburg–Teneriffe, 1963, chs III–VII.
9. Scelle, II, p. 159, note 2.
10. Dahlgren, p. 114.
11. Scelle, II, pp. 110–11.
12. Daubenton to Pontchartrain, 8 August 1705, in Dahlgren, p. 335.
13. 'Libros de registros de ida y venida desde 1701 a 1738,' AGI, Contr. 2901; R. Antúnez y Acevedo, *op. cit.*, p. xxxiii; D. Alsedo y Herrera, *op. cit.*, p. 8.
14. 'Libro de registros,' *cit.*; see also Appendix I to present study.
15. B. de Ulloa, *Restablecimiento de las fábricas y comercio español*, Madrid, 1740, II, pp. 112–13, para. 86.
16. R. D. Hussey, *The Caracas Company, 1728–1784*, Cambridge, Mass., 1934, P. 37; H. Kamen, *op. cit.*, p. 124.
17. On 4 and 5 July 1707, the *consulados de comercio* were asked to send proposals to the king for methods of keeping illicit traders out of the colonies and for the best method of furthering commercial activity in the Indies. 'Remedios del Consulado, núm. 1 [Consulado de Sevilla]', August 5, 1707, AGI, Indif. Gen. 2720. The document in Antúnez y Acevedo, Appendix VI, pp. xvii–xxi, entitled 'Manifiesto que a la Magestad Cathólica de . . . D. Felipe V . . . hace, el capitán de mar y guerra, D. Bartolomé Antonio Garrote,' undated, [1707?], suggesting 'the remedy for the *carrera de Indias*' is probably one of several such pieces presented at the time.

18. R. D. Hussey, *op. cit.*, pp. 8–34.

19. Dahlgren, pp. 225–70.

20. Dahlgren, pp. 322–46; Hussey, p. 37.

21. Dahlgren examines the history of the *Junta de restablecimiento del comercio* chiefly from the point of view of contemporary French diplomacy. Hussey considers the relevance of the various propositions put forward in the *Junta* to the idea of monopolistic trading companies in Spain. Many of the *Junta*'s records are in AGI, Indif. Gen. 2046. See also J. J. Real Díaz, 'Las ferias de Jalapa,' *AEA*, 16, 1959, pp. 169–73.

22. There has been some confusion amongst historians concerning the identity of the commander or commanders of this fleet. The compilers of all the lists of fleets consulted have fallen into the error of believing that there was only one fleet, or at least only one command. The 'Libro de registros' satisfactorily clears up the difficulty. The family's records have revealed the relationship of the two men.

23. 'Inventario de la contratación,' vol. III, AGI; M. Moreyra Paz-Soldán (ed.), *El Tribunal del Consulado de Lima. Cuaderno de juntas*, I (1706–20), Lima, 1956, pp. xxiv–xxvii.

24. H. Kamen, 'The Destruction of the Spanish Silver Fleet at Vigo in 1702,' *BIHR*, 39, 1966, pp. 165–73.

25. Dahlgren, pp. 255–6.

26. *Ibid.*, p. 258.

27. *Ibid.*, pp. 258–9.

28. *Ibid.*, p. 327.

29. *Ibid.*, p. 328.

30. By 'direct French participation' is meant the registering of French goods for exportation to the Indies at the *Casa de Contratación* in the names of the French merchants to whom they belonged, and *not*, as the Spanish law required, in the names of Spanish merchants acting on their behalf. The advantage in this for the French was to cut out the profits of the Spanish middle-man and to give French merchants a direct responsibility in the fitting-out of the fleets. This in its turn brought a share at first hand in the various sharp practices associated with the Indies trade. The widely known French aspirations in this respect are clearly described in a letter from Mr. Secretary Hedges to Governor Handasyde, 17 January 1706, no. 33ii, *COSP, vol. cit.*

31. Dahlgren, pp. 258–9.

32. Governor Handasyde to Mr. Secretary Hedges, 2 August 1706, no 458 in *COSP, vol. cit.* Also 'The merchant vessels . . . which have put in to Cartagena . . . are *nine* in number, and some of them are half laden, and others only a third laden, whereas usually there are . . . sixteen or more fully laden . . . ,' Junta General de Comercio [Lima], 24 September 1706, *Cuaderno de juntas* (1706–20), *cit.*, doc. 4, p. 19.

33. Dahlgren, p. 329.

34. Hedges to Handasyde, January 17, 1706, *cit.*

35. Dahlgren, pp. 341, 348–9.

36. 'Libro de registros,' *cit.*; 'Inventario de la contratación,' *cit.* Details of the equipping and dispatch of these fleets are to be found in AGI, Contr. 1266-9. (Antúnez gives the tonnage of the *flota* as 2653 tons and omits a figure for the *galeones*).

37. Hedges to Handasyde, 20 April 1706, no. 278, *COSP, vol. cit.*

38. Dahlgren, p. 349, note 1, gives 19 April as the date of arrival; 27 April is that given in 'Carta escrita por el tribunal del Consulado y Comercio de Lima al de la Ciudad de Sevilla [25 July 1706] . . . Con otra que también escribió [7 August and 15 October 1706] a los diputados de los Galeones a cargo del General Conde de Casa–Alegre . . . ,' AGI, Indif. Gen. 2720.

39. Handasyde to the Council of Trade and Plantations, 12 May 1706, no. 319, *COSP, vol. cit.*; Whetstone to Hedges, 18 June 1706, *cit.*

40. Scelle, II, p. 128.

41. Hedges to Handasyde, 17 January 1706, no. 33ii, *COSP, vol. cit.*

42. *Ibid.*, no. 376, Whetstone to Hedges, June 18, 1706.

43. *Ibid.* and no. 377, Handasyde to the Council of Trade and Plantations, 18 June 1706; Consejo de Indias to Philip V, 4 April 1707, AGI, México 402.

44. Governor Parke to the Council of Trade and Plantations, 22 September 1706, no. 499, *COSP, vol. cit.*

45. The British in the West Indies made sure that all news of Hapsburg gains in Europe were immediately passed on to the Spanish Americans 'that it [should] encourage them to shake off the yoke of a fforeign Government and to declare for his Catholick Majesty [the Archduke Charles]'. Hedges to Governor Granville, 1 August 1706, no. 454, *COSP, vol. cit.* See also the correspondence on this topic in *COSP, vol. cit.*, January–August, 1706.

46. Parke to Council of Trade, 22 September 1706, *cit.*.

47. Antúnez y Acevedo, p. 104.

48. Mesnager's phrase, quoted by Dahlgren, p. 343.

49. The 19 articles are set out in a résumé, originally by the French minister Mesnager, in Dahlgren, pp. 343–4.

50. Dahlgren, pp. 344, 350, 565.

51. The Archduke Charles was received and proclaimed king in Barcelona in October 1705. The Catalans and most of eastern Spain rallied to his cause, and under Lord Galway (the former French Huguenot leader) the Anglo-Austrian and Catalan army waged a victorious campaign westwards which culminated in the capture of Madrid. One of the organs of government that was immediately set up was a pro-Hapsburg Council of the Indies. See Scelle, II, p. 148.

52. See, for example, Handasyde to Council of Trade, 18 June 1706, no. 377, *COSP, vol. cit.*

53. Dahlgren, p. 350.

54. Handasyde to Council of Trade, 25 October 1706, no. 554, *COSP, vol. cit.*

55. '. . . they'l [the Spaniards in the Indies] hardly ever incline to receive land forces from any other but ye Spaniards themselves, for ye French impoesing that upon them has made them their mortall enemies, when they can have an oppertunity to show it.' Whetstone to Hedges, 18 June 1706, no 376, *COSP, vol. cit.*
56. Handasyde to Council of Trade, 25 October 1706, *cit.*
57. Dahlgren, pp. 352–7.
58. *Ibid.*, pp. 408–20.
59. 'Log books of Admiral Sir Charles Wager's voyage to the West Indies, 1706–8,' *H.M.S. Expedition*, PRO. Because of Britain's continuing use of the Julian calendar the date appears as 28 May 1708, in Wager's log.

Chapter 2

1. 'Carta escrita por el tribunal . . . ,' 7 August and 15 October 1706, *cit.*; Mr. Dummer to Mr. Popple, 13 March 1707, no. 797, *COSP, vol. cit.*; E. W. Dahlgren, *op. cit.*, p. 404; R. Vargas Ugarte, *op. cit.* [III], p. 42; D. Alsedo y Herrera, *Aviso histórico*, in J. Zaragoza (ed.), *Piraterías y agresiones de los ingleses y otros pueblos de Europa en la América española desde el siglo XVI al XVIII . . .* , Madrid 1883, p. 177.
2. For material on the case for and against Castelldosríus, including the *residencia* papers, see: AGI, Lima 408, 482, 483; Escribanía de Cámara 548, 549; 'El *Cuadernillo de noticias* del Virrey del Perú, Marqués de Castelldosríus (agosto de 1708),' published by G. Lohmann Villena, in *Jahrbuch für Geschichte von Staat, Wirtschaft und Gesellschaft Lateinamerikas*, 1, 1964, pp. 207–37; G. Lohmann Villena, *Tres catalanes, virreyes en el Perú*, Madrid, 1962: Vargas Ugarte [III], chs I, II and esp. III; Dahlgren, pp. 397–8; R. Mendiburu, *Diccionario biográfico*, Lima, 1889, articles on Oms de Santa Pau, Flor de Academias; Moreyra, *Cuaderno de juntas* (1706–1720), *cit.*, docs 24, 25.
3. In the many papers on this case in the AGI perhaps the most explicit account of credible charges and evidence is contained in the detailed summary of the statements of the five key witnesses who formed the basis of the secret investigation. The paper, undated, is entitled 'Extracto de lo que resulta de la Inform^{on} secreta que se ha hecho, de orden de S. Mg., sobre los procedim^{tos} del Virrey del Peru Marq^s de Castel dos rius,' AGI, Lima 483.
4. G. Scelle, *op. cit.*, II, p. 147.
5. Governor Handasyde to the Council of Trade and Plantations, 2 August 1706, no. 458, *COSP, vol. cit.*; G. Lohmann Villena, '*Cuadernillo . . .* ,' p. 231, note 57, gives their names and positions.
6. *Recopilación de leyes de los reynos de las Indias*, lib. VIIII, tít. XXVII, ley xij. The Crown was much alarmed by the influx of French subjects into the

viceroyalty under the protection of Castelldosríus and their expulsion was ordered by a 'Real cédula' of 26 June 1708. This was totally ignored and the numbers of Frenchmen in Peru increased considerably over the next few years despite repeated Crown prohibitions. Finally a draconian expulsion order for all French residents in the viceroyalty was printed and served by Castelldosríus's successor, Ladrón de Guevara, on 19 August 1713. BNL, MS C 1837.

7. Handasyde to Council of Trade, 2 August 1706, *cit.*
8. Handasyde to Council of Trade, 8 March 1707, no. 793, *COSP, vol. cit.*
9. It was the complaint of the rightful office-holder, one Francisco Espinosa de los Monteros, dated 12 June 1708, that prompted the Crown to make a full enquiry into the conduct and government of Castelldosríus. His was not the first, nor the last, of several letters of this kind to reach the Crown, but it was the one which first aroused the alarm of the Council of the Indies.
10. See Moreyra, *Cuaderno de juntas* (1706–20), docs 24, 25.
11. Audiencia de Lima to Philip V, 31 December 1706, AGI, Indif. Gen. 2720.
12. D. Alsedo y Herrera, *Memorial informativo . . .* , pp. 62–3.
13. *Ibid.*; Scelle, II, p. 161.
14. Scelle, *loc. cit.*, note 2.
15. *Ibid.*
16. The substance of this account is taken mainly from the 'Extracto . . . ,' *cit.*, AGI, Lima 483, but the 'company' and its activities at Pisco are referred to in guarded terms in a letter from the *consulado* of 2 January 1708, AGI, Lima 482. The 'high rank and privilege' of 'certain' of its members, against whom the merchant body was powerless, is also complained of in a paper of the *consulado* of 12 November 1707, doc. 25, in *Cuaderno de juntas* (1706–20), p. 89; see also Vargas Ugarte, p. 55.
17. 'Extracto . . . ,' *cit.*
18. Castelldosríus to Philip V, 31 August 1707, AGI, Indif. Gen. 2720.
19. A full account of the *asiento de averías* in these years is to be found in Moreyra's prologue to the *Cuaderno de juntas* (1706–20), pp. xxix–xxxii, and docs 22–31, 33–4, 36–8, 50–1 and 55; see also Alsedo y Herrera, *Memorial informativo . . .* , chs 6–10 and 12, and 'Representación del Consulado de Lima,' 1 November 1704, AGI, Indif. Gen. 2720.
20. Alsedo y Herrera, *Memorial informativo . . .* , p. 15.
21. Castelldosríus to Philip V, 31 August 1707, and 'Carta escrita por el tribunal . . . ,' 7 August and 15 October 1706, *cit.*
22. 'Extracto . . . ,' *cit.*
23. G. Céspedes del Castillo, 'Datos sobre comercio y finanzas de Lima, 1707–1708,' *Mercurio peruano*, 333, 1954, pp. 937–45.
24. 'Carta escrita por el tribunal . . . ,' *cit.*; *Cuaderno de juntas* (1706–20), docs 24, 25.
25. Alsedo y Herrera, *Memorial informativo . . .* , pp. 7–8.

26. Handasyde to Council of Trade, 19 January 1707; 25 June 1707; 29 August 1707; 5 December 1707; 30 December 1707, nos. 998, 1005, 1108, 1223, 1250, *COSP, vol. cit.*

27. Handasyde to Council of Trade, 25 June 1707, no. 1005, *COSP, vol. cit.*

28. Vargas Ugarte, p. 46; G. Céspedes del Castillo, *op. cit.*, p. 942.

29. Dahlgren, note 1 on pp. 397–8.

30. A special tax was agreed upon for the year 1708 only, which was levied on goods and money bound from Lima to Panama and known as the *gabela del marchamo* (customs–mark duty). Alsedo y Herrera, *Memorial informativo* . . . , p. 65.

31. Alsedo y Herrera, *Memorial informativo* . . . , p. 9.

32. French interlopers when hindered by honest Spanish officials immediately used force. *Cuaderno de juntas* (1706–20), paper of 12 November 1707, doc. 25, p. 89 and note 50.

33. Castelldosríus to Philip V, 31 July 1708, AGI, Lima 408; Castelfuerte to Philip V, 13 January 1726, AGI, Lima 412.

34. Handasyde to Council of Trade, 14 February 1708, no. 1339, *COSP, vol. cit.*

35. Lohmann Villena, *Tres catalanes* . . . , pp. 4–5.

36. 'Extracto . . . ,' *cit.*; Scelle, II, p. 428.

37. No concise account of this procedure has been found, but see 'Real cédula,' 13 February 1680, in A. Muro Orejón, *Cedulario americano del siglo XVIII*, I, Seville, 1956, pp. 69–71; also J. de Veitia Linage, *Norte de la contratación de las Indias occidentales*, ed. Buenos Aires, 1945, I, xx, 48, and Alsedo y Herrera, *Memorial informativo* . . . , pp. 41–2.

38. Commodore Wager was patrolling the seas between Cartagena and Portobello from December 1707 until June [May] 1708, in hopes of intercepting the *galeones*. Governor Handasyde to the Council of Trade, 5 December 1707 and 31 March 1708, nos. 1223 and 1423, *COSP, vol. cit.*; also Handasyde to Council of Trade, 20 July 1708, no. 56, *COSP*, June 1708–9.

39. Handasyde to Council of Trade, 20 July 1708, no. 56, *COSP*, June 1708–9.

40. Handasyde to Council of Trade, 2 August 1708, no. 68, *COSP, vol. cit.*

41. Alsedo y Herrera, *Memorial informativo* . . . , p. 8; Moreyra, prologue to *Cuaderno de juntas* (1706–20), p. xxviii and doc. 33, p. 134, note 58; Vargas Ugarte, pp. 48–9.

42. Details of these ships' voyages are to be found in AGI, Lima 408. See also Dahlgren, pp. 386–400, 416–19.

43. The incidents involving Fouquet, Chabert, Castelldosríus and Olaurtúa are complex, and accounts contain inconsistencies. Cfr. Vargas Ugarte, pp. 25, 28–9. 44–5, and Lohmann Villena, '*Cuadernillo* . . . ,' p. 218, notes 27–9 and p. 224, note 46, also Dahlgren, *loc. cit.*, and Kamen, *The War of Succession* . . . , pp. 151, 185–6. The present account incorporates material from the 'Extracto . . . ,' *cit.* The official documents relating to the mission are to be found in AGI, Lima 408.

44. Alsedo y Herrera, *Memorial informativo* . . . , pp. 8–9; 'Expedientes del Consulado de Lima sobre quiebras de comerciantes, 1709–10,' AGI, Lima 481.
45. Scelle, II, p. 169, note 1, quoting manuscript by Dernis; Vargas Ugarte, p. 25.
46. Dahlgren, pp. 587–92, 594–5.
47. Handasyde to Council of Trade, 17 December 1709, no. 912, *COSP, vol. cit.*
48. Accounts of French and Spanish shipping in Cartagena, nos. 170, 253, 415, 530, 738, *COSP,* 1710–11 June.
49. Handasyde to Council of Trade, 19 May 1711, reporting Ducasse's intentions as set out in a letter from the Governor of Cartagena to the Viceroy of Mexico, captured by the British, no. 843, *COSP,* 1710–11 June; Consulado de Sevilla to Consejo de Indias, 14 April 1711, AGI, Indif. Gen. 2650.
50. Handasyde to Council of Trade, 2 June 1711, no. 866, *COSP, vol. cit.*
51. Governor Lord Hamilton to Council of Trade, 15 August 1711, no. 75, *COSP, vol. cit.*

Chapter 3

1. E. W. Dahlgren, *op. cit.*, pp. 509-21.
2. *Ibid.*, pp. 352–7, 611. Some of Dahlgren's statements concerning the sailing of vessels, taken from French sources, are contradicted by entries in the Spanish 'Libro de registros,' *cit.* There can be no doubt that the much discussed 'six frigates' sailed with the main New Spain fleet of 1708, and not in December 1707 as stated by Dahlgren.
3. 'Libro de registros' (Antúnez y Acevedo gives no figure).
4. 'Instrucción . . . ,' 10 October 1707, AGI, Indif. Gen. 2642.
5. 'Autos criminales . . . ,' AGI, Contr. 3242.
6. Consejo de Indias to Philip V, 11 March 1710, AGI, Indif. Gen. 2643; Governor Handasyde to the Council of Trade and Plantations, 25 March 1710, no. 170, *COSP,* 1710–11 June; C. Fernández Duro, *Armada española,* Madrid, 1900, VI, p. 422.
7. The Council of Trade and Plantations to Handasyde, 4 April 1710, no. 182, *COSP, vol. cit*; Consejo de Indias to Philip V, 15 March 1710, AGI, Indif. Gen. 2642.
8. Dahlgren, pp. 572–81, 582–8.
9. H. Kamen, *The War of Succession* . . . , pp. 76, 159–61, discusses the financial and commercial consequences in Spain of France's temporary disengagement.
10. 'Real cédula,' 6 March 1710, *Cuaderno de juntas* (1706–20), *cit.,* doc. 53, pp. 272–3; Consejo de Indias to Philip V, 11 March–11 April 1710, AGI, Indif. Gen. 2642; Duque de Linares to Philip V, 15 December 1712, AGI, México 485.

11. Dahlgren, p. 612. These were the unsuccessful negotiations at Geertruidenberg.
12. 'Proyecto . . . ,' 3 March 1712, AGI, Indif. Gen. 2647.
13. 'Indice de los papeles que se remite . . . ,' AGI, Indif. Gen. 2645.
14. 'Libro de registros'; R. Antúnez y Acevedo, *op. cit.*, p. 105; C. Fernández Duro, *op. cit.*, VI, pp. 121, 423.
15. 'Representación del Consulado de Sevilla,' 14 April 1711, AGI, Indif. Gen. 2650; Arriola to Tribunal de la Casa, 31 March 1711, AGI, Indif. Gen. 2649. See also *Arreglamento mandado por Su Magestad observar con las dos fragatas que Su Magestad Christianissima suple para passar a la Nueva España*, undated. (A copy exists in BM)
16. AGI, Indif. Gen. 2649. (A printed copy exists in BM)
17. This method, known as the *palmeo*, was first used from 1695–8. It was partly reintroduced in 1707, was established permanently in 1720, and remained in use until 1778. Antúnez y Acevedo, p. 247.
18. 'Libro de registros' (Antúnez y Acevedo gives no figure for this fleet).
19. The death of Arriola and the promotion of Ribera have confused historians, giving rise to the legend of two separate *flotas* in the years 1711 and 1712. Incorrect and contradictory information is common: see, for example, Antúnez y Acevedo, p. 104 and compare p. xxvii of his Appendix VII. Compare also Fernández Duro, p. 423, and G. Céspedes del Castillo, *La avería en el comercio de Indias*, Seville, 1945, pp. 153–4. The present account is taken from the 'Libro de registros' and the 'Inventario de la contratación,' AGI, *cit.*, and 'Reales órdenes, cartas y expedientes de la flota a cargo de Don Andrés de Arriola, 1711–1713,' AGI, Indif. Gen. 2649–51.
20. AGI, Indif. Gen. 2645, 2647, 2648, and Contr. 3242, contain the principal papers concerning the dispatch and eventual loss of this fleet. Additional information is contained in Duque de Linares to Philip V, 8 August 1714, AGI, México 486B.
21. 'Libro de registros'.
22. *Ibid.* (Antúnez y Acevedo 1202 tons)
23. Antoine Daire to Philip V, 20 January 1712, AGI, Indif. Gen. 2755.
24. Alsedo y Herrera, *Aviso histórico*, p. 189, and Fernández Duro, pp. 125–6, give accounts of the tragedy. Marine archaeologists have worked with great success upon the wrecks of the fleet located a short distance from the Florida beaches. Their finds have proved quite spectacular.
25. Duque de Linares to Philip V, 6 December 1715, AGI, México 486A; Consejo de Indias to Philip V, 3 July 1715, AGI, Indif. Gen. 2648.
26. The contract itself is in AGI, Contr. 3243, and further points of clarification are contained in a letter from Francisco de San Millán to Bernardo Tinajero de la Escalera, 1 November 1711, AGI, Indif. Gen. 2658.
27. Echeverz to Philip V, 24 April 1716, and copy of letter, unsigned, to San Millán, 21 November 1711, AGI, Indif. Gen. 2658.
28. San Millán to Tinajero de la Escalera, 1 November 1711, *cit.*; Echeverz to Philip V, 24 April 1716, and 21 September 1713, AGI, Indif. Gen. 2658.

29. Governor Lord Hamìlton to Council of Trade, 15 May 1712, no. 420, *COSP*, July 1711–June 1712.
30. Echeverz to Philip V, 21 September 1713, *cit.*
31. 'Libro de registros' (Antúnez y Acevedo gives no figure for the tonnage of these ships).
32. *Relazione e giornale del viaggio dell' Eccmo. Sig. Pnpe. di Santo Buono, vice re del Perú con li vascelli che partirono dalla bahia di Cadice li 14 9mbre 1715, sino a Cartagena dell' Indie occidentali. Manoscrito della Biblioteca di San Martino, dato in luce ed annotato da Lorenzo Salazar*, Naples, 1894, quoted by Fernández Duro, pp. 122–5.
33. Echeverz to Philip V, 21 September 1713, *cit.*
34. *Ibid.*
35. Part of the story is recorded by Alsedo y Herrera (who at this time was personal secretary to Ladrón de Guevara) in his *Aviso histórico*, pp. 187–8, 194–5, 315, and other aspects of the affair are recorded in his *Memorial informativo . . .* , p. 22. Further details are to be found in Moreyra, *Cuaderno de juntas* (1706–1720), doc. 57 and notes, and a brief account is given by Vargas Ugarte, pp. 77, 83.
36. Alsedo y Herrera, *Aviso histórico*, p. 189.
37. Curtis Nettels, 'England and the Spanish-American Trade, 1680–1715,' *JMH*, 3, 1931, p. 28.
38. Echeverz to Philip V, 24 April 1716, *cit.*
39. Fernández Duro, p. 126.
40. Echeverz's own words in his moving account of his tragedies to Philip V, 24 April 1716, *cit.* There are further statements by Antonio and Pedro Echeverz about the financial aspects of the affair in AGI, Contr. 2400.
41. This fallacy was first put forward as early as 1740 by B. de Ulloa (see ch. 1, note 15) and it is still repeated (e.g. *The New Cambridge Modern History*, VII, Cambridge, 1963, p. 494).
42. See Appendix I, Tables 3 and 4.

Chapter 4

1. Curtis Nettels, 'England and the Spanish-American Trade, 1680–1715,' *cit.*, p. 28.
2. Governor Handasyde to the Council of Trade and Plantations, 30 December 1707, no. 1250, *COSP*, 1706–8 June.
3. Handasyde to Council of Trade, 19 May 1708, no. 1487, *COSP, vol. cit.* The British ships were probably at Bastimentos, a small bay near Portobello which was used by interlopers at the time of the fair so as to avoid the Spanish fleet yet take advantage of the presence of the Lima merchants on the Isthmus for the fair at Portobello.
4. *Ibid.*
5. Nettels, pp. 29–30.

6. J. O. McLachlan, *op. cit.*, p. 48.

7. Scelle, *op. cit.*, II, pp. 381–414.

8. The question of English trading to the Far East and its relation with the exportation of American silver and British trade in the Indies is the subject of a 'Representación hecha por el Tribunal del Consulado [de la ciudad de México] en razón de que los factores de la Real Compañía de Inglaterra no se internen en este Reino,' 30 October 1723, AGI, Indif. Gen. 2785.

9. See Appendix I, Table 2 of the present study and R. Antúnez y Acevedo, *op. cit.*, Appendix VII.

10. The naval aspects of the siege of Barcelona and the expedition against Majorca are discussed by C. Fernández Duro, *op. cit.*, VI, pp. 109–18.

11. The naval aspects of Alberoni's policies in the Mediterranean are discussed by Fernández Duro, chs IX–X.

12. McLachlan, *op. cit.*; R. Pares, *War and Trade in the West Indies, 1739–1763*, Oxford, 1936; V. L. Brown, 'The South-Sea Company and Contraband Trade,' *AHR*, 31, 1925–6; G. H. Nelson, 'Contraband Trade under the Assiento, 1730–1739,' *AHR*, 51, 1945, and others.

13. *The Assiento; or Contract for Allowing to the Subjects of Great Britain the Liberty of Importing Negroes into the Spanish America. Sign'd by the Catholick King at Madrid, the Twenty sixth Day of March, 1713*, London, 1713, Article 42 (Additional Article).

14. *Tratado de comercio entre Ana, reina de Inglaterra y Carlos III, como rey de España; firmado en Barcelona el 10 de julio de 1707*, in Alejandro del Cantillo, *Tratados, convenios y declaraciones de paz y de comercio que han hecho con las potencias extranjeras los monarcas españoles de la Casa de Borbón*, Madrid, 1843, pp. 48–52.

15. The initial object of England's negotiations with Charles in 1706 had in fact been to obtain an *Asiento de Negros*, and a draft treaty was duly made out. However this assiento was completely disregarded and remained unsigned once the considerably more advantageous treaty of 1707 had been successfully negotiated. Scelle, II, pp. 465–72 and doc. 7, p. 699.

16. McLachlan, p. 61, quotes verbatim Bolingbroke's open admission of this fact.

17. *The Assiento*, Article 42 (Additional Article).

18. 'Convention for explaining the Articles of the *Assiento*, or Contract for Negroes [etc. etc.],' in *A General Collection of Treatys, Declarations of War, Manifestos, and other Publick Papers, relating to Peace and War*, London, 1732, vol. 4, pp. 449–56.

19. 'Contrato que yo Manuel López Pintado . . . ,' 11 November 1712, AGI, Indif. Gen. 2646.

20. 'Proyecto . . . ,' 11 July 1713, AGI, Indif. Gen. 2646.

21. F. Soldevila, *Història de Catalunya*, Barcelona, 1963, p. 1127.

22. López Pintado to Philip V, 24 July 1715, AGI, Indif. Gen. 2645.

23. 'Real cédula,' 9 December 1714, ARAH, D.88/17; 'Allanamiento que hace D^n Manuel López Pintado . . . ,' 17 December 1714, AGI, Contr. 706; Tribunal de la Casa to Philip V, 18 December 1714, AGI, Indif. Gen. 2645.

24. Varas y Valdés to Consejo de Indias, August 25, 1715, AGI, Indif. Gen. 2645.

25. 'Libro de registros,' *cit.*
26. *Ibid.* (Antúnez y Acevedo 1797$\frac{2}{7}$ tons)
27. Duque de Linares to Philip V, 6 December 1715, AGI, México 486A; Consejo de Indias to Philip V, 10 November 1724, AGI, Indif. Gen. 2528; Fernández Duro, p. 423.
28. Consejo de Indias to Philip V, 10 November 1724, *cit.*; 'Representación del Consulado de Cádiz,' 15 October 1725, AGI, Indif. Gen. 2528. See also J. Gutiérrez de Rubalcava, *Tratado histórico, político y legal del comercio de las Indias occidentales . . . 1ª parte: Compendio histórico del comercio de las Indias*, Cadiz, 1750, ch. XIV, p. 235.
29. *Ibid.*
30. 'Representación del comercio de México,' 1 January 1713, AGI, México 2501.
31. 'Representación del comercio de México,' undated [18 November 1713], AGI, México 2501. The Council of the Indies rejected the Mexicans' views and a memo on the matter was drawn up on 27 January 1714. Consejo de Indias to Philip V, 10 November 1724, *cit.*
32. Various aspects of this commercial situation are described in: Consejo de Indias to Philip V, 10 November 1724, *cit.*; 'Acuerdo del Consejo de Indias sobre el despacho de Flotas,' 6 November 1724, AGI, Indif. Gen. 2528; G. de Uztáriz, *Theórica y práctica de comercio y de marina . . .* , Madrid, 3rd ed., 1757, p. 106; J. J. Real Díaz, *op. cit.*, p. 176.
33. Duque de Albuquerque to Philip V, 3 December 1706, AGI, México 477; 'Representación del Consulado de México,' 15 May 1725, AGI, Indif. Gen. 2528.
34. Juan Fr^{co} de la Chica to Félix de la Cruz Haedo, 1 June 1710, AGI, Indif. Gen. 2642.
35. The *alcabala*, a Crown tax on sales of all kinds had from early times formed part of the normal Castilian tax system. It was introduced into the Indies at the end of the sixteenth century and by the eighteenth century various other taxes had been combined with it causing it to be levied at the rate of 10 per cent. In theory the tax was chargeable on all goods for sale, whether actually sold or not, but normally the vendor would rely on his commercial profits for the money to pay the tax. The contract, or *asiento*, for the collection of the *alcabala* was farmed out to the municipalities or to the *consulados* who returned an agreed sum, less than the full product, to the Crown and kept any excess for themselves from the amount which they collected. Farmed out like this the *alcabala* brought in less for the Crown than if the full 10 per cent on all merchandise had been contributed directly, although apparently a greater net return could be relied upon than if the tax had been administered by the royal officials. See C. H. Haring, *The Spanish Empire in America*, p. 228, who follows F. de Fonseca and C. de Urrutia, *Historia general de la real hacienda*, II, pp. 5–118; also see G. de Uztáriz, *op. cit.*, pp. 320–9.
36. Real Díaz, pp. 230–1, quotes at length a document to be seen in AGI,

México 2502, entitled 'Breve historia de los arrendamientos de las alcabalas al Consulado de México'. An outline of the *asiento* in question, covering the years 1709–23, is to be found under the seventh heading of the document. Other details about this *asiento* appear in a letter from Andrés de Pez, Manuel de Silva and Juan de Munaval to Philip V, 2 May 1718, AGI, Indif. Gen. 2771.

37. Although the tax was in theory to be collected on all goods whether sold or not, the *flotista* clearly depended upon the sale of goods to pay the *alcabala*. Money was not brought from Old Spain to New Spain – at least not to the value of 10 per cent of the total cargo of the *flota*. The *alcabala* had therefore to be paid out of the returns from the sale of the goods of the *flota*.

38. Account of the relations at this time between *flotistas*, Mexican merchants, the various *consulados de comercio* and the Council of the Indies is compiled from: Andrés de Pez and others to Philip V, 2 May 1718, *cit.*; 'Acuerdo del Consejo de Indias,' 6 November 1724, *cit.*; Consejo de Indias to Philip V, 10 November 1724, *cit.*; 'Representación del Consulado de Cádiz,' 15 October 1725, *cit.*; and Real Díaz, pp. 176–7.

39. Consejo de Indias to Philip V, 10 November 1724, *cit.*

40. The *consulado* of Mexico in a different context referred to a certain amount of direct trade between the *flotistas* and the *aviadores* (minehead credit traders) in a 'representación' to the viceroy of New Spain, 30 October 1723, AGI, Indif. Gen. 2785, and in the document of 10 November 1724, *cit.*, the Council admitted that this situation could develop if the *flotistas* were obliged to spend a very long time in Mexico City.

41. 'Representación . . . ,' 30 October 1723, *cit.*

42. Consejo de Indias to Philip V, 10 November 1724, *cit.*; Real Díaz, pp. 183–95.

43. Consejo de Indias to Philip V, 10 November 1724, *cit.* Eventually the Mexican merchants succeeded in making life so impossible for the *flotistas* that in the end it was the *consulado* of Cadiz that was petitioning the Crown to suspend the *flotas* to New Spain. Antonio de Sopeña to the Marqués de Valero, 5 November 1722; 'Representación del Consulado de Cádiz,' 15 October 1725, AGI, Indif. Gen. 2528.

44. Alsedo y Herrera, *Aviso histórico*, pp. 186–91, 194–5, 197–202, gives some indication of the extent of the smuggling in Peru from 1712–20. For modern studies see: L. Vignols, 'Le "Commerce interlope" français à la Mer du Sud, au début du XVIIIe siècle,' and L. Vignols and H. Sée, 'La Fin du commerce interlope français dans l'Amérique espagnole,' both in *RHES*, 13, 1925; and S. Villalobos R., 'Contrabando francés en el Pacífico, 1700–1724,' *RHA*, 51, 1961.

45. Moreyra, *Cuaderno de juntas* (1706–20), *cit.*, docs 63 and 66; a fairly complete picture of the situation may be obtained.

46. Unsigned memo, undated, existing in AGI, Indif. Gen. 2771. The ships were certainly sent in 1715, arriving in the Indies towards the end of the year (Andrés de Pez and others to Philip V, 2 May 1718, *cit.*) and not in 1714 as stated by McLachlan, p. 130 and p. 176, note 69.

47. Consejo de Indias to Philip V, 31 October 1716, AGI, Indif. Gen. 2771.
48. 'Resumen de los acuerdos de los comercios de Sevilla y Cádiz sobre el Asiento de ingleses . . . , año de 1722,' AGI, Indif. Gen. 2726; Consejo de Indias to Philip V, 10 November 1724, *cit.*
49. There was evidently some argument about whether the *Bedford* was permitted to sell goods in Cartagena *and* Portobello or Cartagena *or* Portobello. A further royal order of 17 May 1715, stated that the correct reading should be Cartagena *or* Portobello, and it was as a result of this direction that the South Sea Company sent the *Bedford* to Cartagena. Undated, unsigned memo, *cit.*
50. Doc. no. 6, paper dated 18 February 1715, AGI, Contr. 706; 'Libro de registros,' *cit.*; López Pintado to Fernández Durán, 17 June 1715, AGI, Indif. Gen. 2645; Fernández Duro, pp. 122–5, using *Relazione e giornale . . . , cit.* (see ch. 3, note 32)
51. 'Libro de registros' (Antúnez y Acevedo gives no figure for these ships).
52. The governor was Don Gerónimo Valdillo (Echeverz to Philip V, 21 September 1713, *cit.* and declaration of J. Burnet, 3 February 1729, Simancas, Estado 7017) and not Don José de Zúñiga y la Cerda, as stated by Alsedo y Herrera, *Aviso histórico*, p. 189.
53. Consejo de Indias to Philip V, 31 October 1716, *cit.*
54. Declaration of M. Plowes, 1 March 1729, which gives the figure of 75,000 *pesos*, and declaration of J. Burnet, 3 February 1729, which quotes the figure of 80,000 or 85,000 *pesos*. The full story of the buying of these two important South Sea Company officials by the Spanish authorities is told in V. L. Brown, *op. cit.* The declarations (both to be found in Simancas, Estado 7017) were almost certainly made independently, Plowes and Burnet being unaware of each other's treachery.
55. Consejo de Indias to Philip V, 31 October 1716, *cit.*
56. *Ibid.*
57. Full information about the *Elizabeth*, the English case and the claims of the *consulado* of Mexico is contained in the substantial letter from Andrés de Pez and others addressed to Philip V, 2 May 1718, *cit.*
58. Andrés de Pez and others to Philip V, 2 May 1718, *cit.*
59. 'Convention . . . ,' *cit.* at note 18.
60. McLachlan, p. 73.
61. Andrés de Pez and others to Philip V, *cit.*
62. 'Libro de registros'; Fernández Duro, p. 423.
63. 'Inventario de la contratación,' III, *cit.*
64. 'Consulta [del Consejo de Indias] del R^i Decreto de V. M. con que se sirvió remitir el tratado de declaración de alǵunos capítulos del Asiento de negros [1716] y la ratificación de él,' 5 August 1716, AGI, Indif. Gen. 2771.
65. AGI, Indif. Gen. 2020.
66. *Ibid.*
67. Doc. no. 6, 'Carta,' 7 December 1716, AGI, Contr. 706.

68. These are discussed in detail in ch. 5.
69. 'Real decreto,' *cit.* at note 65.
70. AGI, Biblioteca, 305/3. See Appendix III of the present study.
71. Unsigned document (Junta del Asiento de Negros?), 27 April 1718, AGI, Indif. Gen. 2771.
72. *Ibid.*
73. Consejo de Indias to Philip V, 10 May 1717, AGI, Indif. Gen. 2771.
74. 'Libro de registros.'
75. Fernández Duro, p. 423.
76. 'Libro de registros' (Antúnez y Acevedo 2841 tons).
77. 'Libro de registros.'
78 'Real decreto,' *cit.*
79. Andrés de Pez and others to Philip V, 2 May 1718, *cit.*
80. A royal *cédula* of 27 September 1721, AGI, Indif. Gen. 2769, refers to the royal officials' prohibition of goods from the 'Annual Ship' from leaving the port of arrival.
81. Consejo de Indias to Philip V, 10 November 1724, *cit.*
82. 'Representación del Consulado de México,' 30 October 1723, *cit.*
83. It was the usual practice of the South Sea Company to bribe the Spanish commanders of the *flota* and *galeones* to present false statements of the cargoes of the 'Annual Ships'. See declarations of M. Plowes and J. Burnet, *cit.*
84. Consejo de Indias to Philip V, 10 November 1724, *cit.*
85. Consejo de Indias to Philip V, 5 August 1716, AGI, Indif. Gen. 2771.
86. 'Real orden,' 10 March 1718, AGI, Lima 411. General Baltasar de Guevara was given the command, which was never exercised. There is some confusion about a 'phantom' *flota* in 1718 whose command has been attributed to Guevara. The truth may satisfactorily be established from Fernández Duro, chs IX–XI and pp. 181–2, and the 'Inventario de la contratación,' III, AGI. From 1717–19 Guevara was principally involved in naval affairs in the Mediterranean; however, late in 1718 his squadron went to Havana to bring back a large quantity of silver recovered in the second and more successful salvage operation on the wrecks of Ubilla's fleet carried out in the autumn of that year. The first salvage attempt had been made in 1716 under Fernando Chacón. The silver brought back by Guevara in 1718 was re-minted on arrival in Spain, probably giving rise to the *contemporary* (and subsequent) legend that he commanded a New Spain *flota* in 1718. See as an example of this doc. 1, in Moreyra, *Cuaderno de juntas*, II (1721–7), Lima, 1959, and editor's mistaken note 3 on p. 5.
87. Andrés de Pez to Andrés de Corobarrutia, 30 May 1718, AGI, Indif. Gen. 2771.
88. L. Vignols and H. Sée, 'La Fin du commerce interlope . . . ,' *cit.*, pp. 300–3.

Chapter 5

1. R. D. Hussey, *op. cit.*, pp. 8–34, gives an account of these matters.
2. J. M. de Leiva y Lorente, 'La construcción naval en los astilleros cantábricos en los tiempos de D. Blas de Lezo,' in *Conmemoración bicentenaria de D. Blas de Lezo*, Madrid, 1941, pp. 66, 68.
3. Duque de Linares to Philip V, 7 August 1714, AGI, México 485.
4. C. Fernández Duro, *op. cit.*, VI, pp. 111–14. The promotion caused resignations among a number of outraged Spanish naval officials.
5. H. Kamen, *op. cit.*, pp. 379–80.
6. Fernández Duro, pp. 111, 316; G. de Uztáriz, *op. cit.*, p. 187.
7. Kamen, p. 380.
8. This contract has been referred to in a different context in ch. 4, p. 75, and note 19.
9. 'Auto,' 9 December 1712, AGI, Indif. Gen. 2644.
10. Bergeyck to Pontchartrain, 6 April 1713, quoted by Kamen, p. 380.
11. Uztáriz, p. 187.
12. According to Fernández Duro, pp. 316–17, a printed *proyecto* of 1713 attributes the scheme to Tinajero but contains drawings of Gastañeta of 1712. López Pintado's contract of course antedates this document.
13. Bergeyck to Pontchartrain, *cit.*
14. *Ibid.*
15. López Pintado's contract, *cit.*
16. AGI, Indif. Gen. 2020.
17. Kamen, p. 380; M. Moreyra, *Cuaderno de juntas* (1721–7), *cit.*, p. 43, gives details of the first two of these purchases.
18. 'Título primero de Intendente General de Marina a favor de D. José Patiño,' Fernández Duro, pp. 221–3.
19. A. Béthencourt, *Patiño en la política internacional de Felipe V*, Valladolid, 1954, pp. 13–14; J. Mercader, *Felip V i Catalunya*, Barcelona, 1968, pp. 367–8.
20. Fernández Duro, p. 210.
21. *Ibid.*; J. Mercader, *op. cit.*, pp. 209–10.
22. Mercader, pp. 217–21.
23. J. J. Real Díaz, *op. cit.*, p. 172.
24. *Ibid.*, p. 7.
25. J. O. McLachlan, *op. cit.*, p. 147.
26. Uztáriz, ch. LXIII, *passim*; A. Rodríguez Villa, *Patiño y Campillo. Reseña histórico-biográfica de estos dos ministros de Felipe V*, Madrid, 1882, pp. 23–6, quoting Patiño's own words from his 'Exposición reservada'.
27. Fernández Duro, pp. 210–11.
28. *Ibid.*, p. 219.
29. Kamen, pp. 61–2.
30. Fernández Duro, pp. 112–13, reproduces the full text.
31. *Ibid.*; Kamen, p. 380.

32. Fernández Duro, p. 114. See for example officers listed by Fernández Duro, VI, p. 161. Contemporary documents also give this impression.
33. Fernández Duro, pp. 209–10.
34. *Ibid.*, p. 212; 'Cédulas reales' [referring to the College of San Telmo], 1681–1755, in *Colección de documentos y manuscritos compilados por Fernández de Navarrete* [existing in the Naval Museum of Madrid], Liechtenstein, 1971, vol. 24ii, pp. 1337–1484.
35. Fernández Duro, p. 212, quoting an anonymous document.
36. *Ibid.*, and note 2.
37. All these reforms are summarized from Fernández Duro, pp. 211–12, and Uztáriz, pp. 117–22.
38. Account of all that is known of this venture is given by Hussey, pp. 43–8. The 'Libro de registros,' *cit.*, gives details of the departure.
39. See ch. 4, p. 77.
40. These may be roughly rendered as 'Councillor and Inspecting Magistrate of the Department of Control of Trade between Castile and the Indies.' A full account of the outcome of these appointments is given in A. Borges, *Álvarez Abreu y su extraordinaria misión en Indias*, Santa Cruz de Tenerife, 1963, *passim*.
41. López Pintado to Patiño, September 5, 1731, *cit.*; Real Díaz, *op. cit.*, pp. 173–4, 178.
42. A. Mounier, *Les Faits et la doctrine économiques en Espagne sous Philippe V. Gerónimo de Uztáriz, 1670–1732*, Bordeaux, 1919, p. 168.
43. 'Real cédula,' 21 December 1717, reproduced by Uztáriz in ch. LV, pp. 137–41.
44. A. Mounier, *op. cit.*, pp. 102, 104.
45. 'Instrucción de intendentes,' 4 July 1718, reproduced in part by Uztáriz in ch. XLVIII, pp. 113–17.
46. See Mounier, ch. IV, *passim*, and Uztáriz, chs LXIV and C, *passim*.
47. Mercader, pp. 243–5.
48. A. Castro y Rossi, *Historia de Cádiz y su provincia desde los remotos tiempos hasta 1814*, Cadiz, 1858, p. 481; Fernández Duro, p. 220.
49. 'Real decreto,' 12 May 1717, in *Recopilación de diferentes resoluciones . . .* , Madrid, 1722.
50. *Recopilación de diferentes resoluciones . . . , cit.*; 'Representaciones' from merchant bodies of Seville and Cadiz, 1726 and 1727, *Colección de documentos . . . Fernández de Navarrete, cit.*, vol. 30, fols 254–334, 346.
51. A. Castro y Rossi, *op. cit.*, 481–2.
52. R. Antúnez y Acevedo, *op. cit.*, p. 80; 'Real decreto,' 12 May 1717, *cit.*
53. Antúnez y Acevedo, p. 57.
54. Hussey, pp. 43–4.
55. Varas y Valdés to Patiño, 19 April 1734, AGI, Indif. Gen. 2300.
56. J. Gutiérrez de Rubalcava, *op. cit.*, pp. 252–4; Antúnez y Acevedo, p. 118.
57. Vignols and Sée, 'La Fin du commerce interlope . . . ,' *cit.*, p. 300.

58. 'Real cédula,' 3 August 1714, in *Documentos para la historia argentina*, V, Buenos Aires, 1915, No. 3; 'Real despacho,' 5 November 1715, *Cuaderno de juntas* (1721–7), *cit.*, doc. 13.
59. 'Declaración del Rey,' Paris, 29 January 1716, *Cuaderno de juntas* (1706–20), *cit.*, doc. 59.
60. The correspondence of Viceroy Morcillo in AGI, Lima 411, shows how relatively great this French trade still was in the early 1720s.
61. Alsedo y Herrera, *Aviso histórico*, pp. 199–200.
62. *Cuaderno de juntas* (1706–1720), doc. 71, p. 349, also p. 303.
63. López Pintado to Patiño, 1 December 1735, AGI, México 2977.
64. *Cuaderno de juntas* (1706–20), doc. 67.
65. W. L. Schurz, 'Mexico, Peru and the Manila Galleon,' *HAHR*, 1, 1918, p. 390.
66. Uztáriz, pp. 102–3.
67. *Ibid.*
68. *The London Gazette*, 27 July 1723. The prohibitions reached Manila in 1722. Some disturbances had already followed the murder of the previous governor in religious disputes in October 1719 (W. L. Schurz, *The Manila Galleon*, New York, 1959, pp. 51–2).
69. Uztáriz, chs XLVII, XLVIII, L, LXIV.
70. López Pintado to Patiño, 1 December 1735, *cit.*; Real Díaz, p. 178.
71. In 1683, 1706 and 1708; see ch. 4, p. 78, and notes 33 and 34.
72. The basic facts about the establishment of the Jalapa fair are set out by Real Díaz, pp. 178–9. Further material is to be found in López Pintado to Patiño, 1 December 1735, *cit.*, and in Consejo de Indias to Philip V, 10 November 1724, *cit.* Real Díaz, pp. 295–7, reproduces in full the *cédula* of 20 March 1718.
73. A. Rodríguez Villa, *op. cit.*, pp. 44–6, reproduces Patiño's own account of this incident from his 'Exposición reservada'.
74. *Ibid.* See Appendix I, Table 4, years 1718 and 1719, for statistical confirmation of Patiño's allegation.
75. The other two were for the closure of the mercury mine of Huancavelica in Peru and for the abolition of the *mita* in Tierra Firme.
76. Fernández Duro, chs IX–XI, contains a full account of the naval aspects of the war.
77. *Ibid.*, p. 220; Uztáriz, p. 187; Antúnez y Acevedo, p. 49.
78. No *cédula* for the 'Annual Ship' was issued between 1717 and 1721. The *cédula* for 1718 was stopped by royal command (see ch. 4, note 87).
79. The document is reproduced in its entirety in *Documentos para la historia argentina*, V, *cit.*, No. 8.
80. An apparently complete set of the legislation published between 1720 and 1723 on most aspects of the Indies trade is contained in AGI, Indif. Gen. 652. Some important documents are reproduced in *Docs. para la hist. arg.*, V, Nos 9, 10, 11, 12.
81. Gutiérrez de Rubalcava, ch. XVI, *passim* and pp. 332–4, discusses the *Real*

proyecto and explains various points to do with the measuring of ships and the method of taxation which he considers require clarification.

82. *Docs. para la hist. arg.*, V, No. 9.
83. This is Hussey's view (*op. cit.*, p. 200). For other interpretations see S. Villalobos R., *El comercio y la crisis colonial: un mito de la independencia*, Santiago de Chile, 1968, pp. 66–9, and J. Muñoz Pérez, 'La publicación del Reglamento de Comercio Libre de Indias, de 1778', *AEA*, 4, 1947, p. 620.
84. Uztáriz, p. 106.
85. *Ibid.*, pp. 110–11.
86. See for example McLachlan, p. 83.
87. *Cit.* in ch. 4 at note 64.
88. López Pintado to Patiño, 5 September 1731, AGI, Contr. 5102.
89. 'Reales decretos' of 8 January 1718, 20 June 1718, 27 February 1719, referred to and partially quoted by Uztáriz, pp. 101–3.
90. Twenty-three clarifications and additions to the *Real proyecto* of 1720 were published on 28 August 1725, AGI, Indif. Gen. 2528. They outlined the existing *proyecto* (paras 1–4), gave merchants seniority by length of establishment (5), provided for a *visita* to take place thirty days before the departure of a fleet (6), facilitated licences for shipbuilding (7), insisted that one third of the cargo *must* be taken up by Spanish agricultural produce and excluded similar foreign produce from the fleets (8–19), defined the duties of the royal officials (20), provided for the departure of *aviso* ships four months before the sailing of a fleet (21), defined the role of register ships within the pattern of trade (22), and officially declared the above paragraphs to be law (23).

Chapter 6

1. 'Libro de registros,' *cit.* (Antúnez y Acevedo 4428⅚ tons).
2. 'Real cédula,' 20 March 1718, AGI, México 488.
3. C. Fernández Duro, *op. cit.*, VI, p. 423.
4. 'Consulta del Consejo de Indias,' 10 November 1724, *cit.*; J. J. Real Díaz, *op. cit.*, pp. 183 – 95.
5. 'Representación del Consulado de Cádiz,' 15 October 1725, AGI, Indif. Gen. 2528.
6. 'Representación del Consulado de México,' undated (October 1723?), AGI, Indif. Gen. 2785.
7. *Ibid.*
8. *Ibid.*
9. 'Libro de registros'; 'Consulta del Consejo de Indias,' 10 November 1724, *cit.*

10. 'Representación del Consulado de México,' *cit.* Such missions were not infrequent during times of war or national crisis. The coin was raised by the viceroy by means of sizeable loans and gifts, voluntary or enforced, from the merchant bodies and private citizens, by obligatory advance payment of taxes imposed on institutions and private persons, by the sale of leases and other rights, and by the relentless collection of all Crown debts and existing funds. Such operations if ruthless enough could easily upset the monetary balance of a viceroyalty. See E. Rodríguez Vicente in prologue to Moreyra y Paz-Soldán (ed.) *El Tribunal del Consulado de Lima, Cuaderno de juntas*, II (1721–7), Lima, 1959, pp. xxviii, xxix.

11. Real Díaz, p. 231.

12. 'Consulta del Consejo de Indias,' *cit.*

13. *Ibid.*; Real Díaz, pp. 190–1.

14. 'Consulta . . . ,' *cit.*

15. *Ibid.*

16. Unless otherwise stated factual information for this account until note 26 is taken from the 'Representación del Consulado de México,' *cit.* See also R. C. West, *The Mining Community in Northern New Spain: the Parral Mining District*, (Ibero-Americana, no. 30), Berkeley, 1949, pp. 57–91 and D. A. Brading, *Miners and Merchants in Bourbon Mexico, 1763–1810*, Cambridge, 1971, and B. R. Hamnett, *Politics and Trade in Southern Mexico, 1750–1821*, Cambridge, 1971.

17. *Recopilación de leyes de las Indias, cit.*, lib. IIII, tít. XVIIII, leyes j–iij; lib. VIII, tít. X, ley j.

18. F. X. Gamboa, *Comentarios a las ordenanzas de minas*, Madrid, 1761, ch. XII, p. 377.

19. Gamboa, *op. cit.*, pp. 377–83, gives an account of the relationship between *aviador* and miner. It is perhaps a little biased in the miner's favour.

20. *Borrasca* (the opposite of *bonanza*) was the term applied to a period of barrenness in a mine when spar was produced instead of ore, or when a vein became lost.

21. The other viewpoint of the relationship between *aviador* and miner is provided by the 'Representación del Consulado de México,' *cit.* This is perhaps biased in favour of the *aviador*.

22. Gamboa, pp. 382–3, refers to the practice of producing ore from other mines to justify, as the law required, all purchases of quicksilver. It is not surprising that such tricks were also used to convince *aviadores* of rich strikes.

23. Gamboa, p. 380.

24. Gamboa, p. 378, speaks of the rich and expensive cloths and fine cambrics bought and utterly wasted by the miners. See also West, *op. cit.*, pp. 81–2.

25. It must be emphasised that the shortage of coin here discussed was a temporary one and directly related to the circumstances described. In no way does it negate D. A. Brading's conclusions in *Miners and Merchants in*

Bourbon Mexico, 1763–1810, concerning the general rise in silver production in New Spain during this decade.

26. Sopeña to the Marqués de Valero, 5 November 1722, AGI, Indif. Gen. 2528.
27. *Ibid.* No *cédula* was issued for an English 'Annual Ship' for 1722.
28. See J. O. McLachlan, *op. cit.*, pp. 149–50.
29. See ch. 4, III.
30. *The Assiento*, art. 11.
31. 'Real cédula,' 27 September 1721, Simancas, Estado 6865.
32. 'Representación del Consulado de México,' *cit.*
33. 'Consulta del Consejo de Indias,' 10 November 1724, *cit.*
34. 'Representación . . . ,' *cit.*
35. 'Real cédula,' 11 March 1724, Simancas, Estado 6865.
36. These were the *azogues* of Chacón which reached Spain on 8 April 1723. Fernández Duro, p. 423.
37. 'Libro de registros' (Antúnez y Acevedo 4309 $\frac{59}{60}$ tons); *The London Gazette*, 27 July 1723.
38. 'Consulta . . . ,' *cit.*; Fernández Duro, p. 423.
39. *The Daily Journal*, 11 April 1724, reporting a letter from Cadiz of 21 March.
40. *The Post Man*, 25 July 1724; *The Daily Post*, 27 August 1724.
41. 'Memorial del Consulado de Cádiz,' 11 October 1724, AGI, Indif. Gen. 2528; *The Daily Journal*, 4 July 1724.
42. 'Representación del Consulado de Cádiz,' 15 October 1725, AGI, Indif. Gen. 2528.
43. *Mist's Weekly Journal*, 13 April 1723. The date is given as 11 April by the Julian Calendar.
44. 'Relación en orden al comercio ilícito que con el pretexto del Asiento de Negros hacen los ingleses a la Nueva España . . . ,' undated (1725?), and Varas y Valdés to Orandayn, 28 February 1725, Simancas, Estado 6866.
45. *Ibid.*
46. *Ibid.*; *The Weekly Journal*, 2 January 1725.
47. 'Consulta del Consejo de Indias,' 10 November 1724, *cit.*; 'Representación del Consulado de Cádiz,' 15 October 1725, *cit.*
48. Patiño to Sopeña, 13 October 1724, AGI, Indif. Gen. 2528.
49. 'Acuerdo del Consejo de Indias sobre el despacho de flotas,' 6 November 1724, AGI, Indif. Gen. 2528. The decision was upheld by the Crown in the reply to the *consulta* or 10 November 1724, *cit.*: 'Conformándome enteramente con el parecer del Consejo, he mandado que la flota para Nueva España, salga por Mayo del año que viene de 1725 . . . ' (marginalia on the *consulta, cit.*).
50. 'Acuerdo . . . ,' *cit.*
51. 'Memorial del Consulado de Cádiz,' 23 November 1724, AGI, Indif. Gen. 2528.
52. Summary of 'Real orden,' 14 April 1725, AGI, Indif. Gen. 2528.

53. Real Díaz, p. 213.
54. 'Representación del Consulado de México,' 15 May 1725, AGI, Indif. Gen. 2528.
55. 'Libro de registros' (Antúnez y Acevedo 3744 $\frac{21}{40}$ tons).
56. 'Año de 1725. Autos para averiguar si el Rey había revocado la Real Orden de 26 de noviembre de 1724,' AGI, Indif. Gen. 2528.
57. 'Representación del Consulado de Cádiz,' 15 October 1725, *cit.*
58. Details of the voyage of the *Prince Frederick* and its sequel are to be found in 'Negociaciones para la entrega a Inglaterra del Navío "Príncipe Federico," apresado en Veracruz. Años 1727–1728,' Simancas, Estado 6875, 6876.
59. V. L. Brown, 'The South-Sea Company and Contraband Trade,' *cit.*, p. 671.
60. *v. supra*, note 34.

Chapter 7

1. Alsedo y Herrera, *Memorial informativo* . . . , chs. 1, 3, 15, gives a detailed description of these routes of supply and their effects upon the current commercial situation in Peru.
2. Ladrón de Guevara to Philip V, 5 December 1713, AGI, Lima 409.
3. Moreyra, *Cuaderno de juntas*, I (1706–20), doc. 71. See also II (1721–7), p. xxvii and doc. 1 (p. 5).
4. Alsedo, *Memorial*, p. 26.
5. *Ibid.*, ch. 15 is exclusively dedicated to presenting the Lima case in this matter. See also the correspondence of Viceroy Morcillo in AGI, Lima 411, especially letters of 28 May 1721, and 4 January 1724, and the accounts given by S. Villalobos R., *El comercio y la crisis colonial: un mito de la independencia, cit.*, pp. 69–87, and in *Comercio y contrabando en el Río de la Plata y Chile, 1700–1811*, Buenos Aires, 1965.
6. Alsedo, *Memorial, passim*. In 1724 Alsedo was sent to the Court in Spain as the representative of the *consulado* of Lima to plead its case on the tax *asientos* before the Crown. The *Memorial informativo* . . . is that case, and the multitude of matters of which it treats are all germane to the central and complex question of these *asientos*. The greater part of the papers in AGI, Lima 596, are concerned with this matter, as is the lengthy 'Consulta del Consejo de Indias,' 9 October 1723, AGI, Lima 363. See also docs 64 and 66 in Moreyra, I, and twenty six of the docs in Moreyra, II; for brief comment on the issues involved see E. Rodríguez Vicente's prologue to Moreyra, II, pp. xx–xxvii.
7. G. de Uztáriz *op. cit.*, p. 111.
8. Marqués de Campo Florido to Tomás de Idiáquez, 11 December 1720, in Uztáriz, pp. 112–13.

9. 'Libro de registros,' *cit.* (Antúnez y Acevedo 2087 tons)
10. Moreyra, II, doc. 10.
11. *Ibid.*, doc. 9; Alsedo, *Aviso histórico*, p. 204.
12. Alsedo, *Memorial*, pp. 53–8.
13. Moreyra, II, doc. 15.
14. On 11 March 1722, Viceroy Morcillo handed a detailed list of the work to be carried out on the Crown ships. Moreyra, II, doc. 12.
15. This is evident from the relevant docs in Moreyra, II, which indicate the continual insistence of the *consulado* that the viceroy should pledge himself unconditionally to the absolute elimination of smuggling at that time.
16. Moreyra, II, doc. 1 and note 6; Alsedo, *Memorial*, p. 9.
17. These measures included the *bando* of 1 August 1721, threatening execution to collaborators, AGI, Lima 409.
18. Alsedo, *Memorial*, p. 9.
19. *The Daily Journal*, 31 January 1723, quoting a letter from Paris of 29 January 1723.
20. Alsedo, *Presupuestos y consecuencias de la extinción de galeones . . .* (in J. Zaragoza, *Piraterías y agresiones, cit.*), pp. 481–2.
21. Moreyra, II, doc. 37, p. 145.
22. *Ibid.*; Alsedo, *Memorial*, pp. 2, 10, 61, 63–4.
23. Moreyra, II, p. xxiv.
24. These difficulties, mainly of a complicated bureaucratic and financial nature, are explained in minute detail by Alsedo, *Memorial*, pp. 61–4, ch. XI, *passim*.
25. *Ibid.*, pp. 74–5.
26. *Ibid.*, pp. 3, 57–8. See also Alsedo, *Aviso histórico*, pp. 214–15.
27. Alsedo, *Memorial*, pp. 58–64. Alsedo's notes 44, 46, 47 and 48 reproduce the viceroy's orders concerning the procedure to be followed for the transferring of the merchants and their property from Panama to Portobello.
28. *Ibid.*, pp. 83–4.
29. Declaration of Dr. J. Burnet, 3 February 1729, Simancas, Estado 7017.
30. Baltasar de Guevara to Viceroy Morcillo 'noticiándole lo sucedido en Portobelo', 14 September 1722, AGI, Indif. Gen. 2726; Alsedo, *Memorial*, p. 62.
31. *Ibid.*
32. *Ibid.*
33. *Ibid.*
34. Declaration of Burnet, *cit.*; Alsedo, *Aviso histórico*, pp. 204–6.
35. *Ibid.*; Guevara to Andrés de Pez, 23 April 1722, and 'Certificación . . . de las mercaderías alijadas en Cartagena de Indias del navío Real Jorge,' 15 April 1722, AGI, Indif. Gen. 2726.
36. 'Resumen de los acuerdos de los comercios de Sevilla y Cádiz, sobre el

asiento de ingleses, comercios ilícitos, y operaciones del Virrey de Santa F^e,' undated, (1722), AGI, Indif. Gen. 2726.

37. *Ibid.*
38. *Ibid.*; Declaration of Burnet, *cit.*; Guevara to Morcillo, 14 September 1722, *cit.*; Alsedo, *Aviso histórico*, p. 205, all give accounts of the volume of the illicit trade at the time of the fair.
39. *Mist's Weekly Journal*, 6 April 1723.
40. Guevara to Morcillo, 14 September 1722, *cit.*
41. *Ibid.*
42. 'Resumen de los acuerdos de los comercios de Sevilla y Cádiz,' undated, *cit.*
43. Alsedo, *Memorial*, reproduces this *cédula* in full in his note 79 and discusses the matter on pp. 90–2.
44. *Ibid.*, p. 76.
45. See ch. 6, p. 129, and note 31.
46. Morcillo to Presidente de Panamá, 3 July 1722, AGI, Indif. Gen. 2802. This is a classic example of the use of the viceregal formula *'obedezco pero no cumplo'* ('I obey but I do not comply') much maligned by cynical historians of the Spanish Empire.
47. Alsedo, *Memorial*, pp. 71–3.
48. *Ibid.*, p. 48.
49. Declaration of Burnet, *cit.*
50. J. Juan and A. de Ulloa, *Relación histórica del viaje hecho de orden de Su Mag. a la América meridional* . . . , Madrid, 1748, I, pp. 109–10.
51. See Appendix I, Table 3.
52. 'Informe del Tribunal de la Audiencia de la Casa de la Contratación,' 9 November 1728, AGI, Indif. Gen. 2726.
53. Alsedo, *Memorial*, pp. 106–11.
54. Guevara to Morcillo, 14 September 1722, *cit.*
55. 'Resumen de los acuerdos de los comercios de Sevilla y Cádiz,' undated, *cit.*
56. Alsedo, *Aviso histórico*, p. 212.
57. Guevara to Morcillo, *cit.*
58. 'Resumen de los acuerdos . . . ,' *cit.*
59. The details of these negotiations between the *consulados* of Andalusia and the Crown are to be found in 'Proposición y acuerdo del Consulado de Cádiz' 3 October 1722, AGI, Indif. Gen. 2726, and 'Resumen de los acuerdos de los comercios . . . ,' undated (1722), *cit.*
60. 'Proposición y acuerdo . . . ,' *cit.*
61. The figure was later reduced to 4 per cent under a fresh contract of 1732 (reproduced in Antúnez y Acevedo, *op. cit.*, Appendix XV). Alsedo y Herrera in his accounts of these matters (*Aviso histórico*, p. 212, and *Presupuestos* . . . , p. 486) mistakenly gives 4 per cent as the initial rate.
62. Various letters from Castelfuerte to the Crown (eg. 16 November 1724) and *bandos* (eg. 19 June 1724), AGI, Lima 411.

63. The *asientos* were cancelled by a royal order of 13 June 1724, and despite Alsedo y Herrera's intervention were never renewed. 'Informe del Consejo de Indias,' 16 March 1739, AGI, Lima 596.
64. 'Representación de los comercios de Cádiz y Sevilla,' 15 June 1723, AGI, Indif. Gen. 2726.
65. C. Fernández Duro, *op. cit.*, VI, p. 188.
66. *The Daily Courant*, 9 August 1723.
67. *The Daily Journal*, 2 September 1723.
68. *Ibid.*, 17 September 1723.
69. 'Libro de registros' (Antúnez y Acevedo 3127 tons).
70. Details of the problems connected with the sailing of the *Royal George* in 1723 are taken from 'Real orden,' 14 August 1723, AGI, Indif. Gen. 2785; *The Daily Post*, 6 February and 1 June 1724; *The Daily Journal*, 18 July 1724; Declarations of Plowes and Burnet, *cit.*; and J. O. McLachlan, *op. cit.*, p. 176, note 69. Her bill of lading is reproduced in Appendix IV of the present study.
71. Alsedo, *Aviso histórico*, p. 220.
72. A copy exists in AGI, Lima 411.
73. 10 July 1725.
74. Moreyra, II, doc. 39; L. Vignols and H. Sée, 'La Fin du commerce interlope . . . ,' *cit.*
75. Moreyra, II, doc. 36; Alsedo, *Memorial*, pp. 52–3. The letter is dated 15 September 1723.
76. 'Pareceres del fiscal,' 4 December 1728, AGI, Lima 411.
77. Moreyra, II, doc. 39.
78. See relevant docs in Moreyra, II, and Castelfuerte's correspondence in AGI, Lima 411.
79. M. A. Fuentes (ed.), *Memorias de los Virreyes que han gobernado el Perú durante el tiempo del coloniaje español*, Lima, 1859, III, p. 208.
80. *Ibid.*, p. 238; Moreyra, II, doc. 80.
81. The majority of the documents in Moreyra, II, from nos. 34 to 94, illustrate this process.
82. *Memorias de los virreyes* . . . , *cit.*, pp. 234–5; Alsedo, *Memorial*, pp. 51–3; 'Pareceres del fiscal,' *cit.*
83. *Memorias de los virreyes* . . . , p. 237.
84. *Le Journal de Verdun* for September, 1726, p. 188, gives the figure of 12,004,783 *pesos* as the final value of the fleet. The values ex-Callao of the three fleets were 7,120,800 *pesos* (1707), 6,247,414 *pesos* (1722), 11,399,073 (1726), AGI, Lima 412.
85. 'Libro de registros'; Moreyra, II, docs 57, 58 and 59.
86. Castelfuerte to Philip V, 12 and 13 January 1726, AGI, Lima 412; *Memorias de los virreyes* . . . , p. 240.
87. *Le Journal de Verdun, loc cit.; Memorias de los virreyes* . . ., pp. 234 – 5.

88. Declaration of Burnet, *cit.*; Alsedo, *Aviso histórico*, p. 224.

89. Declaration of Burnet.

90. *Ibid.*; Alsedo, *loc. cit.*

91. Fernández Duro, p. 188.

92. Printed document, untitled, undated, being a brief autobiography of López Pintado, existing in the British Museum, Add. Ms. 20,926. Fernández Duro, VI, pp. 188–9, gives a completely distorted account of these events, confusing as he does the return of Serrano's *flota* on 5 March 1727, escorted by Gastañeta, with the return of the *galeones* and *azogues* in 1729 under López Pintado.

93. 'Informe del Tribunal . . . de la Casa de la Contratación,' 9 November 1728, *cit.*

Chapter 8

1. There is no complete or reliable biography of Patiño, but see A. Rodríguez Villa, *op. cit.*; A. Béthencourt, *op. cit.*; J. O. McLachlan, *op. cit.*, Appendix: 'Patiño and the Economic Development of the Spanish Empire,' pp. 146–52; and the relevant entry in the Espasa Calpe encyclopaedia.

2. J. Canga Argüelles, *Diccionario de hacienda con aplicación a España*, Madrid, 1833, p. 123, reproduces Patiño's paper in full.

3. This is Patiño's own assessment. For details of these and other measures aimed in fact towards the stabilisation of currency in Spain see E. J. Hamilton, 'Money and Economic Recovery in Spain under the First Bourbon,' *JMH*, 15, 1943, pp. 196–200, and J. Vicens Vives, *Manual de historia económica de España*, Barcelona, 1964, p. 530.

4. See McLachlan, pp. 150–1.

5. *Ibid.*, quoting Cayley to Newcastle, 25 August 1729.

6. BM, Add. MS 13,974, fol. 383ᵛ.

7. E. Arcila Farías, *El siglo ilustrado en América*, Caracas, 1955, pp. 32–4; W. L. Schurz, *op. cit.*, p. 155.

8. Alsedo y Herrera, *Presupuestos y consecuencias de la extinción de galeones* . . . , in *ed. cit.*, p. 492; J. J. Real Díaz, *op. cit.*, pp. 220–1.

9. AGI, Indif. Gen. 2528. The *cédula* is reproduced in full in Real Díaz, doc. II, pp. 297–9.

10. Alsedo y Herrera, 'Descripción de la extensión, situación . . . ,' NYPL, Rich MSS, vol. 99, fol. 13ᵗ; Alsedo, *Presupuestos* . . . , *cit.*, *Providencias de España* . . . , *Comento geográfico e histórico* . . . , in *ed. cit.*, J. Zaragoza, pp. 277, 371–2, 492–5, 522–3.

11. Tribunal del Consulado de Cádiz to Philip V, 9 November 1728, and 'Pareceres del fiscal,' 4 December 1728, AGI, Indif. Gen. 2726.

12. Tribunal del Consulado de Cádiz to Philip V, *cit.*, quoting Castelfuerte's letter.

13. 'Pareceres del fiscal,' *cit.*
14. Alsedo, *Presupuestos* . . . , pp. 493, 522–3.
15. *Ibid.*, p. 495.
16. Alsedo, 'Descripción de la extensión . . . ,' *cit.*, fol. 12ʳ; *Providencias de España* . . . , p. 277.
17. 'Real orden,' 23 November 1729, in R. Antúnez y Acevedo, *op. cit.*, pp. 297–8.
18. *The New Cambridge Modern History*, VII, Cambridge, 1957, pp. 199–202, 397; J. Carrera Pujal, *Historia de la economía española*, III, Barcelona, 1945, pp. 138–9; G. B. Hertz, 'England and the Ostend Company,' *EHR*, 22, 1907, pp. 255–79.
19. Remember that the records of these discussions were destroyed by fire in 1734.
20. G. B. Hertz, *op. cit.*
21. R. D. Hussey, *op. cit.*, pp. 60–4, reproduced *in extenso* in my Appendix V.
22. Document cited by J. Carrera Pujal, *op. cit.*, p. 140.
23. A. Rodríguez Villa, *op. cit.*, pp. 93–4; Carrera Pujal, pp. 141–2; E. Arcila Farías, *op. cit.*, pp. 32–4.
24. See J. A. La Force Jnr., *The Development of the Spanish Textile Industry, 1750–1800*, Berkeley, 1965.
25. Carrera Pujal, p. 142.
26. Declarations of Dr. J. Burnet and M. Plowes, *cit.*, and see V. L. Brown, *op. cit.*
27. Rodríguez Villa, pp. 72–5; A. del Cantillo, *op. cit.*, gives the full text of the treaty.
28. Rodríguez Villa, p. 74, reproduces the royal decree.
29. *Ibid.*, pp. 92–3.
30. *Ibid.*, p. 93. See McLachlan, pp. 123–6, for British thinking on this matter.

Chapter 9

1. 'Libro de registros,' *cit.* (Antúnez y Acevedo 4882½ tons).
2. Álsedo y Herrera, *Presupuestos* . . . , p. 486; J. O. McLachlan, *op. cit.*, pp. 87–8.
3. J. J. Real Díaz, *op. cit.*, pp. 244–5.
4. 'Bando' published by the Marqués de Casafuerte, 7 November 1729, AGI, México 497. This document is reproduced in full in Real Díaz, pp. 133–42; Casafuerte to Patiño, 18 November 1729, AGI, México 497. See also Real Díaz's discussion of these matters, pp. 299–308.
5. See previous chapter for terms of the *real cédula* of 2 April 1728.
6. See note 30 *infra*.
7. Casafuerte to Patiño, 18 November 1729, *cit.*; 17 December 1729, AGI, México 496; 9 April 1730, AGI, México 497.
8. 'Relación de lo acaecido en Portobelo,' 14 May 1731, AGI, Contr. 5102.

9. 'Tribunal del Consulado de Lima. Cuaderno de Juntas desde el año de 1728 hasta el de 1730,' AMH, MS 0526, fols 221ᵛ–222ʳ.
10. 'Libro de registros' (Antúnez y Acevedo 3862 tons).
11. Printed account of his career written by López Pintado, p. 7, BM, Add. MS 20,926, *cit.*
12. *Ibid.*; 'Relación de lo acaecido en Cartagena y Portobelo, Año de 1731,' AGI, Contr. 5102; 'Relación de lo acaecido en Portobelo,' *cit.*; López Pintado to Varas y Valdés, 28 May 1731, AGI, Contr. 5102; 'Tribunal del Consulado de Lima. Juntas celebradas en Panamá y en Portobelo, Año de 1731' AMH, MS 0549.
13. Keene to Newcastle, 13 April 1731, quoted by McLachlan, p. 90.
14. 'Juntas celebradas . . . ,' *cit.*, 'celebrada en Portobelo en 22 de abril de 1731,' doc. 7.
15. 'Expediente de lo ocurrido entre el gobierno y oficiales reales de Cartagena con el comandante de galeones D. Manuel López Pintado, Año de 1731,' AGI, Santa Fe 476.
16. Alsedo y Herrera in his *Memorial informativo* . . . , pp. 62–3, describes the defrauding of royal revenues in 1708. Echeverz encountered troubles with the authorities there in 1714 and reported malpractice to the Crown. Other incidents came to the Crown's notice in connection with the affairs of the South Sea Company. J. Juan and A. de Ulloa, *Noticias secretas de América*, Buenos Aires, 1953, pp. 158–9, refer to Cartagena's bad reputation during these years.
17. López Pintado to Patiño, 4 December 1730, AGI, Contr. 5102.
18. 'Expediente . . . ,' *cit.*; 'Relación de lo acaecido en Cartagena y Portobelo,' *cit.*
19. 'Cuaderno de Juntas [1728–30],' *cit.*, docs 1–4, fols 1–22.
20. *Ibid.*, doc. 52, fols 130–6; doc. 41, fol. 111 *et seq.* contains the *real cédula* of 2 December 1728, addressed to the Marqués de Villahermosa and his subordinates.
21. *Ibid.*, doc. 65, fols 173–6.
22. *Ibid.*
23. *Ibid.*, docs 65–121.
24. Tribunal del Consulado de Cádiz to Philip V, 9 November 1728, AGI, Indif. Gen. 2726, *cit.*; Castelfuerte to López Pintado referred to in López Pintado to Patiño, 5 September 1731, AGI, Contr. 5102; *Memorias de los virreyes* . . . , III, *cit.*, pp. 237–8.
25. *Memorias de los virreyes* . . . , pp. 241, 262–3.
26. *Ibid.*; 'Tribunal del Consulado de Lima. Cuaderno de Juntas desde el año de 1731 hasta el de 1739,' AMH, MS 610, doc. 11, fols 22–32.
27. *Memorias de los virreyes* . . . , p. 263; Alsedo, *Providencias de España* . . . , p. 278.
28. *Memorias de los virreyes* . . . , pp. 243 –5; 'Nota de los caudales que conduce la Armada del Sur,' AGI, Contr. 5102; 'Relación de lo acaecido en Portobelo,' *cit.*; 'Relación de lo acaecido en Cartagena y Portobelo,' *cit.*, Alsedo alleges

that a sizable amount of this treasure was illegally shipped to the Pacific ports of Realejo, Sonsonate and Acapulco in New Spain and that this appreciably reduced the sum destined for Portobello (*Providencias de España* . . . , *Presupuestos* . . . , pp. 278, 515, *ed. cit.*). No other references to this fact have appeared in the numerous sources consulted, although this practice occurred in 1740 (Blas de Lezo to Varas y Valdés, 5 July 1740, AGI, Contr. 5102). Alsedo probably confused the two occasions.

29. 'Relación de lo acaecido en Portobelo,' *cit.*

30. 'Cuaderno de Juntas [1728–30],' doc. 97, fol. 259, unheaded, unsigned paper (probably from Castelfuerte, about April 1730): 'I am informed that the English "Annual Ship" will not go on this occasion inasmuch as in the Articles of Peace there are still some outstanding points and Don José Patiño will complicate matters as he did with the ship that should have gone to Veracruz for the *flota*. This has been confirmed by recent letters from Spain and I am sure this news will be useful to the merchant body.' Cf. *Fog's Weekly Journal*, 2 May 1730: 'We hear the last Express from the Court of Spain brought nothing to forward the dispatch of the South Sea Company's ship *Prince Wm.* for Porto Bello which still continues in Long Reach. The Spaniards are very complaisant and promise fair, but 'tis fear'd that at best they will delay her Departure so long as to prevent her arriving . . . before the Galleons have sold their cargoes . . . .'

31. 'Relación de lo acaecido en Portobelo,' *cit.*

32. *An address to the Proprietors of the South Sea Capital, containing a discovery of the illicit trade carried on in the West Indies* . . . , London, 1732, pp. 6–9.

33. 'Relación de lo acaecido en Portobelo,' *cit.*

34. López Pintado's account of his career, *cit.*, pp. 8–9; 'Juntas celebradas en Panamá y en Portobelo [1731],' docs 1–3, 5.

35. López Pintado's career, p. 9 'Juntas celebradas . . . ,' docs 4, 7, 9, 15.

36. 'Junta celebrada en Portobelo en 22 de abril de 1731,' *cit.*

37. Details of these disputes are to be found in: 'Relación de lo acaecido en Portobelo' *cit.*; 'Relación de los precios que los dos comercios [ofrecieron] . . . ,' 8 May 1731, AGI, Contr. 5102; 'Juntas celebradas . . . ,' docs 10–17, 9–31 May 1731.

38. *An address to the Proprietors of the South Sea Capital* . . . , *cit.*: '. . . the Spanish Ministers [did not] measure the Goods as they were landed, as they have done in some ships, when they thought proper, . . . but when a Present is deducted . . . expenses . . . and many other charges, there will little if any profit appear. . . .' See also 'Affidavits about the South Sea Private trade relating to the *Prince William's* illicit trade' in *The Gentleman's Magazine*, London, 1732, p. 582.

39. 'Relación de lo acaecido en Portobelo'; Alsedo, *Aviso histórico; Providencias de España* . . . ; *Presupuestos* . . . , pp. 230–1, 278–9, 515–16, *Memorias de los virreyes* . . . , p. 246.

40. Alsedo, *Aviso histórico*, p. 230.

41. López Pintado to Varas y Valdés, 24 December 1731, AGI, Contr. 5102.

42. 'Juntas celebradas . . . ,' *cit.*, 'celebrada en Portobelo en 31 de mayo de 1731,' doc. 17.
43. López Pintado to Patiño, 5 September 1731, AGI, Contr. 5102.
44. 'Relación de lo acaecido en Portobelo,' *cit.*
45. *Ibid.*
46. López Pintado to Patiño, 5 September 1731, *cit.*; 'Libro de registros.'
47. The following account is taken from *Memorias de los virreyes* . . . , pp. 244–50, and the relevant documents in 'Tribunal del Consulado de Lima. Cuaderno de Juntas [1731–9].'
48. This correspondence is discussed in Chapter 10, note 3.
49. AGI, Indif. Gen. 2300. Castelfuerte in his *Memoria* twice gives the date as 9 November 1732, and Alsedo in his *Aviso histórico* gives 9 December 1731. Both are manifestly mistaken.
50. 'Real cédula,' *cit.*
51. *Memorias de los virreyes* . . . , pp. 248–9.
52. Unsigned letter addressed to Don Tomás Geraldino (Sir Thomas Fitzgerald, Spanish Ambassador in London and Spanish Director of the South Sea Company),12 August 1732, AGI, Indif. Gen. 2785; Alsedo, *Aviso histórico*, p. 231.
53. Villagarcía to Blas de Lezo, 26 September 1737, AGI, Contr. 5102; Alsedo, *loc. cit.*
54. 'Libro de registros.'
55. *Ibid.* (Antúnez y Acevedo $4458\frac{29}{100}$).
56. Casafuerte to Patiño, 7 March 1734, AGI, México 2977.
57. 'Bando' signed by Casafuerte, 24 November 1732, AGI, México 298.
58. Casafuerte to Patiño, 7 March 1734, *cit.*
59. 'Minuta de una consulta del Consejo de Indias,' July 1734, AGI, Indif. Gen. 2528.
60. 'Bando' signed by Casafuerte, 22 January 1733, AGI, México 298.
61. Rodrigo de Torres to Patiño, 26 March 1733; Casafuerte to Patiño, 14 May 1733, AGI, México 2977; 'Libro de registros'; 'Minuta . . . del Consejo de Indias,' *cit.*
62. El Comercio de España to Casafuerte, 26 June 1733, AGI, México 2977; Consulado de Cádiz to Patiño, 31 August 1733, AGI, Indif. Gen. 2300.
63. Casafuerte to Patiño, 7 March 1734, *cit.*
64. *Ibid.*; Varas y Valdés to Patiño, 19 April 1734, AGI, Indif. Gen. 2300.
65. Vizarrón to Patiño, 16 November 1734, AGI, México 2977.
66. Real Díaz, pp. 245–7, gives a brief account of these events at Jalapa, but as he makes no mention of the English 'Annual Ship' his interpretation of them varies slightly.
67. McLachlan, pp. 130–1.
68. 'Libro de registros.'
69. *Ibid.*

Chapter 10

1. *Memorias de los virreyes* . . . , III, *cit.*, p. 246.
2. It is worth recalling here López Pintado's words to Patiño, written in 1731: 'I tell Your Excellency that if an efficient remedy is not found [to the arbitrary practices of the colonial merchants], the King will lose authority over both places [Tierra Firme and Peru].' 5 September 1731, AGI, Contr. 5102.
3. 'Consulta del Consejo de Indias,' 30 April 1730, AGI, Lima 364. This was in connection with a long-standing and complex dispute between Castelfuerte and the Crown about whether the merchants of Quito should be allowed to take money to trade with the *galeones* at Cartagena and thus avoid paying the taxes the Lima merchants paid on the movement of their money to Portobello. It is to this that Juan and Ulloa refer, *op. cit.*, p. 159, without understanding fully the issues involved. The argument dragged on until Castelfuerte's retirement in 1736 and in the course of the correspondence (12 October 1728 – 25 June 1736, AGI, Lima 364) the viceroy was often treated quite discourteously by the Council of the Indies.
4. Uztáriz occupied important positions in government until his death in 1732. He was a member of the *Junta de comercio*, secretary of the *Consejo de hacienda* and after leaving this last he served from 1729–32 as one of the two secretaries of the Council of the Indies. A. Mounier, *op. cit.*, pp. 198–9.
5. Artículo XVIII, pp. 214–15, of next cited work published by the Marqués de Santa Cruz de Marcenado.
6. No attempt is here made to summarise or evaluate the thought contained in the works cited; attention is merely drawn to the fact that their publication or composition occurred during the critical decade and a half 1730–45. Some account of their contents may be found in M. Bitar Letayf, *Economistas españoles del siglo XVIII*, Madrid, 1968.
7. Mounier, pp. 178–83, gives a bibliography covering the years 1700–87.
8. 'Tribunal del Consulado de Lima. Cuaderno de Juntas [1731–9],' *cit.*, docs 23, 26, 28–32; Printed 'memorial' undated, AGI, México 2978.
9. Printed account of López Pintado's career, *cit.*, pp. 10–11.
10. *Ibid.*; 'Real cédula . . . ,' 21 January 1735, reproduced by Antúnez y Acevedo, *op. cit.*, Apéndice XX; also in *Docs para la hist. argentina*, V, pp. 115–23. The document refers to the Peruvian representative as Don Juan de Berría; Peruvian sources refer to him as Juan de Verrio or Berrio, and less frequently Berria.
11. 'Real cédula . . . ,' *cit.*
12. 'Tribunal del Consulado de Lima: Juntas celebradas en Panamá y en Portobelo, Año de 1731,' *cit.* The meeting was in fact held in Lima although it is written up as the penultimate item in the Panama and Portobello book.

13. *Memorias de los virreyes* . . . , III, *cit.*, pp. 180, 242; R. Vargas Ugarte, *op. cit.*, pp. 206–7.
14. *Memorias de los virreyes* . . , p. 242.
15. J. J. Real Díaz, *op. cit.*, pp. 252–3.
16. *Ibid.*, pp. 253–4; see 'Real cédula,' 20 November 1738, and 'Real orden', 20 June 1749, in *Docs para la hist. argentina*, V, nos. 30 and 33, and 'Representación del comercio de México,' 25 August 1739, AGI, México 2501.
17. See Chapter 5, p. 111 and notes 84 and 85.
18. *Ibid.*
19. J. O. McLachlan, *op. cit.*, p. 151, quoting Cayley to Newcastle, 8 February 1735.
20. López Pintado, printed account of his career, *cit.*, pp. 11–12; 'Libro de registros.'
21. 'Libro de registros' (Antúnez y Acevedo 3141½ tons).
22. López Pintado's account of his career, p. 12.
23. 'Real orden,' 18 October 1735, AGI, México 2977.
24. López Pintado, p. 12.
25. 'Constancia,' 31 March and 'papel del Sr. D. Joseph Patiño,' 10 April 1735, AGI, Indif. Gen. 2785.
26. The negotiations for the 'equivalent' are discussed in detail by McLachlan, pp. 123–6.
27. López Pintado, p. 12.
28. 'Bando,' 16 June 1736, AGI, México 2977.
29. Vizarrón to Philip V, 10 April 1737, AGI, México 2977.
30. López Pintado, p. 13.
31. López Pintado to Torrenueva, 20 August 1737, AGI, México 2977.
32. López Pintado's account, p. 13.
33. Vizarrón to Torrenueva, 21 August 1737, AGI, México 2977.
34. López Pintado's account, p. 13.
35. López Pintado to Torrenueva, 20 August 1737, *cit.*
36. Alsedo y Herrera, *Aviso histórico*, p. 248.
37. The expedition left on 28 May 1735, 'Libro de registros.' Cf. Alsedo, *Aviso histórico*, p. 237, who mistakes the names of the ships concerned. Later historians (Moreyra, Vargas Ugarte etc.) have unfortunately followed Alsedo.
38. Blas de Lezo to Torrenueva, 30 November 1737, AGI, Contr. 5102. See also Alsedo's explanation of Lezo's strongly held views, *Aviso histórico*, pp. 245–6.
39. 'Apresto de los navíos . . . al mando de D. Blas de Lezo. Año de 1736,' Simancas, Marina 393.
40. 'Libro de registros.'
41. *Ibid.*; M. Moreyra Paz-Soldán, 'La toma de Portobelo por el Almte. Vernon y sus consecuencias económicas,' *Mercurio peruano*, XXIX, Lima, 1948, pp. 301–2.
42. Alsedo, *Aviso* . . . , pp. 248–9.

43. 'Real cédula,' 11 January 1737, 'Libro de cédulas de S.M.,' ATT, Lima, MSS 1–8.
44. Alsedo, *Providencias de España*, p. 280.
45. There are a number of specialised studies of the causes of the War of Jenkins' Ear. See H. M. V. Temperley, 'The Causes of the War of Jenkins' Ear, 1739,' in *Transactions of the Royal Historical Society*, London, 1909, Third Series, 3, pp. 197–236; E. G. Hildner, Jr., 'The Rôle of the South Sea Company in the Diplomacy Leading to the War of Jenkins' Ear, 1729–1739,' *HAHR*, vol. 18, 1938, pp. 322–41; R. Pares, *War and Trade in the West Indies, 1739–1763*, Oxford, 1936, pp. 1–64, and McLachlan, pp. 100–21.
46. Moreyra, 'La toma de Portobelo . . . ,' *cit.*, p. 302, also comes to this conclusion.
47. 'Libro de registros'; Alsedo, *Aviso histórico*, p. 249.
48. 'Libro de registros' (Antúnez y Acevedo 1891 tons).
49. Alsedo, *loc. cit.*
50. 'Tribunal del Consulado de Lima. Cuaderno de Juntas [1731–1739],' *cit.* The *capitana* arrived on 14 March and the remainder on 20 March.
51. *Ibid.*
52. *Ibid.*; Blas de Lezo in his letter of 30 November 1737, *cit.*, describes the extent and damage of the current foreign interloping and betrays the low morale of loyal Spanish officials.
53. The course of these three-year long negotiations may be followed through the 'Cuaderno de Juntas [1731–1739]' and 'Cuaderno de Juntas [1740–1749],' AMH, MSS 610 and 698.
54. Villagarcía to Blas de Lezo, 12 January 1739, AGI, Contr. 5102.
55. 'Nota de los caudales que conduce la Arm^da del Sur,' 1739, AGI, Contr. 5102.
56. Blas de Lezo to Varas y Valdés, 28 August 1739, AGI, Contr. 5102.
57. Relations between Spain and Great Britain at this time are discussed in R. Pares, *op. cit.*, pp. 43–64, and the movements of the British Navy in H. W. Richmond, *The Navy in the War of 1739–48*, vol. I, Cambridge, 1920, pp. 7–47.
58. Blas de Lezo to Varas y Valdés, 28 August 1739, AGI, Contr. 5102; Moreyra, 'La toma de Portobelo . . . ,' pp. 301, 303.
59. For accounts of Vernon's action see Moreyra, 'La toma de Portobelo . . . ,' pp. 297–301, 306–11; H. W. Richmond, *op. cit.*, pp. 46–50; J. F. King, 'Documents. Admiral Vernon at Portobello: 1739,' *HAHR*, 33, 1943, pp. 258–82.
60. *Memorias de los virreyes . . . , cit.*, IV, Conde de Superunda, p. 136.
61. Blas de Lezo to Varas y Valdés, 5 July 1740, and 10 January 1741, AGI, Contr. 5102.
62. 'Tribunal del Consulado de Lima. Cuaderno de Juntas desde el año de 1740 hasta el de 1749' AMH, MS. 698; Moreyra, 'La toma de Portobelo . . . ,' pp. 305–6 *Memorias de los virreyes . . . ,* IV, p. 136.
63. 'Libro de registros,' 1739–70, AGI, Contr. 2902.

Chapter 11

1. Another event, the legendary severing of a certain Captain Jenkins' ear from his head by a Spanish *guardacosta*, although giving its name to the war, actually took place in 1731, but it was recalled with passion by the British parliamentary opposition as justification of its bellicosity in 1738.
2. J. O. McLachlan, *op. cit.*, p. 139.
3. *Ibid.*
4. Andrés de Loyo (of the *consulado* of Cadiz) to the Marqués de la Ensenada, 20 September 1750, BM, Add. MS 13,976; *Memorias de los virreyes . . . , cit.*, IV, Conde de Superunda, p. 137; J. J. Real Díaz, *op. cit.*, p. 260.
5. 'Libro de registros,' 1739–70, *cit.*; R. Pares, *op. cit.*, p. 114, quoting a French source.
6. Andrés de Loyo to the Marqués de la Ensenada, *cit.*
7. *Ibid.*; 'Memorial de los Diputados del Comercio de la Nueva España,' 1756, AGI, México 2980; 'Nota de los factores encomenderos del Comercio de España que residen en la capital de México,' 1 March 1755, AGI, México 2980; Real Díaz, pp. 260–1.
8. Andrés de Loyo to the Marqués de la Ensenada, *cit.*; *Memorias de los virreyes . . .*, IV, pp. 136–40; Moreyra, 'La toma de Portobelo . . . ,' *cit.*, pp. 316–17, 321–8; 'Tribunal del Consulado de Lima. Cuaderno de juntas, 1740–1749,' *cit.*
9. Pares, pp. 114–27.
10. Loyo to Ensenada, *cit.*
11. *Ibid.*
12. *Ibid.*
13. *Ibid.*
14. *Ibid.*; Real Díaz, p. 260; *Memorias de los virreyes . . . ,* p. 137.
15. Loyo to Ensenada.
16. R. Vargas Ugarte, *op. cit.*, pp. 264–74; *Memorias de los virreyes . . . ,* pp. 305–7.
17. Alsedo y Herrera, *Comento anual geográfico e histórico, ed. cit.*, pp. 321, 327–8.
18. Morevra, 'La toma de Portobelo . . . ,' p. 314. The Conde de Superunda spent 234,726 *pesos* on the fortifications and his successor Amat 370,942 *pesos*. This made only 605,668 *pesos* over more than 25 years.
19. Loyo to Ensenada, *cit.*
20. *Memorias de los virreyes . . . ,* pp. 139–40.
21. J. Zaragoza, *Piraterías y agresiones de los ingleses, cit.*, p. 125; J. H. Parry, *The Spanish Seaborne Empire*, London, 1966, p. 288.
22. *Memorias de los virreyes . . . ,* p. 141.
23. See Chapter 10, pp. 198–9 and notes 15 and 16.
24. *Memorias de los virreyes . . . ,* p. 141. See also G. Céspedes del Castillo, 'Lima y Buenos Aires. Repercusiones económicas y políticas de la creación del virreinato del Plata', *AEA*, 3, 1946, pp. 677–874; S. Villalobos, *El comercio y la crisis colonial . . . , cit.*, and *Comercio y contrabando . . . , cit.*, and V. Vázquez de

Prada 'Las rutas comerciales entre España y América en el s. XVIII', *AEA*, 25, 1968, pp. 197–237.

25. *Ibid.*

26. *Ibid.*

27. 'Freedom of trade' in this context does not refer to our modern concept of 'free trade', but rather to a relative lack of restriction upon the trading practices of one (authorised) individual or group of merchants with another (authorised) individual or group. Within the terms of the concept, trade would always be controlled by the Crown as regards the routes it followed, the individuals who could engage in it and to some extent the merchandise with which it was carried on.

28. Compare for example the following statements of 1728, 1730 and 1732 with that of Campillo in 1743: 'el comercio se mueve donde halla interés . . . por ser el modo de vivir de los comerciantes' (the *fiscal* of the Council of the Indies, 4 December 1728, AGI, Indif. Gen. 2726); 'siendo el comercio libre, existen ya bastantes impedimentos' ('Consulta del Consejo de Indias,' 30 April 1730, AGI, Lima 364); 'atendiendo principalmente a la libertad en que se debe mantener a los comercios para su mayor conservación' ('Consulta del Consejo de Indias,' 9 February 1732, AGI, Lima 364); 'Hay que mirar a la libertad como el alma del comercio, sin la cual no puede florecer ni vivir' (Campillo, *op. cit.*, [written in 1743], p. 64).

29. Campillo, p. 19.

30. All factual information in the following paragraphs is taken from Real Díaz, pp. 269–80; J. Muñoz Pérez, 'La publicación del Reglamento de Comercio Libre de Indias, de 1778,' *AEA*, IV, 1947, pp. 615–64; R. Antúnez y Acevedo, *op. cit.*, Apéndice VII, p. xxix.

List of sources cited in the text and notes

A. Manuscript sources

Archivo General de Indias, Seville.
  Biblioteca: 305/3.
  Sección de Contratación, *legajos*: 706, 1266, 1267, 1268, 1269, 2400, 2901, 2902, 3242, 3243, 5102, 5800.
  Escribanía de Cámara, *legajos*: 548, 549.
Sección de Indiferente General, *legajos*: 652, 2020, 2046, 2300, 2528, 2642, 2643, 2645, 2646, 2647, 2648, 2649, 2650, 2651, 2658, 2720, 2726, 2755, 2769, 2771, 2785, 2802.
  Inventario de la Contratación, vol. III.
  Audiencia de Lima, *legajos*: 363, 364, 408, 409, 411, 412, 481, 482, 483, 596.
  Audiencia de México, *legajos*: 298, 402, 477, 485, 486A, 486B, 488, 496, 497, 2501, 2502, 2977, 2978, 2980.
  Audiencia de Santa Fe, *legajo*: 476.
Archivo General de Simancas, Valladolid.
  Sección de Estado, *legajos*: 6865, 6866, 6875, 6876, 7017.
  Sección de Marina, *legajo*: 393.
Archivo del Ministerio de Hacienda, Lima.
  MSS 0526, 0549, 0610, 0698.
Archivo del Palacio de Torre Tagle, Lima.
  MSS 1–8.
Archivo de la Real Academia de la Historia, Madrid. MS D 88/17
Biblioteca Nacional, Lima.
  MS C 1837.
British (Museum) Library.
  Additional MSS 13,974; 13,976; 20,926.
New York Public Library, N.Y.
  Rich MSS, vol. 99.

B. Printed sources

Alsedo y Herrera, D., *Memorial informativo . . . del Consulado de la ciudad de los Reyes . . . sobre diferentes puntos tocantes al estado de la real hacienda, comercio, etc.,* without place or date [Madrid, 1726(?)].

——, *Aviso histórico*, 1740 (in J. Zaragoza, *Piraterías y agresiones . . .* , *q.v.*).

——, *Incursiones y hostilidades de las naciones extranjeras en la América meridional . . .* (including *Providencias de España para defender y guardar el paso de la Mar del Sur . . .* and *Comento anual geográfico e histórico . . .*), 1770–1 (in J. Zaragoza, *Piraterías y agresiones . . .* , *q.v.*).

——, *Presupuestos y consecuencias de la extinción de galeones . . . y retardación de las flotas . . . y de la continuación de los registros*, 1771(?) (in J. Zaragoza, *Piraterías y agresiones . . .* , *q.v.*).

An Address to the Proprietors of the South Sea Capital, containing a discovery of the illicit trade carried on in the West Indies . . . , London, 1732.

Antúnez y Acevedo, R., *Memorias históricas sobre la legislación y gobierno del comercio de los españoles en sus colonias en las Indias occidentales*, Madrid, 1797.

Arcila Farías, E., *El siglo ilustrado en América*, Caracas, 1955.

Assiento, The; or Contract for Allowing to the Subjects of Great Britain the Liberty of Importing Negroes into the Spanish America, London, 1713.

Baudrillart, M. A., *Philippe V et la cour de France*, (5 vols) Paris, 1890–1900.

Béthencourt, A., *Patiño en la política internacional de Felipe V*, Valladolid, 1954.

Bitar Letayf, M., *Economistas españoles del siglo XVIII*, Madrid, 1968.

Borges, A., *Álvarez Abreu y su extraordinaria misión en Indias*, Teneriffe, 1963.

——, *La Casa de Austria en Venezuela durante la guerra de Sucesión Española (1702—1715)*, Salzburg-Teneriffe, 1963.

Brading, D. A., *Miners and Merchants in Bourbon Mexico, 1763—1810*, Cambridge, 1971.

Brown, V. L., 'The South-Sea Company and Contraband Trade,' *American Historical Review*, 31, New York, 1925–6, pp. 662–78.

Calendar of State Papers, Colonial Series, America and the West Indies, 1706—1730, London, 1916–37.

Campbell, J., *The Spanish Empire in America by an English Merchant*, London, 1747.

Campillo y Cossío, J., *Nuevo sistema de gobierno económico para la América, con los males y daños que le causa el que hoy tiene . . .* , Madrid, 1789.

Canga Argüelles, J., *Diccionario de hacienda con aplicación a España*, Madrid, 1833.

Cantillo, A. del, *Tratados, convenios y declaraciones de paz y de comercio que han hecho con las potencias extranjeras los monarcas españoles de la Casa de Borbón*, Madrid, 1843.

Carrera Pujal, J., *Historia de la economía española*, (5 vols) Barcelona, 1943–7.

Castro y Rossi, A., *Historia de Cádiz y su provincia desde los remotos tiempos hasta 1814*, Cadiz, 1858.

Céspedes del Castillo, G., *La avería en el comercio de Indias*, Seville, 1945.

——, 'Datos sobre comercio y finanzas de Lima, 1707–1708,' *Mercurio peruano*, 333, Lima, 1954, pp. 937–45.

——, 'Lima y Buenos Aires. Repercusiones económicas y políticas de la creación del virreinato del Plata', *Anuario de Estudio Americanos*, 3, Seville, 1946, pp. 677–874.

Chaunu, P. and H., *Séville et l'Atlantique, 1504–1650*, (8 vols) Paris, 1955–7.

Colección de documentos y manuscritos compilados por Fernández de Navarrete [existing in the Museo Naval, Madrid], (32 vols) Liechtenstein, 1971.

Cooke, E., *Voyage to the South Seas and Around the World . . .*, *1708–9–10–11*, London, 1712.

Daily Courant, The, London, 1712– .

Daily Journal, The, London, 1712– .

Daily Post, The, London, 1712– .

Dahlgren, E. W., *Les Relations commerciales et maritimes entre la France et les côtes de l'Océan Pacifique (commencement du XVIIIe siècle)*. Vol. 1 (only one publ.): *Le Commerce de la Mer du Sud jusqu'à la paix d'Utrecht*, Paris, 1909.

Documentos para la historia argentina, (45 vols) Buenos Aires, 1913– .

Fernández Duro, C., *Armada española*, (9 vols) Madrid, 1885–1903.

Fog's Weekly Journal (continuation of *Mist's Weekly Journal*), London, 1720– .

Fonseca, F. de, and Urrutia, C. de, *Historia general de la real hacienda, escrita . . . por orden del virrey, Conde de Revillagigedo*, (6 vols) Mexico, 1845–53.

Fuentes, M. A., (ed.) *Memorias de los Virreyes que han gobernado el Perú durante el tiempo del coloniaje español*, (6 vols) Lima, 1859.

Gamboa, F. X., *Comentarios a las ordenanzas de minas*, Madrid, 1761.

General Collection of Treatys, Declarations of War, Manifestos, and other Publick Papers, relating to Peace and War, (4 vols) London, 1732.

Gentleman's Magazine, The, London, 1731– .

Gutiérrez de Rubalcava, J., *Tratado histórico, político y legal del comercio de las Indias occidentales . . . l^a parte: Compendio histórico del comercio de las Indias*, Cadiz, 1750.

Hamilton, E. J., 'Spanish Mercantilism before 1700,' *Facts and Factors in Economic History*, Cambridge Mass., 1932, pp. 214–39.

——, *American Treasure and the Price Revolution in Spain, 1501–1650*, Cambridge Mass., 1934.

——, 'Money and Economic Recovery in Spain under the First Bourbon,' *Journal of Modern History*, 15, Chicago, 1943, pp. 192–206.

——, 'The Decline of Spain,' *Essays in Economic History* (ed. E. M. Carus-Wilson), vol. I, London, 1954, pp. 215–26.

Hamnett, B. R., *Politics and Trade in Southern Mexico, 1750–1821*, Cambridge, 1971.

Haring, C. H., *Trade and Navigation between Spain and the Indies in the Time of the Hapsburgs*, Cambridge Mass., 1918.

——, *The Spanish Empire in America*, New York, 1947.

Hertz, G. B., 'England and the Ostend Company,' *English Historical Review*, 22, London, 1907, pp. 255–79.

Hildner, E. G., Jnr., 'The Rôle of the South Sea Company in the Diplomacy Leading to the War of Jenkins' Ear, 1729–1739,' *Hispanic American Historical Review*, 18, Durham N.C., 1938, pp. 322–41.

Hussey, R. D., *The Caracas Company, 1728–1784*, Cambridge Mass., 1934.

Journal de Verdun, Le, (Journal historique sur les matières du tems . . .) Verdun, Paris, 1714– .

Juan, J., and Ulloa, A. de, *Noticias secretas de América*, Buenos Aires, 1953.

——, *Relación histórica del viaje hecho de orden de Su Mag. a la América meridional* . . . , Madrid, 1748.

Kamen, H., 'The Destruction of the Spanish Silver Fleet at Vigo in 1702,' *Bulletin of the Institute of Historical Research*, 39, London, 1966, pp. 165–73.

——, *The War of Succession in Spain, 1700–1715*, London, 1969.

King, J. F., 'Documents. Admiral Vernon at Portobello: 1739,' *Hispanic American Historical Review*, 33, Durham N.C., 1943, pp. 258–82.

La Force, J. A., Jnr., *The Development of the Spanish Textile Industry, 1750–1800*, Berkeley, 1965.

Leiva y Lorente, J. M. de, 'La construcción naval en los astilleros cantábricos en los tiempos de D. Blas de Lezo,' *Conmemoración bicentenaria de D. Blas de Lezo*, Madrid, 1941, pp. 59–87.

Lohmann Villena, G., *Tres catalanes, virreyes en el Perú*, Madrid, 1962.

——, 'El *Cuadernillo de noticias* del Virrey del Perú, Marqués de Castelldosríus (agosto de 1708),' *Jahrbuch für Geschichte von Staat, Wirtschaft und Gesellschaft Lateinamerikas*, 1, Cologne, 1964, pp. 207–37.

London Gazette, The, London, 1712– .

McLachlan, J. O., *Trade and Peace with Old Spain, 1667–1750*, Cambridge, 1940.

Mendiburu, R., *Diccionario biográfico*, Lima, 1889.

Mercader, J., *Felip V i Catalunya*, Barcelona, 1968.

Mist's Weekly Journal, London, 1712– .

Moreyra Paz-Soldán, M., 'La toma de Portobelo por el Almte. Vernon y sus consecuencias económicas,' *Mercurio peruano*, 29, Lima, 1948, pp. 289–329.

——, (ed.) *El Tribunal del Consulado de Lima. Cuaderno de Juntas*, I (1706–1720), Lima, 1956; II (1721–1727), Lima, 1959.

Mounier, A., *Les Faits et la doctrine économiques en Espagne sous Philippe V. Gerónimo de Uztáriz, 1670–1732*, Bordeaux, 1919.

Muñoz Pérez, J., 'La publicación del Reglamento de Comercio Libre de Indias, de 1778,' *Anuario de Estudios Americanos*, 4, Seville, 1947, pp. 615–64.

Muro Orejón, A., *Cedulario americano del siglo XVIII*, I, Seville, 1956, II, Seville, 1969.

Nelson, G. H., 'Contraband Trade under the Assiento. 1730–1739,' *American Historical Review*, 51, New York, 1945, pp. 55–67.

Nettels, C., 'England and the Spanish-American Trade, 1680–1715,' *Journal of Modern History*, 3, Chicago, 1931, pp. 1–32.

New Cambridge Modern History, The, (14 vols) Cambridge, 1957–70.

Pares, R., *War and Trade in the West Indies, 1739–1763*, Oxford, 1936.

Parry, J. H., *The Spanish Seaborne Empire*, London, 1966.

Post Man, The, London, 1712– .

Real Díaz, J. J., 'Las ferias de Jalapa,' *Anuario de Estudios Americanos*, 16, Seville, 1959, pp. 167–314.

Recopilación de diferentes resoluciones, y órdenes de Su Magestad . . . sobre si la Casa de Contratación . . . debe residir en Sevilla, Cádiz J en otra perte . . . , Madrid, 1722.

Recopilación de leyes de los reynos de las Indias, ed. Consejo de la Hispanidad, Madrid, 1943.

Richmond, H. W., *The Navy in the War of 1739–48*, (3 vols) Cambridge, 1920.

Rodríguez Villa, A., *Patiño y Campillo. Reseña histórico-biográfica de estos dos ministros de Felipe V*, Madrid, 1882.

Santa Cruz de Marcenado, Marqués de, *Rapsodia económica-política-monárquica*, Madrid, 1732.

Scelle, G., *La Traite negrière aux Indes de Castille*, (2 vols) Paris, 1906.

Schurz, W. L., 'Mexico, Peru and the Manila Galleon,' *Hispanic American Historical Review*, 1, Durham N.C., 1918, pp. 389–402.

——, *The Manila Galleon*, New York, 1959.

Soldevila, F., *Història de Catalunya*, Barcelona, 1963.

Temperley, H. M. V., 'The Causes of the War of Jenkins' Ear, 1739,' *Transactions of the Royal Historical Society*, 3rd series, 3, London, 1909, pp. 197–236.

Ulloa, B. de, *Restablecimiento de las fábricas y comercio español*, Madrid, 1740.

Usher, A. P., 'Spanish Ships and Shipping in the Sixteenth and Seventeenth Centuries,' *Facts and Factors in Economic History*, Harvard, 1932, pp. 203–5.

Uztáriz, G. de, *Theórica y práctica de comercio y de marina en diferentes discursos . . . que . . . se procuran adaptar a la Monarquía española para su pronta restauración*, 3rd ed., Madrid, 1757.

Vargas Ugarte, R., *Historia del Perú*. [vol. III] *Virreinato (siglo XVIII), 1700–1790*, Lima, 1956.

Vázquez de Prada, V., 'Las rutas comerciales entre España y América en el siglo XVIII', *Anuario de Estudios Americanos*, 25, Seville, 1968, pp. 197–237.

Veitia Linage, J. de, *Norte de la contratación de las Indias occidentales*, ed. Buenos Aires, 1945.

Vicens Vives, J., *Manual de historia económica de España*, Barcelona, 1964.

Vignols, L., 'Le "Commerce interlope" français à la Mer du Sud, au début du XVIIIe siècle,' *Revue d'Histoire Économique et Sociale*, 13, Paris, 1925, pp. 240–99.

Vignols, L., and Sée, H., 'La Fin du commerce interlope français dans l'Amérique espagnole,' *Revue d'Histoire Économique et Sociale*, 13, Paris, 1925, pp. 300–13.

Villalobos R., S., *Comercio y contrabando en el Río de la Plata y Chile, 1700–1811*, Buenos Aires, 1965.

——, *El comercio y la crisis colonial: un mito de la independencia*, Santiago de Chile, 1968.

——, 'Contrabando francés en el Pacífico, 1700–1724,' *Revista de Historia de América*, 51, Mexico, 1961, pp. 49–80.

Ward, B., *Proyecto económico . . .* , Madrid, 1779.

West, R. C., *The Mining Community in Northern New Spain: the Parral Mining District*, (Ibero-Americana, no. 30), Berkeley, 1949.

Zaragoza, J., *Piraterías y agresiones de los ingleses y otros pueblos de Europa en la América española desde el siglo XVI al XVIII . . .* , Madrid, 1883.

Zavala y Auñón, M. de, *Representación al Rey N.S. Felipe V, dirigida al más seguro aumento del real erario . . .* , Madrid, 1732.

Index